Sustainable Development Indicators in Ecological Economics

CURRENT ISSUES IN ECOLOGICAL ECONOMICS

Series Editors: Sylvie Faucheux, *Professor of Economic Science* and Martin O'Connor, Associate *Professor of Economic Science, C3ED, Université de Versailles – Saint Quentin en Yvelines, France*, John Proops, *Professor of Ecological Economics, School of Politics, International Relations and the Environment, Keele University, UK* and Jan van der Straaten, *Retired Senior Lecturer, Department of Leisure Studies, Tilburg University, The Netherlands*

The field of ecological economics has emerged as a result of the need for all social sciences to be brought together in new ways, to respond to global environmental problems. This major new series aims to present and define the state-of-the-art in this young and yet fast-developing discipline.

This series cuts through the vast literature on the subject to present the key tenets and principal problems, techniques and solutions in ecological economics. It is the essential starting point for any practical or theoretical analysis of economy–environment interactions and will provide the basis for future developments within the discipline.

Titles in the series include:

Greening the Accounts
Edited by Sandrine Simon and John Proops

Nature and Agriculture in the European Union
New Perspectives on Policies that Shape the European Countryside
Edited by Floor Brouwer and Jan van der Straaten

Waste in Ecological Economics
Edited by Katy Bisson and John Proops

Environmental Thought
Edited by Edward A. Page and John Proops

The Ecological Economics of Consumption
Edited by Lucia A. Reisch and Inge Røpke

Modelling in Ecological Economics
Edited by John Proops and Paul Safonov

Sustainable Development Indicators in Ecological Economics

Edited by

Philip Lawn

Flinders University, Adelaide

CURRENT ISSUES IN ECOLOGICAL ECONOMICS

Edward Elgar

Cheltenham, UK • Northampton, MA, USA

Published by
Edward Elgar Publishing Limited
Glensanda House
Montpellier Parade
Cheltenham
Glos GL50 1UA
UK

Edward Elgar Publishing, Inc.
136 West Street
Suite 202
Northampton
Massachusetts 01060
USA

A catalogue record for this book
is available from the British Library

Library of Congress Cataloguing in Publication Data
Sustainable development indicators in ecological economics / edited by
  Philip Lawn.
      p. cm. – (Current issues in ecological economics)
   Includes bibliographical references.
    1. Environmental economics. 2. Sustainable development–Statistics.
  3. Economic indicators. I. Lawn, Philip A. II. Series.

  HC79.E5S866854 2006
  338.9′27–dc22   2005046143

ISBN-13: 978 1 84542 099 4
ISBN-10: 1 84542 099 3

Printed and bound in Great Britain by MPG Books Ltd, Bodmin, Cornwall

Contents

v

PART IV: SUSTAINABLE DEVELOPMENT AND NATURAL
           CAPITAL ACCOUNTING

PART V: SUSTAINABLE DEVELOPMENT AND INDICATORS
          OF HUMAN–ENVIRONMENT INTERACTION

PART VI: CONCLUDING ASSESSMENTS OF SUSTAINABLE
           DEVELOPMENT INDICATORS

Contributors

H. Asbjørn Aaheim, Centre for International Climate and Environmental Research, University of Oslo, Oslo, Norway.

Matthew Clarke, School of Social Science and Planning, RMIT University, Melbourne, Australia.

Rudolf de Groot, Environmental Systems Analysis Group, Wageningen University, Wageningen, The Netherlands.

Simon Dietz, Department of Geography and Environment, London School of Economics and Political Science, London, United Kingdom.

Salah El Serafy, Independent Economic Consultant, Arlington, VA, USA.

Richard W. England, Department of Economics, University of New Hampshire, Durham, USA.

Stefan Giljum, Sustainable Europe Research Institute, Vienna, Austria.

Lars Hein, Environmental Systems Analysis Group, Wageningen University, Wageningen, The Netherlands.

Janne Hukkinen, Laboratory of Environmental Protection, Helsinki University of Technology, Helsinki, Finland.

Nigel Jollands, New Zealand Centre for Ecological Economics, Landcare Research and Massey University, Palmerston North, New Zealand.

Carolien Kroeze, Environmental Systems Analysis Group, Wageningen University, Wageningen, The Netherlands.

Philip Lawn, School of Business Economics, Flinders University, Adelaide, Australia.

Rik Leemans, Environmental Systems Analysis Group, Wageningen University, Wageningen, The Netherlands.

John Lintott, London South Bank University, London, United Kingdom.

Dan Moran, Global Footprint Network, Oakland, USA.

Michael Murray, Global Footprint Network, Oakland, USA.

Eric Neumayer, Department of Geography and Environment, London School of Economics and Political Science, London, United Kingdom.

David Niemeijer, Environmental Systems Analysis Group, Wageningen University, Wageningen, The Netherlands.

Murray Patterson, New Zealand Centre for Ecological Economics, Massey University, Palmerston North, New Zealand.

John Peet, Department of Chemical and Process Engineering, University of Canterbury, Christchurch, New Zealand.

David Rapport, Principal, Ecohealth Consulting, Salt Spring Island, BC and Honorary Professor, Faculty of Medicine and Dentistry, The University of Western Ontario, London, Ontario.

Ola Ullsten, Former Prime Minister of Sweden, Senior Fellow, The International Institute for Sustainable Development (IISD), Winnipeg, Canada.

Mathis Wackernagel, Global Footprint Network, Oakland, USA.

Sahm White, Global Footprint Network, Oakland, USA.

PART I

Introduction to sustainable development indicators

1. Introduction

Philip Lawn

Sustainable development is a concept that almost everybody has heard of but few understand. That so many people are familiar with the term is quite remarkable considering it was virtually unknown until the release of the Brundtland Report by the World Commission on Environment and Development in 1987 (WCED, 1987). Indeed, it was not until the 1992 Earth Summit in Rio de Janeiro and the widespread promotion of the United Nations' Agenda 21 that sustainable development became firmly established as a desirable policy objective (UN, 1993). Since this time, many national governments have introduced a range of new policy measures in an attempt to steer their economies along a more sustainable path. On the surface, at least, this appears to be a positive trend. But should we be scratching the surface and asking whether nations have been successful in moving toward the sustainable development goal? Is it possible that we have focused too heavily on policy measures and have forgotten to supplement the means to achieving sustainable development with a suitable range of indicators to assess a nation's sustainable development performance? Or, alternatively, do we now have appropriate sustainable development indicators at our disposal but the policies implemented to achieve sustainable development have been horrendously conceived and/or inadequately implemented? Either way, we could be aimlessly moving along a catastrophic pathway or, as Costanza (1987) describes it, be caught in a 'social trap' because of a reliance on misleading signals or a failure to heed the warning signs revealed by recently established indicators.

Given the questions asked above, the main aim of this book is to provoke academics, policy-makers, civil servants, business leaders, and activists to think more seriously about: (1) the importance of sustainable development indicators; (2) the potential value and shortcomings of the sustainable development indicators already in use; and (3) how sustainable development indicators can be improved so as to better inform us of the impact of past policies and what is required to avoid past failings. The book contains chapters on indicators that have been specifically designed to measure sustainable development. Each invited contributor is either a practitioner in

3

the field of sustainable development indicators or has intimate knowledge of sustainable development indicators given their research and/or professional background.

The range of contributions and the means by which the book is presented is designed to allow readers to make their own mind up about the policy-guiding value of sustainable development indicators. Despite the weaknesses of some indicators, the consistent message revealed by the contributors suggests, if nothing else, that the quest for appropriate sustainable development indicators is critically important. But the need to refine and improve upon existing sustainable development indicators remains acute. So, too, is the responsibility of the advocates of sustainable development indicators to discard an unworthy or misleading indicator.

The book is divided into six sections of which the chapters contained in each of the four main sections – Parts II, III, IV and V – share a common theme. Part I, as the introductory section of the book, includes a foundational chapter on the sustainable development concept and sustainable development indicators (Chapter 2). The aim of this chapter is to employ a linear throughput model in the context of a coevolutionary worldview to establish a broad definition of sustainable development. Narrower definitions of sustainable development are then put forward to serve as the theoretical and philosophical justification for each of the sustainable development indicators discussed in the book.

Part II, on green national accounting, focuses on how conventional macroeconomic indicators can be adjusted to provide a more accurate assessment of a nation's sustainable development performance. In Chapter 3, Salah El Serafy argues that the aim of green national accounting should be the proper estimation of a nation's sustainable output for economic policy purposes. It should not, according to El Serafy, be used to estimate the welfare generated by a nation's economic activity or serve as a guide to environmental policy. El Serafy particularly warns against the 'strong sustainability' practice of fully expunging the value contributed by the resource extraction sector. Only when national accounting adjustments involve a deduction of the 'user cost' of natural resource depletion – which constitutes a portion of all resource extraction losses – do we obtain a proper measure of national income that can help policy-makers to steer national economies in the right direction.

As for welfare, El Serafy argues that national welfare assessment is an entirely different exercise to national product calculations. As such, national accounts should not be adjusted in the false hope of obtaining better indicators of the welfare generated by a nation's economic activity. Although El Serafy does not explicitly argue against national welfare assessments, he is adamant that welfare calculations – such as the Index of

Sustainable Economic Welfare – should remain outside the conventional national accounting framework.

In the following chapter (Chapter 4), John Lintott points out that successful policy-making requires a source of statistical information to assist in the planning for and assessment of policy outcomes. Since environmental accounts provide a valuable statistical framework in the case of policies that affect the natural environment, Lintott argues that environmental accounts should be elevated to the core of the overall statistical system.

Since this raises issues as to what type of statistical framework can contribute to more appropriate policy-making, Lintott questions the development and use of consumption-based indicators – particularly given the tenuous link between consumption and welfare once a certain level of affluence is reached. Lintott therefore believes it is efficacious to combine accounts in physical units with a set of social and environmental indicators and to make a coherent connection between these and the existing monetary-based accounting system.

In Chapter 5, Asbjørn Aaheim, in demonstrating how green national accounts can incorporate natural resource and environmental valuations, discusses some of the problems associated with the numerical assessment of values. According to Aaheim, a major problem arises because although traditional national accounts are based on readily observable prices and quantities, the prices applicable to environmental standards and natural resources are rarely apparent. Aaheim therefore focuses on the role of prices and the fundamental differences in the valuation techniques used.

To arrive at an appropriate set of prices for green national accounting, Aaheim believes that one must first take account of any reallocation of initial endowments that may result from environmental stress. According to Aaheim, this can be achieved through the use of general equilibrium models whereby prices can be calculated endogenously. By considering some of the potential impacts of climate change on forest productivity, and personal demand for various transport modes in Norway, Aaheim shows how assessments of environmental change can be used to establish relationships between environmental stresses and economic activities. Aaheim concludes that the indirect macroeconomic effects of climate change are not only significant, but an assessment of this type can itself provide a far richer understanding of the economic consequences of climate change.

In Chapter 6, Simon Dietz and Eric Neumayer critically appraise the Genuine Savings (GS) approach to sustainability assessments. Dietz and Neumayer reveal some of the weaknesses inherent in GS estimates and, consistent with El Serafy's conclusions regarding green adjustments to GDP, show that GS measures are only meaningful with respect to the weak sustainability paradigm. Despite this, Dietz and Neumayer believe that existing GS estimates are sufficiently robust to indicate that many resource-dependent countries are already failing to invest sufficiently in the establishment of suitable replacement assets. This, they argue, undermines their capacity to sustain current income levels.

Part III deals with two sustainable development indicators designed to measure sustainable economic welfare at the national level – namely, the Index of Sustainable Economic Welfare (ISEW) and the Genuine Progress Indicator (GPI). In Chapter 7, Philip Lawn addresses three of their perceived weaknesses: (1) the lack of a sound theoretical foundation; (2) the shortcomings associated with the valuation methods used in their construction; and (3) the dubious interpretation of ISEW and GPI results. By focusing on the individual items of which the ISEW and GPI are comprised, Lawn demonstrates that both indexes are, theoretically at least, soundly based on Fisher's (1906) concept of income and capital. While agreeing with many of the criticisms relating to (2) and (3), Lawn believes the ISEW and GPI are more reliable measures of sustainable economic welfare than mainstream macroeconomic indicators, such as GDP. Notwithstanding this, Lawn urges all ISEW and GPI advocates to establish a more consistent and robust set of valuation methods to increase their mainstream acceptance.

In Chapter 8, Matthew Clarke presents the results of an ISEW study of Thailand. By incorporating systems analysis into the calculation of the ISEW, Clarke shows that the threshold point at which macroeconomic growth begins to lower economic welfare need not be confined to industrialised countries. Moreover, Clarke believes the ISEW demonstrates why there is a need to broaden the policy prescriptions beyond the current predilection with continuing economic growth. Clarke concludes his chapter by highlighting the strengths and weaknesses of the ISEW and what is required to increase its policy appeal.

In Chapter 9, Simon Dietz and Eric Neumayer warn of the potential pitfalls when interpreting studies involving the ISEW and GPI. Given the inadequate nature of some of the valuation methods and assumptions used to calculate the ISEW and GPI, Dietz and Neumayer believe the two indexes can misleadingly support the 'threshold hypothesis' put forward by Max-neef (1995) and respectively referred to by Lawn and Clarke in Chapters 7 and 8.

Few would doubt the critical role played by the natural environment in achieving ecological sustainability. Because of it, Part IV is devoted to natural capital accounting. In Chapter 10, Richard W. England employs classical thermodynamics and ecological principles to establish a conceptual framework for theorising about economy–environment interactions.

England uses this framework to outline three useful definitions of natural capital. By showing that the capitalised value of natural capital can vary significantly depending, firstly, on how natural capital is defined, and secondly, on how the future stream of benefits it generates is discounted, England believes a high research priority should be given to improving the ISEW discussed in Part III of the book. Having said this, England stresses that the sheer magnitude of the capitalised value of natural capital – irrespective of how much estimates have tended to vary – is sufficient to indicate that its continued depletion will have tragic consequences for humanity.

In Chapter 11, de Groot et al. show how natural capital can be classified and measured to facilitate ecological sustainability. Using the concept of 'critical natural capital', they present a framework to select indicators that can be used to systematically assess the criticality of ecosystems in terms of their ecological, economic and cultural importance. The framework is developed on the basis that since ecological indicators exist in a variety of forms, common denominators need to be found to describe (1) the *threat* to natural capital (pressure–state–impact), and (2) the *importance* of natural capital in terms of ecosystem services and values.

Following the presentation of a European-based study involving the calculation of a natural capital index (NCI), four individual case studies are revealed as examples of how the proposed indicator framework can assist in determining the criticality of natural capital. Finally, de Groot et al. conclude by stressing that critical natural capital indicators must take account of the important environmental services provided by natural capital as well as the link between these services and the overall condition of the natural capital that generates them.

A different approach to natural capital accounting is outlined by Wackernagel et al. in Chapter 12. Using the well-known ecological footprint concept, Wackernagel et al. provide evidence to suggest that humankind is eroding the natural resource base upon which it depends (i.e. per capita ecological footprint is exceeding the planet's per capita biocapacity). Following a brief explanation of what the ecological footprint means in terms of ecological 'overshoot', Wackernagel et al. focus on the limitations of their estimates and respond to some of the criticisms levelled at the ecological footprint concept. Wackernagel et al. then give an interpretative account of their ecological footprint estimates to illustrate how the concept can guide policy-makers to institute the reforms necessary to achieve ecological sustainability.

In Chapter 13, the final chapter on natural capital accounting, David Rapport and Ola Ullsten respond to the lack of readily communicable information on the state of the environment by proposing a forest capital index (FCI). Although the FCI would be designed to assess the ecological sustainability of forest ecosystems, Rapport and Ullsten believe the FCI represents an opportunity to develop indices for communicating the status of other critical environmental assets.

Following a discussion on such concepts as ecological footprints, ecological integrity, and ecosystem health – each with its own unique focus and particular strengths and weaknesses – Rapport and Ullsten describe, in considerable detail, how the FCI might be constructed. According to Rapport and Ullsten, critical factors to consider include: (1) the selection of existing forest-related indicators; (2) the development of ecological thresholds and targets upon which to base the FCI; (3) an explanation as to how the chosen indicators can be suitably aggregated; and (4) how changes in the FCI should be interpreted. In addition, Rapport and Ullsten believe the FCI, in order to be of value, must be capable of reaching an appropriate audience and, most importantly, have the capacity to be linked to existing indices of sustainable development at both the national and international levels.

Part V of the book moves onto indicators of human–environment interaction, whereby the second and third chapters of this section focus specifically on measures of eco-efficiency. In Chapter 14, Janne Hukkinen demonstrates how alternative sustainability scenarios can serve as interpretive frameworks for indicators of human–environment interaction. Hukkinen adopts this approach on the basis that scenarios of the future can provide a series of reference points against which specific indicator values can be assessed.

According to Hukkinen, many existing sustainability indicators are deficient because the framework from which they emerge is often based on a specific sustainability scenario. Yet, as Hukkinen points out, there are many possible ecologically sustainable states as well as different socio-cultural dimensions to the sustainability issue. Should policy-makers assess sustainability indicators from the perspective of a single sustainability scenario, they run the risk of adopting a partisan position as to what constitutes ecological sustainability.

By employing the Pressure–State–Response (PSR) framework with reference to reindeer management in Finland, Hukkinen outlines a new set of indicators designed to measure the technological, institutional and path-dependent nature of the conditions influencing reindeer management. Hukkinen concludes that the incorporation of alternative scenarios into the indicator framework can signal the increased vulnerability and/or reduced resilience of the interdependent systems under analysis and therefore assist policy-makers to design adaptive policies to cope with surprising events.

Moving onto eco-efficiency indicators, Nigel Jollands (Chapter 15) argues that the policy-guiding value of eco-efficiency indicators rests on the resolution of four theoretical issues: (1) properly defining the eco-efficiency concept; (2) determining what is meant by an eco-efficiency indicator; (3) establishing appropriate criteria for choosing suitable eco-efficiency indicators; and (4) recognising the strengths and weaknesses of eco-efficiency indicators, particularly as they relate to policy-making. Unless these issues are adequately resolved, Jollands believes the likelihood of the eco-efficiency concept being corrupted by poorly conceived and constructed indicators is extreme. This, Jollands adds, has the potential to condemn the eco-efficiency concept to policy oblivion.

Mindful of the caveats posited by Jollands, Lawn puts forward a range of eco-efficiency indicators as a means of assessing the effectiveness with which a country transforms natural capital to human-made capital. The eco-efficiency indicators outlined by Lawn in Chapter 16 are developed on the understanding that: (1) natural capital and human-made capital are complements not substitutes; (2) humankind cannot overcome its dependence on the natural environment by 'dematerialising' economic activity; and (3) since humankind cannot control the evolutionary pathway of the global system, eco-efficiency solutions must be in keeping with a coevolutionary view of the world. By calculating the outlined eco-efficiency indicators for Australia, Lawn shows that Australia's use of its natural capital assets has progressed very little since the mid-1960s – a consequence of Australia's failure to embrace the notions of sufficiency, equity and natural capital maintenance.

In echoing the message stressed by the majority of the contributors, Stefan Giljum (Chapter 17) argues that new approaches to environmental governance must take a systemic view of the economy–environment relationship where, importantly, recognition needs to be given to the fact that current environmental problems are as much a consequence of the overall scale of resource use as they are individual micro-activities. As such, Giljum believes that any monitoring of eco-efficiency policies requires appropriate information on the relationship between socio-economic activities and their subsequent environmental impact.

Although a number of approaches have been developed to provide the necessary relational information in biophysical terms, Giljum emphasises that one particular approach – namely, economy-wide material flow accounting and analysis (MFA) – allows for the direct integration of monetary and physical information within one particular accounting framework. In doing so, the MFA facilitates the compilation of consistent databases for policy-oriented analyses of economy–environment interactions.

With the above in mind, Giljum focuses on the policy relevance of the MFA approach and the derived material flow indicators. Giljum undertakes this task by presenting selected examples to reveal how the MFA indicators can be used for the evaluation of sustainability-oriented policies. Finally, Giljum discusses the main deficiencies of the MFA approach and introduces possible extensions to the current MFA framework to overcome them.

Part VI, the concluding section of the book, begins with a chapter by John Peet focusing on the importance of 'goal-setting' when determining an appropriate set of sustainable development indicators (Chapter 18). In particular, Peet places great emphasis on the issue of *need*, pointing out that needs are not just confined to individual people, but extend to communities, economies, humanity and nature as a whole. In keeping with an holistic worldview, Peet explains why society's over-arching goal must be based on satisfying the needs of each and every interconnected system. Furthermore, Peet believes these needs must be consistent with a community-based ethic of how to best move towards the goal. According to Peet, the adoption of this approach facilitates the emergence of 'red-light' indicators that can: (1) reveal a society's failure to satisfy the critical needs of each system, and (2) indicate the need for urgent action that must be taken before attention can be directed to less critical areas of concern.

Peet's chapter is a sobering reminder that existing sustainable development indicators may not satisfactorily reveal whether the critical needs of each interconnected system are being adequately satisfied. I have deliberately positioned Peet's chapter in Part VI in the hope that each reader will not only be better equipped to make a judgment about the policy-guiding value of each sustainable development indicator discussed in the book, but of sustainable development indicators generally.

The final chapter, Chapter 19, is specifically aimed at evaluating the policy-guiding value of some of the sustainable development indicators covered in the book. By reflecting on New Zealand's search for headline indicators, Murray Patterson begins with a short summary of the history and rationale for sustainability indicators. Then, having considered what constitutes a headline indicator, Patterson surveys the theoretical basis of sustainability indicators from ecological, economic, thermodynamic, and public policy perspectives.

With the various sustainability interpretations in mind, Patterson puts forward an eight-point criteria for evaluating the following indicators:

- the 'ecological footprint';
- the Environmental Sustainability Index (ESI);

- green GDP, including the Index of Sustainable Economic Welfare (ISEW) and Genuine Progress Indicator (GPI);
- the Genuine Savings (GS) index;
- Material Flows indicators;
- the Consumption Pressure Index (CPI);
- a Living Planet Index (LPI);
- a Composite Environmental Performance Index (CEPI) based on the aggregation of various environmental themes;
- and a Composite Sustainable Development Index (CSDI) that integrates economic, social, and environmental performance.

Since the ecological footprint and the GPI rank highest across the eight evaluation categories, Patterson suggests that both indexes offer the greatest potential in terms of measuring a nation's sustainable development performance. Drawing from the evaluation results, Patterson makes the following recommendations:

1. The ecological footprint should be implemented as a stand-alone headline indicator of ecological sustainability.
2. A more comprehensive indicator of ecological sustainability – existing in the form of a composite index – should be established to supplement the ecological footprint indicator and, in so doing, encapsulate a greater range of ecosystem functions and services.
3. A nation-specific GPI should be calculated to encompass the economic, social, and environmental dimensions of sustainable development into a single index number.
4. A composite index of sustainable development – involving the aggregation of three already existing indicators – should be established explicitly to measure the economic, social, and environmental aspects of a nation's progress.

Patterson concludes by suggesting that the evaluation and recommendations he presents can provide lessons that are invaluable and applicable to all nation states.

As this Introduction suggests, this book covers a wide but not exhaustive range of sustainable development indicators. Exactly what policy-guiding value these indicators possess will no doubt continue to be debated regardless of how successful the book is in clarifying the ambiguities surrounding them. However, should this book broaden people's knowledge of sustainable development indicators and contribute to indicators that are both increasingly informative and policy-relevant, it will have served a very useful purpose at a time when the need for policy redirection is more urgent than ever.

REFERENCES

Costanza, R. (1987), 'Social traps and environmental policy', *BioScience*, **37** (6), 407–12.
Fisher, I. (1906), *Nature of Capital and Income*, New York: A.M. Kelly.
Max-Neef, M. (1995), 'Economic growth and quality of life', *Ecological Economics*, **15** (2), 115–18.
United Nations (1993), *Agenda 21*, New York: UN.
World Commission on Environment and Development (WCED) (1987), *Our Common Future*, Oxford: Oxford University Press.

2. Sustainable development: concept and indicators

Philip Lawn

IN SEARCH OF A DEFINITION OF SUSTAINABLE DEVELOPMENT

Sustainable development means different things to different people. There are many reasons for this. To begin with, the concept of sustainable development is used in many locations and contexts, by people from varying cultural backgrounds and disciplinary schools of thought, and for different purposes. Second, the sustainable development concept has evolved rapidly and over a relatively short period of time. Finally, debates about sustainable development have been influenced by a wide range of underlying views regarding the relationship between human beings, economic systems, and the natural environment of which they are a part. As such, there are various opinions as to how sustainable development should be measured and what is required to move toward the sustainable development goal.

To accommodate the various interpretations of sustainable development, it is necessary to define sustainable development in broad terms. This, unfortunately, makes the task of measuring sustainable development a very difficult one. Thus, the concept of sustainable development used to assess a nation's sustainable development performance is likely to differ from the one we might use to describe the sustainable development process generally. The former is likely to be defined in considerably narrower terms in order to establish operational rules of thumb to serve as the basis for a congruent set of sustainable development indicators. Of course, when defining sustainable development more narrowly, there is the inherent danger of losing sight of its broader meaning and the need to accommodate the diverse cultural interpretations of the sustainable development process. Clearly, an appropriate balance between inclusiveness and specificity needs to be struck. While this is not easily achieved, the accomplishment of such is one of the central aims of this chapter.

The Coevolutionary Worldview as a Concrete Representation of the Socio-Economic Process

The quest for broad and narrow definitions of sustainable development must begin within the context of a concrete representation of the socio-economic process. Unfortunately, a number of past interpretations of sustainable development have been falsely premised on the view that ecological, social and economic spheres of influence are independent systems. The circular flow model of the macroeconomy that forms the centrepiece of the mainstream economic view of the sustainable development process is a case in point. The inadequacy of this approach has led many observers to introduce linkages between the three major systems, usually depicted in the form of something akin to Figure 2.1 below.

Although Figure 2.1, with arrows drawn to represent the transfer of material, energy and informational flows between the three separately demarcated systems, is an improvement on isolationist models, it remains deficient because it reflects an atomistic–mechanistic view of the world. As such, it fails to recognise the coevolutionary nature of economic, social, and ecological change (Mulder and van den Bergh, 2001). Coevolution is

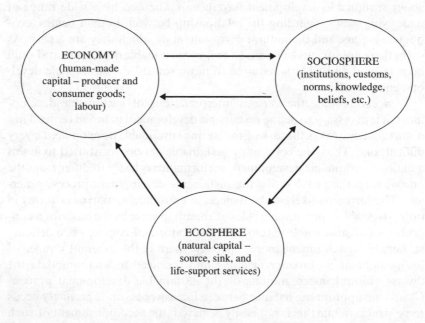

Figure 2.1   An atomistic–mechanistic depiction of the relationship between the economy, sociosphere and ecosphere

a term used to describe the evolving relationships and feedback responses typically associated with two or more interdependent systems. Coevolution takes place when at least one feedback loop is altered by within-system activity that, in turn, initiates an ongoing and reciprocal process of change (Norgaard, 1985). A coevolutionary worldview provides a more realistic and concrete understanding of the many critical relationships that bind together the various systems that make up the global system.

There are a number of basic features of the coevolutionary worldview worthy of elaboration. First, the coevolutionary paradigm begins from the premise that the Earth is a system comprised of closely interacting and interdependent subsystems. Second, it recognises the Earth and its constituent systems as dissipative structures[1] – i.e. the Earth as a dissipative structure that is open with respect to energy (a solar gradient); and the Earth's constituent subsystems as dissipative structures that are open with respect to energy, matter, and information.[2] Third, since each system is connected to and dependent in some way on all others, everything evolves together over time. Even the rules governing the relationships between systems are in a constant state of flux. Most importantly, however, the global system is a system far greater and richer than the sum of its constituent parts. Fourth, coevolution is characterised by path-dependency – a proclivity of systems to be inextricably related to past characteristics and events and to thus exhibit structural inertia (Arthur, 1989; David, 1985). Fifth, the coevolutionary worldview regards disequilibria and change as the rule rather than the exception. For many people accustomed to atomistic–mechanistic paradigms, this sounds at best unsettling, and at worst debilitating. But this need not be the case. As Norgaard (1985) has pointed out, disequilibria and change should be seen as an ongoing process offering a plethora of opportunities for humankind to engage in *positive coevolution* which, for the purposes of this chapter and the remainder of the book, can be construed as a coevolutionary process commensurate with the sustainable development objective. Finally, the coevolutionary worldview is based on a principle of system embeddedness that is sometimes referred to as the *logos* of nature. Metaphorically, 'logos' is a term used as a principal concept embracing the natural order of the universe. By acknowledging the logos of the global system, the coevolutionary worldview recognises, firstly, that the world is characterised by self-organisation (Capra, 1982). Second, it recognises that systems exist at varying levels of complexity and, as such, are characteristically stratified and multi-levelled (Laszlo, 1972). The logos of the global system and the embedded relationship between the three major spheres of influence – the macroeconomy, sociosphere and ecosphere – are illustrated by way of Figure 2.2 below.

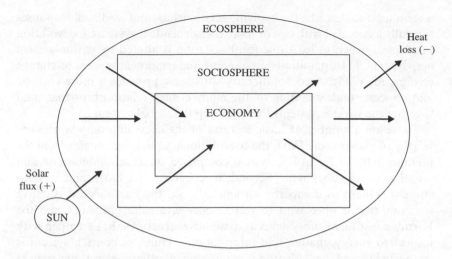

*Figure 2.2   A coevolutionary depiction of the interdependent relationship
between the economy, sociosphere and ecosphere*

In Figure 2.2, the three major spheres of influence represent different
systems at varying degrees of complexity. Each can be considered a *holon*
insofar as they manifest the independent and autonomous properties of
wholes and the dependent properties of parts.[3] Thus, each sphere consists
of smaller parts while simultaneously acting as the part of a larger whole
(i.e. the macroeconomy serves as a component of the sociosphere while
the sociosphere serves as a component of the ecosphere). In a sense,
Figure 2.2 represents the sociosphere as the interfacial system between the
macroeconomy and the larger ecosphere, thereby highlighting the crucial
role played by institutions and social capital in promoting stable human
behaviour in the face of indeterminacy, novelty and surprise (Capra,
1982; Hodgson, 1988; Faber et al., 1992). More on the role of institutions
later.

The Linear Throughput Representation of the Socio-economic Process

In order to diagrammatically convey the coevolutionary worldview in
greater detail, consider the linear throughput representation of the socio-
economic process in Figure 2.3. In keeping with the coevolutionary paradigm, the linear throughput model: (1) depicts the macroeconomy as a
subsystem of the sociosphere that, in turn, is depicted as a subsystem of
the ecosphere; (2) recognises the ongoing exchange of matter, energy and

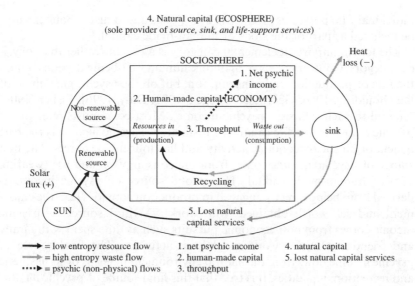

4. Natural capital (ECOSPHERE)
(sole provider of *source, sink, and life-support services*)

➤ = low entropy resource flow	1. net psychic income
➤ = high entropy waste flow	2. human-made capital
▸ = psychic (non-physical) flows	3. throughput

4. natural capital
5. lost natural capital services

Figure 2.3   Linear throughput depiction of the socio-economic process

information between the three major spheres of influence and all constituent subsystems; and (3) acknowledges the evolving relationships and
feedback responses typically associated with coevolutionary change.

Although the dynamics of the linear throughput model involve a multitude of elements, each element can be conveniently classified into five broad
elemental categories. The first elemental category, *natural capital*, constitutes the initial source of all human endeavour. This is because natural
capital is the only source of low entropy resources; it is the ultimate waste
assimilating sink; and it is the sole provider of the life-support services that
maintain the human habitability of the Earth.[4] The second elemental category is the *throughput of matter-energy* – that is, the input into the macroeconomy of low entropy resources and the subsequent output of high
entropy wastes. The throughput flow is the physical intermediary connecting natural and human-made capital. *Human-made capital* is the third
elemental category and is needed for human welfare to be greater than it
would otherwise be if the socio-economic process did not take place.
Conventionally, human-made capital is confined to producer goods such as
plant, machinery and equipment. From a Fisherian perspective, capital is
interpreted as all physical objects subject to ownership that are capable of
directly or indirectly satisfying human needs and wants (Fisher, 1906).
Hence, human-made capital best refers to durable consumer goods as well
as producer goods. Although not subject to ownership (other than by the

individual who possesses productive knowledge and skills), labour can also be included as part of the stock of human-made capital.

The fourth important elemental category is a psychic rather than physical category. Contrary to some opinions, human well-being depends not on the rate of production and consumption, but on the psychic enjoyment of life (Boulding, 1966; Georgescu-Roegen, 1971; Daly, 1996). Fisher (1906) referred to such a flux as 'psychic income'. Most economists refer to the psychic enjoyment of life as utility satisfaction. Psychic income is the true benefit of all socio-economic activity and has four main sources. The first source of psychic income comes from the consumption and use (wearing out) of human-made capital. The second source of psychic income is derived from being directly engaged in production activities (e.g. the enjoyment and self-worth obtained from work). A third source of psychic income comes from non-economic pursuits such as time spent with family and friends, volunteer work and leisure activities. The final source of psychic income flows from the natural environment in terms of its aesthetic and recreational qualities. It is true that this final source of psychic income does not come directly from socio-economic activity. If anything, such activity tends to destroy rather than enhance such values. It is therefore better that these values be taken as a given and their subsequent destruction be counted as an opportunity cost of the socio-economic process.

This last point reminds us that not all socio-economic activity enhances the psychic enjoyment of life. Consumption of some portion of human-made capital can reduce the psychic enjoyment of life if consumers make bad choices or if needs and wants have been inappropriately ranked. In addition, while benefits can be enjoyed by individuals engaged in production activities, for most people, production activities are unpleasant. Unpleasant things that lower one's psychic enjoyment of life (e.g. noise pollution and commuting to work) represent the 'psychic outgo' of economic activity. It is the subtraction of psychic outgo from psychic income that leads to a measure of *net psychic income* – the fourth elemental category. Net psychic income is, in effect, the 'uncancelled benefit' of socio-economic activity (Daly, 1979). Why? Imagine tracing the socio-economic process from natural capital to its final psychic conclusion. Every intermediate transaction involves the cancelling out of a receipt and expenditure of the same magnitude (i.e. the seller receives what the buyer pays). Once a physical good is in the possession of the final consumer, there is no further exchange and, thus, no further cancelling out of transactions. Apart from the good itself, what remains at the end of the process is the uncancelled exchange value of the psychic income that the ultimate consumer expects to gain from the good plus any psychic disbenefits and other costs associated with the good's production. Note, therefore, that if the costs are subtracted from the good's final selling price, the difference constitutes the 'use value' added to low entropy matter-energy during the production process. Presumably the difference is positive otherwise the socio-economic process is a pointless exercise.

The fifth and final elemental category is the cost of *lost natural capital services* and arises because, in obtaining the throughput to produce and maintain human-made capital, natural capital must be manipulated and exploited both as a source of low entropy and as a high entropy waste absorbing sink. Perrings has shown that no matter how benignly human beings conduct their exploitative activities, the resultant disarrangement of matter-energy and inevitable coevolutionary feedback responses has deleterious impacts on the natural environment (Perrings, 1987). Consequently, human beings must accept some loss of the free source, sink and life-support services provided by natural capital as some portion of the low entropy it provides is transformed into physical goods and returns, once they have been consumed, as high entropy waste. In a similar way to net psychic income, lost natural capital services constitute the 'uncancelled cost' of socio-economic activity (Lawn and Sanders, 1999). Why? Imagine tracing the socio-economic process from its psychic conclusion back to natural capital. Once again, all transactions cancel out. What remains on this occasion is the opportunity cost of resource use or, more definitively, the uncancelled exchange value of any natural capital services sacrificed in obtaining the throughput of matter-energy to fuel the socio-economic process.[5]

In sum, the linear throughput model illustrates the following. Natural capital provides the throughput of matter-energy that is needed to produce and maintain the stock of human-made capital. Human-made capital is needed to enjoy a level of net psychic income greater than what would otherwise be experienced if the socio-economic process did take place. Finally, in manipulating and exploiting natural capital for the throughput of matter-energy, the three instrumental services that natural capital provides are, to some degree, unavoidably sacrificed.

ASPECTS FUNDAMENTAL TO UNDERSTANDING WHAT IS REQUIRED TO ACHIEVE SUSTAINABLE DEVELOPMENT

The above discussion now places us in a more advantageous position to reflect on the aspects central to both defining and achieving sustainable development and, ultimately, how sustainable development might be measured. These aspects can be categorised as ecological/biophysical, psychological, economic, and social/cultural.

Ecological and Biophysical Factors

As previously mentioned, the throughput of matter-energy is the physical intermediary connecting natural and human-made capital. It was also pointed out that natural capital constitutes the tap-root of the socio-economic process because natural capital is the only source of low entropy resources; it is the ultimate waste assimilating sink; and is a critical generator of the life-support services that maintain the human habitability of the planet. Given the obvious importance of natural capital in achieving ecological sustainability, one must ask oneself the following questions:

- How much natural capital is required to ensure the ecological sustainability objective is not recklessly put at risk?
- Should natural capital maintenance be a necessary sustainability tenet, what rules-of-thumb should human beings adhere to in order to prevent the wholesale decline in both the quantity and quality of natural capital stocks?

I will endeavour to answer the first question by beginning with a consideration of production possibilities. Since Hicks (1946) defined income as the maximum amount that can be produced and consumed in the present without comprising the ability to produce and consume the same amount in the future, it has been widely recognised that sustaining the production of a particular quantity of physical goods requires the maintenance of income-generating capital. Where debate has raged is in relation to the form in which the capital should exist. While some observers believe natural and human-made capital should be individually maintained ('strong' sustainability), others believe it is only necessary to maintain an appropriately combined stock of both forms of capital ('weak' sustainability). Which of the two approaches stands as the most appropriate form of action depends critically upon whether human-made capital and the technology embodied within it are able to serve as an adequate substitute for the low entropy matter-energy that only natural capital can provide. Should it fail to do so, the requisite capital maintenance policy is that advocated by the strong sustainability proponents.

It is undeniably true that advances in the technology embodied in human-made capital can, for some time at least, reduce the resource flow required from natural capital to produce a given physical quantity of goods. However, for three related reasons, this does not amount to substitution (Lawn, 1999). First, technological progress only reduces the high entropy waste generated in the transformation of natural capital to human-made capital. It does not allow human-made capital to 'take the place of' natural capital. Second, because of the first and second laws of thermo-dynamics, there is a limit to how much production waste can be reduced by technological progress. This is because 100 per cent production efficiency is physically impossible; there can never be 100 per cent recycling of matter; and there is no way to recycle energy at all.[6] Third, a value of one or more for the elasticity of substitution between human-made and natural capital is necessary to demonstrate the adequate long-run substitutability of the former for the latter. It has recently been shown that the value of the elas-ticity of substitution derived from a production function obeying the first and second laws of thermodynamics is always less one (Lawn, 2004a). Thus, the production of a given quantity of human-made capital requires a minimum resource flow and, therefore, a minimum amount of resource-providing natural capital (Meadows et al., 1972; Daly, 1996; Pearce et al., 1989; Costanza et al., 1991; Folke et al., 1994; Lawn, 2003). It is for this reason that some observers believe the strong sustainability approach to capital maintenance is necessary to achieve sustainability of the socio-economic process.

But before one can give a satisfactory answer to the first of the above questions, it is still necessary to consider what constitutes the minimum amount of natural capital that needs to be kept intact to ensure ecological sustainability. It is at this point that we must go beyond production pos-sibilities and turn our attention to the life-support function of natural capital.

The ability of natural capital or the ecosphere to support life exists because, as a far-from-thermodynamic-equilibrium system characterised by a range of biogeochemical clocks and essential feedback mechanisms, it has developed the self-organisational capacity to regulate the tempera-ture and composition of the Earth's surface and atmosphere.[7] There has, unfortunately, been a growing tendency for human beings to take for granted the conditions for life – a consequence of technological optimism and the growing detachment most people have from the vagaries of the natural world. In particular, two falsely held beliefs have emerged. The first is a widely held belief that the Earth's current uniqueness for life was preordained. This is not so since, as Blum (1962) explains, had the Earth been a little smaller or a little hotter, or had any one of an infinite number of past events occurred only marginally differently, the evolution of living organisms on Earth might never have eventuated. Moreover, the coevolu-tionary process need not have included the participation of human beings. Second, it is widely believed that organic evolution is confined to living organisms responding to exogenously determined environmental factors. However, it is now transparently clear that 'fitness' is a byproduct of the coevolutionary relationship that exists between the ecosphere and its constituent species. Indeed, the ecosphere is as uniquely suited to existing species as are the latter to the ambient characteristics of the ecosphere. Hence, according to Blum (1962, p. 61), it is 'impossible to treat the environment as a separable aspect of the problem of organic evolution; it becomes an integral part thereof'. Unequivocally, just as past and current environmental conditions were not preordained, nor are the environmental conditions of the future. They will always be influenced by the evolution of constituent species and, in particular, the actions of recalcitrant species.

An awareness of the above brings to bear a critical point. While human intervention can never ensure the Earth remains eternally fit for human habitability, humankind does have the capacity to bring about a premature change in its prevailing comfortable state. Many people believe that global warming, ozone depletion and acid rain are already the first signs of a radical change in the planet's comfortable conditions. Nonetheless, there are some observers who argue that these events, if they are occurring at all, are of no great concern since they are little more than symptoms of a benign coevolutionary adjustment brought on by the eccentricities of humankind. That is, any malady caused by human activity is short-lived because whatever threatens the human habitability of the planet will simply induce the evolution of a new and more comfortable environmental state. For such observers, humankind is potentially immune to the consequences of its own actions.

Nothing, however, could be further from the truth. The quasi-immortality of the ecosphere prevails only because of the informal association that exists between the global system and its constituent species. But quasi-immortality in no way extends to any particular species. Indeed, historical evidence indicates a tendency for the global system to correct ecological imbalances in ways that are invariably unpleasant for incumbent species. Hence, while the Earth has revealed itself to be immune to the emergence of wayward species (e.g. oxygen bearers in the past), individual species – including human beings – are in no way immune from the consequences of their own collective folly. We can therefore conclude that the minimum amount of natural capital required to ensure ecological sustainability may greatly exceed the quantity necessary for production purposes alone. Of course, this still leaves the first of the above questions unanswered.

Deeper insight into the minimum required natural capital can be gained by considering what bestows natural capital with the unique capacity to support life. Is it the quantity of natural capital or is it some particular aspect of it? Lovelock leaves us in no doubt by emphasising that a minimum number and complexity of species are required to establish, develop, and maintain the Earth's biogeochemical clocks and essential feedback mechanisms. To wit:

> The presence of a sufficient array of living organisms on a planet is needed for the regulation of the environment. Where there is incomplete occupation, the ineluctable forces of physical or chemical evolution soon render it uninhabitable. (Lovelock, 1988, p. 63)

It is, therefore, the convoluted interactions and interdependencies between the various species in combination with their sheer diversity and the complexity of ecological systems – in all, the *biodiversity* present in natural capital – that underpins its life-supporting function. That is not to say that the quantity of natural capital is unimportant. It is important if only because the biodiversity needed to maintain the Earth's habitable status requires a full, not partial, occupation by living organisms. But the quantity of natural capital, itself, should never be equated with biodiversity.

If the sheer magnitude of natural capital is an inadequate indication of the effectiveness with which it can foreseeably support life, what is the minimum level of biodiversity needed to maintain the ecosphere's life-support function? Unfortunately, this is not known, although there is general agreement that some semblance of a biodiversity threshold does exist. What we do know about biodiversity is that in the same way biodiversity begets greater biodiversity, so diminutions beget further diminutions.[8] It is also known that the present rate of species extinction is far exceeding the rate of speciation – indeed, so much so that biodiversity has, on any relevant time scale, become a non-renewable resource (Daily and Ehrlich, 1992). Given that a rise in the global rate of extinction will unquestionably increase the vulnerability of human beings to its own extinction, a sensible risk-averse strategy for humankind to adopt is a rigid adherence to a biodiversity 'line in the sand'. Ehrlich (1993) provides a hint as to where this line should be drawn by pointing out that humankind knows enough about the value of biodiversity to operate on the principle that 'all reductions in biodiversity should be avoided because of the potential threats to ecosystem functioning and its life-support role'. As a corollary of Ehrlich's dictum, humankind should draw a line at the currently existing level of biodiversity. Conscious efforts should also be made to preserve remnant vegetation and important ecosystems.[9] In all, a systematic decline in both a nation's natural capital and the biodiversity contained within such stocks should be viewed as a failure on the part of government policy to achieve ecological sustainability.

We are now in a position to answer the second of our above questions – that is, what sustainability precepts must we follow to prevent the decline in both the quantity and quality of natural capital stocks? While there are many possible precepts, the four fundamental rules-of-thumb requiring adherence are that:

1. the rate of renewable resource extraction should not exceed the regeneration rate of renewable resource stocks;
2. the depletion of non-renewable resources should be offset by using some of the depletion proceeds to cultivate renewable resource substitutes;
3. the rate of high entropy waste generation should not exceed the ecosphere's waste assimilative capacity; and
4. native vegetation and critical ecosystems must be preserved, rehabilitated, and/or restored. In addition, future exploitation of natural capital should be confined to areas already strongly modified by previous human activities.

As we shall see soon, these sustainability precepts can be used to ascertain both broad and narrow definitions of sustainable development. Moreover, and provided the rate of resource use, the regeneration rates of renewable resource stocks, and the ecosphere's waste assimilative capacity can be reliably measured, the above precepts can also serve as a useful means for establishing sustainability indicators. They can also be employed to estimate the cost of lost natural capital services. More on the value of this later.

Psychological Factors

It has already been explained that human well-being depends critically on the psychic enjoyment of life. Despite having a good sense of what contributes directly towards net psychic income – the fourth elemental category of the linear throughput model – it is important to consider the extent to which each of the contributing factors is likely to advance the human condition. Although this will differ from culture to culture, and between each individual in any particular society, a greater understanding can be arrived at by contemplating Maslow's hierarchy of human needs (1954) as depicted in Figure 2.4.

Beginning with the lowest form of human need, the hierarchy is classified below in accordance with Maslow's ranking of lower to higher-order needs:[10]

- *Physiological needs* – this category of need includes one's basic requirement for food, clothing, and shelter.
- *Safety needs* – this includes the need for physical and mental security; freedom from fear, anxiety and chaos; and the need for stability,

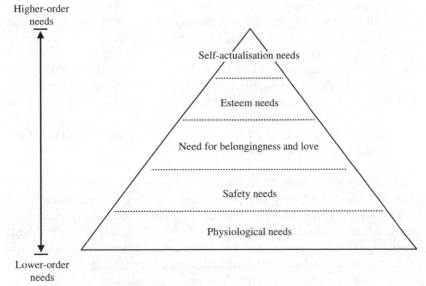

Higher-order needs

Lower-order needs

Figure 2.4   Maslow's needs hierarchy

dependency and protection. It also includes the need for a comprehensive and overarching philosophy that organises one's view of the
universe into a satisfactory, coherent and meaningful whole.
Satisfying safety needs necessitates such things as: (1) a minimum
level of income and an appropriate welfare safety net – overall,
a strict adherence to the principle of intragenerational equity and
justice; (2) the establishment of institutions based around the need
for social coherence and stability; and (3) ecological sustainability
and the continuation of the evolutionary process to ensure physiological needs are safely sustained in the future.

• *The need for belongingness and love* – this includes the need for
affectionate relationships with people in general; the hunger for
contact and intimacy; the desire for a sense of place in one's group,
family and society; and the urgent need to overcome or avoid the
pangs of loneliness, of ostracism, of rejection and of rootlessness.
A true and fully encompassing sense of belongingness and love also
necessitates a strong sense of identity with posterity. Hence, satisfying the need for belongingness and love demands a corresponding
adherence to the principle of intergenerational equity and justice.

• *The need for esteem* – this includes the need for a stable and high
evaluation of oneself, for self-respect and for the esteem of others.
It essentially involves: (1) the desire for strength, achievement,

adequacy, mastery and competence; (2) the need for independence and freedom; (3) the desire for recognition, attention, importance, dignity and appreciation; and (4) a sense of personal contribution to society at large.

- *Self-actualisation needs* – the need for self actualisation relates to an individual's ultimate desire for self-fulfilment, that is, one's desire to become fully actualised in what he or she is capable of becoming. At the pinnacle of the hierarchy of human needs, Maslow regards self-actualisation needs as the most 'creative and rewarding phase of the human development process'.

By organising human needs into a hierarchy of relative prepotency, Maslow's needs hierarchy not only reflects the multi-dimensionality of human existence, it paints a picture of the human personality as an integrated whole in which every part, level and dimension is interdependent. Most importantly, however, the needs hierarchy indicates that once basic physiological needs have been satisfied, desires originating from a higher level of existence begin to emerge. As they do, an individual's desires are no longer dominated by the need for food, clothing, and shelter, but by the need to satisfy emerging psychological needs. It is at this point that a healthy human existence requires the emerging higher-order needs to be satisfied along with basic physiological needs – what Weisskopf (1973) refers to as a healthy *existential balance*.

It is important to recognise that should the lower-order needs of the majority of a nation's citizens be satisfied, the socio-economic process need not operate in a manner consistent with the adequate satisfaction of emerging higher-order needs. In other words, it is possible for the socio-economic process to continue its emphasis on physiological need satisfaction at the expense of psychological need satisfaction. Why might this be so when it perceptibly results in many people experiencing an unhealthy existential imbalance? A couple of points need to be made here. First, and unlike psychological need satisfaction, physiological need satisfaction (such as being well fed) has no enduring qualities. Hence, satisfying lower-order needs requires one to engage frequently in what is required to satisfy them (such as eating often). Second, if higher-order or psychological needs are being inadequately satisfied, an equilibrium – albeit an unhealthy one – can be obtained by engaging in more physiological need-satisfying activities (such as increased production and consumption). Because physiological need satisfaction quickly evaporates, the desire for more production and consumption significantly reduces one's ability and the time available to fully satisfy higher-order needs. In doing so, it further increases the desire for higher rates of production and consumption that usually manifests itself in the form of a physical expansion of the economic subsystem. Consequently, an illusionary need for continued growth has the potential to become self-perpetuating. In a coevolutionary world characterised by path dependency, a growth addiction can arise even though it may be contrary to the betterment of the human condition. This growth addiction is commonly referred to as 'consumerism' or the 'treadmill of production' (Schnaiberg, 1980).

What does this all mean in terms of the human developmental process? To begin with, it is self-evident that need satisfaction aimed continuously at increasing the supply of means along one level that neglects needs on a different level is likely to disturb the balance of human existence (Kenny, 1999).[11] Since human development or the improvement in the total quality of life demands a balanced system of need satisfaction, the accumulation of human-made capital should only continue if, having largely satisfied lower-order needs, it does not come at the expense of higher-order needs. Finally, it would seem that human development demands, at the very least, a deep respect for the continuation of the evolutionary process plus a widespread concern for posterity and intragenerational inequities and injustices. Clearly, this entails having to invoke and uphold various universal rights and privileges, one of which should be the eradication of absolute poverty. Not only does poverty alleviation ensure the satisfaction of basic physiological needs, it constitutes a prerequisite for the attainment of the higher-order needs necessary for a balanced and healthy human existence.

Economic Factors

Many of the economic factors central to both defining and achieving sustainable development also emanate from Maslow's needs hierarchy. Basic physiological needs at the lower end of the needs hierarchy are, as previously explained, satisfied by way of the consumption and use of human-made capital. Therefore, just as natural capital maintenance is required to ensure ecological sustainability, so must human-made capital remain intact once its accumulation reaches a 'sufficient' quantity. The stock of human-made capital must also be equitably distributed and, in order to both maximise the benefits it yields and reduce the throughput required to keep it intact, must be efficiently produced.

Unemployment is an economic factor that has long been a weakness of contemporary socio-economic processes. While unemployed people in countries with a social security safety net are rarely deprived of their ability to satisfy basic lower-order needs, they are often deprived of the capacity to satisfy their safety and esteem needs. In almost all instances, they are starved of their potential to satisfy self-actualisation needs.

Indeed, for many long-term unemployed people, self-actualisation needs are grotesquely suppressed. This often leads to disillusionment, depression, and an increased likelihood of committing a serious crime.[12] Unemployment also results in a major loss of valuable skills and the subsequent depreciation of a nation's productive capacity (Mitchell, 2001). Indisputably, the impact of unemployment and underemployment should be counted as a welfare-reducing cost. In addition, full employment must be viewed as an obligatory macroeconomic objective for any nation wanting to achieve a comprehensive form of sustainable development.

There is, however, the potential for the full employment and ecological sustainability objectives to conflict (Lawn, 2001). Under the institutional arrangements currently existing in most countries, there is a well-established link between gross domestic product (GDP) and employment. This link compels such countries to continually expand the economic subsystem in order to prevent unemployment from rising. Compounding the fact that growth can eventually be existentially undesirable, it is unquestionably unsustainable. It is therefore critical to discover ways and means to sever the GDP–employment link so that full employment can be achieved without the perceived need for continued growth (Lawn, 2004b).

It is unfortunate that many beneficial economic factors are ignored because they fail to be assigned a market price. Unpaid household work and other forms of voluntary work yield enormous benefits in terms of both the economic goods and services they provide and the psychological need satisfaction obtained by those who engage in such work. Clearly, any worthwhile indicator of sustainable development must, where possible, include the value of unpaid as well as paid forms of employment.

Finally, debt is an economic factor all too often overlooked when both the concept of sustainable development is discussed and when indicators of sustainable development are constructed. Of particular significance is overseas debt. In most instances, the increase in a nation's foreign debt reduces its long-term capacity to sustain current levels of economic welfare. While it is true that a net borrower can use the inflowing funds to both augment its stock of human-made capital and improve the technology embodied within it, productive capacity is ultimately limited by the stock of natural capital. Unfortunately, many countries with burgeoning foreign debts are forced to liquidate their natural capital assets in order to service their debt repayments. This has the disastrous effect of eroding their sustainable productive capacity. Worse still, heavily indebted Third World countries are increasingly required to accept loans from the International Monetary Fund (IMF) that, as a consequence of attached conditions, compel their respective governments to rein in spending on the provision of vital public services (Pitt, 1976; George, 1988; Daly and Cobb, 1989).

Social/Cultural Factors

Critical social and cultural factors are to be found and expressed in a society's institutions. By institutions, I mean norms, customs, habits, support networks and various non-price rules embodied in a range of formal and informal structures and arrangements. There has been a tendency in recent times to downplay the importance of institutions, particularly with regard to the relationship between institutions and the market place. Many free-marketeers, for example, view institutions as constraints or impediments to the free and effective operation of markets. Some observers have gone so far as to say that a nation's well-being can be deleteriously affected by a condition referred to as 'institutional sclerosis' (Olson, 1982). While one should never doubt the likely existence of ill-conceived institutions or institutional arrangements that become obsolete over time, the economic value of the majority of institutions lie in their capacity to serve as a cognitive framework for both interpreting reality and understanding the sense data upon which choices and exchanges are made (Hodgson, 1988). Furthermore, institutions act as an informational guideline without which a complex economic environment would be largely devoid of meaningful and purposeful action (McLeod and Chaffee, 1972). Hence, it is only through a culturally-defined institutional framework – society's *moral capital* – that market-based arrangements between buyers and sellers can be of a qualitative nature sufficient to facilitate mutually advantageous exchange (Boulding, 1970; O'Connor, 1989). From a non-economic perspective, social and moral capital constitute much of the foundation upon which many higher-order needs, such as a sense of belongingness, contribution and social inclusion, are ultimately satisfied.

The importance of moral capital helps explain why market economies, once they became widely established, were so successful in advancing the human condition. Either by good luck or good design, the moral capital presupposed by a market economy was largely in place at the time when markets first emerged as prominent institutional mechanisms – a legacy of a pre-capitalist past when morality played a critical role in the establishment of built-in restraints on individual self-motivated behaviour. This ensured that market outcomes were beneficially influenced by shared morals, religion, custom and education (Daly, 1987). However, there is increasing evidence to suggest that the individualistic ethos that has since become an integral part of modern capitalism is slowly undermining the market's moral capital foundations (Hirsch, 1976). It is for this reason that some observers believe that markets do not accumulate moral capital, they have a tendency to deplete it. As a consequence, the continued success of any market economy, in particular, its ability to achieve sustainable development, could well depend on society's capacity to regenerate moral capital, just as it relies on the ecosphere to regenerate natural capital (Daly and Cobb, 1989; Lawn, 2000).

The importance of moral capital has one other important implication for the sustainable development process. It has already been argued that human development involves having to invoke and uphold various universal rights and privileges. Exactly what these rights and privileges entail is, again, a cultural-specific issue. Nonetheless, very few would argue against the principle that while the needs of posterity should take priority over the extravagant desires of the present, they should always remain subordinate to the latter's basic needs. There is a good reason for this. People currently alive can experience the pain of severe deprivation. People yet to exist cannot. Whether we like it or not, sentience unambiguously serves as a means for determining what rights accrue to whom and when. But, of course, human beings are not the only sentient creatures on the planet. To overlook the moral concerns and rights of sentient non-human creatures simply because they are incapable of expressing preferences in the same way as human beings is entirely unjustifiable (Pearce, 1987). Indeed, as Johnson (1991) stresses, the genuine interests of sentient non-human beings must carry at least some moral weight otherwise human interests carry no moral weight at all. The consequent need to recognise the 'intrinsic value' of sentient non-human beings visibly warrants the limited rights of subhuman species to be included in the general domain of human rights. Although the rights of sentient non-human beings would in no way equal the rights of humans, one would expect an extended principle of justice to include the dignified and, where plausible, cruelty-free treatment of sentient non-human beings.

This leads to an important question: is it possible that a moral obligation to include the rights of subhuman species in the general domain of human rights – a so-called *biocentric* view of the world – could limit humankind's capacity to exploit natural capital for its own instrumental purposes? The answer is a probable yes, since the application of an extended principle of justice would, in some way, restrict the ability of humankind to augment the regenerative and waste assimilative capacities of the natural capital stock. For example, the prohibition of inhumane means of incarceration, transportation, and exploitation of livestock would greatly limit the capacity to augment the maximum sustainable yields of meat, dairy and poultry products. And while certain logging practices do not threaten sustainable timber yields, they can result in unacceptable losses of wildlife and old growth forests (e.g. the replacement of slow growing native forests with rapidly growing exotic timber plantations). Any subsequent banning of such logging practices would significantly reduce sustainable timber yields. In both instances, the regulation of human exploitative activities on biocentric grounds could dramatically restrict the sustainable rate of resource extraction from the supporting ecosphere.

One of the difficulties associated with a biocentric view of the sustainable development process is that is difficult to devise a general rule-of-thumb to uphold the limited rights of sentient non-human beings. Pearce (1987) suggests that natural capital intactness and biodiversity preservation and restoration – essentially an adherence to the four previously listed sustainability precepts – are sufficient to continue the evolutionary process and protect the habitats of sentient non-human creatures. Hence, according to Pearce, there is no need to make allowances above what is already required to maintain the source, sink and life-support functions of natural capital. Unfortunately, such advice does not prevent the unwarranted removal of sentient non-humans from their habitats nor any ill-treatment that may arise out of their subsequent exploitation. A strict adoption of a biocentric stance obviously demands more than mere natural capital intactness. However, from a measurement perspective – which is important when pondering the value of sustainable development indicators – Pearce's recommendation probably suffices. Without doubt, it is more amenable to measurement. Furthermore, in view of the atrocious record that most countries have in terms of natural capital maintenance, designing policy on evidence revealed by indicators that account for changes in the quantity and quality of natural capital constitutes an enormous step towards protecting the rights of sentient non-human creatures.

If social and moral capital are fundamentally important to achieving sustainable development, how do we go about measuring them? There have been a number of attempts at measuring social capital but all are in the embryonic stage of development (Spellerberg, 1997; World Bank, 1998; Kreuter et al., 1999; Lochner et al., 1999; Stone, 2001). It is probably more constructive at this stage to measure the impact of its deterioration, particularly given that it can be more readily observed in the form of such undesirables as high unemployment, reduced volunteer labour and increasing rates of crime and family breakdown. Notably, the cost of many of these undesirables have already been estimated and employed in the calculation of alternative measures of economic welfare, such as the Index of Sustainable Economic Welfare (ISEW) and Genuine Progress Indicator (GPI). Unfortunately, these costs are excluded from measurements of GDP or, if incorporated, are perversely counted as benefits.

Defining Sustainable Development in Broad Terms

Taking account of the aforementioned, I propose the following as a very broad definition of sustainable development: a nation is achieving sustainable development if it is undergoing a pattern of development that improves the total quality of life of every citizen, both now and into the future, while ensuring its rate of resource use does not exceed the regenerative and waste assimilative capacities of the natural environment. It is also a nation that safeguards the survival of the biosphere and all its evolving processes while recognising, to some extent, the intrinsic value of sentient non-human beings.

As indicated at the beginning of the chapter, such a broad definition of sustainable development may not, by itself, be particularly conducive to the establishment of sustainable development indicators. But it is a useful definition for a number of reasons. First, by equating human development with an improvement in the total quality of life, it reminds us of how important it is to satisfy the full spectrum of human needs. Second, by referring to every citizen, both now and into the future, it obliges the current generation to adhere to the principles of intra- and intergenerational equity. Third, it captures the two main aspects relating to the sustainability imperative – namely, the fundamental need to operate within the limits imposed by the ecosphere's source and sink functions, and the importance of preserving biodiversity and critical ecosystems. Fourth, it reminds us that rights accrue to creatures other than ourselves that, if upheld, limit humankind's share of the planet. Finally, it serves as an important basis for defining sustainable development in narrower terms insofar as any subsequent focus on a particular sustainable development aspect (such as ecological sustainability) must simultaneously conform to the relevant sustainable development principle (natural capital maintenance) while eschewing violation of all remaining principles (it must avoid leaving a section of society grossly disadvantaged).

DEFINING SUSTAINABLE DEVELOPMENT NARROWLY TO FACILITATE THE EMERGENCE OF SUSTAINABLE DEVELOPMENT INDICATORS

Sustainable Development as Increasing Hicksian Income – Sustainable Net Domestic Product (SNDP)

In seeking narrower definitions of sustainable development to facilitate its measurement, it is worth beginning with a reconsideration of the Hicksian definition of income. To recall, Hicks (1946) defined income as the maximum amount that can be produced and consumed in the present without comprising the ability to do likewise in the future. Whether a nation should specifically aim to continue the production and consumption of a given quantity of physical goods is, of course, a debatable issue.

But there is one aspect of Hicksian income that cannot be denied – it automatically subsumes the sustainability principle. Combined with the fact that the consumption of physical goods relates in some way to human well-being, the first of our narrower definitions of sustainable development can thus be: sustainable development is a case of *increasing Hicksian income*.

Given the widespread use of GDP as a measure of income at the national level, it is instructive to consider how well it does or does not reflect Hicksian income. GDP is a monetary measure of the goods and services annually produced by domestically located factors of production (i.e. by the natural and human-made capital located in a particular country). The best way to determine whether GDP constitutes Hicksian income is to ask the following question: can a nation consume its entire GDP without it undermining its ability to produce and consume the same GDP in the future? For a number of reasons, the answer is an obvious no. First, some of the annual GDP must be set aside to replace worn out human-made capital. Second, production and consumption involve activities that are, in many cases, ecologically destructive. Consequently, a portion of the annual GDP – namely, some of the profits generated from the depletion of natural capital – must be invested to restore the stock of income-generating capital. Finally, many economic activities are designed, not with consumption in mind, but for rehabilitative purposes (e.g. medical procedures and vehicle accident repairs). Others are conducted with the specific intention of defending a nation's citizens from the side-effects of past and present human endeavours (e.g. flood mitigation projects and crime prevention measures). Clearly, GDP overstates Hicksian national income. In all, a better measure of Hicksian income or what is variously referred to as Sustainable Net Domestic Product (SNDP) or 'green' Net Domestic Product (gNDP) can be calculated by adhering to the following formula (Daly, 1996):[13]

$$SNDP = GDP - DKh - DKn \quad DRE, \tag{2.1}$$

where SNDP = Sustainable Net Domestic Product, GDP = Gross Domestic Product, DKh = depreciation of human-made capital (producer goods plus labour), DKn = depletion of natural capital and DRE = defensive and rehabilitative expenditures.

Exactly what measure of SNDP one obtains when using equation (2.1) depends on the deduction made with regards to the depletion of natural capital. A simple but ingenious formula has been put forward by El Serafy (1989) to calculate the portion of the profits generated from resource extraction that must be set aside to establish a replacement capital asset. The set-aside component of depletion profits constitutes the 'user cost' or replacement cost of resource depletion. It is this amount that should be deducted when ascertaining a nation's SNDP.

Significantly, the user cost will differ depending on whether one adopts the weak sustainability or strong sustainability approach to capital maintenance. How? Included in the El Serafy formula is a discount rate that ought to reflect the interest rate generated by the replacement asset. If a weak sustainability approach is adopted, whereby substitutability between human-made and natural capital is assumed, it is highly probable that a human-made capital asset will be established. The chosen interest rate – commonly around 6 or 7 per cent in present value calculations involving human-made capital – is likely to be much higher than the interest rate used when a natural capital asset is established as per the strong sustainability approach. This is because the interest rate generated by a cultivated substitute resource is equivalent to its natural regeneration rate. For most renewable resources, this rate is approximately 2 to 3 per cent and therefore considerably lower than the rate of return on human-made assets (although strong sustainability advocates will point out that the return on a human-made capital asset is entirely dependent on the availability of natural capital, but not vice versa).

Consider, then, a non-renewable resource with a mine life of thirty years. At a discount rate of 2 percent, the user cost constitutes 54 per cent of depletion profits (i.e. 46 per cent constitutes income in the Hicksian sense). However, at a discount rate of 7 percent, the user cost constitutes just 12 per cent of depletion profits (i.e. 88 per cent constitutes income). Clearly, the user cost deducted in the calculation of SNDP will be much higher when the strong sustainability stance is embraced. SNDP will be correspondingly lower.

Sustainable Development as Non-Declining Capital (Weak Sustainability) – Genuine Savings (GS)

As valuable as Hicksian national income is as an indicator of weak or strong sustainable development, it has two glaring weaknesses. To begin with, it does not tell us with any precision whether the quantity of goods produced and consumed can be sustained in the long run. This is because Hicksian income assumes that capital replacement has been undertaken, or that it ought to have been undertaken, and that whatever remains constitutes the monetary value of what can be sustainably produced and consumed. However, it is an estimation only. Worse still, the stock of income-generating capital may have declined over the accounting period. Consider the following hypothetical example. A nation manufactures an insufficient quantity of new producer goods to replace worn out plant, machinery and equipment. Instead, it significantly increases the manufacture of consumption goods: indeed, so much so that it exceeds the net depreciation of human-made capital. Due to prudent resource management, the stock of natural capital remains unchanged. This country will experience a rise in Hicksian national income yet a decline in income-generating capital. Should this pattern continue, the former will be unsustainable in the long run. Clearly, the short-term rise in Hicksian national income would not be indicative of a nation achieving sustainable development.

There is a way to deal with this measurement problem. Since Hicksian income is based on the notion of keeping income-generating capital intact, we can focus on the stock of capital rather than the total quantity of goods produced. So long as income-generating capital does not diminish, the socio-economic process can be regarded as sustainable. Thus we arrive at our second narrow definition of sustainable development: sustainable development is a case of *non-declining capital*.

The change in a nation's income-generating capital can be measured in terms of an economic algorithm called 'genuine savings' (GS). There are many formulae available to calculate GS (Pearce and Atkinson, 1993; Hamilton, 1994; Pearce et al., 1996). For the purposes of this chapter, GS is given by the following:

$$GS = \text{Investment in Kh} - \text{NFB} - \text{DKh} - \text{Dkn} + q.\Delta\text{EHI}, \quad (2.2)$$

where GS = genuine savings, NFB = net foreign borrowing, DKh = depreciation of human-made capital (producer goods plus labour), DKn = depletion of ecosphere's source and sink functions and $q.\Delta\text{EHI}$ = value of ecosphere's augmented/diminished life-support function (q = marginal value of ecosystem health; ΔEHI = change in the ecosystem health index) (Costanza, 1992).

Sustainability is denoted by a non-negative measure of GS. As with Hicksian income, the value of GS will depend on whether one adopts the weak or strong sustainability approach to capital maintenance. Because the user cost of resource depletion is much higher when the strong sustainability stance is taken, GS is lower. There is, therefore, a greater likelihood of GS being negative and the socio-economic process, as a whole, appearing to be unsustainable under the strong sustainability approach.

Sustainable Development as Non-Declining Natural Capital (Strong Sustainability)

Not unlike Hicksian income, GS has a number of deficiencies. First, using optimisation principles, it has been theoretically shown that a positive value for genuine savings is a necessary but insufficient condition for achieving sustainability (see Chapter 6 for a full explanation) (Asheim, 1994; Pezzey and Withagen, 1995). Second, despite the strong sustainability approach involving a more austere estimation of the user cost of natural capital depletion, it is still possible for natural capital to decline and for GS to be positive.[14] Since strong sustainability demands natural capital maintenance, this result is counter-intuitive. As such, a positive value for GS is only meaningful in the weak sustainability sense. Advocates of the strong sustainability approach might therefore call for the following as a third narrow definition of sustainable development: sustainable development is a case of *non-declining natural capital*.

From an indicator perspective, this definition leads us to the problem of how to measure natural capital. One solution is to compile a natural capital account. Ideally, this account would exist as an inventory of: (1) the two major forms of low entropy providing natural capital – namely, renewable and non-renewable resources; (2) waste absorbing sinks; and (3) important ecosystems. The greatest difficulty associated with the construction of a natural capital account is determining the means by which its various elements should be measured. Does one use monetary values or physical estimates of the quantity of natural capital? Unfortunately, neither bears any precise relationship to the capacity of natural capital to sustain its source, sink and life-support functions. In response, a number of observers believe it is more pertinent to identify the specific aspects of the natural environment that perform critical and irreplaceable functions – what might be called 'critical' natural capital.[15]

There is one last weakness of GS that requires mentioning. While a measure of GS indicates something about the capital stock, it doesn't tell us if what we wish to sustain is rising or falling. Despite the logical desirability of a constant or rising stock of capital, one is still left asking: Is the total quality of life improving?

Sustainable Development as Increasing Economic Welfare – the Index of Sustainable Economic Welfare (ISEW) and the Genuine Progress Indicator (GPI)

The last weakness of GS brings us to the second deficiency of Hicksian income and, therefore, of SNDP – namely, it is not a particularly good way to conceptualise income. Very early on in the consideration of national income, Fisher (1906) argued that the annual national dividend does not consist of the physical goods produced over a particular year. As explained in relation to the linear throughput model, Fisher believed it to be the services enjoyed by the ultimate consumers of physical goods – what is, after subtracting the psychic costs of irksome activities, net psychic income.

The implications of adopting Fisher's distinction between income and capital are significant. To begin with, any durable producer or consumer good manufactured during the current year is not part of this year's income. It simply constitutes an addition to the stock of human-made capital. Only the services rendered by the non-durable goods consumed in the current year and the durable goods manufactured in previous years that have depreciated through use over the current year are part of this year's income. Unfortunately, since the calculation of SNDP counts all additions to human-made capital as current income, it wrongly conflates the services rendered by capital (income) with the capital that renders them. While it is true that psychic income cannot be experienced without the existence of physical goods, it is certainly not determined by the rate at which goods are produced and consumed. It is, in part, determined by the quantity of human-made capital (at least up to a certain amount), the quality of the stock, and its ownership distribution – all of which can be favourably adjusted without the need for an increased rate of production and consumption.

It is interesting to note that one of the forefathers of national income accounting, A.C. Pigou (1932), believed Fisher's approach was both mathematically attractive and logically correct. Pigou opted not to follow Fisher's approach because he believed 'the wide departure it makes from the ordinary use of language involves disadvantages that seem to outweigh the gain in logical clarity'. Given that this observation was made at a time when the rise in production benefits clearly exceeded the rise in production costs, one can hardly be critical of Pigou. However, emerging evidence suggests the latter are now surpassing the former and so the great weight of disadvantage rests with the maintenance of the present system of national income accounting (Max-Neef, 1995).

Fisher's distinction between income and capital has one further implication. By keeping the two separate, it forces one to recognise that since the stock of human-made capital depreciates and wears out through use, its continual maintenance is a cost, not a benefit. It constitutes a cost because the maintenance of human-made capital requires the production of new goods that, as the linear throughput model revealed, can only occur if there is an ongoing throughput of matter-energy (the input of low entropy resources and the output of high entropy wastes). This, of course, results in the inevitable loss of some of the source, sink and life-support services provided by natural capital – the uncancelled cost of the socio-economic process. As equation (2.1) showed, the calculation of SNDP requires the cost of natural capital depletion to be subtracted. Nevertheless, because

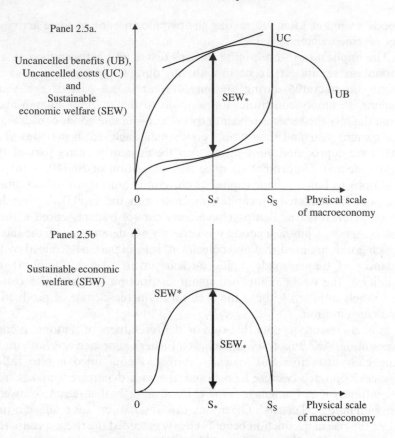

Figure 2.5   The sustainable economic welfare generated by a growing macroeconomy

Fisher's distinction between income and capital treats the production of replacement goods as the cost of keeping human-made capital intact, SNDP effectively stands as an index of sustainable cost. While an index of sustainable cost is preferable to an index of unsustainable cost, such as GDP, it scarcely serves as a quality of life indicator.

It is at this point that the two elemental categories of net psychic income (uncancelled benefits) and lost natural capital services (uncancelled costs) prove invaluable. Both can be presented diagrammatically to demonstrate the impact of a growing macroeconomy. Consider Figure 2.5 where, for the moment, it is assumed that there is no technological progress.

The uncancelled benefit (UB) curve in Panel 2.5a represents the net psychic income generated as a national economy expands. The character-istic shape of the UB curve is attributable to the law of diminishing marginal benefits which, barring technological improvements, is equally applicable to the total stock of wealth as it is to individual items. The cost of a growing macroeconomy is represented in Panel 2.5a by way of an uncancelled cost (UC) curve. It represents the natural capital services lost in the process of transforming natural capital and the low entropy it provides into human-made capital. The shape of the UC curve is attributable to the law of increasing marginal costs. Why does this law apply to a macroeconomic system? First, it is customary to extract the more readily available and higher quality resources first and be left with the more complicated task of having to extract lower quality resources later. Second, the cost of the undesirable ecological feedbacks associated with each incremental disruption of natural capital increases as the macroeconomy expands relative to a finite natural environment. Note that the UC curve is vertical at a physical economic scale of S_S. This is because S_S denotes the *maximum sustainable scale* – what is, for given levels of human know-how, the largest macroeconomic scale that a nation can physically sustain while still adhering to the four sustainability precepts.

Since economic welfare is the difference between the benefits and costs of the socio-economic process, the vertical distance between the UB and UC curves represents the *sustainable economic welfare* applicable to various macroeconomic scales. Sustainable economic welfare is also illustrated by way of the SEW curve in Panel 2.5b. In this particular case, a nation's sustainable economic welfare is maximised by operating at the macroeconomic scale of S_* (i.e. where sustainable economic welfare equals SEW_*). For this reason, S_* constitutes the *optimal macroeconomic scale* although, in a coevolutionary world characterised by disequilibria, such a point would not precisely exist nor be precisely attained.

Importantly, when technological progress is assumed to be fixed – that is, when the UB and UC curves are stationary – growth is only desirable in the early stages of a nation's developmental process. Continued physical expansion of the economic subsystem beyond the optimal scale is antithetic to the sustainable development goal because it eventually leads to a decline in sustainable economic welfare. This subsequently brings us to our fourth narrow definition of sustainable development: Sustainable development is a case of *increasing economic welfare* and occurs only while the macroeconomy is growing between the physical scales of zero and S_*.

Economic welfare at the national level is now conveniently revealed by the previously mentioned Index of Sustainable Economic Welfare (ISEW) and Genuine Progress Indicator (GPI). Both indicators involve the estimation of a range of economic, social and environmental benefits and costs deemed applicable to the socio-economic process (see Chapter 7 for a list of the benefit and cost items used). The costs are subtracted from the benefits to

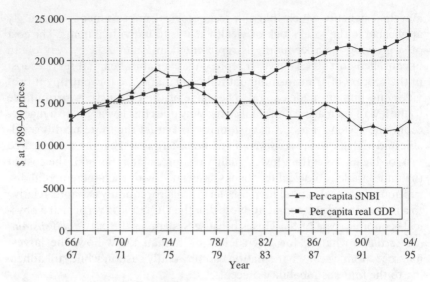

*Figure 2.6   Per capita SNBI and per capita real GDP for Australia,
1966/67 to 1994/95*

obtain an index number equivalent to the vertical difference between the UB
and UC curves in Panel 2.5a. As such, the ISEW and GPI conform to the
Fisherian definition of income rather than Hicksian income.[16]

Why are there two indicators of sustainable economic welfare?
Essentially the indicators differ in name only – the latter name adopted in
the mid 1990s to increase the indicator's appeal – although there are slight
variations in some of the valuation methods used to estimate the benefit
and cost items that make up the indexes (Neumayer, 1999). It should be
noted that a third index, a sustainable net benefit index (SNBI), has been
recently developed to highlight the Fisherian foundation underlying these
new measures of economic welfare. In this example, the various items are
organised into separate 'uncancelled benefit' and 'uncancelled cost'
accounts (Lawn and Sanders, 1999). The sum total of the cost account is
subtracted from the sum total of the benefit account to obtain the final
index value.

Figures 2.6 and 2.7 reveal the SNBI for Australia and the ISEW for the
USA and a number of European countries. In each case, the alternative
index begins to decline once the growth of the macroeconomy reaches what
amounts to a 'threshold' level of GDP (Max-Neef, 1995). Thus, the macro-
economies of each of these countries appear to have exceeded their optimal
scale.

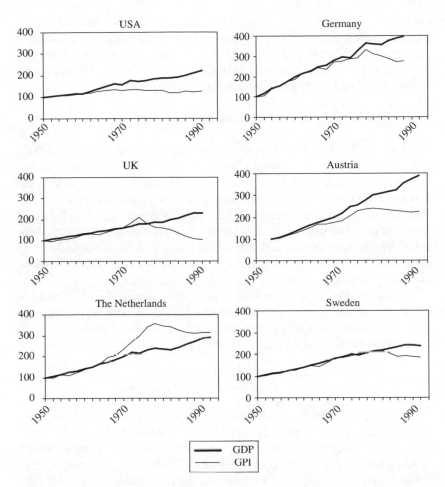

Source: Jackson and Stymne, 1996.

Figure 2.7 The ISEW for the USA and a range of European countries

There have been a number of criticisms levelled at the ISEW, GPI and SNBI. Some of these criticisms are dealt with in Chapters 7 and 9. At this point, I shall bring to the reader's attention one important weakness. While the ISEW, GPI and SNBI count the cost of resource depletion and environmental degradation, the final index figures do not indicate whether the economic welfare being enjoyed is sustainable in the long run. This is because environmental costs, whether reflected by the market or estimated by way of shadow prices, do not automatically become infinite once the macroeconomy exceeds the maximum sustainable scale (i.e. as per the UC curve at S_S in Panel 2.5a). Thus, it is difficult to tell if a declining index figure means: (1) a nation has surpassed its optimal scale; (2) a nation is operating inefficiently and therefore experiencing a narrowing of the gap between its UB and UC curves; and/or (3) a nation's UB and UC curves are widening but at a lesser rate than the rate of macroeconomic expansion.

Sustainable Development as Increasing Eco-Efficiency

The need to distinguish between the possibility of excess growth and shifts in the UB and UC curves would indicate a need to gain a greater understanding of the impact of both technological progress – which can shift the UB and UC curves – and the efficiency with which natural capital is transformed into human-made capital. The latter is commonly referred to as 'eco-efficiency'. In view of the desirability of improving the efficiency of the transformation process, a fifth narrow definition of sustainable development emerges, namely: Sustainable development is an example of *increasing eco-efficiency*.

To examine the eco-efficiency concept in more detail, the two elemental categories of net psychic income and lost natural capital services can be arranged to arrive at a measure of ecological economic efficiency (EEE).[17] Consider the following EEE ratio (Daly, 1996, p. 84):

$$EEE = \frac{net\ psychic\ income}{lost\ natural\ capital\ services} \qquad (2.3)$$

For a given physical scale of the macroeconomy, an increase in the EEE ratio indicates an improvement in the efficiency with which natural capital and the low entropy resources it provides is transformed into benefit-yielding human-made capital. A multitude of factors can be shown to contribute to an increase in the EEE ratio. To demonstrate how, the EEE ratio is decomposed to reveal four eco-efficiency ratios. The EEE ratio thus becomes the following identity:

$$\text{Ratio 1} \quad \text{Ratio 2} \quad \text{Ratio 3} \quad \text{Ratio 4}$$

$$EEE = \frac{NPY}{LNCS} = \frac{NPY}{HMK} \times \frac{HMK}{RT} \times \frac{RT}{NK} \times \frac{NK}{LNCS} \qquad (2.4)$$

where EEE = ecological economic efficiency, NPY = net psychic income, LNCS = lost natural capital services, HMK = human-made capital, RT = resource throughout, NK = natural capital.

Starting from Ratio 1 and progressing through to Ratio 4, each eco-efficiency ratio cancels the ensuing ratio out. This leaves the basic EEE ratio on the left-hand side. The order in which the four eco-efficiency ratios are presented is in keeping with the conclusions drawn from the linear throughput representation of the socio-economic process – i.e. net psychic income is enjoyed as a consequence of human-made capital (Ratio 1); human-made capital requires the continued throughput of matter-energy (Ratio 2); the throughput of matter-energy is made possible thanks to the three instrumental services provided by natural capital (Ratio 3); and, in exploiting natural capital, the three instrumental services provided by natural capital are, to some degree, sacrificed (Ratio 4). Each eco-efficiency ratio represents a different form of efficiency pertaining to a particular sub-problem of the larger ecological economic problem of sustainable development. The four eco-efficiency ratios are discussed in considerable detail and calculated for Australia in Chapter 16. Also provided in this later chapter is an explanation of how increases in the eco-efficiency ratios can beneficially shift the UB and UC curves shown in Figure 2.5.

Sustainable Development as Overshoot Avoided – Ecological Footprint Not to Exceed Biocapacity

As with any indicator, eco-efficiency ratios have their inherent weaknesses (see Chapters 15 and 16 on the potential pitfalls of eco-efficiency indicators). I will endeavour to focus on one crucial weakness. Not unlike SNDP and Fisherian measures of income, eco-efficiency indicators are unable to reveal whether a nation's macroeconomy has exceeded its maximum sustainable scale. While eco-efficiency can reflect the effectiveness with which natural capital is transformed into human-made capital, it says nothing about the long-run capacity of natural capital to sustain the socio-economic process. This, of course, comes at no surprise to some observers who have long demonstrated that efficiency does not guarantee ecological sustainability (Norgaard, 1990; Bishop, 1993; Daly, 1996; Lawn, 2000 and 2004c).

The need for an indicator to reveal whether the macroeconomy is nearing or has surpassed the maximum sustainable scale has led many observers to call for the compilation of a natural capital account (Jansson et al., 1994). As alluded to above, natural capital accounting is an exercise much easier said than done. Because it is impossible to add heterogeneous physical quantities, difficulties arise when measuring the total stock of any form of capital. For instance, how does one add timber, oil, fish stocks, wetlands and ecosystem services to obtain a single, well behaved physical index of natural capital? One possible way of getting around this problem is to aggregate the individual components of natural capital into a single quantitative index expressed in real monetary values. However, in what is known as the 'Cambridge controversy', some observers question whether an index of this kind can adequately represent the physical and, in particular, qualitative aspects of natural capital. This issue is taken up in more detail by Richard England in Chapter 10.

Because of the potential problems associated with the compilation of a natural capital account, it is has been suggested that an alternative means of ascertaining whether the macroeconomy has overshot its maximum sustainable scale be established (Catton, 1980). One such approach is a comparison of a nation's 'ecological footprint' with its available biocapacity. A country's ecological footprint is the equivalent area of land *required* to generate the renewable resources and absorb the high entropy wastes needed to sustain its socio-economic activity at the current level (Wackernagel and Rees, 1996). Biocapacity refers to the amount of *available* land a nation has to both generate an on-going supply of renewable resources and absorb its own and other nation's spillover wastes. Unsustainability occurs if a nation's ecological footprint exceeds or overshoots its biocapacity. This leads us to the next of our narrow definitions of sustainable development: sustainable development is a case of *overshoot avoided*.

There have been a number of criticisms levelled at the methodology used to calculate the ecological footprint (van den Bergh and Verbruggen, 1999; Ayres, 2000; Moffatt, 2000; Opschoor, 2000; van Kooten and Bulte, 2000; van Vuuren and Smeets, 2000). While methodological issues related to the ecological footprint are far from resolved, some of the criticisms have been addressed via the development of more credible valuation approaches (Lenzen and Murray, 2001). This has significantly increased the worthiness of ecological footprint estimates.

Having said this, some observers believe that ecological footprint assessments reveal only half of the sustainability story. As Rapport (2000) stresses, human survivability depends on more than the ability of the planet to meet the resource demands of socio-economic activity. It also depends upon the maintenance and restoration of ecosystem health – i.e. the life-support function of natural capital (Vitousek et al., 1997; Rapport et al., 1998). Since studies reveal little more than humankind's demand for resources, an indication of whether humankind has overshot the Earth's sustainable carrying capacity requires ecological footprint estimates to be complemented by diagnostic assessments of the health of the Earth's ecosystems.

As important as they no doubt are, ecological footprint and ecosystem health assessments suffer a similar fate as the natural capital account – they do not tell us whether the quality of the human condition is improving. Clearly, ecological footprint/biocapacity comparisons plus ecosystem health assessments serve only as a potential indicator of ecological sustainability.

THE POLICY-GUIDING VALUE OF SUSTAINABLE DEVELOPMENT INDICATORS

One doesn't have to think long and hard to acknowledge a fundamental weakness characterising all the indicators so far presented – they either reveal something about the sustainability of the socio-economic process or something about the quality of life it generates. No single indicator can adequately reflect both sides of the sustainable development coin. Regardless of what indicators are ultimately devised, inherent deficiencies always exist that, in some way, diminish their policy-guiding value. Despite this, each indicator has the potential to provide policy-makers with important information about past and present activities. This, in turn, can assist them to introduce the policies most likely to move a nation towards the sustainable development goal.

The policy-guiding value of sustainable development indicators can be further increased by examining them collectively rather than individually. For example, the ISEW, when combined with ecological footprint/biocapacity comparisons, can provide policy-makers with substantial insight as to whether a country is approaching or has exceeded its optimal macroeconomic scale (S_* in Figure 2.5) or, more crucially, its maximum sustainable scale (S_S in Figure 2.5). Hence, although the indicators revealed in this chapter are unable to reflect concrete reality with great precision, the message they convey can warn policy-makers of impending socio-economic decline or ecological catastrophe. This, alone, makes the quest for sustainable development indicators worthwhile. But the advocates of the various sustainable development indicators must never rest on their laurels. There is always room for improvement or, if need be, the eventual rejection of an unworthy indicator. Given the quality of the chapters in this book, I am confident that our capacity to do just that will be greatly enhanced.

NOTES

1. Dissipative structures are dynamic systems that draw in low entropy matter-energy from their parent system. In doing so, they exploit their capacity to change their physical form, to grow, and, potentially at least, to develop. Provided a dissipative structure is fulfilling its thermodynamic potential, it will tend toward a state of increasing order. But it can do so only at the expense of a much greater degree of increasing disorder of the parent system upon which it depends.

2. In the natural world, information exists as genetic information coded in the DNA molecule. In the anthropocentric world, information exists as knowledge encoded in various institutions and organisations.

3. A holon is a term made popular by Arthur Koestler. See Capra (1982), p. 303.

4. To understand what is meant by low and high entropy matter-energy, the importance of the first and second laws of thermodynamics must be revealed. The first law of thermodynamics is the *law of conservation of energy and matter*. It declares that energy and matter can never be created or destroyed. The second law is the *Entropy Law*. It declares that whenever energy is used in physical transformation processes, the amount of usable or 'available' energy always declines. While the first law ensures the maintenance of a given quantity of energy and matter, the Entropy Law determines that which is usable. This is critical since, from a physical viewpoint, it is not the total quantity of matter-energy that is of primary concern, but the amount that exists in a readily available form. The best way to illustrate the relevance of these two laws is to provide a simple example. Consider a piece of coal. When it is burned, the matter-energy embodied within the coal is transformed into heat and ash. While the first law ensures the total amount of matter-energy in the heat and ashes equals that previously embodied in the piece of coal, the second law ensures the usable quantity of matter-energy does not. In other words, the dispersed heat and ash can no longer be used in a way similar to the original piece of coal. To make matters worse, any attempt to reconcentrate the dispersed matter-energy, which requires the input of additional energy, results in more usable energy being expended than that reconcentrated. Hence, all physical transformation processes involve an irrevocable loss of available energy or what is sometimes referred to as a 'net entropy deficit'. This enables one to understand the use of the term *low entropy* and to distinguish it from *high entropy*. Low entropy refers to a highly ordered physical structure embodying energy and matter in a readily available form, such as a piece of coal. Conversely, high entropy refers to a highly disordered and degraded physical structure embodying energy and matter that is, by itself, in an unusable or unavailable from, such as heat and ash. By definition, the matter-energy used in economic processes can be considered low entropy resources whereas unusable by-products can be considered high entropy wastes.

5. There are two things worthy of note here. First, uncancelled costs are often undervalued because many natural capital values escape market valuation. Second, uncancelled costs should reflect the highest of two classes of opportunity costs – the first being the cost of transforming an extracted unit of low entropy into physical goods in terms of alternative goods forgone (e.g. if an extracted unit of low entropy resource X is used to produce good A, it cannot be used to produce goods B, C or D, etc.); the second in terms of the reduced capacity of natural capital to provide a future flow of low entropy resources that is required to produce physical goods in the future (e.g. if the extraction of a unit of low entropy resource X reduces the capacity of natural capital to provide a continuous flow of a unit of X over time, a unit of X will be unavailable to produce goods of any type in the future).

6. The technical efficiency of production (E) can be written as the ratio of energy-matter embodied in physical goods (Q) to the energy-matter embodied in the low entropy resources used to produce them (R) – i.e. $E = Q/R$. While the value of E can be reduced by technological progress, E must be something less than a value of 1.

7. It is the self-organisational capacity of the Earth to maintain the conditions fit for life that has led Lovelock to develop his 'Gaian hypothesis' – an hypothesis based on the notion that the Earth, or Gaia, behaves like an immense quasi-organism. See Lovelock (1988).

8. It has been estimated that for every one plant species lost, approximately 15 animal species will follow. See Norton (1986), p. 117.

9. Of course, the mere preservation or 'locking up' of large and small ecosystems will not, by itself, ensure biodiversity maintenance. Given the interdependent relationships between systems of all types, individual ecosystems are not entirely self-supporting (Lovelock, 1988). Their continued existence and the well-being of the biodiversity they contain is conditional upon the exchanges of both matter-energy with and between

neighbouring and far-distant systems. This applies to systems of all kinds, whether they be relatively pristine, moderately disturbed or totally refined. Above all else, maintaining biodiversity requires the exploitation of natural capital to be conducted on the principle of respecting the holistic integrity of geographical land and water resource units.

10. It should be pointed out that Max-Neef, while agreeing with Malsow's notion that all human needs are inter-related, does not believe in the existence of a needs hierarchy. Except for basic subsistence needs, Max-Neef (1991) believes in the presence of a horizontal spectrum rather than vertical hierarchy of human needs.

11. Kenny (1999) provides ample evidence to show that once a certain 'standard of living' is attained, the relationship between growth and happiness breaks down.

12. Evidence provided by the Australian Bureau of Statistics shows an alarmingly high rate of mental disorders amongst unemployed people relative to the remaining population. See Australian Bureau of Statistics (1997).

13. Equation (2.1) is just one of a number of varieties of Hicksian income equations.

14. This is due largely to the fact that the GS equation exists in a purely additive/subtractive form. The GS equation therefore implies potential substitutability of one element in the equation for another. The equation requires a 'subject to' which, in the strong sustainability case, is the need for a non-negative change in natural capital.

15. See Chapter 11 and the special section on 'Identifying critical natural capital' in Volume 44 (2–3) of *Ecological Economics* (2003).

16. For example, SNDP, as a measure of Hicksian income, starts with GDP as its base value (see equation (2.1)). Conversely, the ISEW and GPI start with consumption expenditure as the base value – because it is the major psychic income item – and avoid adding any net additions to the capital stock.

17. It should be pointed out that this is just one way of defining and measuring eco-efficiency.

REFERENCES

Arthur, W. (1989), 'Competing technologies, increasing returns, and lock-in by historical events', *The Economic Journal*, **99**, 116–31.

Asheim, G. (1994), 'Net national product as an indicator of sustainability', *Scandinavian Journal of Economics*, **96**, 257 65.

Australian Bureau of Statistics (1997), *Mental Health and Well-being: Profile of Adults*, Catalogue No. 4326.0, AGPS, Canberra.

Ayres, R. (2000), 'Commentary on the utility of the ecological footprint concept', *Ecological Economics*, **32** (3), 347–9.

Bishop, R. (1993), 'Economic efficiency, sustainability, and biodiversity', *Ambio*, May, 69–73.

Blum, H. (1962), *Times Arrow and Evolution*, 3rd edn, Princeton: Harper Torchbook.

Boulding, K. (1966), 'The economics of the coming spaceship Earth', in H. Jarrett (ed.), *Environmental Quality in a Growing Economy*, Baltimore: John Hopkins University Press, pp. 3–14.

Boulding, K. (1970), *A Primer on Social Dynamics*, New York: Free Press.

Capra, F. (1982), *The Turning Point*, London: Fontana.

Catton, W. (1980), *Overshoot*, Urbana: University of Illinios Press.

Costanza, R. (1992), 'Toward an operational definition of ecosystem health', in R. Costanza, B. Norton and B. Haskell (eds), *Ecosystem Health: New Goals for Environmental Management*, Washington DC: Island Press, pp. 239–56.

Costanza, R., H. Daly and J. Bartholomew (1991), 'Goals, agenda, and policy recommendations for ecological economics', in R. Costanza (ed.), *Ecological Economics: The Science and Management of Sustainability*, New York: Columbia University Press, pp. 1–20.

Daily, G. and P. Ehrlich (1992), 'Population, sustainability, and Earth's carrying capacity', *BioScience*, **42** (10), 761–71.

Daly, H. (1979), 'Entropy, growth, and the political economy of scarcity', in V.K. Smith (ed.), *Scarcity and Growth Reconsidered*, Baltimore: John Hopkins University Press, pp. 67–94.

Daly, H. (1987), 'The economic growth debate: what some economists have learned but many have not', *Journal of Environmental Economics and Management*, **14**, 323–36.

Daly, H. (1996), *Beyond Growth: The Economics of Sustainable Development*, Beacon Press, Boston.

Daly, H. and J. Cobb (1989), *For the Common Good: Redirecting the Economy Toward Community, the Environment, and a Sustainable Future*, Boston: Beacon Press.

David, P. (1985), 'Clio and the economics of QWERTY', *American Economic Review*, **75** (2), 332–7.

Ehrlich, P. (1993), 'Biodiversity and ecosystem function: need we know more?', in E.D. Schulze and H. Mooney (eds), *Biodiversity and Ecosystem Function*, Berlin: Springer-Verlag.

El Serafy, S. (1989), 'The proper calculation of income from depletable natural resources', in Y. Ahmad, S. El Serafy and E. Lutz (eds), *Environmental Accounting for Sustainable Development*, Washington DC: World Bank, pp. 10–18.

Faber, M., R. Manstetten and J. Proops (1992), 'Toward an open future: ignorance, novelty, and evolution', in R. Costanza, B. Norton and B. Haskell (eds), *Ecosystem Health: New Goals for Environmental Management*, Washington DC: Island Press, pp. 72–96.

Fisher, I. (1906), *Nature of Capital and Income*, New York: A.M. Kelly.

Folke, C., M. Hammer, R. Costanza and A. Jansson (1994), 'Investing in natural capital – why, what, and how', in A. Jansson, M. Hammer, C. Folke and R. Costanza (eds), *Investing in Natural Capital*, Washington DC: Island Press, pp. 1–20.

George, S. (1988), *A Fate Worse Than Debt*, New York: Grove.

Georgescu-Roegen, N. (1971), *The Entropy Law and the Economic Process*, Cambridge MA: Harvard University Press.

Hamilton, K. (1994), 'Green adjustments to GDP', *Resources Policy*, **20** (3), 155–68.

Hicks, J, (1946), *Value and Capital*, Second Edition, London: Clarendon.

Hirsch, F. (1976), *The Social Limits to Growth*, London: Routledge and Kegan Paul.

Hodgson, G. (1988), *Economics and Institutions*, Cambridge: Polity Press.

Jackson, T. and S. Styme (1996), *Sustainable Economic Welfare in Sweden: A Pilot Index 1950–1992*, Stockholm: Stockholm Environment Institute.

Jansson, A., M. Hammer, C. Folke and R. Costanza (eds) (1994), *Investing in Natural Capital*, Washington DC: Island Press.

Johnson, L. (1991), *A Morally Deep World*, Cambridge: Cambridge University Press.

Kenny, C. (1999), 'Does growth cause happiness or does happiness cause growth?', *Kyklos*, **52**, 3–26.

Kreuter, M., L. Young and N. Lezin (1999), *Measuring Social Capital in Small*

Communities, study conducted by Health 2000 Inc., Atlanta GA in cooperation with the St Louis School of Public Health, Atlanta, Georgia.

Laszlo, E. (1972), *The Systems View of the World*, New York: G. Braziller.

Lawn, P. (1999), 'On Georgescu-Roegen's contribution to ecological economics', *Ecological Economics*, **29** (1), 5–8.

Lawn, P. (2000), *Toward Sustainable Development: An Ecological Economics Approach*, Boca Raton: Lewis Publishers.

Lawn, P. (2001), 'Full employment in a low-growth or steady-state economy: A consideration of the issues', *Australian Bulletin of Labour*, **28** (1), 20–38.

Lawn, P. (2003), 'To operate sustainably or to not operate sustainably? – that is the long-run question', *Futures*, **36** (1), 1–22.

Lawn, P. (2004a), 'How important is natural capital in sustaining real output? Revisiting the natural capital/human-made capital substitutability debate', *International Journal of Global Environmental Issues*, **3** (4), 418–35.

Lawn, P. (2004b), 'Reconciling the policy goals of full employment and ecological sustainability', *International Journal of Environment, Workplace, and Employment*, **1** (1), 62–81.

Lawn, P. (2004c), 'How well are resource prices able to serve as indicators of natural resource scarcity?', *International Journal of Sustainable Development*, **7** (4).

Lawn, P. and R. Sanders (1999), 'Has Australia surpassed its optimal macroeconomic scale? Finding out with the aid of benefit and cost accounts and a sustainable net benefit index', *Ecological Economics*, **28** (2), 213–29.

Lenzen, M. and S. Murray (2001), 'A modified ecological footprint method and its application to Australia', *Ecological Economics*, **37** (2), 229–55.

Lochner, K, I. Kawachi and B. Kennedy (1999), 'Social capital: a guide to its measurement', *Health and Place*, **5**, 259–70.

Lovelock, J. (1988), *Ages of Gaia: A Biography of our Living Planet*, New York: Norton and Company.

Maslow, A. (1954), *Motivation and Personality*, New York: Harper and Row.

Max-Neef, M. (1991), *Human Scale Development*, New York: Apex Press.

Max-Neef, M. (1995), 'Economic growth and quality of life', *Ecological Economics*, **15** (2), 115–18.

McLeod, J. and S. Chaffee (1972), 'The construction of social reality', in J. Tedeschi (ed.), *The Social Influence Processes*, Chicago: Aldine-Atherton.

Meadows, D.H., D.L. Meadows, J. Randers and W. Behrens III (eds) (1972), *The Limits to Growth*, New York: Universe Books.

Mitchell, W. (2001), 'The pathology of unemployment', in W. Mitchell and E. Carlson (eds), *Unemployment: The Tip of the Iceberg*, Centre for Applied Economic Research, Sydney: University of New South Wales Press, pp. 11–32.

Moffatt, I. (2000), 'Ecological footprints and sustainable development', *Ecological Economics*, **32** (3), 359–62.

Mulder, P. and J. van den Bergh (2001), 'Evolutionary economic theories of sustainable development', *Growth and Change*, **32**, 110–34.

Neumayer, E. (1999), 'The ISEW – not an index of sustainable economic welfare', *Social Indicators Research*, **48**, 77–101.

Norgaard, R. (1985), 'Environmental economics: an evolutionary critique and a plea for pluralism', *Journal of Environmental Economics and Management*, **12**, 382–94.

Norgaard, R. (1990), 'Economic indicators of resource scarcity: a critical essay', *Journal of Environmental Economics and Management*, **19**, 19–25.

Norton, B. (1986), 'On the inherent danger of undervaluing species', in B. Norton (ed.), *The Preservation of Species*, Princeton: Princeton University Press.

O'Connor, M. (1989), *Non-Market Codependencies and the Conditions of Market Performance*, Working Papers in Economics No. 63, Department of Economics, University of Auckland.

Olson, M. (1982), *The Rise and Decline of Nations*, New Haven: Yale University Press.

Opschoor, H. (2000), 'The ecological footprint: measuring rod or metaphor?', *Ecological Economics*, **32** (3), 363–5.

Pearce, D. (1987), 'Foundations of ecological economics', *Ecological Modelling*, **38**, 9–18.

Pearce, D. and G. Atkinson (1993), 'Capital theory and the measurement of sustainable development: an indicator of weak sustainability', *Ecological Economics*, **8**, 103–8.

Pearce, D., K. Hamilton and G. Atkinson (1996), 'Measuring sustainable development: progress on indicators', *Environment and Development Economics*, **1** (1), 85–101.

Pearce, D., A. Markandya and E. Barbier (1989), *Blueprint for a Green Economy*, London: Earthscan.

Perrings, C. (1987), *Economy and Environment: A Theoretical Essay on the Interdependence of Economic and Environmental Systems*, Cambridge: Cambridge University Press.

Pezzey, J. and C. Withagen (1995), 'The rise, fall and sustainability of capital-resource economies', *Scandinavian Journal of Economics*, **100**, 513–27.

Pigou, A. (1932), *The Economics of Welfare*, London: MacMillian.

Pitt, D. (1976), *The Social Dynamics of Development*, Oxford: Pergamon.

Rapport, D. (2000), 'Ecological footprints and ecosystem health: complementary approaches to a sustainable future', *Ecological Economics*, **32** (3), 367–70.

Rapport, D., R. Costanza, P. Epstein, C. Gaudet and R. Levins (eds) (1998), *Ecosystem Health*, Malden MA: Blackwell Science.

Schnaiberg, A. (1980), *The Environment: From Surplus to Scarcity*, New York: Oxford University Press.

Spellerberg, A. (1997), 'Towards a framework for the measurement of social capital', in D. Robinson (ed.), *Social Capital and Policy Development*, Institute of Policy Studies, Victoria University of Wellington, Wellington, NZ.

Stone, W. (2001), *Measuring Social Capital: Towards a Theoretically Informed Measurement Framework for Researching Social Capital in Family and Community Life*, Australian Institute of Family Studies Research Paper No.24, AIFS, Melbourne.

van den Bergh, J. and H. Verbruggen (1999), 'Spatial sustainability, trade, and indicators: an evaluation of the ecological footprint', *Ecological Economics*, **29** (1), 61–72.

van Kooten, G. and E. Bulte (2000), 'The ecological footprint: useful science or politics?', *Ecological Economics*, **32** (3), 385–9.

van Vuuren, D. and E. Smeets (2000), 'Ecological footprints of Benin, Bhutan, Costa Rica, and the Netherlands', *Ecological Economics*, **34** (1), 115–30.

Vitousek, P., H. Mooney, J. Lubchenco and J. Melillo (1997), 'Human domination of the earth's ecosystems', *Science*, **277**, 494–9.

Wackernagel, M. and W. Rees (1996), *Our Ecological Footprint: Reducing Human Impact on the Earth*, Gabriola Island: New Society Publishers.

Weisskopf, W. (1973), 'Economic growth versus existential balance', in H. Daly (ed.), *Towards a Steady State Economy*, San Francisco: W.H. Freeman, pp. 240–51.
World Bank (1998), *The Initiative of Defining, Monitoring, and Measuring Social Capital: Overview and Program Description*, Social Capital Initiative Working Paper No. 1, Washington DC: World Bank.

PART II

Sustainable development and national accounting

3. The economic rationale for green accounting

Salah El Serafy

INTRODUCTION

The gross domestic product (GDP) and the gross national product (GNP) are the standard indicators used by economists for judging the level of economic activity and its changes over time. They are often used in sophisticated models that attempt to cull the subtlest lessons from them – lessons regarding past macroeconomic performance, from which spring recommendations for future policies – and all manners of analysis for testing economic hypotheses. And yet, rarely are these numbers questioned for accuracy, not just for errors of measurement, but more fundamentally on conceptual grounds. GDP, the central quantity of the national accounts, should be made up purely of value added, and must not contain any capital elements. And yet for many developing countries the conventionally estimated accounts do not distinguish between returns to the original factors of production, which are 'value added', and receipts arising from natural asset sales. In addition the erosion and degradation of the natural resource base that sustains most economies are ignored. Whether natural resources are 'depletable' or 'renewable' (according to the standard classification) mining them amounts in economic terms to 'disinvestment' that should be understood and properly reflected in the accounts.[1]

Green accounting has come to mean adjusting the national accounts to make them mirror natural asset deterioration as far as possible. But the course of using the national accounting system in this way has not run smoothly. Using different methods for adjustment inevitably yielded different results, and the variability of the results has led some critics to question the usefulness of the whole initiative.[2] In the present state of confusion over greening methods, and putatively authoritative endorsements of wrong approaches, it is not surprising that a climate of 'green accounting fatigue' has set in.

When the early debates on green accounting began to settle, attention focused for a while on whether any adjustment of the conventional estimates should involve the basic accounts themselves (i.e. those centring on GDP), or alternatively be relegated to extraneous accounts, leaving the basic accounts unchanged. Early experience in the Netherlands and Norway pointed in the direction of the latter alternative. A number of developing countries, however, had a different perspective, being aware that estimates of their national incomes were economically unhelpful and needed radical overhauling, but their influence on standardising universal accounting methods has understandably been limited. For a variety of reasons, the decision was taken to the effect that any adjustment to the conventional estimates had to be confined to what came to be known as 'satellite accounts'. The mantle of greening the accounts fell naturally on the United Nations Statistics Division (UNSD), for long the accepted arbiter of statistical techniques and the propagator of accounting methods throughout most of the world. It is of great concern, therefore, to find that in its latest guidelines for greening the accounts, UNSD itself has questioned the very notion as to 'whether a measure of green GDP is desirable, practicable or feasible' (United Nations et al., 2003, p. 415).

THE 'ECONOMIC' AND THE 'ENVIRONMENTAL'

The signs may have been evident early on when the revised System of National Accounts, SNA, (Commission of the European Communities et al., 1993) and its offshoot, the companion volume of guidelines on how to compile environmental 'satellite accounts' (United Nations, 1993) came out in December of that year. A decision seems to have been taken then to keep the conventional estimates of national income and expenditure virtually unchanged, curiously describing them as 'economic', while any adjustment, if made, would only be 'environmental'; hence the incongruously overused phrase, *Integrated Environmental and Economic Accounting*, the title under which the initial 'Interim Version' of the guidelines was issued. Thus green accounting was presented as an 'environmental' device, depriving it of economic significance. This language has continued until the present.

In order to ensure that the process of greening the accounts should meet with acceptance, it should produce results that make economic sense. Wrong methods would only produce unconvincing indicators that might be ignored altogether – a fate that has doomed the 'genuine savings' initiative of the World Bank (see below). During the 1980s' efforts to explore green accounting, while it was not difficult to garner support for the argument that environmental losses should be reflected in the national accounts, the method of effecting such an adjustment proved problematic. As controversy over the proper methods persisted (see Ahmad et al., 1989), it made sense, at least initially, to leave the unadjusted numbers alone, banishing debatable matters to satellite accounts. Because of the importance of method in this respect, this chapter will be intentionally tilted towards questioning popular procedures that spell confusion and threaten to sink the whole quest for adjusting the national accounts to mirror environmental losses.

'Integrating' the Environment

The stated function of the satellite accounts is to explore 'points of contact between the environment and the economic system', and provide a conceptual basis for forming a system that 'describes the interrelationships between the natural environment and the economy'. A principal justification for confining the adjustments to satellite accounts was to avoid 'overburdening the central framework' of the system (United Nations, 1993).[3] Opponents of a genuinely integrated approach that would alter the 'central framework' had a good excuse. The methods proposed for the adjustments had not settled, and confining them to satellite accounts would, in addition, safeguard the continuity of the previously estimated time series of the economic magnitudes. It was difficult for national accountants to have the validity of the old numbers impugned, and for them to face the inevitable discontinuity between the old series and the new. The argument will be made that the unadjusted numbers were in many cases wrong and economically misleading, particularly for economies containing significant primary production sectors where appreciable natural resource losses were occurring. Since the 'central framework' was being kept intact, confining any adjustments to satellite accounts provided a convenient shield against criticism, and afforded a haven for proposals that in many respects lacked rigour. There was nothing fundamentally wrong with this procedure when methods were offered as experimental, but rigidity tended in time to replace flexibility as the recommended methods for adjustment began to harden and reduce the available options.

The UNSD derives its authority from the Statistical Commission of the United Nations, and its recommendations tend to carry weight. But as the greening field has continued to be methodologically controversial, and as the 1993 SNA itself had imposed certain constraints that were naturally viewed by the UNSD as binding, further refining of the earlier guidelines has proved difficult. Two updated versions of the guidelines have come out, and more revisions are in store. In United Nations et al. (2003, p. 415), the statement is made that: 'The whole of this handbook is likely to be subject to significant revision in the short to medium terms . . .' A telling indication of the difficulties encountered is the fact that successive handbooks

gained steadily in length as they lost in clarity.[4] The initial 1993 guidelines
had come out in 182 pages; the 2000 version (UN, 2000) in 235 pages; and
the latest, the 2003 update, has no less than 572 pages – more than triple
the first version.

DIFFERENCES IN OUTLOOK

In hindsight it is possible to discern a dichotomy that had plagued the green
accounting initiative from the start. During the 1980s series of workshops
that was organised by the United Nations Environment Programme
(UNEP) and the World Bank with the aim of exploring concepts and
method, participants were probably under the illusion that they all had the
same objective in mind. There appeared no conflict between hitting both
targets of reform, whether economic or environmental, using the same
'greening' weapon. At least, the pursuit of the environmental objective did
not necessarily preclude achieving the economic one also. Divisions on
outlook, however, emerged, but these did not become really evident until
later. Gradually the split became unmistakable as disputes raged over
such issues as 'sustainability', and whether it is weak (economic) or strong
(environmental) sustainability that should be pursued in the greened
accounts, and whether one method or the other implicitly assumed that
natural capital and produced capital were substitutes or, at least to some
extent, complements.

Put differently, the environmentalists were looking for indicators of
natural resource change, whereas the economists had broad, and as yet,
uncrystallised intentions. Within the 'economist camp' there existed critical
subdivisions, perhaps the most important of which was whether the economic purpose of greening the accounts was to gauge *welfare* changes, or
less ambitiously, just to get a firmer grasp on the aggregate *product* and the
other macroeconomic magnitudes associated with it. There were also other
divisions which will be discussed later.

A DISCOURSE ON WELFARE

Welfare was to become a major source of conflicting views on green
accounting, deflecting attention away from properly estimating output, and
in the direction of the elusive pursuit of consumer preferences. Estimating
output, most national accountants would avow, is what they try to do, and
welfare assessment is none of their business. It is the re-estimating of
output that should be the primary goal of green accounting since welfare

is a derivative of output, not the other way around. Natural asset losses, being tantamount to disinvestment, should in the first instance reduce the conventionally estimated product before the impact of such losses on welfare can be considered. There is only one qualification to this statement when an ecological loss, such as biodiversity deterioration, totally escapes the national accounts since it is unlikely to be 'transacted in the market-place'. In this case, focusing attention on welfare would be justified, but this, of course, is not a green accounting matter.

With proper adjustments, the disinvestment associated with natural asset losses (or more accurately, only the 'user cost' part of these losses, see below) ought to be deducted from conventionally reckoned capital formation, and hence from GDP, leaving welfare interpretations to be made freely outside the national accounting framework. And yet, many economists, believing they were 'doing' green accounting, have taken naturally to the mistaken view, the one favoured by many environmentalists, namely of conflating domestic product with domestic welfare. These economists were eager to make use of a thoroughly worked field, welfare economics, attempting to employ it, *mutatis mutandis*, for shaping the course of green accounting. Helping this endeavour has been the emergence of the discipline of cost–benefit analysis, an offshoot of welfare economics, as an acknowledged practical tool for appraising new investments.

The 'official' history of welfare economics, we are told (Hicks, 1975), must begin with Pigou[5] whose name is quite familiar to environmentalists, not least for his analysis of pollution externalities. Pigou's role as the progenitor of welfare economics is well recognised by mainstream economists. Interestingly, his contribution to the subject came out co-mingled with the measurement of the social product, to which he repeatedly referred as the 'national dividend'. Pigou even attempted, though rather unsuccessfully, to depict the whole of economics as a study of 'economic welfare' which he defined, in a well known phrase, as that 'part of human welfare which can be brought, directly or indirectly, into relation with the measuring rod of money'. This definition was rightly disparaged on the grounds that welfare, or happiness, could not be divided into separate compartments of which one may be designated 'economic'.[6] Criticism also came later from another direction. Individual utilities, measured on a cardinal scale (the scale Pigou implicitly used for aggregating utilities), could not be added up meaningfully to produce a measure of 'collective utility'.[7] The debate over cardinal and ordinal utility was to open up a 'superstructure' of a 'new welfare economics', even when the sub structure, made up of cardinal utilities and segmented welfare, crumbled under criticism. The new welfare economics, armed with ordinal utility, veered away from its Pigouvian moorings as economists busied themselves with devising and debating 'compensation tests' to compare welfare in different situations. Then paradoxes began to emerge: a movement from point A to point B on a combined preference–production frontier could be pronounced as raising welfare, whereas by the same test, moving back from B to A would also raise welfare. Gradually trust in welfare comparisons along such lines began to be shaken (see Hicks, 1975 and 1989). Some index of cardinal utility, however theoretically imperfect, seems to be needed in order to make welfare propositions. But the Pareto optimum was to survive, appearing later in the guise of cost–benefit analysis.

Pigou in fact had issued explicit warnings against confusing the 'national dividend' with welfare. He stressed all along that it was important to think of 'real income' (or the goods and services that make up the national dividend such as 'beer, beef, concerts etc.', not as a total, but as per head of population. He enumerated three factors that affected translating aggregate income into welfare. First, the bigger the size the higher the welfare; secondly, the more evenly it is distributed the more welfare a given size would yield; and thirdly, the more evenly real income is spread through time, the greater welfare is likely: sharp temporal fluctuations would impair welfare (Pigou, 1952, pp. 66–7). Needless to say that viewing the principal aggregate that the annual national accounts churn out as synonymous with welfare (which many economists tend to do) will not satisfy Pigou's provisos.[8] The pursuit of welfare indicators, based on some measure of green accounting, became quite popular as evidenced by the search for an index of sustainable economic welfare, a human development index, and similar yardsticks, often meant to contrast higher product estimates with reduced happiness.

The Cloud-Capped Castles of the Mathematicians

Still on the welfare trail, a formidable hurdle has emerged. Interpreting the social product as an indicator of welfare managed not just to divert attention away from the central purpose of greening the accounts, but threatened to drag the whole initiative in the direction of what Hicks called the 'cloud-capped castles of the mathematicians'.[9] The practical pursuit of greening the accounts by altering the statistical measurements was sidetracked by influential economists who raised interesting welfare issues – issues, however, that are rather irrelevant to the rough art of income estimation. This has been distracting on a deeper level because the national income statisticians tend to pride themselves on being guided by the thoughts of the economists. Again through welfare, the concept of the Hamiltonian was bound sooner or later to enter the discussion of national income estimation. The versatility of Hamiltonian dynamics for analysing optimisation problems under conditions of perfect foresight – problems that are clearly far removed from the rough estimates sought by the national accountant – was brought to bear on greening the national accounts. The Hamiltonian was probably introduced in economics by Samuelson and Solow (1956), but was later articulated for national accounting purposes, especially by Weitzman who gave an unmistakable welfarist flavour to income (Weitzman, 1976 and 2000).[10] It is significant that Weitzman became a member of the panel chaired by William Nordhaus on integrated environmental and economic accounting – the panel that produced *Nature's Numbers* (Nordhaus and Kokkelenberg, 1999). Membership of that panel included theoretical economists with little familiarity with practical accounting methods, and a sample of national accountants who favoured 'strong sustainability' – the same strong sustainability that, in my view, had wrecked the USA initial efforts to green the American accounts (Bureau of Economic Analysis, 1994; El Serafy, 1997). Associating welfare-oriented theoretical economists with this report, though they had much of value to say, and despite the fact that they came out commendably in support of the resumption of empirical green accounting, eventually led the report along a strong sustainability path – a path, as a later part of this chapter shows, is inappropriate for national accounting. Briefly stated, pursuit of strong sustainability ends in wiping out from a greened net product any contribution made by mining – a result that was later judged untenable even by the chairman of this panel.[11]

WEALTH VERSUS INCOME

It seems almost self-evident that the 'wealth' of an individual or a group has more bearing on welfare than income which can naturally fluctuate from year to year. In lean years a person of wealth can draw on that stock to sustain annual welfare. Whether this obvious fact needed mathematical proof is questionable. But wealth became the focus of a line of thinking that again distracted attention away from attending to the flow accounts, and reinforced the strong sustainability approach rooted in stock valuation, stock being correctly identified as wealth. An important supporter of the wealth approach has been Dasgupta who, however, could find no better way of estimating the 'wealth' of a number of countries than multiplying the available income estimates by a factor of four (Dasgupta, 2001, p. C11) while at the same time surprisingly misinterpreting Adam Smith's wealth (as in *Wealth of Nations*, 1776) as if it meant other than the 'income of nations'.[12] Hardly any country has in fact successfully estimated its wealth, even just its wealth of *produced* assets such as machinery and equipment, roads, dams or other structures whose estimation in money terms is tricky.

The book values of some of these may be available, but economists, and hence the national accountants, are justifiably reluctant to set much store on these historical numbers. Here it can safely be asserted that a comprehensive measure of wealth has not been obtained for any country, however 'advanced'.

As to ecological wealth, which is presumed to be part of the national wealth, it comes in a vast variety of shapes, extending from a share in the protective ozone layer to biodiversity; from fish in streams, lakes and adjacent oceans, to forests of disparate types; from natural springs to rainfall to subsoil aquifers; and to complex ecological systems that are not easy physically to delineate. How can we be expected to be able to count the fish, quantify the forestry stock, or get some measure of biodiversity in physical terms let alone attach values to them in order to be able to calibrate ecological wealth? And yet, the latest guidelines for compiling the satellite accounts (United Nations et al., 2003, Chapters 7 and 10) cheerfully gloss over the obvious difficulties and reiterate a theoretical approach which is put forward as a recommended 'method'. Projections are to be made of the future use of this wealth, year by year, with annual prices predicted for valuation before discounting this conjectured stream in order to arrive at an estimate of current wealth.

Overlooked in this tortuous procedure is the fact that an estimate of wealth is not needed to gauge the flow accounts, and changes in total wealth, even if they could be reliably estimated, should not be mixed indiscriminately with the annual product or the latter would lose its economic significance. What is more relevant for greening the accounts is the physical change in the stock being accounted for, not its value. Physical changes in stocks due to economic activity can be valued at current prices as they occur. The total value of the stocks will always be debatable, and in fact it is of little use to economists. It would understandably interest its owners, the authorities assessing inheritance tax liability, and lending institutions when considering loan collaterals. If economists need to estimate wealth they can do this freely outside national accounting. The imaginative view, attributed to Irving Fisher, that national income is in fact the interest society earns annually on its wealth, is no doubt true, but hardly provides any guidance for reliable measurements.[13]

THE QUESTION OF POLLUTION

Pollution damage appears to be the major environmental concern of the richer countries,[14] but addressing it requires little help from national accounting. Assessing the impact of pollution on the national accounts is not easy, but pollution could be evaluated with profit outside them.[15] Where this has been attempted, its impact on the social product has been found to be relatively small – a finding that has probably lessened the presumed worth of greening the accounts still further. But in many poorer countries it is by no means small, and tends to be locally concentrated where it would have devastating effects. Direct counter-pollution measures have been applied with some success, both with market-based instruments and with regulatory devices. With higher levels of education, the availability of financial resources and better gathering and analysis of information, pollution can be indicated, its sources identified, and ameliorative measures instituted. Cases of significant success in this regard have not been scarce.[16]

Sidestepping pollution, what is seriously missing for the natural resource-dependent countries is accounting for the economically germane erosion of their natural resources. In what follows the focus will be largely on natural resource-dependent developing countries. The point is worth repeating: the flow accounts would be misleading if a country runs down its natural stocks and the accountants treat asset sales as a contribution to the domestic product. We must not forget that this is still the practice followed in the national accounts to this day – a practice that is surprisingly being accepted as producing 'economic measurements'. Even the satellite accounts, we have recently been told (United Nations et al., 2003), need not be used to adjust the domestic product on that or any other score. In addition to the commercial exploitation of stocks of minerals, timber and the like, there are also other forms of natural asset declines that need consideration, such as falling water tables, eroding top soils, receding forest cover and similar erosions that are not directly sensed by the market, and following the traditions of the national accounts could not be covered, though they lead to the under-pricing of primary products in the marketplace. Accounting for these may be difficult though not entirely intractable. Until some consensus forms on method, these may be left out of green accounting, but perhaps flagged in the satellite accounts. Being left out presents no serious problem: after all, no system of accounts is ever comprehensive.

THE INCONGRUITY OF STRONG SUSTAINABILITY

The attention given by environmentalists to the need to preserve natural resource stocks is certainly defensible. At least it raises awareness of the enormous losses that are occurring in natural stocks everywhere.[17] But physical measurements are perfectly capable of expressing these losses, perhaps more effectively than dressing them up in a money garb. Take, for example, a stock that at the end of an account period is physically lower

than it had been at the beginning, but whose price has in the interval risen
sufficiently to more than offset its physical decline. Using current prices –
a more recent usage now in vogue among national accountants – the stock
will be counted as having risen, and this questionable rise, if carried to the
flow accounts as an increase in income, will in effect license devoting it to
consumption. And if consumed, capital will be eroded in violation of the
basic accounting tenet of 'keeping capital intact' that has guided the estimation of income since accountancy began.[18]

The argument is doubtless important that natural resources have no
ready substitutes, or more accurately they lack *near-enough* substitutes. But
in the current context, substitutability or otherwise is essentially an economic facet that needs to be analysed in economic terms, and cannot just
be asserted as an inherent attribute of things beyond economic analysis. It
is not an invariable quality, but it varies in practice (among other things) in
response to changes in relative prices, consumer preferences and technology. Accepting at their face value the assertions made of the absolute
'uniqueness' of natural resources would stultify economic reasoning. And
economics is nothing if it is not a discipline of trade-offs and opportunity
costs, a medium that pits alternatives against each other for evaluation with
the economic calculus. Greening the accounts is obviously an economic
process, and denying the possibilities of substitution to invoke 'strong sustainability' methods for adjustment is certainly unhelpful. The 'user cost'
method which is an expression of so-called 'weak sustainability' does not
deny the possibilities of substitution between categories of capital. But in
its application to national accounting it is confined to a limited temporal
horizon – a year at a time – and is limited also to the entity for which the
accounts are being compiled. In its defence it could be viewed as a step in
the right direction: towards the sought-after strong sustainability which, of
course, cannot be obtained by national accounting (El Serafy, 1996).

That strong sustainability cannot be achieved through green accounting
may be demonstrated with the help of a simple example.[19] Take an imagin-
ary economy that depends totally on the extraction of a depletable natural
resource and where no other productive activity exists. Assume further that
extraction is carried out without capital equipment and totally without cost.
Let the conventional gross product of this hypothetical economy, which is
made up entirely of the proceeds of natural asset sales, be written as GP.

Since no capital equipment is involved, there is no capital depreciation.
The only 'depreciation' is the depletion of the natural asset, to be written
here as D. But D is one and the same as GP, so that if we seek a net product,
NP, this will be:

$$NP = GP - D = 0 \qquad\qquad (3.1)$$

Adopting this popular method for greening the accounts would result in negating any contribution made by the extractive activity to the net product. In other words, this hypothetical country, which may be viewed as an extreme case of a Saudi Arabia, has no net income, and is thus denied, by this kind of green accounting, any consumption from its revenues. Another point that needs emphasis here is that GP, being made up of asset sales, and NP, estimated as zero, are economically meaningless, both representing a faulty method of estimation.

Needless to say that the user cost method will always indicate a positive 'net' product that will be available for consumption. As argued in El Serafy (1993), a better view is to consider extraction not as depreciation, but as drawing down of inventories, to be accounted for at the level of the determination of the gross product which, if adjusted accordingly, will obviate any need to adjust the net product. Employing the user cost method, Neumayer (2000) was able to challenge the highly pessimistic estimates of genuine savings published by the World Bank (1997) which suffered – apart from other weaknesses Neumayer identified – from the use of a strong sustainability approach,[20] thus misleadingly indicating the economic unsustainability of a large number of countries. By employing the weak sustainability instrument of the user cost method, Neumayer was able to reverse many of the World Bank's conclusions. Interestingly, the genuine savings estimates, while published as indicators of sustainability, have been ignored in the country macroeconomic work of the World Bank itself.

STEERING BY THE WRONG COMPASS[21]

The foregoing was a rather lengthy introduction to the argument that greening the accounts has to follow an acceptable path in order for it to produce economically convincing green estimates. Using the wrong methods will not only produce faulty numbers, but might also continue to plague the account greening initiative. Green accounting, in physical terms, is straightforward and raises less controversy. It has to be done anyway as a preliminary to any green accounting in money terms, whether within or without the framework of national accounting. *Ex officio*, the sifting and propagation of 'acceptable' green accounting methods is the responsibility of UNSD which, however, seems to need the support of powerful associates to lend credibility to the debatable greening methods it has recently put forward. Why 'Studies in Method', previously proposed solely under the aegis of UNSD, should suddenly need powerful endorsements by institutions not especially known for special expertise in statistical methods, is unclear, and may in fact be interpreted as a defensive attempt to conceal the lack of confidence in what is being proposed.

If the above arguments are accepted, then the methods that are being recommended should be seen as unsuited to the conditions and requirements of the poorer countries. They may reflect the mature experience of a number of developed countries possessing few natural resources, but they must be seen as having been tailored primarily for addressing their special circumstances, characterised by the dominance of their economies by secondary and tertiary activities. It may suffice for their needs to pursue a NAMEA-type path to green accounting,[22] or impound environmental impacts in satellite accounts, but this will not meet the basic requirements of the developing countries, at least those which are anxious to know if their economies are growing or declining. The relevance of rich country experience and the applicability of their methods to the poorer countries need to be closely examined before these methods can be enshrined into a global accounting system.

The importance of adequately estimated national accounts cannot be overestimated. National accounts have been used quite productively in most countries for short- and medium-term economic management. Their greatest usefulness has been proved in relation to monetary and fiscal policies, for price stabilisation, setting interest rates, promoting employment, sustaining business confidence and influencing consumer behaviour. But their most profound failure has been for managing economic development in natural resource-dependent economies. If the macroeconomic magnitudes of the national accounts disregard serious losses of natural capital, they are bound to impart faulty messages about the economy concerned and indicate the wrong corrective policies. The fact that programme after programme of 'structural adjustment' supported, if not actually designed, by the World Bank and the International Monetary Fund (IMF) during the past two decades have failed, most spectacularly in the natural resource-dependent countries of Sub-Saharan Africa, suggests that the economic management of these countries may indeed have been 'steered by the wrong compass'. If we cannot judge from the accounts if an economy is growing or declining, living significantly on selling its natural assets, or on the unaccounted-for erosion of assets, how can we identify the economic weaknesses we seek to redress, locate sources of potential strengths to be promoted, or test the sustainability through time of current economic behaviour? If we fail to read the signs of the Dutch Disease (see below) in a resource-liquidating economy, we will continue to lead unsuspecting countries along a disastrous path of economic policies that not only hinder development, but will actually promote 'de-development'.

Policies Misled by Faulty Accounting

The principal purpose of this chapter is to argue that the conventional estimates of the national accounts, in providing imperfect indicators of macroeconomic change, can mislead economic policy (El Serafy, 1997a). Serious
ecological losses must be incorporated in the accounts for them to make
economic sense. Leaving aside the problematic issue of pollution, which
fortunately can be handled directly without help from national accounting,
it is obvious that when a country sells its forests as timber, depletes its
aquifers, over-exploits its fish stocks, and exhausts its mineral deposits, this
must not be seen as indicating economic progress. The accounts if adjusted
will in this case show a lower product, and in the process could indicate a
different growth.[23] Such asset losses as mentioned earlier are in fact disin-
vestments that should be incorporated in the accounts for the benefit of
veracity, and for providing a solid basis on which to build serious economic
analysis for the resource-losing countries. If these losses are overlooked, as
they tend to be in the conventional measurements, not only will the macroeconomic variables be faulty, but many other economic details will be
adversely affected also. Techniques for assessing input productivity, for
instance, will not yield reliable insights if the contribution of nature (the
'user cost') is not counted as a cost. The apparatus of project appraisal,
which has developed directly from earlier work on welfare, and which has
evolved into an apparently reliable discipline, has often in application fallen
short of reliability. Project analysts of extractive ventures rarely if ever
attribute any cost to nature's contribution to output, thus exaggerating
their profitability and luring capital away from more deserving undertak-
ings. At least since Marshall (*Principles*, 1920), economists had been
warned that mining comes at the cost of diminishing nature's store.

Valuation of inputs and outputs in cost–benefit analysis often depends
on the estimation of shadow prices, sometimes with the help of refined
methods, including computable general equilibrium models. But despite
the sophistication of techniques, the elementary notion that the apparent
net benefits of the investment are exaggerated is usually overlooked. On top
of the appraisal itself being faulty, the investment will additionally accel-
erate natural resource liquidation. The affected projects do not only fall in
the categories of mining and extraction, but they are also ventures that
involve soil erosion or falling water tables which remain concealed from the
accountants' view. Over-estimated project benefits inflate the sectoral and
domestic products too, thus licensing unwarranted consumption.

Beneficiaries of extractive activities, especially governments in developing
countries in which the rights of many natural resources are usually vested,
tend to believe, or affect to believe, their economists when they assure

them that financial flows associated with the deterioration of their natural endowment constitute economic income. The celebrated 'Hartwick Rule' (Hartwick, 1977), it may be recalled, cautioned against such a view, but went to the other extreme of regarding them *entirely* as capital – a reflection, as argued earlier, of a strong sustainability outlook. Hartwick urged that these revenues, representing capital erosion, should be excluded from estimates of current income, and re-invested in new projects to yield future income. The fact that he did not specify that the new projects should aim at the restoration of the natural assets that were being liquidated, or the generation of close substitutes for them, earned him the opprobrium of environmentalists who labelled him, rather inappropriately, a 'weak sustainablist'. Mainstream economists, denying the growing scarcity of natural resources, are at least consistent when they regard the surpluses of extraction as 'resource rents' or income, made up of value added, thus conjuring up the vision of Ricardo's definition of rent which clearly is not applicable in this case. In practice, squandering 'resource rents' on unwarranted consumption has been common, producing in many instances economic after-effects that have been tragic. And instead of finding the fault in false accounting, a curious query has often been raised as to whether exhaustible natural resources, which can be commercially exploited, are a blessing or a curse for the country in question. This assumes that a country that is fortunate enough to stumble on hidden subsoil treasures, affording it a chance to enhance its development, must inevitably be doomed 'as if by a law of nature' to subjecting them to consumption and wasteful investments. Their exploitation is often associated with deleterious effects of a Dutch Disease nature (see below), which if correctly diagnosed, are capable of being abated by economic policies. But above all correct methods of accounting need to be employed.

THE DUTCH DISEASE

The Dutch disease is a complex economic syndrome that, unless checked by proper policies, will undermine the very structure of an economy that is otherwise lucky enough to locate natural assets, thus enjoying unrequited financial receipts not arising from the value added by the use of its original factors of production. It is usually associated with a sudden flourishing of a booming sector, such as happened in the Netherlands on the discovery of substantial deposits of natural gas in the 1960s. But it is also manifested in economies that are depleting and degrading their natural wealth and, in the process, causing the inflow of receipts that should not all be counted as recurrent income. The impact of the 'disease' is more severe the higher such revenues are in relation to the economy as a whole.

As the Dutch enjoyed the influx of the gas windfalls, they lavished them on consumption, pushing up wages and pensions, and raising other social benefits. But their good fortune was soon to be tempered by disadvantages that gradually emerged, reflected in rising real estate values, higher costs of production all round and an alarming shrinkage of secondary industry. Exports of manufactures suffered with the appreciation of the guilder, which also encouraged imports and led to imbalances in external payments generally. This phenomenon has been analysed extensively (Corden, 1984) with emphasis on the flow of funds away from 'tradeable' activities that produce goods for export or for substituting for imports, in the direction of 'untradeables', such as construction and services, to the detriment of employment and the balance of trade. It is instructive to see how this sequence of events has been repeated in the oil exporting economies, while income statisticians continued to portray asset-sales proceeds as income. The effect has been less drastic, though not unappreciable, in the case of other natural resource-losing countries, varying in proportion of the actual natural losses to their economies.

Even if the actual disease is not correctly diagnosed, or not diagnosed in time, its symptoms will out, thus calling for remedial policies. An obvious sign of sickness is the exchange rate as the local currency rises in value in terms of the currencies of the economy's trading partners. As exports of natural resources rise ahead of imports, the currency appreciates. The forces of the market cannot distinguish between flows that are 'requited' and others that are fortuitous and unpaid for, being 'windfall' transfers of essentially a capital nature. The appreciation of the currency, not only impedes the other exports, but induces imports that tend to displace the products of domestic industry, so that the effect on domestic employment can be devastating. A good flow-of-funds analysis would reveal the nature of the flows, their size and direction, indicating the appropriate amount of the inflows that the monetary authorities need to 'sterilise', keeping them apart from the reserves that sustain the money supply. Alternatively, sterilization may be attained if the surpluses, or the requisite part of them, could be held abroad in isolation from the domestic money supply. Such an analysis could be part of the account greening process.

If economic policy framers and those who advise them overlook the Dutch Disease (and, remarkably, institutions such as the World Bank have shown scant interest in it), the exchange rate may be out of kilter and remain so for long periods doing damage to the afflicted economy. Furthermore, as imports flow in, encouraged by a favourable exchange rate, the domestic price level, at least for tradeable goods, will not show rises that may cause alarm, and the authorities therefore will not think of devaluation as necessary. A method favoured by the IMF for testing whether devaluation is indicated or not is roughly the following. A past year is selected when the exchange rate is judged to have been 'right', and used as a base. Domestic inflation is then estimated and compared with a weighted average of inflation in the country's major trading partners. If domestic inflation appears to have been higher than foreign inflation, devaluation would be indicated, and if found to be lower, devaluation would be ruled out as a policy option. The idea that inflation might, in the latter case, be suppressed by the inflow of imports, made cheap by an overvalued currency, often escapes notice.

Perhaps the most effective weapon in the armoury against the Dutch Disease is devaluation. Economic development in countries like Indonesia in the 1970s and 1980s profited greatly from progressive adjustments of the exchange rate with a view to aiding non-natural-resource-based exports, and to check imports. Whether or not this important weapon of devaluation was wielded in this case to abate specific economic symptoms that appeared unfavourable, or consciously as part of a wider war against the Dutch Disease, is difficult to discern and probably of minor importance.

It may be argued that national accounting, even if properly done, will fail to identify a Dutch Disease. But the greening process could still be a necessary first step to lay the groundwork for corrective policies. A downward adjustment of the conventional estimates of the national product would certainly be indicative, and with it also other adjustments in savings and investment, the fiscal balance and maybe exports and other balance of payments items too. The balance of payments on current account may wrongly show surpluses of a capital nature due to exporting natural assets when these should be recorded in the capital account.[24] But apart from adjusting the aggregates, subdivisions could also be adjusted. Social accounting matrices (SAMs) would certainly be helpful if they are made to reveal the flows of funds between the various components of the economy, specifically identifying their nature and whether they are flows of an income or a capital nature. SAMs are well known as useful for national accounting, and they receive ample coverage in Chapter XX of the SNA (Commission of the European Communities et al., 1993) though without reference to natural resources. But the topic is picked up in Chapter 6 of United nations et al. (2003) which, however, treats it essentially in an input–output framework, with pollution given greater emphasis than the management of natural resources.

Fiscal Policy

Lastly, a word on fiscal policy: in many countries that export depletable natural resources, taxes and royalties and other duties, and maybe also a share in profits, accrue to the government directly and are mixed up with other fiscal collections. This source of revenue will only last as long as the natural resource activity lasts and will fall *pari passu* with its decline. Many countries in that situation behave as if fiscal policies can be neglected, after all their Treasuries are flush with natural resource revenues. But again, during the years of plenty, when there is room for manoeuvre, the fiscal policy makers should be thinking of structural reforms in the tax system, with changes that would guard against falling revenues later.

A SUMMING UP

Green accounting is a powerful economic tool, needed for understanding resource dependent economies and for guiding them along a sustainable development path. But the greening method adopted should be a robust one in order for the results to be convincing. Methods that are applicable to countries with minor primary production sectors may not be very useful for numerous developing countries that are losing their natural resources on a significant scale, while this loss is counted perversely as value added and contributing to growth. Pollution issues seem to dominate the attention given to the environment by the richer countries, but pollution does not need much help from national accounting as it can be addressed directly without it. It is not always easy to devise methods for translating ecological losses into money values for ready incorporation in the national accounts, but progressively improved methods are bound to emerge if interested economists, instead of chasing grandiose concepts of welfare optimality, would devote some of their energies to understanding and refining practical valuation methods. Attempting to put a value on existing stocks is unnecessary for this purpose, and Marshall's injunction as to the need to distinguish between rent and royalty (Marshall, 1920)[25] should be heeded.

The user cost method, which is synonymous with Marshall's royalty, is a versatile instrument, applicable to both exhaustible resources and to renewable ones when the latter are being 'mined'. The user cost method is the only available one that does not obliterate the contribution made by extraction to net value added. Its estimation does not require any valuing of the stocks, nor does it rely on any projection of future extraction. It is simply a year-by-year 'positive' instrument. However, its calibration is highly sensitive to the interest rate used to convert extraction revenue into a permanent income stream that defines economic income. That is why careful thought needs to be given to what interest should be used, and justification offered for its selection. It is not a hoped-for target rate for yields from the new investments, but a realistic, cautiously expected rate, probably of around

3 or 4 per cent. Once chosen, it should be explicitly stated in order for mean-ingful comparisons to be made of adjustment methods. Employing ambi-tiously high interest rates would reduce the user cost and bring it close to negating nature's contribution to net income. Such negation, perhaps unconsciously intended, is implicit in the inadequate methods being pro-posed for greening the accounts.[26] Though associated with 'weak sustain-ability', there is nothing feeble about the user cost method. It is a tool needed for ensuring sustainability from year to year, and thus fits snugly into national accounting procedures. It is not an *ex ante* device for long term sustainability, but an *ex post* descriptive tool to account for the past year's economic performance. It certainly does not lay down a definite future which is not the business of accountants in any case. The currently popular adjustment method, that which is rooted in 'strong sustainability' (calling for incorporating 100 per cent of stock declines in the flow estimates at the net level) should be seen as incompatible with national accounting since it indicates a zero net value added in extraction.

Welfare considerations should be left out of the quest for greening the accounts for they manage to cloud the vision of the primary need to adjust the estimates of the product. Welfare is a derivative of output, and a more accurate assessment of output must take precedence over inferring welfare gains or losses from it. Impounding the adjustment in satellite accounts, not only saves it from careful scrutiny, but also depreciates its economic worth, especially if the enclave used for such impounding is labelled 'envir-onmental'. The danger is that economists will continue to ignore the adjusted accounts whatever method is used for greening them, and persist in using for their analysis the unadjusted variables which have been mis-leadingly described as 'economic'.

The national accounting framework is an economic framework needed for economic purpose. Environmental objectives are better achieved through physical accounting which can be instructive, using 'strong sustainability' methods that would periodically disclose resource stocks and their likely life expectancy at current deterioration rates.

If a convincing method is used for greening the accounts, the results will have a better chance of being taken seriously. Unless properly greened, eco-nomic management would be 'steered by the wrong compass'. Development economists are seldom conscious of the ecological basis of the macroeco-nomic numbers they use uncritically, and tend to be oblivious to the relevance of natural resource deterioration to the apparent economic per-formance as it shows through the unadjusted national accounts. The most insidious economic ailing associated with natural resource losses is often the Dutch Disease since it is all enveloping and corrosive. It affects monetary and fiscal policies, price stabilization, exchange rates and the balance of payments. Unless suppressed it will generate and enforce a process of 'de-development'. This is an area which needs greater economist attention. The present chapter merely indicated directions at a general level, but the necessary work has to be undertaken piece-meal, case by case, since each country is almost unique: in history, governance, institutions, factor endowment, economic structure, population size, composition and consumer preferences, as well as much else besides.

NOTES

1. Mining of non-renewable resources (such as minerals) *ceteris paribus* reduces their stocks; mining of renewable resources (such as fish, or forests as a source for timber) means extraction that exceeds their regeneration. In both cases stocks decline and the decline, instead of being counted as disinvestment, is wrongly reckoned as value added. The proper way to account for this disinvestment is set out in detail in El Serafy (1989).
2. See Common and Sanyal (1998), and my comment (El Serafy, 1999).
3. See the preface of this work for more detail.
4. Though the 1993 SNA itself was described as 'flexible' (United Nations, 1993, preface) it was in many respects rather rigid, and it is understandable that the UNSD could not deviate much from the constraints it imposed. The SNA was, after all, issued under the signatures of the heads of five imposing institutions, including the Secretary General of the United Nations. Constraints in my view include: (1) the advocacy of a stock approach that focuses on compiling environmental asset accounts in *current* value terms, and carrying annual changes in these values into the flow accounts; and (2) adoption of an environmental, strong sustainability stance, that should be seen as incompatible with meaningful accounting, as shown in a later part of this chapter.
5. Pigou published his *Wealth and Welfare* in 1912, to be followed later (1920) by his magnum opus which he labelled *The Economics of Welfare*. Two later versions of this work came out before his 'definitive' fourth edition appeared in 1932. See Hicks (1990, p. 537, note 8).
6. Robertson (1963, pp. 16–17) quotes in defense of Pigou a statement by the latter to the effect that economic welfare and total human welfare will *'probably'* (Pigou's emphasis) move in the same direction, but not necessarily in the same magnitude.
7. Hicks used the phrase 'collective utility' to refer to the aggregate of individual utilities of members of a group, contending that this aggregate corresponded to what Pareto, the arch utility 'ordinalist', called 'ophelimity' (cf. also Georgescu-Roegen, 1987). Hicks credits Kaldor with providing a way of escape from this Paretian conundrum by linking aggregate utility to the concept of the 'Pareto optimum' (Hicks, 1975, p. 220).
8. It may be worthwhile to mention here a variation attributed to Irving Fisher whose definition of income excluded investment which obviously does not contribute to current welfare, thus directing attention to *consumption* as the relevant quantity that should express welfare (see Hicks, 1940, reprinted 1981, p. 95). This welfare-oriented Fisherian view has recently been revived in the green accounting literature, and thus became a new source of diversion.
9. This memorable phrase was coined in a different context by Hicks (1966, p. 21).
10. The Hamiltonian, which began to appear in the literature on green accounting with some frequency, is described as being equal to a level of 'stationary utility' obtained by discounting future utilities, using discount rates as weights (see Heal and Kriström, forthcoming).
11. An e-mail from Nordhaus to the author, dated 19 December 2002, contained the statement that 'It is going too far to argue that there is zero value added in the extractive

sector'. Needless to say that this 'outlandish argument' was the very one favoured by the Nordhaus Panel. Reference should also be made to a different, yet comparable, work, that by Heal and Kriström (forthcoming). This interestingly combines admirable theoretical analysis with a less satisfactory handling of practical approaches to greening the accounts. In this paper, 'strong sustainability' is implicitly accepted as the guiding principle for adjusting the accounts. In both these works the user cost method, while mentioned, is not advocated in application.

12. On p. C4 Dasgupta (2001) writes, 'The moral is this: whether we are valuing or evaluating, the object of study should be wealth. Viewed in terms of this finding, it should not surprise that Adam Smith inquired into the wealth of nations, not the gross or net national product of nations, nor the Human Development Index of Nations.' Contrast this with Hicks's statement, reinforcing other authorities on Smith: 'We are nowadays so accustomed to thinking of wealth as capital wealth that it may not be easy to realize that in Smith wealth is normally taken in a "flow" sense' (Hicks, 1975, p. 224, note 9).

13. If Dasgupta (2001) had followed Fisher, instead of multiplying national income by a factor of four to arrive at wealth, he could have instead divided income by a hypothetical interest rate; but of course the choice of a relevant interest rate would have been awkward. The factor-of-four assumption implies a Fisherian interest rate of 25 per cent, provided of course that human and ecological 'wealth' is excluded from the calculation.

14. The admirable survey entitled 'The Environment in Economics' (Fisher and Peterson, 1976), while touching lightly on natural resources as a source, said to be covered in a mimeograph paper, is tellingly dominated by pollution issues.

15. A useful method was put forward by Hueting (see Tinbergen and Hueting, 1992), whereby standards are set for an acceptable level of pollution, the cost of meeting which are theoretically imputed as a charge against the unadjusted GDP. Arbitrariness, however, butts in when defining such standards, and again in respect of the technology to be applied for attaining them. If behaviour improves and such standards are observed in practice by the perpetrators themselves, no correction for pollution would be necessary.

16. Pollution optimists, overestimating the self regulating forces of *laissez-faire* market mechanism, have argued that as countries' income per capita rises, they climb up a kind of a Kuznets curve that ushers a tendency towards the abatement of pollution. In respect of income distribution – a totally different context – Kuznets had observed that as countries move up the income scale, income disparity initially sets in up to a per capita income level after which it begins to fall. Applying this argument to pollution (which many specialists have since found faulty), overlooks the fact that income per capita has to rise to a high enough level that is likely to remain out of reach of the bulk of humanity for the foreseeable future.

17. A relevant point usually stressed by the environmentalists is that a base of natural resources needs to be preserved on which to build any 'value added'. As argued here, value added is the stuff from which income is made.

18. A long-established accounting rule for income estimation is to value stocks at the close of an account period at the current market price or the price at the beginning of the period 'whichever is less'. Petroleum prices, for instance, have more than doubled in the course of 2004. For oil exporting countries, bringing changes in stock values (when stocks are often orders of magnitudes greater than current extraction) into their flow accounts would reduce the latter to near meaninglessness.

19. I have used a version of this example in El Serafy (2002).

20. This is my own interpretation, however, since Neumayer did not identify the approach he criticised as one reflecting strong sustainability (see Neumayer, 2001).

21. This phrase was coined by Hueting (see Tinbergen and Hueting, 1992). But Hueting, while drawing attention to the inadequacy of the unadjusted accounts for managing an economy, has favoured leaving the unadjusted estimates without modification, and using the alternative numbers to show how deviating from sustainability is the path taken by an economy.

22. NAMEA is a hybrid system combining physical indicators with money values of environmental deterioration. It is an acronym for National Accounting Matrix including

Environmental and Economic Accounts. This was developed in Statistics Netherlands, and avoids any change in the macroeconomic aggregates. See Keunig and de Haan (1996), and also El Serafy (1999a).

23. The adjusted rates of growth may be either the same, higher, or lower than rates based on the conventional estimates of the product (see El Serafy, 1993a). It is interesting that many economists tend to focus on the effect of account greening on growth, disregarding the more important effect on the absolute magnitudes themselves. This work (El Serafy, 1993a) contains a reworking of the estimates for Indonesia (Repetto et al., 1989) – a reworking that produced radically different results.

24. This point was raised originally by Haberler (1976) in relation to petroleum exports, but has not subsequently been made use of.

25. In several places in Marshall's *Principles* he insisted that the economic surplus derived from mining is part rent and part royalty, likening the latter in respect of coal mining to 'taking a ton out of nature's store' (Marshall, 1920, p. 439).

26. Comparisons are almost invariably made between the 'net price' and 'user cost' methods for adjusting the conventionally estimated national accounting magnitudes without mentioning the interest rate used for calculating the user cost. This often revealed a lack of understanding of the methods themselves. In fact it is common for authors of empirical studies not to disclose the interest rate used, seemingly unaware of its decisive effect on the results. Remarkably, the trial runs for 'United Nations 1993' – the studies conducted for Papua New Guinea and Mexico (Lutz, 1993) – do not show this important parameter. Recently, on enquiring from Lutz (who had participated in these two studies on behalf of the World Bank), he could not recall the interest rate used, or who actually selected its magnitude, and suggested that the rate may have been as high as 10 or 12 per cent. (E-mail from Lutz to the author dated 26 May 2004.)

REFERENCES

Ahmad, Yusuf J., S. El Serafy and E. Lutz (eds) (1989), *Environmental Accounting for Sustainable Development*, A UNEP–World Bank Symposium, Washington DC: World Bank.

Bureau of Economic Analysis (1994), 'Accounting for Natural Resources: Issues and BEA's Initial Estimates', *Survey of Current Business*, Washington DC: United States Department of Commerce, pp. 50–72.

Commission of the European Communities, Eurostat, International Monetary Fund, Organisation for Economic Co-operation and Development, United Nations and World Bank (1993), *System of National Accounts 1993*, Brussels/Luxembourg, New York, Paris, Washington DC.

Common, M. and K. Sanyal (1998), 'Measuring the depreciation of Australia's non-renewable resources: a cautionary tale', *Ecological Economics*, **26** (1), 23–30.

Corden, M. (1984), 'Booming sector and Dutch disease economics: survey and consolidation', *Oxford Economic Papers*, **36**, 359–80.

Dasgupta, P. (2001), 'Valuing objects and evaluating policies in imperfect economies', *Economic Journal*, **111** (471), C1–C29.

El Serafy, S. (1989), 'The proper calculation of income from depletable natural resources', in Yusuf J. Ahmad, S. El Serafy and E. Lutz (eds), *Environmental Accounting for Sustainable Development*, a UNEP–World Bank Symposium, Washington DC: World Bank, pp. 10–18

El Serafy, S. (1993), 'Depletable resources: fixed capital or inventories', in A. Franz and C. Stahmer (eds), *Approaches to Environmental Accounting* (proceedings of the IARIW Conference on Environmental Accounting, Baden, near Vienna, Austria, 27–9 May 1991), New York: Physica-Verlag Heidelberg and Springer-Verlag, pp. 245–58.

El Serafy, S. (1993a), *Country Macroeconomic Work and Natural Resources*, Environment Working Paper No. 58, Washington DC: World Bank.

El Serafy, S. (1996), 'In defence of weak sustainability: a response to Beckerman', *Environmental Values*, **5** (1), 75–8.

El Serafy, S. (1997), 'Environmental and resource accounting: impact on macro-economic policy – Part II', *Environmental Taxation and Accounting*, **1** (2), 38–59.

El Serafy, S. (1997a), 'Green accounting and economic policy', *Ecological Economics*, **21**, 217–29.

El Serafy, S. (1999), 'Depletion of Australia's non-renewable resources: a comment on Common and Sanyal', *Ecological Economics*, **30**, 357–63.

El Serafy, S. (1999a), 'Natural resource accounting', in Jeroen C.J.M. van den Bergh (ed.), *Handbook of Environmental and Resource Economics*, Cheltenham UK and Northampton MA, USA: Edward Elgar, pp. 1191–206.

El Serafy, S. (2002), 'La contabilidad verde y la sostenibilidad', in *Revista de Economia*, Num. 800, Junio-Julio, Madrid: Información Commercial Española, de Economia, pp. 15–30.

Fisher, A.C. and F.M. Peterson (1976), 'The environment in economics: a survey', *Journal of Economic Literature*, **14** (1), 1–33.

Georgescu-Roegen, N. (1987), 'Ophelimity', *The New Palgrave*, in J. Eatwell, M. Milgate and P. Newman (eds), UK: Macmillan Press Limited, pp. 716–17.

Haberler, G. (1976), 'Oil, inflation, recession and the international monetary system', *Journal of Energy and Development*, **1** (2), 177–90.

Hartwick, J. (1977), 'Intergenerational equity and the investing of rents from exhaustible resources', *American Economic Review*, **67** (5), pp. 972–4.

Heal, G. and B. Kriström (forthcoming), 'National income and the environment', in Karl-Göran Mäler and J.R. Vincent (eds), *Handbook of Environmental Economics*, Amsterdam: North Holland.

Hicks, J. (1940), 'The valuation of the social income', *Economica*, **14** (26) (New Series), reprinted as 'Valuation of social income' in J. Hicks, *Wealth and Welfare* (Collected Essays on Economic Theory, Volume 1), Cambridge, MA: Harvard University Press, 1981, pp. 78–99.

Hicks, J. (1966), 'Dennis Holme Robertson, A Memoir', reprinted in Dennis H. Robertson, *Essays in Money and Interest*, Manchester: Collins Fontana Library.

Hicks, J. (1975), 'The scope and status of welfare economics', originally published in *Oxford Economic Papers*, and reprinted in J. Hicks, *Wealth and Welfare* (*Collected Essays on Economic Theory*) Volume 1, Cambridge, MA: Harvard University Press, 1981, pp. 218–42.

Hicks, J. (1989), 'The assumption of constant returns to scale', *Cambridge Journal of Economics*, **13** (1), 9–17.

Hicks, J. (1990), 'The unification of macro-economics', *Economic Journal*, **100** (401), 528–38.

Keuning, S. and M. de Haan (1996), 'What is in a NAMEA?', *National Accounts Occasional Paper*, Voorburg, the Netherlands: Statistics Netherlands.

Lutz, E. (ed.) (1993), *Toward Improved Accounting for the Environment*, a UNSTAT–World Bank Symposium, Washington DC: World Bank.

Marshall, A. (1920), *Principles of Economics*, 8th edn (1947), London: Macmillan.

Neumayer, E. (2000), 'Resource accounting in measures of unsustainability: challenging the World Bank's conclusions', *Environmental and Resource Economics*, **15**, 257–78.

Neumayer, E. (2001), 'The Human Development Index and sustainability – a constructive proposal', *Ecological Economics*, **39**, 101–14.

Nordhaus, W. and E. Kokkelenberg (1999), *Nature's Numbers: Expanding the US National Economic Accounts to Include the Environment*, Washington DC: National Academy Press.

Pigou, A.C. (1952), *Essays in Economics*, London: Macmillan & Co. Ltd.; London.

Repetto, R., W. Magrath, M. Wells, C. Beer and F. Rossini (1989), *Wasting Assets: Natural Resources in the National Income Accounts*, Washington DC: World Resources Institute.

Robertson, D.H. (1963), *Lectures on Economic Principles*, Fontana Press: London and Glasgow.

Samuelson, P.A. and R.M. Solow (1956), 'A complete model including heterogeneous capital goods', *Quarterly Journal of Economics*, **70** (4), 537–62.

Smith, A. (1776), *An Inquiry into the Nature and Causes of the Wealth of Nations*, (1937), ed. Edwin Cannan, New York: Random House.

Tinbergen, J. and R. Hueting (1992), 'GNP and market prices: wrong signals for sustainable economic success that mask environmental destruction', in R. Goodland, H. Daly and S. El Serafy (eds), *Population, Technology and Lifestyle*, Washington DC: Island Press, pp. 52–62.

United Nations (1993), Handbook of National Accounting, *Integrated Environmental and Economic Accounting* (Interim Version), Studies in Methods, Series F. No. 61, New York: United Nations.

United Nations (2000), Handbook of National Accounting, *Integrated Environmental and Economic Accounting: an Operational Manual*, Studies in Methods, Series F, No. 78, New York: United Nations.

United Nations, European Commission, International Monetary Fund, Organisation for Economic Co-operation and Development and World Bank (2003), *Integrated Environmental and Economic Accounting 2003* (Handbook of National Accounting), Final draft prior to publication.

Weitzman, M. (1976), 'On the welfare significance of national product in a dynamic economy', *Quarterly Journal of Economics*, **90**, 156–62.

Weitzman, M. (2000), 'The linearized Hamiltonian as comprehensive NDP', *Environment and Development Economics*, **5**, 55–68.

World Bank (1997), *Expanding the Measure of Wealth: Indicators of Environmentally Sustainable Development*, Washington DC: World Bank.

4. Environmental accounting and policy making

John Lintott

INTRODUCTION

For more than 50 years national income accounting has played a key role in economic development. It has provided a target and a measure of success, the gross national product (GNP),[1] as well as a framework for tracing monetary flows, which has been at the core of economic policy making. In both these roles, however, national accounting has been increasingly perceived as inadequate. Environmental concern has focused attention on the physical flows of resources and pollutants which underlie the money flows, but which the latter reflect only partially and inadequately. Since the 1960s at least, for a variety of reasons, GNP has been criticised as a target for development, as it became clear that GNP could easily grow while welfare stagnated or declined.

It is in this context that environmental accounting has been proposed as a supplement or replacement for national accounting. Policy making requires a framework of statistics as a source of information for analysis and planning, and of targets for judging success. Environmental accounts are intended to provide such a framework in the case of decisions affecting the natural environment. Since this essentially means all decisions, environmental accounts should be at the centre of the overall statistical system. This raises such issues as what type of framework is appropriate and how it may contribute to policy-making? These issues are the principal subject matter of this chapter.

The chapter is organised as follows. After a brief review of approaches to environmental accounting, three related issues are raised, which are of critical importance in assessing its potential. First, like other statistics, the accounts are policy tools, and so can only be evaluated in relation to how they are to be used in designing and carrying out policy. Second, they are intended to serve a new type of development and it is necessary to ask what this type of development entails, in particular whether it involves continued growth of output. Third, proposals to construct environmental accounts in monetary units and derive from them a Green National Income or similar measure have all in effect been consumption based. Yet there are strong grounds for questioning the close link between consumption and welfare which this implies: unless there is a close link it makes little sense to measure development using an indicator based on consumption. Discussion of these three issues leads to an assessment of the approach most favoured by environmental economists, that of environmental accounts in money terms, as well as to looking at one possible alternative, that of combining accounts in physical units with a set of social and environmental indicators.

APPROACHES TO ENVIRONMENTAL ACCOUNTING

Environmental accounting encompasses a variety of attempts to apply accounting principles to environmental sources and sinks, and thus trace energy and materials through the economic system in much the same way that business accounting and national accounting trace monetary stocks and flows. There are a number of possibilities for accounts in physical units, largely based on the materials balance approach originally put forward by Ayres and Kneese (1969). These include attempts to create 'satellite' accounts, linked to the national income accounts, notably the French Natural Patrimony Accounts (Theys, 1990), and the Norwegian Natural Resource Accounting system (Lone et al., 1993). A number of countries have constructed environmental input–output systems where natural resource inputs and waste/pollution outputs are linked to the standard economic input–output tables via common industry or commodity classifications. A prominent pioneering example is the Dutch NAMEA system (De Haan and Keuning, 1996). The United Kingdom has followed a similar approach (Vaze, 1998).

For most environmental economists however – and many activists – accounts in physical terms are merely a first step. By imputing money values to environmental goods which currently have none, it is possible to construct accounts in money terms which complement, or even replace, the present national income accounts. As a result, GNP can be replaced by a more valid measure of economic success. National Income, as presently measured, includes a large element of natural capital depreciation which, like manufactured capital depreciation, should be omitted.[2] This takes the form of including defensive expenditures – that is, expenditures which offset declining welfare rather than provide a genuine increase in welfare – and failing to subtract the cost of resource depletion and environmental degradation. To arrive at a Green National Income, these costs all need to be expressed in money terms, and subtracted from existing National Income. In other respects, this approach leaves the traditional economics view of the environment unchanged. Economic activity is not seen as inevitably damaging the environment. On the contrary, so the theory suggests, thanks to sufficient substitution possibilities, environmental damage per unit of output can be reduced to any desired level, provided the market is allowed to work. As far as welfare is concerned, the traditional view is maintained, that consumption is closely related to welfare and should therefore be maximised.[3] Economic growth and sustainability, on this view, can and should be reconciled.

There have been a number of academic attempts at modifying the national accounts to incorporate environmental costs in money terms. An early attempt was Nordhaus and Tobin's measure of economic welfare (Nordhaus and Tobin, 1973), a version of which was implemented by the Economic Council of Japan (1973). More recently Daly and Cobb's Index of Sustainable Economic Welfare[4] (Daly and Cobb, 1990) has gained some prominence and been implemented in a number of countries. Such efforts are mainly intended to challenge the picture painted by the existing national accounts, and succeed in doing so in spite of many failings and objections which might be raised against the methods used (Cobb and Cobb, 1994).[5]

The purpose of the satellite accounts proposed by the United Nations, the Satellite System for Integrated Environmental and Economic Accounting (SEEA), is different. It represents an international and official consensus about how the UN System of National Accounts might be extended into environmental accounts. Originally proposed in 1993 (UN, 1993a), these accounts are intended as policy tools, and the issues of how they are to be used, and what the implications of their use are for economic development, are crucial. The UN system is made up of a number of versions, ranging from environment-related disaggregation of the existing national accounts, through incorporating environmental factors in physical units, and on to increasingly ambitious proposals for monetary valuation of these factors. Not surprisingly these also raise increasing difficulties, and as a result, the latest version of the UN proposals (UN, 2003)[6] which is based on discussion and experience over the last decade, puts more emphasis on the less ambitious and controversial versions, and their practical uses, and is more cautious regarding monetary valuation. It is of course possible to stop short of the monetary version, but that is not what was originally intended by the accounts' authors. As one of them suggests (Bartelmus, 1994, p. 45), 'Introducing a monetary valuation for environmental goods and services facilitates choices between economic goods and services and environmental ones. This is what economics is all about.'

POLICY USES OF NATIONAL ACCOUNTS AND ENVIRONMENTAL ACCOUNTS

Surprisingly, most discussion of environmental accounts makes little or no reference to their purpose. Often they are seen more as a matter of implementing economic theory, for example, providing better measures of key concepts such as income. Yet statistics are policy tools, collected or constructed at considerable expense, with particular purposes in view. Although debates about them are often conducted in terms of theory, they arise from practical policy concerns.

Past statistical development can only be explained, and proposals for the future evaluated, in the light of these concerns. This is clear if we consider the development of national income accounting, which in many ways is the model for proposals for environmental accounts. Much of the development of early national income estimates was in response to the emergence of centralised nation states, with the type of estimates required varying over time and among different countries. Early estimates of national income in England (Petty, 1690; King, 1696), for example, largely reflected the need to raise taxes in war time, and so measure the size of the tax base. German estimates were used for descriptive and comparative purposes; while in France the emphasis was on distribution among the social classes (Lazarsfeld, 1961; Schumpeter, 1954).

In the case of modern national income accounting much of the discussion about choice of frameworks can be understood as a debate between neoclassical economists and Keynesians; the latter were concerned with implementing demand management policies while the former saw the accounts as essentially about welfare measurement (Seers, 1976). The clearest example of this was the treatment of government expenditure, which neoclassical economists wanted to exclude as not contributing to welfare.[7] But for Keynesian economists and policy makers the object of the accounts was to measure, not economic welfare, but aggregate demand and its main components. Excluding government expenditure – the component which a Keynesian government could directly control – would have made no sense at all. It was the Keynesian national accounting framework which was adopted, not because Kuznets and the neoclassicals were 'wrong' in some absolute sense, but because by the time the accounts were implemented Keynesian ideas, objectives and policies had gained official acceptance in the industrial capitalist countries. Nevertheless the same framework has come to be used as the source for the principal measure of economic progress, GNP, the per capita growth of which has become the major overall goal of economic policy (Lintott, 1996).

These developments illustrate several key points. First, the evolution of statistics is in accordance with policy requirements rather than a matter of technical or conceptual improvement. Tax collection, war finance, short-term forecasting and similar concerns provide the stimulus. Although it plays a part, economic theory is not the driving force. Second, statistics constructed for one purpose may well then be used for another purpose – in many cases inappropriately. Third, there seem to be two general categories of use, one being the monitoring of welfare (well-being, happiness, progress and so on), and the other providing data for modelling and planning. Thus the national income accounts are used to trace monetary flows across the economy – for example, with a view to demand management – but also in practice, in spite of caveats, as a source of measures of economic success such as GNP.[8]

Economists freely acknowledge many of the deficiencies of GNP as a general welfare indicator. But in practice they and others treat it as a fair approximation to welfare, with GNP growth the main aim of economic policy (Daly and Cobb, 1990, ch. 3). This role for GNP is of particular importance since it has done much to encourage policies promoting economic growth, leading to environmental deterioration – which is the main motivation for environmental accounts. GNP growth has been pursued with little regard to environmental or other costs; 'society has been sailing by the wrong compass' (Hueting, 1991).

The ways that the national accounts have been used suggest some conclusions for environmental accounting. They can both be used for two distinct purposes: to keep track of various stocks and flows which are important for policy making, and the modelling and forecasting this requires; and as a source of measures of welfare which can be used to monitor and guide development.[9] To the extent that the national accounts are a way of tracing monetary flows – something likely to be useful in any complex monetary economy – they should be left as they are; including the cost of environmental damage expressed in terms of money, even though there is no actual flow of money, as is done in monetary environmental accounts, would defeat the purpose. Environmental accounts in physical units have a parallel purpose, to trace environmental flows, and since monetary and environmental flows are related, there are good reasons to find ways to link up the two accounts. But this purpose can be served by accounts in physical units and provides no reason for monetary imputation. On the other hand, to the extent that the national accounts are used (or misused) as a source of welfare measures, there is a strong case for another approach. But, as the following sections argue, what is required is a break with national accounting rather than its replacement by environmental accounting.

WHAT TYPE OF DEVELOPMENT: WEAK OR STRONG SUSTAINABILITY?

Environmental accounts are intended to promote a new kind of development – sometimes called 'sustainable development' – and the question arises what this entails. In particular does it involve continued, though modified, economic growth, or on the contrary, movement towards a steady state economy? The terms 'sustainability' and 'sustainable development' have been much abused, to the point where many people avoid their use altogether. Nevertheless the concepts of 'weak' and 'strong' sustainability, which have been the subject of much discussion among environmental economists (for example, Pearce et al., 1989, ch. 2; Daly, 1992, ch. 13), are useful in discussing environmental accounting, since they are an attempt to make the notion of sustainability operational. 'Weakly' sustainable development requires total capital (manufactured plus natural) not to decrease, while 'strongly' sustainable development additionally requires natural capital not to decrease.

Weak sustainability treats manufactured and natural capital simply as sources of income, actual or imputed, in effect implying that it is always possible to substitute one for the other – environmental degradation can be offset by additional factory building, for example. It is then possible to envisage sustainable GNP growth in spite of apparent resource and pollution limits. Using some kind of Green National Income, derived from monetary accounts, as a policy target requires that one accepts the weak sustainability view, since Green National Income growth is consistent with continued environmental degradation provided investment in manufactured capital is sufficient. Not only does monetary environmental accounting require weak sustainability; weak sustainability requires monetary environmental accounting, if it is to be implemented. Only if natural capital, or at least changes in it, is measured in terms of money can one know whether environmental degradation is offset by manufactured capital formation, and so whether development is on a (weakly) sustainable path.

On a strong sustainability view, however, there is no particular necessity or advantage in monetary valuation. Implementing strong sustainability policies requires following a set of rules limiting use of the different natural resources and release of the various pollutants to what is sustainable (Daly, 1996, ch. 4). What is then needed, in order to monitor these policies, is separate measurement of the different aspects of the environment, which can be in appropriate physical units.[10]

Choosing the monetary approach to environmental accounting therefore depends on accepting the weak sustainability view. But this is unsatisfactory from several points of view. Manufactured and natural capital are complements rather than substitutes; economic growth inevitably involves increasing use of both. Moreover, as even economists usually associated with a weak sustainability view have accepted (for example, Pearce et al., 1989, ch. 2), there is a strong case for treating some natural capital as 'critical', and thus requiring special treatment, because of a combination of factors such as lack of substitutes, uncertainty and irreversibility of damage – in other words, the weak sustainability view certainly cannot be applied to all environmental services.

There are thus plausible reasons for rejecting weak sustainability and the possibility of sustainable growth. But, in addition, arguing for weak sustainability presupposes that increasing manufactured capital, and thus future income and consumption, is at least in most cases a good thing. For a wide range of consumption this is open to question, as the next section argues.

CONSUMPTION AND WELFARE[11]

Attempts to construct a Green National Income or similar measure have all in effect been consumption based. They start from consumer spending, as defined in the national accounts, and then apply various modifications both in terms of what is included and how it is valued; but consumption remains the major item. A close link between consumption and welfare is assumed.[12]

Yet consumption is not a goal in itself. As Schumacher put it, '. . . since consumption is merely a means to human well-being, the aim should be to obtain the maximum of well-being with the minimum of consumption' (1974, pp. 47–8). While there is no doubt that some consumption is essential to welfare, there is much evidence to suggest that such a link is the exception rather than the rule in rich countries: evidence from studies of self-reported happiness, from commonly accepted social indicators, from disciplines such as psychology and anthropology, and from historical and cross-cultural comparisons. There is even some support from unorthodox strands in economics.

A large body of research on income and 'subjective well-being' (SWB) has accumulated, over the last four decades, based on surveys of self-reported happiness. Although there is some variation in methods, as well as in the detailed findings, the results show broad unanimity. In a given country at a given time, there is some correlation between income and well-being: the rich are happier than the poor. The correlation is however quite weak, indicating that other factors are more influential; health, social relationships and leisure activities seem to be particularly important (Argyle,

1999). Comparisons between countries yield a more mixed conclusion. For low income countries, there does seem to be some correlation – though again, rather low – between income and well-being; but there is no correlation among high income countries (see, for example, Inglehart and Klingemann, 2000).

The most significant and striking result however is that where income and SWB in individual countries are tracked over time, there is no correlation whatever between the two. The proportion of US respondents who declare themselves 'very happy' has fluctuated between 30 and 40 per cent over the period 1972–91. Japanese self-reported happiness was flat for almost three decades (1961–87) in spite of more than quadrupled income (Frank, 1999, pp. 72–3). In contrast EU data (1973–98) shows large fluctuations (and big differences among member countries) but no clear trend and no relationship to income (Inglehart and Klingemann, 2000, p. 167).

The pattern shown by these results was first pointed out by Easterlin (1972), and dubbed the 'Easterlin paradox': happiness appears to be related to income on the basis of cross-sectional, but not time series, data. The explanation, suggested by Easterlin himself, and elaborated in one form or another by many others since (notably Hirsch, 1977; Scitovsky, 1976; Cross and Guyer, 1980; and Wachtel, 1983), seems to be that it is principally income *relative to others* which determines happiness; in that case an increase in income over time, which necessarily leaves individuals' relative position on average unchanged, cannot by itself result in increased happiness.

This conclusion is reinforced by commonly used indicators of basic welfare in areas such as health and nutrition, which tend to stabilise at levels of consumption much lower than those of present day industrialised countries. Studies of other times and places suggest that consumerism is exceptional, a feature of modern capitalism. Early industrialists found they had to cut pay to force workers to work a 'full' working day; previously self-employed artisans chose leisure over luxury (Gorz, 1989; Smith, 1993). And, until the Second World War, it was generally thought that rising productivity would lead to increased leisure rather than consumption (Cross, 1993).

Evidence about the relation between consumption and welfare can never be absolutely conclusive, given the general and intuitive nature of concepts like welfare and well-being. Nevertheless all the evidence points in the same direction, and taken together it is very persuasive. The goal of ever increasing consumption, far from being universal, is mostly a feature of post-Second World War industrialised societies. But even where consumerism rules, factors other than consumption are more important for welfare. And in so far as welfare is related to consumption at all, once basic material needs are satisfied, it is an individual's relative, not absolute, consumption level that counts for his or her welfare. It follows that in rich countries increases in consumption do not and cannot, in the aggregate, lead to improvements in overall welfare. And – the key point for our argument – it would be perverse to put the consumption–welfare equation at the very core of policy making or of policy tools such as environmental accounts.[13]

PROBLEMS OF MONETARY ENVIRONMENTAL ACCOUNTS

Problems of Monetary Valuation

In addition to the issues discussed so far there are the difficulties of imputing a money value to goods and bads for which there is no market, and therefore no market price. These are well-known and the subject of a large literature. Most imputation methods proposed are based on estimating the 'willingness to pay' of individuals for environmental services, most often through survey methods (the contingent valuation approach).[14] Willingness to pay methods are required to implement the most inclusive and ambitious version of the UN satellite accounts.

In practice these methods result in a wide range of estimates, even in relatively 'easy' cases. Comparison over time is quite unreliable: '. . . even small variations in approach and data availability may affect the indicator more than actual changes in what it purports to measure' (Bartelmus, 1994, p. 53). There is a risk that in practice the more difficult cases will be left out altogether, or that arbitrary guesses will be introduced. These issues are often seen as merely technical, that is, as simply requiring further research and improvement in techniques. But at the heart of the problem seems to be the fact that monetary imputation based on willingness to pay is a matter of invention, not discovery. Exchange values are created by exchange; they do not exist in the absence of markets. Willingness to pay imputations are an averaging of individual decisions taken in the completely different context of survey research, and sensitive to variations in that context.

Willingness to pay is also in practice often limited by ability to pay. One result of this is that large discrepancies are found between willingness to pay for an environmental good and willingness to accept compensation for its loss, which is not limited in the same way and which in some cases is infinite. Even more seriously, environmental goods are systematically assigned a greater weight, the richer the people enjoying them or suffering from their loss.

In response to criticisms of willingness to pay, a 'maintenance cost' approach has also been proposed, where the value of an economic activity is its value as currently calculated, less the hypothetical cost of avoiding any environmental damage which results from it (either by repairing the damage or by not carrying out the activity in the first place). The maintenance cost approach, while avoiding the problems of willingness to pay methods, raises difficulties of it own. In particular, where the cost of clearing up environmental damage is greater than the value of the activity causing it (or where the damage cannot be cleared up at all), the activity is assigned a zero value. This is arbitrary and perverse since, for example, the activity can then become even more damaging without this being reflected in the accounts (Aaheim and Nyborg, 1995).

Other problems occur even if no monetary imputation is attempted. Subtracting defensive expenditures from total expenditure requires deciding what is 'defensive'. This is a difficult line to draw: as the UN themselves (1993b, p. 14) point out, in the extreme case all expenditure can be regarded as defensive. If anything even more intractable, is the problem of uncertainty, which frequently affects whether environmental damage is thought to result from an activity at all, its seriousness and eventual consequences, whether it can be repaired, who will suffer, and much else. In these circumstances no valuation method will help us. Introducing 'best guesses' will only ensure that the resulting series fluctuates wildly, and that changes in the situation measured are drowned out by changes in our knowledge of it. The problem of large fluctuations in the value of environmentally adjusted output affects even the UN's least ambitious version of monetary environmental accounts which involves subtracting from output the value of natural resource depletion. The value of depletion of course depends on the price of the resource, which can vary widely, making adjusted output quite unstable, particularly in the case of more resource based economies (Aaheim and Nyborg, 1995; Repetto et al., 1992).

Using Monetary Environmental Accounts to Monitor Progress

Constructing environmental accounts in money terms thus raises a number of difficulties, to do both with practical implementation and, perhaps more fundamentally, with what the impact of using them would be. In particular, if there is little reason to think that higher aggregate consumption leads to greater welfare, once basic material needs are met, then there is no justification for using a consumption based measure to monitor progress. The combination of basing environmental accounts on consumption and assuming that more investment in manufactured capital can offset (rather than increase) environmental damage – the weak sustainability approach – means continuation of growth-promoting policies. There may be some shift towards more environmentally efficient consumption (less damage per unit of consumption) but this will be easily overwhelmed by increased consumption and damage.

Problems of definition and monetary valuation are likely to lead to a bias towards omitting the more uncertain (but not necessarily less serious) environmental costs, as well as a broad spread of valuations which allows everyone to choose the figure which suits them. The influence of powerful pressure groups is likely to lead to emphasis on the valuations which most favour growth. The result is that adoption of a greener National Income as overall policy target will favour continued economic growth, perhaps even reinforce it by making it appear more legitimate.

The Reaction of Policy Makers

The UN's original SEEA proposals (UN, 1993a) offered, as we have seen, a menu of options regarding environmental accounts, ranging from relatively simple modifications of the national income accounts, to comprehensive accounts in money terms, the whole presented however as a progression, with money accounts the eventual objective. The following decade saw various opportunities for member countries' policy makers to debate the various options, and of course, to demonstrate their preferences by the choices they made for their own statistical development.[15]

Much of this discussion is reflected in the revised proposals (UN, 2003), which depart from the original document in a number of respects. The link between monetary accounts and the weak interpretation of sustainability is acknowledged (p. 7), as is the problematic and controversial nature of monetary imputations. Indeed the most ambitious option for arriving at a Green National Income (Eco Domestic Product, version IV.3 in UN (1993a)), involving using contingent valuation to express all environmental degradation in monetary terms, is dropped completely. On the other hand, there is more emphasis on accounts in physical terms, and on linking them to monetary flows, and on the various policy uses these may serve (UN, 2003, ch. 10). Examples include the use of environmental input–output tables (described as 'hybrid' accounts by the UN) to predict the environmental effects of changes in consumption, or conversely to suggest the changes in consumption required to achieve certain environmental goals; the use of environmentally-related disaggregation to assess the cost of environmental policies; the use of asset accounts to monitor sustainability; and more generally, using the various accounts taken together to monitor environmental damage and the impact of policies to reduce it. There is also emphasis on the potential for physical accounts as a source of environmental indicators (see next section). Meanwhile, discussion of the uses of monetary valuation emphasises such things as setting appropriate user charges and pollution taxes, and cost–benefit analysis, rather than arriving at an adjustment to National Income.

National statistical offices have been reluctant to get involved in monetary imputations. In the United Kingdom, for example, while there is progressive integration between the national accounts, environmental input–output tables, and environmental accounts in physical terms, the available monetary valuation methods are not considered 'sufficiently robust or comprehensive' (Harris, 2000, p. 38), and the only instances of monetary accounting are where there are actual money flows, as with environmental protection expenditures, or environmental taxes. This situation seems likely to persist, given the difficulties of monetary valuation discussed above.

SOCIAL AND ENVIRONMENTAL INDICATORS

If the objective of development is ensuring welfare while limiting environmental damage, and the strong sustainability view is adopted, then a better welfare monitoring tool would be a set of social and environmental indicators.[16] The indicator approach has a number of attractions, particularly the flexibility and coverage it can provide. It can allow for a variety of influences on welfare to be included, economic in the traditional sense, environmental or social. It provides for both the welfare benefits and the environmental costs of activities to be evaluated, and reflects a view of both as having a number of distinct dimensions.

Indicators can be expressed in terms of any suitable unit of measurement, thus avoiding the many problems associated with arriving at monetary measures for non-marketed goods. They can be formulated in a number of ways, for example as averages, inequality measures, or as a proportion reaching a critical threshold. Choices about the form of any indicator system – welfare aspects to be included, the indicators and their operational definitions – would depend on the type of development envisaged and the decision-making mechanisms instituted to set social goals. In particular it would be possible to move away from the idea of *maximising* some indicator of well-being. Maximisation seems desirable, almost by definition, in the case of general concepts such as welfare, progress or health. But as soon as these are broken down into specific, concrete sources of well-being – what we eat, our education, and so on – maximisation makes little sense; what is desirable is achieving a certain optimum standard.

There is a considerable literature on social indicators, going back to the 1960s (one review of the issues is Carley (1981)). The experience of the social indicator movement of the 1960s and 1970s has suggested a number of directions as well as problem areas.[17] However these problems are even greater in the case of Green National Income. It may be difficult, for example, to arrive at a small set of indicators which between them provide a complete and direct description of aspects of welfare such as 'health' or 'environmental quality', with the risk that policy will neglect what is omitted. But the situation is certainly no better with accounts which show spending figures, perhaps combined with questionable willingness to pay estimates, which at most have some perceived relevance to these aspects. Similar conflicts also arise from the different purposes of social indicators – on the one hand welfare measurement and on the other rather ambitious ideas put forward, but abandoned, for their use in planning and social control (Bauer et al., 1969; Nectoux et al., 1980). But such problems may be inherent in the tasks which such statistical systems are set, and only amenable to political, not technical, solutions.

Aggregating social and environmental indicators into one index of 'social growth' would raise some of the same problems as with economic growth, by concealing what is happening to the various components and offsetting them against each other. Of course trade-offs have to be made, and the different dimensions of welfare represented by indicators have to be weighed against each other. But this is not a technical matter of devising a 'correct' index but rather a political issue of who chooses: whether it is specialists employed to do so, or those affected by the decisions. Thus while there are all kinds of problems with finding or deciding on appropriate indicators in certain areas the main difficulty is to devise and bring about an appropriate political process. Many of the technical problems that orthodox social science sees in arriving at a small set of indicators which represent a consensus, as well as meeting other criteria, in reality mask political issues.

CONCLUSIONS

Policy making should be concerned with increasing welfare while reducing or limiting environmental damage, and the value of environmental accounts depends on the contribution they can make to this objective. At the same time, like other statistics, they are a policy tool, and their merits can only be evaluated in terms of their uses. The uses envisaged seem to fall into two categories.

One type of use for environmental accounts is as a source of data for planning and modelling. From this perspective, there is a strong case for developing accounts in physical terms. Just as a complex money-using society is likely to want to trace money flows, as in the national accounts, so any society concerned with environmental damage is likely to want to trace resource and pollution flows and stocks. To the extent that there is a significant relation between the two flows, it makes sense to connect the respective accounting systems. It will help, for example, to determine which economic activities are most responsible for which forms of pollution, and predict the environmental effects of expanding or reducing various consumption categories. But this type of use does not require environmental accounts in money terms; on the contrary, accounts in physical units are much more appropriate.

The other use for environmental accounts is as a way to construct a Green National Income which would replace GNP as a target of policy, and would thus play a key role in guiding development. But the kind of development which would result from using the accounts in this way would involve continued association of welfare and progress with increasing consumption, continued growth of output, and very limited concessions to environmental concerns, compared to what is required. It would thus achieve little in terms of promoting welfare in a sustainable way. The case for constructing environmental accounts in money terms is therefore quite weak, particularly since there is a better alternative. The development of social and environmental indicators seems more promising for evaluating policies aiming at sustainable welfare.

NOTES

1. Gross National Product has now been officially renamed Gross National *Income*; however I refer to GNP throughout this chapter, since the term is still in widespread usage, and since it avoids confusion with proposals for a 'Green National Income'. Gross *Domestic* Product is also used as an indicator of economic success; but the difference between GDP and GNP is irrelevant to the issues discussed here.
2. Although this terminology may be objectionable, 'In referring to the environment as capital, there is an implicit assumption that it can be substituted by other forms of capital, that it is reproducible, and that it is there to be managed in much the same way as manufactured capital' (Victor, 1991, p. 210).
3. Of course the concept of welfare is the subject of a variety of interpretations and much debate. For the purposes of the discussion in this chapter, the orthodox economic view of welfare as preference satisfaction can be accepted: individuals are to be regarded as the best judges of their own welfare. What is not accepted is the view that markets (or the ballot box) ensure that preferences are satisfied. The argument that (present, human) consumption and welfare are only weakly linked is of course strengthened if welfare is expanded to include future generations and non-human nature.
4. Also known as the Genuine Progress Indicator.
5. In particular, for the countries where it has been implemented, the ISEW suggests that there has been little or no increase in welfare in the last 40 years, in spite of substantial GNP growth; this is mainly the result of making allowances for environmental degradation and for income inequality.
6. This is a final draft circulated for information prior to official editing, and available from the internet site http://unstats.un.org/unsd/envAccounting/seea.htm

7. Thus Kuznets, one of the US pioneers of National Accounting, argued that 'most government activities are designed to preserve and maintain the social framework and are thus a species of repair and maintenance which cannot in and of itself produce net economic returns' (1951, p. 184).

8. It has been suggested by some economists (for example, El Serafy, 1997) that national accounting has another purpose, distinct from both indicating welfare and tracking monetary flows, namely the measurement of income, which should be defined as the maximum amount that can be sustainably consumed. Correct measurement of maximum sustainable consumption (thus income) then requires adjustment for running down of natural capital. It is apparent however, that for these economists, the goal of economic policy should be to maximise income thus adjusted. So in effect, they take the view that, by measuring income correctly, the national accounts serve the purpose of measuring welfare, and that this should be equated with (maximum sustainable) consumption. The latter view is questioned in the following sections.

9. A similar view is expressed by Peskin (1998), who refers to 'management' and 'score-keeping' as the two main functions of environmental accounting (and indeed of accounting generally, whether national accounting or business accounting).

10. Interpretation of strong sustainability is the subject of a good deal of debate, some arguing, for example, that the requirement to use *every* resource sustainably would be far too stringent, while others point to uncertainty over what constitutes sustainable use in the case of many resources. But the key point here is that if the natural environment provides a number of services, for which, in each case, there is no substitute, then what is required is a set of indicators for each aspect, rather than an aggregated index such as Green National Income.

11. The argument in this section is presented in more detail in Lintott (1998) and Carr-Hill and Lintott (2002, ch. 4).

12. One way in which equating consumption and welfare is misleading has long been the subject of discussion (Fisher, 1906; Boulding, 1949; Daly, 1996). According to this line of thought, it is people's stock of assets that is a source of welfare, rather than the flow of new consumption goods that is regrettably necessary to replenish the stock when it is depleted through wearing out of old consumption goods. This point of view has some attraction for environmentalists since it recognises the value of durability. In accounting terms, it would lead to an emphasis on balance sheets measuring the stock of consumers' assets, rather than, as now, monetary flows which decline, other things being equal, when the durability of goods improves. The argument here is intended to apply to both the flow and the stock of consumption goods: neither is closely related to welfare.

13. Questioning the benefits of consumption is not inconsistent with an economic approach. One classic definition of economics describes it as 'the science which studies human behaviour as a relationship between ends and scarce means which have alternative uses' (Robbins, 1932). But the way that the 'ends' of human behaviour are interpreted is crucial. The pursuit of economic growth has entailed interpreting 'ends' in terms of income and consumption, making increased resource use and environmental damage inevitable. Reducing the scale of rich economies requires re-interpreting the ends in terms of welfare – as well as arriving at better measures of the scarce means.

14. This is unsatisfactory even in principle since it means mixing estimates of consumer surplus with exchange values (Vanoli, 1998). But the latter are themselves unsatisfactory. As Scitovsky (1976, p. 141) puts it, 'The inclusion of $1000 in the national accounts implies that (1) someone did work, the discomfort of which was worth less than $1000 to him or her, and (2) services were rendered worth more than $1000 to someone else. Thus the sum of worker's and consumer's net gains could be much less or much more than the $1000 included in the accounts.'

15. For a brief description of the various organisations and forums involved, see http://unstats.un.org/unsd/envAccounting/histbground.htm

16. Bartelmus, one of the architects of the UN's SEEA, accepts something like this view, but only for non-economic and non-environmental goods and services: 'Further welfare effects result from non-economic goods and services used for the satisfaction of other

human needs and aspirations . . . In general, these goods are not or cannot be valued or costed in markets. Consequently, social evaluation will have to complement or replace monetary (market) valuation. Social evaluation can be carried out in principle by setting targets, thresholds or standards for non-economic development objectives' (1994, p. 65). There seems no reason not to extend this argument to environmental services.

17. For example, problems of partial coverage, of indirect measurement, and of combining indicators into indices (Etzioni and Lehman, 1967).

REFERENCES

Aaheim, A. and K. Nyborg (1995), 'On the interpretation and applicability of a Green National Product', *Review of Income and Wealth*, **41** (1), 57–71.

Argyle, M. (1999), 'Causes and correlates of happiness', in D. Kahneman, E. Diener and N. Schwarz (eds), *Well-Being: The Foundation of Hedonic Psychology*, New York: Russell Sage Foundation.

Ayres, R.U. and A.V. Kneese (1969), 'Production, consumption and externalities', *American Economic Review*, **69**, 282–97.

Bartelmus, P. (1994), *Environment, Growth and Development*, London and New York: Routledge.

Bauer, R., R. Rosenbloom and L. Sharp (1969), *Second-Order Consequences*, Cambridge, MA: MIT Press.

Boulding, K. (1949), 'Income or Welfare', *Review of Economic Studies*, **17**, 77–86.

Carley, M. (1981), *Social Measurement and Social Indicators*, London: Allen and Unwin.

Carr-Hill, R. and J. Lintott (2002), *Consumption, Jobs and the Environment*, London: Palgrave.

Cobb, C. and J. Cobb (1994), *The Green National Product*, Lanham, MD: University Press of America.

Cross, G. (1993), *Time and Money: The Making of Consumer Culture*, London: Routledge.

Cross, J. and M. Guyer (1980), *Social Traps*, Ann Arbor: University of Michigan Press.

Daly, H. (1992), *Steady-State Economics*, London: Earthscan.

Daly, H. (1996), *Beyond Growth*, Boston: Beacon Press.

Daly, H. and J. Cobb (1990), *For the Common Good*, London: Green Print.

De Haan, M. and S. Keuning (1996), 'Taking the environment into account: the NAMEA approach', *Review of Income and Wealth*, **42**, 131–48.

Easterlin, R. (1972), 'Does economic growth improve the human lot? Some empirical evidence', in P. David and M. Reder (eds), *Nations and Households in Economic Growth*, Stanford: Stanford University Press.

Economic Council of Japan (1973), *Measuring Net National Welfare of Japan*, Tokyo: Economic Council of Japan.

El Serafy, S. (1997), 'Green accounting and economic policy', *Ecological Economics*, **21**, 217–29.

Etzioni, A. and E. Lehman (1967), 'Some dangers in "valid" social measurement', *Annals of the American Academy of Political and Social Science*, September, 1–15.

Fisher, I. (1906), *The Nature of Capital and Income*, London: Macmillan.

Frank, R. (1999), *Luxury Fever: Money and Happiness in an Era of Excess*, Princeton and Oxford: Princeton University Press.

Gorz, A. (1989), *Critique of Economic Reason*, London: Verso.

Harris, R. (2000), 'Recent developments in environmental accounting', *Economic Trends*, **563**, October.

Hirsch, F. (1977), *The Social Limits to Growth*, London: Routledge.

Hueting, R. (1991), 'Correcting national income for environmental losses: a practical solution for a theoretical dilemma', in R. Costanza (ed.), *Ecological Economics: The Science and Management of Sustainability*, New York: Columbia University Press.

Inglehart, R. and H.-D. Klingemann (2000), 'Genes, culture, democracy and happiness', in E. Diener and E. Suh (eds), *Culture and Subjective Well-Being*, Cambridge, MA: MIT Press.

King, G. (1696), 'Natural and political observations and conclusions upon the state and condition of England', reprinted in G. Barnett (ed.) (1936), *Two Tracts*, Baltimore: John Hopkins Press.

Kuznets, S. (1951), 'Government product and national income', in International Association for Research in Income and Wealth, *Income and Wealth Series I*, London: Bowes and Bowes.

Lazarsfeld, P. (1961), 'Notes on the history of quantification in sociology – trends, sources and problems', *Isis*, **168**, 277–333.

Lintott, J. (1996), 'Environmental accounting: useful to whom and for what?', *Ecological Economics*, **16** (1), 179–90.

Lintott, J. (1998), 'Beyond the economics of more: the place of consumption in ecological economics', *Ecological Economics*, **25**, 239–48.

Lone, O., K. Nyborg and A. Aaheim (1993), 'Natural resource accounting: the Norwegian experience', in A. Franz and C. Stahmer (eds), *Approaches to Environmental Accounting*, Heidelberg: Physica-Verlag.

Nectoux, F., J. Lintott and R. Carr-Hill (1980), 'Social indicators for individual well-being or social control?', *International Journal of Health Services*, **10** (1), 89–113.

Nordhaus, W. and J. Tobin (1973), 'Is growth obsolete?', in M. Moss (ed.), *The Measurement of Economic and Social Performance'*, New York: National Bureau of Economic Research.

Pearce, D., A. Markandya and E. Barbier (1989), *Blueprint for a Green Economy*, London: Earthscan.

Peskin, H. (1998), 'Alternative resource and environmental accounting approaches and their contribution to policy', in K. Uno and P. Bartelmus (eds), *Environmental Accounting in Theory and Practice*, Dordrecht: Kluwer.

Petty, W. (1690), 'Political arithmetick, or a discourse concerning the extent and value of lands, people, buildings', reprinted in C. Hull (ed.) (1899), *Economic Works of Sir William Petty*, Cambridge: Cambridge University Press.

Repetto, R., W. Magrath, M. Wells, C. Beer and F. Rossini (1992), 'Wasting assets: natural resources in the national income accounts', in A. Markandya and J. Richardson (eds), *Environmental Economics*, London: Earthscan.

Robbins, L. (1932), *An Essay on the Nature and Significance of Economic Science*. London: Macmillan.

Schumacher, E. (1974), *Small is Beautiful*, London: Abacus.

Schumpeter, J. (1954), *History of Economic Analysis*, London: Allen and Unwin.

Scitovsky, T. (1976), *The Joyless Economy*, New York: Oxford University Press.

Seers, D. (1976), 'The political economy of national accounting', in A. Cairncross and M. Puri (eds), *Employment, Income Distribution and Development Strategy: Problems of the Developing Countries*, London: Macmillan.

Smith, G.A. (1993), 'The purpose of wealth: a historical perspective', in H. Daly and K. Townsend (eds), *Valuing the Earth*, Cambridge, MA: MIT Press.

Theys, J. (1990), 'Environmental accounting in development policy: the French experience', in Y. Ahmad, S. El Serafy and E. Lutz (eds), *Environmental Accounting for Sustainable Development*, Washington DC: World Bank.

UN (1993a), *Integrated Environmental and Economic Accounting*, New York: United Nations.

UN (1993b), *System of National Accounts*, New York: United Nations.

UN (2003), *Integrated Environmental and Economic Accounting*, New York: United Nations.

Vanoli, A. (1998), 'Modelling and accounting work in national and environmental accounts', in K. Umo and P. Bartelmus (eds), *Environmental Accounting in Theory and Practice*, Dordrecht: Kluwer.

Victor, P. (1991), 'Indicators of sustainable development: some lessons from capital theory', *Ecological Economics*, **4**, 191–213.

Vaze, P. (ed.) (1998), *UK Environmental Accounts 1998*, London: Stationery Office.

Wachtel, P. (1983), *The Poverty of Affluence*, New York: Free Press.

5. Estimating the economic impacts of climate change by means of green accounting

H. Asbjørn Aaheim

INTRODUCTION

The attention given to the establishment of green national accounts and the estimation of an Eco-Domestic Product (EDP) over the past decades is understandable: the aggregate information provided by the national accounts is widely accepted, used and understood, but fails to reflect changes in primary production factors other than labour and real capital.[1] In order to include indications of environmental change, green accounts that include a valuation of natural resources and the environment as well as changes in these stocks should be established. This would provide decision-makers with more comprehensive and better information about social and economic development.

There is theoretical support to the view that if the national accounts are being used to indicate the welfare of a nation, and there is a change in environmental standards or in the stock of natural resources, 'green' national accounts provide a better overview of economic activities than the traditional accounts. However, there are considerable problems in finding practical solutions to the numerical assessment of values. The reason is, in general, that while the traditional national accounts are based on observations of prices and quantities, the prices applicable to environmental standards and natural resources can seldom be observed. Prices have to be estimated by means of some other observation and updated annually in order to reflect changes resulting from a combination of variations in both volumes and prices.

Monetisation of environmental standards and the stock of natural resources is a linear transformation of physical quantities that allows fish and trees to be added into a meaningful measure of natural resources. This is a useful exercise in many respects, but one has to be aware of the limitations. When a price is attached to something, we may get to know the value of the quantity to which the price is attached, but cannot tell the value of any other quantity. Nor can we claim that the value of a change is this particular price times the quantity of change. This complicates the establishment of green accounts because it not only requires a considerable effort in establishing reliable prices on environmental qualities, but also it is worthless if not updated regularly.

The usefulness of a green national account where prices are not updated regularly lies in the interpretation of the national accounts figures as volumes, which make physical quantities comparable. Green accounting may then serve as a necessary step to parameterise the relationships between economic activities and the physical environment. But if the changes in the prices are not observed, the value of environmental change will have to be determined endogenously by integrated macroeconomic models.

The aim of this chapter is to show how and why the changes resulting from such a modelling procedure differ from changes in green national accounts where the prices are assumed fixed. The next and second major section briefly surveys possible aims of green national accounts and discusses the alternative ways to provide appropriate information. The following section discusses the role of prices and some basic differences between valuation techniques. The determination of damage costs of environmental degradation is discussed in the fourth major section, and the fifth section shows how the national accounts can be used in the determination of these costs. In order to focus the issues, examples will be taken from damage costs of climate change. The sixth section shows how assessments of impacts of environmental change, exemplified by climate change, can be used to establish relationships between environmental stresses and economic activities, while the seventh section presents some illustrative examples of macroeconomic consequences. The final section provides some concluding remarks.

AIMS OF GREEN ACCOUNTS AND APPROPRIATE MEASUREMENT

If it is accepted that production and welfare are somehow related to the state of the environment and to the availability of natural resources, the aim of providing relevant information about the economic development of a country is itself reason enough to work out green national accounts (see Hartwick, 1990; and Mäler, 1991).

It is much more difficult to be precise about what information green accounts ought to provide and what the best measures representing this information is. For example, national income is not easily defined. Hicks (1946) suggested the maximum amount a population could consume over a year without being worse off by the end of the period than it was in the beginning. He emphasises that this definition may apply in a static context, but is much more problematic if used in a dynamic perspective, where the consumption-saving decision needs to be dealt with. Weitzman (1976) shows that the national product may be defined as a measure of income opportunities, provided that the consumption programs are optimal. However, Asheim (1994) and Brekke (1994) show that this result applies only under very restricted assumptions. In practice, the net national product is just a proxy for income, which again is only an indication of welfare. Accordingly, corrections to account for changes in environmental standards and natural resources are also subject to the purpose of greening the national accounts.

One possible purpose is to provide an estimate of the value-added of a country, net of the depreciation of primary production factors (Peskin et al., 1992). This is often said to be the main purpose of measuring the traditional net national product. Since primary production factors are traditionally restrained to labour and capital, green national accounts would imply adjustments for depreciation and appreciation of natural resources and environmental assets, with the aim of estimating how the provision of commodities and services would change if the use of natural resources and environmental change were to be compensated.

Hueting et al. (1992) propose a green national product based on green accounts that provide a measure for sustainable development. Bartelmus (1999) points out that one might define sustainability such that it coincides with a 'green' measure for the value added, but sustainability may be defined in different ways. Thus, the adjustments of the national product needed to indicate sustainable development depend on how sustainable development is defined, for example, with respect to extraction of irreplaceable natural assets. Sustainability also means that dynamic aspects have to be considered. This involves the problems in defining income in a dynamic context, which were pointed out by Hicks.

Some have pursued the relation to welfare economics in Hicks's definition, including Mäler (1991). Then, the usefulness of national accounts in developing national welfare is emphasised. In this sense, the primary aim of green national accounts could be to indicate the severity of environmental degradation or, as Bartelmus and van Tongeren (1994) suggest, to provide early warning signals about the trends and limits of sustainable economic growth. This implies a broadening of the perspectives mentioned above, for example, by including the considerations of future risks and risk management.

In this present chapter, the provision of an appropriate measure for the value added in an economy is taken to be the main purpose. This is mainly because this definition seems to be the least dependent on concepts such as sustainability, welfare, or consumption programs for which the appropriate measure depends significantly on the definition. At the same time, a 'green' value-added constitutes an important step in telling us how environmental change affects sustainability, welfare, or consumption programs. A limitation is, however, that it includes only changes in the availability of natural resources and environmental change of relevance for the value added of the economy. Hence, we deal with what can be considered purely economic impacts.

NATIONAL ACCOUNTS AND THE ROLE OF PRICES

The national accounts measure the values of activities in an economy and the contributions from different production factors. The valuation serves as a means to aggregate widely different things on to one denominator, or to add apples and oranges to obtain a meaningful measure on fruit. Clearly, natural resources and environmental services can be included in the national accounts only if it is possible to attach appropriate prices to them. If so, one is in principle able to compare the contributions from natural resources and the environment with the contributions from labour and capital to all economic activities.

Observations of environmental standards and stocks of natural resources are measured in physical terms. In most cases, a physical measure of use or extraction over an accounting year can be observed. The challenge when it comes to valuation is therefore to attach appropriate prices, both to standards and stocks and to their use and extraction. In some cases, prices can be observed from market transactions, such as for extraction of many natural resources, but this is very often not the case, for example, when it comes to environmental standards. In these cases one will have to rely on valuation techniques.

A range of techniques apply to the valuation of non-marketable assets, but one cannot say in general which techniques are 'better' or 'worse'. It depends on the subject and what information is obtainable. One cannot, therefore, recommend one particular technique for green accounting, but the aim is always to attach the price to natural resources and environmental assets that would be observed if they were traded in competitive markets. The techniques approximate a price under different assumptions. A number of alternatives are described in United Nations (1993). They can also be distinguished by the following four methodological approaches:

- supply-side valuation;
- demand-side valuation;

- valuation by analogy;
- shadow prices.

Supply-side valuation means that the price of an asset is set equal to the marginal cost of providing it. For example, if air pollution is regulated, the marginal cost of emissions control can be considered an approximation of the value of clean air. This method applies if the amount of the asset can be considered close to the optimal, for example, if the air quality under current emissions control is considered to be acceptable, or if the marginal cost is more or less horizontal, such that the observed marginal cost of control would not change significantly even if the emission cuts are far from optimal.

Demand-side valuation means that the price is set equal to the price those who use the asset are willing to pay for it. Different techniques can be used, but the most prominent one is contingent valuation, which can be carried out by surveying people's willingness to pay for environmental assets. The method applies, in particular, for assets considered to be free goods, but subject to externalities, for example if air pollution is not controlled, or far from optimal. If the current situation is far from optimal, the willingness to pay is an estimate for the demand only if demand functions are more or less horizontal.

Valuation by analogy means that observed or approximate prices of similar assets are attached to the asset. This method applies when there is knowledge about the value of one asset which can be generalised to a broader class of similar assets. In some cases, prices observed within a geographically limited location can be taken to apply also within the region or the country. Sometimes information from one country can be used to estimate values in other countries as well. Also, for an aggregate of environmental or natural assets, an observation of a subset may give sufficient information about the price of the aggregate.

Shadow prices imply that the value of an asset is approximated by modelling the interactions between natural resources, environmental assets, and the rest of the economy, and solving the prices endogenously. If the model is 'perfect' the correct prices will be found, but it all depends on the quality of the model.

An advantage of all these methods is that prices are related to physical measures. This allows us, in principle, to take advantage of any knowledge about the physical state and changes in the environment from one year to the next. Thus, if the accountants are provided with assessments of physical changes, appropriate price estimates can be used to calculate asset values, and the required adjustments of the traditional national accounts can, in principle, be made.

The valuation techniques provide, however, only point estimates for the price of the assets valid for the observed stock of natural resources and the observed standard of the environment. A change in stocks or standards always requires two price estimates: one before and one after the change has taken place. Only shadow price valuation allows the two prices to be estimated on the basis of one observation. Then, the point estimate can be used to calibrate the relationships between the economy and the natural environment. Changes in prices following variations in stocks and standards can then be estimated by means of a model. It is, of course, possible also to utilise the other three kinds of point estimates to calibrate relationships between the economy and nature, but the change of prices will still have to be estimated by models. In that case one may of course question whether the concept of accounting can be used if in fact based on modelling.

The message is that the value of a change is, in principle, different from the physical change multiplied by a price observed or estimated at a certain point. This may seem a little peculiar, but is in fact vital, not because the estimate of the value of a change will turn out to be dramatically different but because prices no longer express values in an economic sense. In other words, adding changes in the quantities of apples and oranges multiplied with point estimates of prices no longer gives a meaningful measure of the change in the quantity of fruit. This can be stated without further inquiry because prices do not only express values in market equilibrium. They are also a means of reallocating resources: a change in physical quantities is a result of reallocation, and reallocation is a result of a change in relative prices. Thus, physical change cannot be explained by economic theory unless there is a change in relative prices.

GREEN ACCOUNTING AND DAMAGE ASSESSMENTS

Aaheim and Nyborg (1995) discuss possible consequences of neglecting this relationship between changes in quantities and changes in prices. The conclusion is that the information provided is easily misinterpreted, for example, that a warning about serious degradation may fail to be detected, and that policy-makers may be provided with biased information if compared with the consistent information from traditional national accounts. This undermines one of the basic ideas of establishing green accounts – namely, to provide policy-makers with consistent comparisons of economic and environmental changes. If green accounts cannot be made consistent, it may be better to present the traditional economic accounts and instead provide supplementary information about the environment, for example, in terms of physical indicators. Valuation in itself is not necessary for policy-making.

However, national accounts aim not only at presenting easily interpretable and statistically based indicators of economic development for the purpose of policy-making. Equally important is its role as a database for economic analysis. In that case, inclusion of environmental change and changes in the stock of natural resources in so-called integrated analysis requires valuation of environmental impacts or changes in natural resources in order to compare the contributions from the different factors of production. Although integrated analysis seldom aims at a comprehensive description of environmental change and natural resource development in the same manner as green accounting, the problem related to valuation and the available approaches are very much the same. In recent years, integrated models have been used to study the interaction between economic development and climate change. The impacts of climate change are usually represented by damage functions. These are relationships between a change in mean temperature and economic consequences expressed in monetary terms. As a parallel, one may consider green accounts as an attempt to estimate total environmental damage in economic terms.

Most climate cost functions are based on physical estimates of changes at a fixed change in the climate, for example, a doubling of the concentrations of greenhouse gases relative to pre-industrial time, usually denoted $2 \times CO_2$. The value of the resulting economic change, or the damage cost, is found by attaching a price, evaluated at present, to these changes and then multiplying with the estimated physical change. It is emphasised that the damage cost is evaluated as if concentrations increased to $2 \times CO_2$ 'today', and that future changes in the basic prices are disregarded. The point estimate is then used to calibrate a relationship between costs and concentrations under some assumption about the functional form of this relationship. We know, of course, very little about the functional form but the standard choice of a logarithmic function with exponent between 2 and 3 may be just as good as any other function.

Leaving aside other problems in doing integrated analysis with cost functions in this manner, we can concentrate on the cost estimate. What in actual fact is being done is a price believed to be representative of the value of various climate-sensitive assets today is multiplied with the expected physical change of these assets. Note, however, that even if it is accepted that a non-changing climate in the future can be evaluated at today's prices, the prices would change as a result of climate change. Therefore, if a change should suddenly take place, the prices observed prior to the change could no longer be justified as economic values. For the same reason, damage cost functions estimated on the basis of observed prices do not represent the true cost.

The biases inherent in these damage cost functions are basically the same as those pointed out for the green national accounts above. The main difference is perhaps that green accounting is supposed to represent a system of statistical information, whereas future damage from climate change is unequivocally subject to model analysis. Thus, possible scepticism with respect to a mingling of accounting and modelling no longer applies when analysing damages from climate change.

On the other hand, a main drawback in doing integrated analyses based on aggregate cost functions is that the representation of damages is more or less disconnected from the rest of the economy. Thus, the damages become insensitive to structural change and adaptation to climate change can be taken into account only exogenously. Moreover, the qualities of the physical assessments of effects of climate change from which damage cost functions have to be estimated are poor. There is a lot of uncertainty about the effects of climate change, but the uncertainty increases substantially the more aggregated are the effects accounted for. A consequence is that there is a strong tendency in the scientific community to focus more on local effects or impacts of single events or on particular sectors in order to come up with more accurate predictions. This means that it is difficult to implement new results in aggregated damage cost functions.

As an alternative, Aaheim and Schjolden (2004) suggest to utilise the ideas underlying the greening of national accounts by establishing relationships between the natural environment and economic activities. It is important, though, that prices are endogenously determined in order to reflect the change of value following climate change. This serves three purposes. First, the estimated cost of climate change becomes consistent, at least in principle. Second, adaptation becomes subject to, and consistent with, economic behaviour. Third, it becomes easier to take advantage of advances in scientific knowledge about the effects of climate change. In the remainder of this chapter, we illustrate how climate impacts may be integrated in accordance with this idea, and provide numerical examples of the differences between the various approaches to assess damage costs.

THE ACCOUNTING FRAMEWORK

A simple but remarkably powerful way to use the national accounts for the purpose of macroeconomic analysis is the input–output scheme developed by Leontief (1941). By the assumption of fixed input coefficients, the relationship between the total economic activity measured by the value of production and the value-added of an economy is explained with an explicit reference to observed data. In an economic sense, the main shortcomings of the input–output scheme are that economic activities are assumed to be independent of relative prices and that the activity can increase without limitations because primary production factors are always assumed to be available.

The interpretation of the input–output structure as a snapshot of the technology of the economy applies, however, irrespective of these shortcomings. Price sensitivity and resource constraints becomes important only if the issue at stake is what is going to happen if some change takes place. A test of any model, sophisticated or not, is to check whether it generates the observed input–output coefficients – defined as the technology – under the prevailing set of prices and resource constraints.

Referring to the discussion above, the input–output scheme thereby allows prices to be considered only as a means to aggregate physical quantities. If the observed input and output change for reasons other than changes in prices and resource availability, it should be interpreted as a change in the technology, that is, the required quantity of input to produce a given quantity of output at constant prices. Consider, now, impacts of climate change as estimated by damage cost functions. Since they are evaluated at present prices, they cannot represent 'costs' or 'benefits' but rather a change of technology, which results from a different climate. The costs and benefits can be expressed only by comparing the economic responses resulting from a change of technology.

Thus, knowledge from studies of economic impacts of climate change can be used to recalibrate the technology of the economy described by the input–output scheme. Define by $\mathbf{A}$, the matrix of input coefficients, where the element α_{ij} gives the quantity of input of factor i to produce one unit of output in activity j. In general, $\mathbf{A}$ is a representation of the technology of the economy at a given set of prices and resource availabilities. Climate change affects these input coefficients irrespective of changes in prices and resources. An impact assessment can be viewed as the task of establishing a relationship $\{f: \alpha_{ij} \rightarrow \beta_{ij}\}$ for all i and j, where $\beta_{ij} \in \mathbf{B}$ is the quantity input of factor i per unit of output in activity j, or per unit of final demand, at a given change in climatic conditions, and $\mathbf{B}$ is the matrix of input coefficients, or technology, posterior to climate change.

The establishment of these relationships is, in principle, the same as the process of 'greening' the national accounts. With reference to the input–output scheme, adjustments that may take place can be divided into three classes. The first is the change in intermediate deliveries between production sectors. For example, Askildsen (2004) points out that road transport is regularly hampered by closed roads during winter storms in Norway, and that land transport systems are vulnerable to landslides in extreme conditions. Climate change may, in general, affect man-made capital particularly if there is a shift in the frequency of extreme events. This will affect the building and construction sector directly, both in terms of repairs of destructions, or in terms of a change in building standards and habits in response to the climatic change.

The second class of effect is the immediate change in final deliveries. Households may change their composite of consumer goods in order to maintain exactly the same standard of living. At a very basic level, clothing is of course climate dependent. The choice of holiday activity is in many cases subject to climatic conditions, and the demand for energy for heating purposes is sensitive to temperature. Personal transport demand may depend on the climate, both when it comes to distance and to choice of transport mode.

The third class of effect relates to the productivity of primary input factors, which are usually excluded from the ordinary input–output scheme, but constitute an important part of the national accounts. There are potential impacts of climate change on the return on real and human capital. For example, diseases or injuries caused by climate change affects the productivity ('return') on human capital, and material damage affects the return on real capital. However, the major impacts are expected to relate to the economic return on natural resources, which is not explicit in traditional national accounts. Thus, greening the national accounts is important, if not essential, to capture the economic impacts of climate change adequately.

SECTOR STUDIES APPLIED TO NATIONAL IMPACTS ASSESSMENT

A comprehensive inclusion of possible impacts of climate change requires extensive studies. To the economist, the easy part is to detect physical effects at the sector level, because this information will usually have to be provided from experts in fields other than economics. The aggregation of impacts by means of observed or simulated market prices constitutes only one of several steps in examining the economic impacts of climate change. To illustrate and exemplify this whole process, this section shows how micro- and sector-based knowledge about the response to climate change can be analysed and prepared for implementation in the national accounts framework, and further utilised for the purpose of macroeconomic analysis. Below we focus on two of the three categories of impacts noted above – namely, a change in the productivity of natural resources, exemplified by forestry, and an immediate change in a household's final demand, more precisely the response to climate change on the demand for different modes of transport.

*Table 5.1   Expected changes in average annual and seasonal temperatures
and precipitation between the periods 1980–2000
and 2030–50 by region in Norway*

Region		Temperature (°C)		Precipitation (mm/day)	
		Level*	Change	Level*	Change
Northern	Year	2.8	1.6	2.8	0.3
	Spring	1.7	1.4	2.0	0.2
	Summer	10.6	1.2	2.4	0.1
	Autumn	2.8	1.7	3.7	0.8
	Winter	−3.9	2.0	3.2	0.2
Western	Year	7.6	1.0	6.2	0.8
	Spring	6.5	0.9	4.3	0.1
	Summer	13.9	0.7	5.1	1.0
	Autumn	8.2	1.1	8.9	1.5
	Winter	1.6	1.2	6.4	0.6
Eastern	Year	6.2	1.1	3.1	0.2
	Spring	5.0	1.0	2.3	−0.1
	Summer	15.6	0.6	3.5	0.1
	Autumn	8.0	1.3	4.3	0.3
	Winter	−3.8	1.3	2.5	0.4

Note: * Average levels for Tromsø (Northern), Bergen (Western) and Oslo (Eastern).

Source: RegClim.

The scenario for the future climate will be taken from results of the RegClim project for Norway, published by Førland and Nordeng (1999), which is based on a downscaling of results from global circulation models (GCM). They predict that climate change over the coming 50 years will lead to higher average temperature and more precipitation. The main predictions are displayed in Table 5.1. Temperature increase varies from 1.0 to 1.6°C, with the most substantial change in the Northern region. The expected increase in daily precipitation ranges between 0.2 and 0.8 mm/day on an annual basis, but may increase by 1.5 mm/day in the autumn in the Western region.

Choice of Transport Modes Under Variations in Climate

It is probably uncontroversial to claim that people's choice of transport mode is to some extent dependent on the weather when travelling short distances. It is much more difficult to say how and to what extent, because individuals consider a wide range of factors important to them, but they emphasise them differently. One difficulty in analysing the choice of mode is to identify factors of relevance. Another, perhaps more challenging task, is to define tractable observations of them.

Travelling habit surveys collect a broad range of information about single journeys within a region at a certain period of time. The survey of travelling habits for the city of Bergen in Norway in 2000 (Bergen Fylkeskommune, 2000) provides information about where, when, why, how and by whom journeys are made, that can be used to derive structural patterns in travelling habits. These data can be coupled with weather observations at the time the journey took place in order to examine possible causal relationships between weather and choice of mode.

However, despite the details recorded for each single journey, a number of problems in identifying explanatory variables were encountered. For example, it turned out to be impossible to identify where journeys started and ended. Whether or not public transport was a real option could not therefore be considered. Travelling distance had to be approximated with reference to the time spent on each journey and the choice of transport mode. Moreover, the weather observations applied as daily averages or daily totals, which might differ from the weather at the point in time when the choice of mode was made. Thus, even if there were clear causal relationships between weather and choice of mode, we could not trace them from the dataset.

As a proxy for differences in the availability of public transport, the observations were stratified into one set representing journeys starting in the city centre, and the other set starting outside the centre. Moreover, the journeys were stratified according to their purpose. Journeys in connection with work, school and leisure were grouped together. Since only short distances were recorded, journeys in connection with leisure includes visits to the cinema or to friends, but those for holidays are excluded. The other group included journeys in connection with errands, such as shopping. A more detailed discussion of the stratification and alternative mode choices is given in Aaheim and Hauge (2005).

The choices of mode were estimated as logit choice probabilities, explained by daily average wind, daily average temperature, daily precipitation, gender, age group and distance travelled. Although there are tendencies in the data, only a few parameters related to the weather were significantly different from zero. However, the motivation here is primarily to show how possible relationships can be implemented in a national accounting framework rather than making completely accurate estimates of the impacts of climate change.

Figure 5.1 displays the probabilities of mode choice for journeys in connection with work and leisure starting from the city centre. As expected,

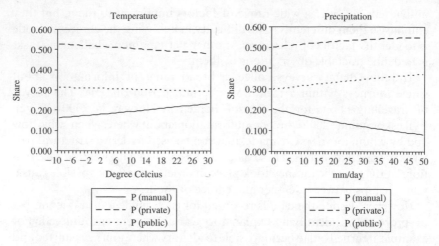

*Figure 5.1   Micro behaviour choice – probabilities of mode choice
              (work and leisure from city centre)*

higher temperature and low rain makes people shift from private and public
transport to walking or bicycling. The switch between public transport and
walking and bicycling is somewhat stronger than between private transport
and walking and bicycling, both when the temperature changes and when
precipitation changes. A similar pattern was found for travels from the suburban areas.

Travels in connection with errands, however, exhibit a different pattern.
More precipitation makes people switch, in particular, from private to
public transport, whereas walking and bicycling in suburban areas is limited
because of the distance travelled. In all strata, travelling distance also tends
to shorten when it rains more.

If the estimated change of mode choice is taken to represent responses to
climate change, the results of this study may be used to estimate the impact
on personal transport use. Under the assumption that these patterns represent individual responses in 11 of the largest cities in Norway, the results for
Bergen were transmitted to the other ten cities, but adjusted for differences
in city size, distribution of population in urban and suburban areas and
the initial composition of mode choice and travelling purpose, as well as
differences in the aforementioned explanatory factors used in the estimation of the choice probabilities.[2] The resulting change of mode following
the predicted climate change for all the cities are shown in Figure 5.2.

Figure 5.2 displays the relatively complex pattern in the changes. Thus,
while walking and cycling take over from private transport regardless of
purpose in the centres, private transport takes over from walking and cycling

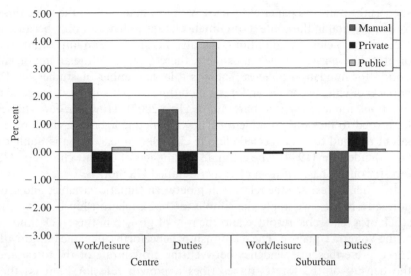

Figure 5.2   Change of transport mode pattern for short journeys following predicted climate change (all cities)

for journeys connected to duties in suburban areas. The most substantial increase is in public transport for these journeys in city centres. Most cities exhibit similar patterns, with more vigorous changes in the cities where the weather is expected to change the most – such as Bergen. A pattern somewhat different from the other cities emerges in Stavanger and Trondheim, which end up with very small shifts.

In total, the estimated change of mode for all the nine cities were calculated as a 0.6 per cent increase in journeys by walking or bicycling, a 0.2 per cent reduction in private transport and a 0.6 per cent increase in public transport. The reduction in private transport implies that private households have reduced their expenditure on fuel and road charges in the largest cities. The total savings were estimated at 77.7 million NOK (Norwegian Kroner). Higher demand for public transport implies an increase in expenditure on services, which was estimated to be 39.9 million NOK for all households. The increase in walking and bicycling indirectly leads to an increase in disposable income, which is a result of the difference between the extra expenditure on public transport and the reduction in private transport.

Impact of Climate Change on Forestry

Forestry constitutes an important part of the Norwegian economy, partly because of the harvesting, but mainly because it supplies other industries, such as the pulp and paper industries, with raw material. At the same time, forestry is vital in the context of climate change policy, not only because it is sensitive to climatic conditions, but also because it is an important sink of greenhouse gases in the atmosphere, thereby representing an important option for mitigation policies. There is a large number of studies on the impacts of climate change on forests including assessment for damage cost functions for forestry (see particularly Tol, 2002). However, few studies have tried to tackle the problem of how economic agents in the forestry might respond to the expected climate changes. An exception is Sohngen and Mendelsohn (1999), who estimate the impacts of climate change on US forestry on the basis of a set of rather detailed US models.

In order to describe the relationship between climatic variables and economic responses, we apply the simple textbook relationship between the stock of a renewable resource and the rate of growth in this stock, known as the Volterra equation. The relationship, henceforth called the bio-growth curve, prescribes a dependency between the growth rate of the forest and the density of the forest. It describes a growth rate for biomass that increases for increasing densities when the density is low, and reaches a maximum at a certain point, called the maximum sustainable yield. Beyond this point, the growth rate declines with higher densities. At some point, the stock of biomass is mature, meaning that the growth is choked. In Aaheim (2004), the stock of a standing forest within a region – for example, a country – is interpreted as the density. National statistics are then used to calibrate a bio-growth curve for Norwegian forests, which is shown by the reference case in Figure 5.3.

The effect of climate change on the forests can now be characterised by changes in the bio-growth curve. There are no available estimates of the effects of the expected climate changes shown in Table 5.1 that can be plugged directly into a bio-growth curve. Strand (2002) has estimated that the forested area will grow by more than 55 000 km^2 at a temperature increase of 1.0°C, but this constitutes nearly 50 per cent of the potential increase of forest area regardless of how favourable the climatic conditions should turn out. Moreover, a large part of this area is currently at high latitudes or in the north of the country, where the potential for bio-growth is limited. Schjolden (2004) notes that although there is some knowledge about the physical responses of climate change on forests, there are no economic estimates available at the moment. What follows is, therefore, a brief discussion of how economic agents may respond to improvements in the bio-growth of forests.

The expectation is that climate change will have a positive effect on the forests, partly because a longer growth season may increase growth in forested areas, but mainly because new areas of forestry will emerge. These

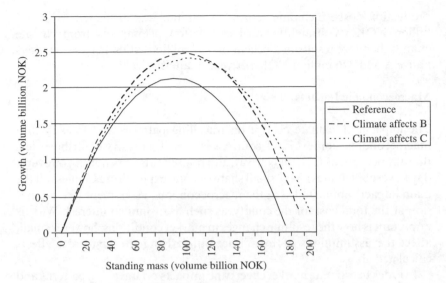

Figure 5.3   *The bio-growth curve and possible effects of climate change (standing mass and growth in volumes of billion NOK)*

two effects may, on the other hand, affect bio-growth differently. Figure 5.3 illustrates this by two positive shifts. In one case, maximum sustainable yield increases by more, however, the choking point is higher in the other case. The difference between the two may illustrate that an increase in the growth of formerly forested areas contributes more to an increase in maximum sustainable yield than an expansion of areas covered by existing forests.

In order to maximise profits, economic agents take into account the cost of harvesting; the possible value of a standing mass (for example, for recreational purposes); and the alternative cost, which is to cut and sell the whole forest and invest the proceeds in some other activity. The optimal harvest is at the point on the bio-growth curve where the net income of leaving the tree to grow for one more year yields exactly the same return as cutting it and reinvesting the income in the best alternative. The problem is further discussed in Aaheim (2004).

The economic model briefly presented here allows for a study of the forest owner's adaptation to climate change. In the first step, this may be regarded as a reconsideration of the present harvest from the perspective of the micro level – that is, as if prices and costs are unaffected by climate change. The effects illustrated in Figure 5.3 imply an increase in harvest at 15.8 per cent in alternative A and 18.4 per cent in alternative B. The forest rent in the reference case, which is the difference between income and production costs, including return on capital, was estimated to be 1.5 billion NOK. A straightforward calculation of impacts from climate change therefore results in a benefit of 737 million NOK per year in alternative A and 776 million NOK per year in alternative B.

Macroeconomic Impacts

The impacts of climate change on travelling patterns and forestry in a macroeconomic context is, of course, very small. Forestry contributes less than 0.1 per cent of GDP in Norway, and households' expenditure on everyday travel contributes a very small share of total expenditures. Unless all the main impacts are included in the macroeconomic assessment, the estimation of the total cost for the county, as such, is of limited interest. What is important is how the resulting changes in market conditions, however small, affect the assumptions of fixed prices underlying the first-order effects calculated above.

In order to estimate market effects, the impacts on travelling patterns and the forestry management problem were implemented in a small macroeconomic model for Norway (Aaheim and Rive, 2005). The model consists of six production sectors: forestry, wood products, other manufacturing industries, fossil fuel production, electricity production and services. It has an ordinary nested Constant Elasticity of Substitution (CES) production structure, as well as a nested CES utility structure. The forestry sector is subject to biotic constraints and is further presented in Aaheim (2004).

The macroeconomic results indicate how the reduction in expenditure on private transport in households is allocated. The demand for fossil fuels in the private sector is reduced by 0.5 per cent, but this is partly counteracted by an increase of 0.1 per cent in the demand for fossil fuels in the service sector, which includes public transport. All in all, energy prices decrease. This implies a 4.5 million NOK increase in the disposable income in households, two-thirds of which is spent on services with one-third spent on products from other industries, including electricity. The point is that although the macroeconomic impacts are negligible, they bring an important new aspect when compared with the sector assessment on which the recalibration of the model was based. First, the reduction in energy prices adds to the expenditure savings calculated in the sector assessment, and second, we can tell how the savings are spent.

Implementing the forestry module in the macroeconomic model has basically two effects. One is that higher growth makes it profitable to expand the area of the accessible part of the forest. This can be arranged by investments in infrastructure. The other is that an increase in timber supply will lead to a reduction in timber prices. The total benefit from climate change is therefore lower than indicated by the increase in the biomass. Because of the optimal management of the forest, the two cases depicted in Figure 5.3 result in highly different economic benefits. Owing to assumptions about extraction costs and willingness to pay for standing mass, the optimal point of harvest is found at a relatively high standing mass, where the increase in case B exceeds that of case A. Thus, case A increases the forestry rent by 67 million NOK, and case B by 181 million NOK, which is considerably lower than the simple fixed price assessment indicated.

CONCLUSIONS

It is easy to find support for the view that 'greening' the national accounts would provide better information about the socio-economic development of a country than the ordinary national accounts. The problem is to attain appropriate data about the value of environmental change and changes in the stock of natural resources. Most of the efforts to solve this problem deal with the task of attaching one single price to these assets. This is, however, insufficient because changes in quantity cannot be explained straightforwardly by economic theory unless there is has been a change in prices. What is needed is one set of prices prior to the change and another set of prices after the change has taken place.

Estimation of the economic value of environmental change by means of one single set of prices is, nevertheless, quite standard. For example, various assessments of the economic impacts of climate change are, nearly without exception, based on it. In this chapter, it has been argued that the idea of adjusting national accounts figures in accordance with expected environmental change, such as impacts of climate change, might be useful if interpreted as changes in quantity or volume. Then, the set of prices on which the estimates are based are used as a *means to aggregate* different impacts on to a common denominator. In order to arrive at the values, one has to take into account the resulting *reallocation of initial endowments* and their uses. This problem may be solved by general equilibrium models, where the prices are determined endogenously. Hence, methods developed to establish green national accounts turn out to be useful, for example, in estimating the socio-economic impacts of climate change.

The difference between a fixed price assessment and a general equilibrium assessment has been illustrated by comparing economic impacts estimated in sector oriented bottom-up studies and impacts resulting from an implementation of the bottom-up studies in a macroeconomic model. With examples from assessments of the impact of climate change on personal transport and forestry in Norway, we found that the indirect macroeconomic effects are not only significant, but the assessments also provide richer and more easily interpretable results for the understanding of the economic impact of climate change. In the case of personal transport, a sole calculation of benefits minus costs in the bottom-up assessment could be analysed in the light of its contribution to disposable income in the top-down assessment. Thus, both the increase in income following a lower price of energy and the allocation of the savings on different consumer goods could be analysed. In the case of forestry, the significant price effect following an increase in the supply of timber reduced the economic benefit by 10 per cent in the top-down assessment when compared with the bottom-up assessment.

Over the past decades, politicians, policy-makers and the public in general have demanded vast amounts of socio-economic analysis of environmental change. Although the issues at stake have been dealt with in economic theory for a long time, the variety and details of the problems that were raised often made it necessary to base the analyses on rather strong assumptions. When the first-order approximations have been made, however, it is time to go back and reconsider the shortcuts to see if a more appropriate set of assumptions do make a difference. Viewed in such a perspective, this chapter argues that the assumption that environmental change is evaluated on the basis of fixed prices is strong, indeed, and that it may make a big difference if prices instead are determined endogenously, not only for the numerical results, but also for the interpretation of the results.

NOTES

1. Changes in labour and capital are, in fact, also poorly treated, but are taken into account, at least in principle.
2. The cities are Oslo, Bergen, Trondheim, Stavanger, Tromsø, Kristiansand, Tønsberg, Skien, Porsgrunn, Fredrikstad and Sarpsborg.

REFERENCES

Aaheim, H.A. (2004), 'Impacts on climate change on forestry and the macro economy', presented at the Second International Workshop on Integrated Climate Models: An Interdisciplinary Assessment of Climate Impacts and Policies, Trieste, 29–30 November 2004, available at http://www.ictp.trieste.it/~eee/workshops/smr1579/smr1579.htm.

Aaheim, H.A. and K. Hauge (2005), 'Dependencies between weather and the choice of transport mode, and possible impacts of climate change', CICERO working paper (forthcoming).

Aaheim, H.A. and K. Nyborg (1995), 'On the interpretation and applicability of a "green national product" ', *The Review of Income and Wealth*, **41** (1), 57–71.

Aaheim, H.A. and N. Rive (2005), 'An integrated computable general equilibrium model for analyses of impacts of climate change', CICERO working paper (forthcoming).

Aaheim, H.A. and A. Schjolden (2004), 'An approach to utilise climate change impacts studies in national assessments', *Global Environmental Change*, **14**, 147–60.

Asheim, G.B. (1994), 'Net National Product as an indicator of sustainability', *Scandinavian Journal of Economics*, **96** (2), 257–65.

Askildsen, T.C. (2004), 'Ekstremværsituasjoner og transporteffekter: næringslivets transportilpasninger til klimaendringer' (Extreme weather events and transport effects: the transport industry's adaption to climate change), CICERO Report 2004: 10, Oslo (in Norwegian).

Bartelmus, P. (1999), 'Greening the national accounts: approach and policy use', DESA discussion paper no. 3, New York: United Nations.

Bartelmus, P. and J. van Tongeren (1994), 'Environmental accounting: an operational perspective', working paper series, No. 1. ST/ESA/1994/WP.1, New York: United Nations.

Bergen Fylkeskommune (2000), *Reisevaneundersøkelse for Bergen 2000* (Travelling Habits Survey for Bergen 2000), Bergen (in Norwegian).

Brekke, K.A. (1994), 'Net National Product as a welfare indicator', *Scandinavian Journal of Economics*, **96** (2), 241–52.

Førland, E.J. and T.E. Noredeng (1999), 'Framtidig klimautvikling i Norge' (Future Climate Development in Norway), *Cicerone* No. 6, CICERO Oslo (in Norwegian).

Hartwick, J.M. (1990), 'Natural resources, national accounting and economic depreciation', *Journal of Public Economics*, **43**, 291–304.

Hicks, J. (1946), *Value and Capital*, 2nd edn, Oxford: Oxford University Press.

Hueting, R., P. Bosch and B. de Boer (1992), 'Methodology for the calculation of sustainable national income', *Statistical Essays* M44, Gravenhage: Centraal bureau voor de statistiek.

Leontief, W. (1941), *The Structure of the American Economy 1919–1939*, New York: Oxford University Press.

Mäler, K.-G. (1991), 'National accounts and environmental resources', *Environmental and Resource Economics*, **1**, 1–15.

Peskin, H., W. Floor and D.F. Barnes (1992), 'Accounting for traditional fuel production: the household energy sector and its implication for the development process', Energy series paper no. 49, Washington DC: Industry and Energy Department, World Bank.

Schjolden, A. (2004), 'Towards assessing socioeconomic impacts of climate change in Norway. Sensitivity in the primary sectors: fisheries, agriculture and forestry', CICERO report 2004: 3, Oslo: CICERO University of Oslo.

Sohngen, B.L. and R. Mendelsohn (1999), 'The impacts of climate change on the US timber market', in R. Mendelsohn and J.E. Neumann (eds), *The Impact of Climate Change on the United States Economy*, Cambridge, New York, Melbourne: Cambridge University Press.

Strand, G.-H. (2002), 'Beregning av areal som kan bli tresatt ved temperatureheving' (Calculation of potential area covered by forests at a temperature increase), *Rapport* 05/2002, Norsk Institutt for Jord- og Skogbruksforskning, Ås (in Norwegian).

Tol, R.S.J. (2002), 'Estimates of damage costs of climate change: Part I: benchmark estimates', *Environmental and Resource Economics*, **21**, 47–73.

United Nations (1993), 'Integrated environmental and economic accounting, interim version', *Handbook of National Accounting*, Series F, No. 61, New York: Statistical Division, Department of Economic and Social Development.

Weitzman, M.L. (1976), 'On the welfare significance of the Net National Product in a dynamic economy', *Quarterly Journal of Economics*, **90**, 156–62.

6. A critical appraisal of genuine savings as an indicator of sustainability

Simon Dietz and Eric Neumayer

INTRODUCTION

Chapters 3, 4 and 5 have introduced the tradition of green national accounting that has now become well established. The basic principles of this tradition are commonly understood by most practitioners to involve accounting for the consumption and accumulation of produced, human and natural capital, assuming the different capital stocks are infinitely substitutable (weak sustainability). One particular indicator that shares this basis and has been the subject of considerable attention and data gathering over the last decade is genuine savings (hereafter GS). In this chapter, we introduce and critically appraise GS.

THE BASIC MEANING OF GENUINE SAVINGS

GS sets out to measure whether we are dis-saving. That is, whether we allow depreciation of total capital to exceed investment in all forms of capital. The term 'genuine' was coined by Hamilton (1994) to reflect the fact that GS includes all forms of capital, not just produced capital.[1] In common with the wider green national accounting literature, GS traces its roots back to the work of neoclassical economists Robert Solow (1974) and John Hartwick (1977), who were concerned with modelling a development path in which social welfare or well-being does not decline in an economy exploiting a non-renewable resource. The problem is one of maximising the present value of social welfare over all time, given a range of simplifying assumptions that will be critically discussed below. Solving this maximisation problem yields green net national product or gNNP, which is equal to society's consumption plus the sum of net changes in all the capital stocks valued at their shadow prices. These shadow prices are the prices that would exist in an inter-temporally efficient economy without externalities (this is one such assumption):

gNNP = consumption + net investment in produced capital
      − net depreciation of natural capital
      + investment in human capital.   (6.1)

Subtracting consumption leaves us with net changes in all the capital stocks valued at their shadow prices, which is GS. Without pursuing a formal derivation (see Hamilton and Clemens, 1999):

GS = net investment in produced capital
      − net depreciation of natural capital
      + investment in human capital.   (6.2)

In what equates to a modification to the so-called Hartwick rule,[2] the aim of the sustainability planner is to keep GS above or equal to zero. This is a necessary (but not sufficient) condition for ensuring sustainability under the weak sustainability paradigm. If GS is persistently below zero, then the economy is not sustainable, since future utility must be below current utility at some point (Hamilton and Clemens, 1999). Keeping GS greater than or equal to zero is necessary but not sufficient to ensure sustainability. Asheim (1994) and Pezzey and Withagen (1995) showed that, if the economy has had persistently negative GS in the past, then positive GS at some later point in time is insufficient to guarantee sustainability. But the sustainability planner does not have the luxury of hindsight. This means that GS is at best a one-sided indicator. We will reprise this issue below.

EMPIRICAL ESTIMATES OF GENUINE SAVINGS

Pearce and Atkinson (1993) produced initial GS estimates for 18 countries. Since then, the GS mantle has very much been assumed by the World Bank (see, for example, World Bank, 2003), which now regularly publishes a comparatively comprehensive GS measurement exercise for over 150 countries.[3] In simplified form, the World Bank operationalises GS, which it now calls 'adjusted net saving' − as follows:

GS = investment in man-made capital − net foreign borrowing
      + net official transfers − depreciation of man-made capital
      − net depreciation of natural capital
      + current education expenditures   (6.3)

- Investment in produced capital, net foreign borrowing and net official transfers are obtained from the national accounts. Although depreciation of produced capital is not, estimates can be derived from data on produced capital formation. The World Bank uses estimates from the United Nations Statistics Division.

- Net depreciation of natural capital can be divided at a basic level into resource extraction on the one hand and environmental pollution on the other. The World Bank estimates resource extraction for a range of fossil fuels (oil, natural gas, hard coal and brown coal), minerals (bauxite, copper, iron, lead, nickel, zinc, phosphate, tin, gold and silver), and one renewable resource (forests). Depreciation of these resources is computed as the product of price minus average costs of extraction multiplied by the volume of extraction:

$$(P - AC)^*R \tag{6.4}$$

where P is the resource price, AC is average cost and R is the volume of extraction (in the case of a renewable resource, R represents harvest beyond natural regeneration). Environmental pollution is conceptualised as the use of sink capacity in order for it to be equivalent to capital depreciation. Until recently, environmental pollution was taken to be the estimated damage cost of carbon dioxide emissions where each ton of carbon emitted is valued at US\$20 per metric tonne of carbon (from Fankhauser, 1995). In its most recent estimation (2003), it added the damage costs of particulates in the air.

- Investment in human capital is calculated as net educational expenditure. This includes both capital expenditure as well as current expenditure that are counted as consumption rather than investment in the traditional national accounts. This is certainly rather crude, but it is difficult to see how investment in human capital could be estimated otherwise for so many countries over such a long time horizon. Dasgupta (2001a, p. C9 f.) argues that it is an overestimate since human capital is lost when people die. But part of the human capital stock might be passed on when people die or, to be precise, leave the workforce. In any case, such a correction would be difficult to undertake.

Figure 6.1 shows estimated GS for the major world regions and global GS between 1976 and 2000. Global GS and GS in the OECD countries, East Asia and South Asia have always been positive. In practicality then, these regions and the world as a whole have passed the one-sided GS test: they have apparently not been unsustainable over the past 25 years or so. Latin

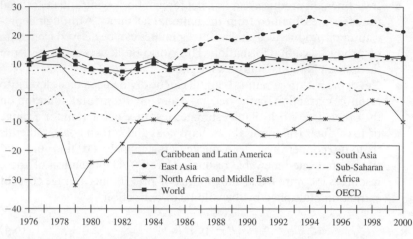

Source: World Bank (2004).

Figure 6.1   Genuine savings rates as a percentage of GNP

America and the Caribbean had negative GS for a time during the early 1980s, but the worst savers have been Sub-Saharan Africa, North Africa and the Middle East. In Sub-Saharan Africa, GS has been negative since the early 1980s. In North Africa and the Middle East, they have always been negative.

One conclusion we can draw from this data is that the regions with the greatest natural resource extraction are also the poorest performers in terms of GS (Neumayer, 2003). This is also true at the national level of analysis. Figure 6.2 plots time-averaged national GS rates against an indicator of resource abundance: the share of fuel and mineral exports in total exports. With the exception of Algeria and Guinea, for whom GS was just above zero for the period 1970–2001, every country with an average share of fuel and mineral exports in total exports of over 60 per cent had negative GS. In contrast, most resource-poor countries, especially the cluster of countries with an average share of fuel and mineral exports in total exports of under 20 per cent, had positive GS. In Sub-Saharan Africa, it must also be said that net produced capital investment is often negative too. In other words, the total 'man-made' wealth of these countries is also decreasing, and the World Bank's estimates of net natural capital depreciation simply worsen the situation. This is the case in Guinea-Bissau, for example. The surprising element of the World Bank's results is that some heavy resource extractors appear more unsustainable than intuition would suggest (Neumayer, 1999, 2003). Saudi Arabia is the clearest example of this. It is

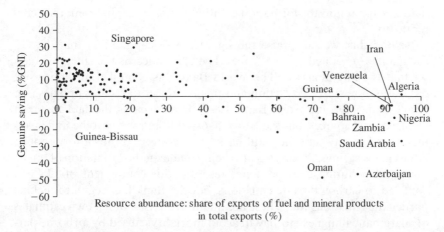

Source: World Bank (2004).

Figure 6.2 *Resource abundance and genuine savings between 1970 and 2001*

hugely unsustainable according to the World Bank, but still has vast reserves of oil and natural gas. It turns out that calculating natural capital depreciation according to a different method produces a more plausible outcome (see below).

THE POSITIVE CONTRIBUTION OF GENUINE SAVINGS

As we have pointed out, one of the strongest aspects of GS, at least from the perspective of influencing policy, is the fact that it acts as a counterweight to traditional systems of national accounting. Although GNP and GDP do not (and indeed were never intended to) measure welfare, in practice they tend to be construed in exactly that way and thus GS is a related but much more holistic indicator. For example, in 2001 global gross savings amounted to 23.9 per cent of global gross income, whereas global genuine savings were only 12.9 per cent of global gross income. In the Middle East and North Africa, gross savings were 26.9 per cent of gross income, whereas genuine savings were −5.9 per cent of gross income (World Bank, 2003), indicating unsustainability. Furthermore, although we have reservations about the very low GS estimates in certain resource-rich countries, the basic empirical outcome is a valid one for policy: certain resource-rich countries need to invest more of the proceeds of natural capital into the formation of other forms of capital than they currently do.

Beyond this, we can praise the significant research effort that the GS agenda has generated on two fronts. The first concerns the emerging data set that is being amassed. The World Bank has compiled an impressive database on resource extraction and this is subject to regular updates (see Kunte et al., 1998 and World Bank, 1997). In most cases, the data are taken from external sources, but the effort involved in this is not to be underestimated and in any case they still have to be converted into a form apt to adjust gross savings. Progress is also being made on the estimation of environmental pollution damage. Until recently, this component of GS was confined to carbon dioxide emissions, but the Bank has begun to include particulate emissions too. These are quantified based on its own estimates of marginal willingness-to-pay to avoid mortality caused by airborne particulates (equivalent to the shadow price of the stock of particulate emissions: Pandey et al., 2003). Hopefully we will see more pollutants included in the near future. For example, tropospheric ozone pollution would be a valuable addition, as would organic pollution of waterways.

The second impressive outcome of the GS research effort is the theoretical development of the topic, which has advanced knowledge not only about GS, but also about weak sustainability in general. Of course, it might seem rather odd to praise the development of a research area, something that is after all an inherent property of all research. But research on GS has meaningfully advanced since its initial development in the early 1990s. We are now better placed to understand, for example, the implications of different methods for calculating natural resource rents, and our understanding of the significance of per capita estimates of GS versus aggregate GS is also improving. Both of these issues are discussed below. We have also chosen not to mention the theoretical development of the Hartwick rule, and the implications of the optimal growth model. Important contributions include Asheim et al. (2003). Taking on board these improvements leads to a more sophisticated indicator than that initially advanced.

CRITICISMS OF GENUINE SAVINGS

GS has come in for a series of criticisms since its inception, much as its competitors have. These have been discussed in the past by Neumayer (1999, 2003). We will now outline a series of the most significant problems. We do not, however, discuss the general advantages and disadvantages of green national accounting and other indicators of weak sustainability in comparison with indicators of strong sustainability (which assumes at least some natural capital is non-substitutable). The interested reader is directed to Part IV in this volume. It is nevertheless important to remember that the merit of GS as a policy-guiding indicator depends to a great extent on the wider paradigms to which it belongs.

GS is Based on a Model of an Inter-temporally Efficient Economy

We have already explained that, because GS is a point measure of total wealth in the economy, it can only be a one-sided indicator of sustainability. The problem is then that an economy with positive GS is not necessarily sustainable. This is compounded by the violation of a basic assumption behind the model of GS: the economy develops along an optimal path over all time. In this inter-temporally efficient economy, there is 'a complete set of property rights (that is, no externalities) with competitive households and firms and a full set of forward markets where perfectly rational agents have perfect information and households take full account of the welfare of their actual or prospective descendants' (Neumayer, 1999, p. 155). None of these conditions will hold in reality. Markets fail, especially markets for natural assets, which often do not exist. Hence it is entirely possible that positive GS is associated with, among other things, non-optimal natural resource prices, such that these assets are in fact being extracted unsustainably. This is of course hardly a revelation for environmental and resource economists, whose discipline is founded in large part on the notion that natural resources are under-priced in the economy (see, for example, Pearce and Turner, 1989).

In the present context at least, knowing that the economy is inter-temporally inefficient might suggest a preference for those indicators of (strong) sustainability that set some exogenously defined environmental standard and then measure the opportunity cost of attaining that standard. This so-called hybrid technique for measuring sustainable development was pioneered by Roefie Hueting (1992) and advanced, using multisectoral economic modelling, by Brouwer et al. (1996), Brouwer and O'Connor (1997a, 1997b) and O'Connor and Ryan (1999).[4]

Exogenous Shocks to the GS Model

Quite apart from the unrealistic assumption of intertemporal efficiency, the GS model is vulnerable to shocks from outside the system. The difficulty with exogenous shocks is that the prices existing at the outset will no longer be optimal and will not adequately reflect economic scarcities (Neumayer, 1999). Looking forward from the base year into the future, there is once again no guarantee that GS is giving the correct signals vis-à-vis sustainability. What should therefore happen after such a shock is that prices should be re-estimated. Understandably, Hamilton (1995) rejects this approach as impracticable, and instead proposes that the assumption of efficient pricing is simply dropped. The paradox one ends up in, however, is that the whole method of accounting remains on some level dependent on efficient pricing. Three particular types of exogenous shock are:

1.   exogenous technological progress;
2.   terms-of-trade effects;
3.   a non-constant discount rate.

Exogenous technological progress

The GS model assumes stationary technology. This does not mean that there is no technological progress at all. In fact, as long as progress is embodied in one or other form of capital (in other words is endogenous to the GS model) its effect is accounted for in GS estimates. Instead, it is that fraction of future technological progress that is exogenous, that requires the re-estimation of GS. Equally, exogenous technological progress will only be of interest provided it is non-constant: otherwise it is simply the level of utility (gNNP) that is altered and not the rate of change with time (GS). Presuming technological change does alter the rate of change of utility with time, GS can still be negative even with expanded welfare possibilities, which means that society is losing its capacity to attain that higher level of well being. Alternatively, if exogenous technological progress is contributing less over time to welfare relative to the base year, then even zero GS is insufficient for ensuring sustainability and positive GS is necessary (Neumayer, 1999). In principle, it is possible to treat technological change as an externality and quantify it, but it is very difficult even to approximate unanticipated future change.

Terms-of-trade effects

The effects of changes in future terms of trade are obviously quite different for importing and exporting countries, and are intuitive. If resource rents rise, then the resource exporting country will be better off and the resource importing country worse off than initially predicted. Hence it is theoretically possible at least that the exporting country is not unsustainable, even though its GS rate is negative. Exactly the opposite is true if resource rents unexpectedly fall, due, for instance, to breakthroughs in the development of a substitute so-called backstop technology (for example, solar energy in the case of oil).

A non-constant discount rate

Where the discount rate is non-constant, the meaning of GS estimates becomes similarly ambiguous. In particular, Asheim et al. (2003) show that negative GS at any moment in time need not imply an economy is unsustainable.

The Assumption of Constant Population

The basic model of GS, and our discussion thus far, has focussed on total wealth, and population has been assumed constant. Dasgupta (2001b) points out that this is a reasonable assumption over the very long run, but over the shorter run and especially in the developing world it is less tenable. Thus attention has recently been cast on the question of measuring GS on a per capita basis. The reason for this is rather obvious: one can envisage a situation in which GS is positive, but if population is growing at an even faster rate, then per capita wealth will actually be decreasing. On the face of it, the adjustment to GS that is required is conceptually straightforward (Hamilton, 2003, p. 426):

$$
\frac{d}{dt}\left(\frac{W}{P}\right) = \frac{\frac{dW}{dt}}{P} - \frac{\frac{dP}{dt}}{P}\frac{W}{P}, \tag{6.5}
$$

where W = total wealth, P = population and dW/dt = GS. Thus the per capita measure of GS is equal to the net change in total wealth per capita minus the product of total wealth per capita and the population growth rate.

Hamilton (2003) makes preliminary empirical estimates of GS per capita for 110 developed and developing countries. But first he conducts a sensitivity analysis of the results of GS per capita according to different population growth rates for the USA in 1997. He concludes that GS per capita is responsive to population growth, and an increase in p from 0.8 per cent p.a. to 1.0 per cent p.a., *ceteris paribus*, is sufficient to push GS per capita below zero. On a country-by-country basis, the pattern of per capita estimates reflect the World Bank's aggregate estimates: it is the resource-rich countries of Sub-Saharan Africa, the Middle East and Northern Africa that tend to have the most negative GS per capita. Clearly, having negative GS on aggregate automatically translates into negative GS per capita (unless population growth is negative). But crucially some countries with positive GS on aggregate have negative GS per capita: for example, Jordan and Niger, for whom of course population growth rates are high. This emphasises the value in computing GS per capita alongside GS on aggregate.

Yet the problem of accounting for population growth may not be as simple. Dasgupta (2001b) and Arrow et al. (2003) derive a fundamentally different formula for GS per capita, based on the inclusion of the stock of population in the social welfare (utility) function as a capital asset. As Asheim (2004) puts it, following this reasoning makes instantaneous well being (which is what point estimates of GS measure) dependent on population size. This is the position of 'total utilitarianism'. A simplified version of Arrow et al.'s (2003) GS per capita is therefore:

$$GS = \frac{\text{net investment in capital (various forms)} + \text{population growth}}{\text{population size}}$$

(6.6)

One might immediately object to the idea that a larger future population should be given greater welfare weight because of just that. Arrow et al. (2003) argue that this weighting is in keeping with the simple principle of treating people equally (discounting notwithstanding), and Dasgupta (2001b) also showed that the alternative position of 'average utilitarianism' has its own implications that may not be ethically defensible.[5] It is in any case not necessarily true that a larger future population receives more weight, *ceteris paribus*, because population growth is valued in the GS function at its shadow price, and this could be negative. The only restriction on the shadow price of population growth according to their derivation is that it may not equal zero.

If the above formula is applied, then an important question is what rate of population growth to choose. A common assumption in models with a growing population is that population growth is constant: that is, population grows exponentially. In this case, Arrow et al. (2003) show that the GS formula simply collapses to per capita GS as in Hamilton (2003). But this is also an untenable assumption, because population growth is slowing worldwide. A more reasonable growth function to impute is logistic growth, where population initially grows exponentially, but later converges to a constant level. In this case, if one decides to retain population in the social welfare function, then the modified Arrow et al. method is the correct one. This is an emerging research agenda, and important contributions are expected to follow in the next few years. In the meantime, we conclude that the relatively straightforward adjustment made in equation (6.5) is worthwhile.

Calculating Natural Capital Depreciation

The World Bank's method for calculating resource rents based on price minus average cost is problematic. This much was suggested by its empirical results, some of which appeared superficially odd. As we have mentioned, GS rates seem to be remarkably low in certain resource-rich countries. Neumayer (2000) in particular asked if GS in North Africa and the Middle East truly was as low as -30 per cent of gross income at the end of the 1970s, and if GS in Saudi Arabia, a nation with reserves of oil and natural gas that are still enormous even now, was plausibly lower than -20 per cent of gross income over most of the Bank's 25-year measurement period? If these results were true, then the regions and countries in question would consume the better part of their total capital stock within a matter of decades, leading to economic collapse. Needless to say, we see no signs of this happening.

In an inter-temporally efficient economy, calculating the depreciation of natural capital is theoretically straightforward, being equal to the so-called total Hotelling rent (Hotelling, 1931; Hartwick, 1990; Hamilton, 1994; Neumayer, 1999, 2003):

$$(P - MC)^*R \tag{6.7}$$

where MC is marginal cost. But data on marginal costs are very difficult to obtain in reality, so the Bank falls back on average costs as in equation (6.4). In fact, the Bank's method is just one of several. Of these, El Serafy (1981, 1989 and 1991) estimated natural capital depreciation according to the following formula:

$$(P - AC)^*R^*\left[\frac{1}{(1+r)^{n+1}}\right] \tag{6.8}$$

where $r =$ the discount rate and $n =$ the number of remaining years of the resource stock.

The tendency is for n to be set equal to the static reserves to production ratio, which is the number of years the reserve stock would last if production were maintained equivalent to the base year. Comparing (6.4) and (6.8), we can clearly see that if both r and n are large, then the 'El Serafy' method will produce a smaller estimate of natural capital depreciation, and it follows that GS rates will be more positive, *ceteris paribus*. The 'El Serafy' method in effect partitions the rents from resource extraction into the 'user cost' of resource extraction – that is, the share of resource receipts that should properly be considered as capital depreciation – and 'sustainable income' (in a Hicksian sense), which is a level of consumption that can be sustained indefinitely.[6]

The rather important difference between the 'El Serafy' method and the Bank's method is that the former does not depend on the assumption of inter-temporal efficiency and hence optimal prices. Since there is no reason to presume resource pricing is efficient (see above), it is more defensible to employ a method that does not depend on it.[7] Furthermore, the Bank's method is in any case at best an approximation of the theoretically correct method, because it substitutes average costs for marginal costs. To the extent that marginal costs are increasing (it becomes increasingly costly to extract successive units of a resource), then the application of average costs should overestimate the depreciation of natural capital. The 'El Serafy' method, on the other hand, uses average costs without apology, because it does not depend on marginal costs.

In response to questioning the realism of GS estimates for certain regions and nations, Neumayer (2000) re-estimated GS using the 'El Serafy' method. Applying a discount rate (r) of 4 per cent p.a., the regions of Sub-Saharan Africa, North Africa and the Middle East no longer had negative GS, and most individual countries also passed from negative GS into positive GS, particularly those with large remaining reserves relative to production. Other countries that continued to record negative GS had negative savings irrespective of natural capital depreciation, while only a handful of countries could still be said to be weakly unsustainable due in itself to unsustainable natural resource extraction. Auty and Mikesell (1998) provided similar results in the case of Indonesia.

All this seems to suggest that the 'El Serafy' method is superior to the Bank's method, but this may not be true in all cases. The method is very sensitive both to r and n, and there are problems associated with arriving at both values (Auty and Mikesell, 1998). What is the correct discount rate is always an open question, and taking a high value of, say, 10 per cent p.a. leads 'El Serafy' GS estimates to deviate even more from the Bank's estimates (Neumayer, 2000). It is equally unclear what values n should take, since it requires predictions into the future and is thus troubled by uncertainty. We explained above that n is generally estimated as the static reserves to production ratio, but reserves data are much less reliable in general than production data. Broadly, if r and n are *both* small, then the Bank's and the 'El Serafy' method converge somewhat, and the adjustment may not be meaningful. This will be true of r if it is of the order of 4 per cent p.a. or lower, and of n if it is around 20 years or lower. Scanning data from the US Bureau of Mines (various years) tends to reveal that n lies between 20 and 30 in the case of many resources for many countries, so the Bank's method will not normally be far off the mark. Vis-à-vis Saudi Arabia and other countries with very large remaining reserves relative to production, the results generated by applying the Bank's method are nonsensical, but otherwise the Bank's method can still be usefully regarded as imposing a conservative sustainability standard.

Accounting for Environmental Pollution

The World Bank estimates the depreciation of natural capital due to environmental pollution as the total damage cost of national carbon dioxide emissions. Fine particulate emissions were added in 2003, though the retrospective estimates of GS from 1970 to the present day that we use do not include these. This is quite clearly a restrictive approach, and the Bank knowingly omits many other types of pollutant (including air pollutants such as sulphur dioxide and oxides of nitrogen, water pollutants such as faecal coliforms, and ground contaminants such as heavy metals). The upshot of this may well be, among other things, that developed countries are not as sustainable as one might presume. Hamilton and Atkinson's (1996) results suggest this is the case: they estimated the damage cost of air pollution in the UK to be between 3 per cent and 5 per cent of GDP during the 1980s, enough to push the UK's GS below zero for most of the early 1980s.

The Bank sees its hands tied in this respect: there simply are not enough data available to estimate a comprehensive set of damage costs. It would be fair to say that, in general, of all the components of GS the damage costs of environmental pollution are the most incomplete and 'approximate'. There is even some debate as to how the value of environmental pollution should be calculated in the first place. Hamilton and Atkinson (1996) and the World Bank apply the damage cost approach, where emissions of the relevant pollutant (net of natural dissipation) are multiplied by their shadow price. Other studies have focussed on so-called maintenance costs, which reflect the cost of returning the environment to some previous state based on marginal abatement costs (e.g. Prince and Gordon, 1994). In an optimal economy, the two methods should amount to the same, but we know this is not the case and it is hence likely that maintenance costs, based on marginal pollution abatement costs, will understate the costs of pollution (Prince and Gordon estimate the cost of air *and* water pollution in the USA in the early 1980s to be only 1 per cent of GDP: this is considerably lower than the Hamilton and Atkinson estimate). But damage costs are not beyond censure themselves. Most are estimated in a partial equilibrium context as part of a cost–benefit analysis (CBA), but what is required for estimates to be compatible with systems of national accounting is a general equilibrium estimate. More research and practice is required here too, but for the moment we can conclude that GS estimates, particularly in developed countries, may be too high, *ceteris paribus*.

In the context of costing environmental pollution, there is also the controversial issue of transboundary and global pollution and how it is integrated into green national accounting. This particularly affects carbon dioxide emissions. Either one simply estimates the damage cost of pollution wherever it occurs, and hence certain countries will pay the welfare price for others' emissions, or the damage cost of pollution is attributed to the emitting country. The latter is a basic application of the 'polluter pays principle' that now wields considerable influence in international environmental policy-making. On the other hand, the damage cost of emissions is not strictly speaking equivalent to the environmental capital stock that determines the impact of climate change on a country's economy. Instead, it is the global concentration of carbon dioxide in the atmosphere, a function of global emissions, which does so (Ferreira and Vincent, 2003). Clearly this decision will exert a considerable influence on GS rates.

In fact, it has a corollary in the case of accounting for resource extraction, insofar as some have argued that the resources depleted in developing countries of the South for the purpose of consumption or capital accumulation in developed countries of the North should properly be debited from the national accounts of the developed country. Again this adjustment significantly changes the distribution of GS rates, being more positive for resource exporters and more negative for importers (Proops et al., 1999). In this latter case, however, there is no real argument for adjustment. The purpose of estimating GS is to find out the magnitude of a nation's natural capital depreciation as a share of total national capital formation. Negative GS rates, *especially* if caused by excessive exports to developed countries of the North, should indicate that developing countries of the South need to invest more of the proceeds of natural capital into the formation of other forms of capital than they currently do. And the results should also affect policy-making in the North. Developed countries should assist developing countries experiencing negative GS rates in attempting to become sustainable.

There is no real case for following the same logic in respect of environmental pollution, however. Strictly from the perspective of whom the natural capital (sink resource) belongs to, deductions should be made from the recipient country's GS. But this is hardly the policy signal one wants to give in this context. Instead, it seems difficult in principle to reject the notion that the polluter should 'pay', which is in accordance with the way the Bank values pollution. Also from a practical perspective, it is easier and safer to calculate damage cost estimates based on national emissions rather than ambient emissions concentrations.

CONCLUSIONS ON THE POLICY USEFULNESS OF GENUINE SAVINGS

Whether one believes in the policy-guiding value of GS depends at the outset on whether one subscribes to the weak sustainability paradigm.

Admittedly there have been moves towards dealing with the non-substitutability of natural capital within the GS framework. Atkinson et al. (2003) propose that, as the asset base of some natural resource is depleted up to its critical level, the shadow price of the asset should approach infinity. In practical terms, the magnitude of the term for natural capital depreciation becomes very large indeed. But there are at present limits to this approach. The loss of critical natural capital still needs to be measured through marginal WTP, and this is difficult enough for incremental as opposed to very large losses of welfare. In essence, we are not currently equipped to measure the welfare value of losses of critical natural capital. In that case, if one is concerned with strong sustainability, then GS results are largely uninteresting.

Within the confines of the weak sustainability paradigm, we have praised GS as a meaningful counterweight to gross product in the measurement of social welfare (understanding, of course, that gross product was never intended to be a measure of social welfare), and as an indicator with a direct (if one-sided) sustainability criterion. On the other hand, the thrust of our discussion is that GS is a very rough measure of sustainability. The assumption of an inter-temporally efficient economy is undoubtedly problematic, and thus even non-negative GS rates cannot really rule out unsustainable development. In much the same way, the validity of point estimates of GS depends on the absence of external shocks to the system. If there are any, then all prices, and in turn GS, would have to be re-estimated. These are fundamental problems for GS and we recommend all estimates be accordingly interpreted with a great deal of caution. If one seriously objects to the optimality assumption, then it may be preferable to set exogenous environmental standards and model the opportunity cost of reaching them as the so-called hybrid indicators do. In this context, modelling opportunity costs in a dynamic framework (e.g. O'Connor and Ryan, 1999) is the most appropriate method. However, although there is insufficient scope here, it should be noted that the problems apparent in the hybrid approach are no less grave (see Neumayer, 1999, 2003).

The measurement of natural capital depreciation is another problem for GS. We have shown that GS estimates are sensitive to the method of calculating rents from resource extraction. The World Bank's estimates, by their own admission, are at the high end, and probably overestimate the unsustainability of certain resource-dependent regions and countries. Even patchier is the estimation of the value of environmental pollution damage. At present, the World Bank judges there to be so few data that it can only estimate the values of carbon dioxide and particulate pollution damage. Even in these cases, the estimates of marginal pollution costs are very rough. In fact, this patchy data coverage is also an issue for extractive resources. It is striking that the least sustainable regions and countries according to the World Bank are those heavily dependent on fossil fuels and minerals.

To summarise, the most useful policy suggestion to emerge from GS studies is that certain resource-dependent countries need to invest more of the proceeds of natural capital into the formation of other forms of capital than they currently do. On the other hand, the debate over calculating resource rents means that countries with still large remaining reserves of fossil fuels – mainly Saudi Arabia and some other Gulf States – are almost certainly more sustainable than the World Bank suggests. Other countries, however, that are heavily dependent on resources not included in the analysis such as fish or soil (via agriculture) may well be less sustainable. One can, for example, ask if Sub-Saharan Africa would be even less weakly sustainable after calculating the depletion of soils? In any case, the fact that its main results become reversed for some countries if another, and not inferior, method for calculating natural capital depreciation is used, sheds great doubt on the validity and reliability and therefore on the policy usefulness of the measure.

For developed countries, GS produces the result that everywhere weak unsustainability is avoided. This may or may not be true. These countries are not especially resource-dependent, and do tend to invest significantly in capital formation, but including a more comprehensive range of environmental pollutants would undoubtedly drive GS downwards. Hence the really interesting policy outcome that currently evades us is that some developed countries might be unsustainable on the grounds of excessive pollution.

At the present time then, GS provides some interesting if *generic* policy guidance to sustainability planners. Given improved coverage and estimation of natural resource depletion in the future, we may obtain more interesting and accurate results. Given the restrictive assumptions of the method, however, and the fact that few if any environmental data can ever be considered truly accurate, it would be a mistake to interpret GS rates too literally.

NOTES

1. Dasgupta (2001a, 2001b) and Neumayer (1999, 2003) share the view that genuine *investment* would be a better term to use than genuine savings, because in macroeconomics savings tends to be defined as private savings. As GS applies it, savings means the sum of private plus public savings (the latter being taxes minus public expenditures), hence genuine savings equals genuine investment.
2. Hartwick (1977) showed that a resource-dependent economy could maintain its consumption level over time if it invested all the rents from resource extraction in produced capital.

3. This is presumably at least in part due to Kirk Hamilton's affiliation with the World Bank's Environment Department.
4. Most hybrid indicators have been developed to measure strong sustainability, insofar as environmental standards are set in order to protect what equates to critical natural capital. However, the method is inherently flexible and the opportunity costs of attaining a range of environmental standards, differing in their stringency, can be modelled simultaneously.
5. In a simple timeless economy with two populations, keeping population out of the social welfare function allows a result where the government distributes less to each member of the larger population (Dasgupta, 2001b, pp. 99–100).
6. See Neumayer (2000) for a formal derivation.
7. The Bank is in any case inconsistent in its assumption of optimal prices, since it presumably rejects optimality when deciding to ignore terms-of-trade effects.

REFERENCES

Arrow, K.J., P. Dasgupta and K.-G. Mäler (2003), 'The genuine savings criterion and the value of population', *Economic Theory*, **21**, 217–25.

Asheim, G. (1994), 'Net national product as an indicator of sustainability', *Scandinavian Journal of Economics*, **96**, 257–65.

Asheim, G. (2004), 'Green national accounting with a changing population', *Economic Theory*, **23**, 601–19.

Asheim, G., W. Buchholz and C. Withagen (2003), 'The Hartwick rule: myths and facts', *Environmental and Resource Economics*, **25**, 129–50.

Atkinson, G., K. Hamilton and W. Nalvarte (2003), *Sustainability, Green National Accounting and Deforestation*, London: Department of Geography and Environment, London School of Economics and Political Science, mimeo.

Auty, R.M. and R.F. Mikesell (1998), *Sustainable Development in Mineral Economies*, Oxford: Clarendon.

Brouwer, R., M. O'Connor and W. Radermacher (1996), *Defining Cost-effective Responses to Environmental Deterioration in a Periodic Accounting System*, proceedings of the third meeting of the London Group on Natural Resource and Environmental Accounting, Stockholm, 28–31 May 1996, Stockholm: Statistics Sweden.

Brouwer, R. and M. O'Connor (1997a), *Final Summary Report of Research Project No. EV5V-CT94-0363, Methodological Problems in the Calculation of Environmentally Adjusted National Income Figures*, C3ED.

Brouwer, R. and M. O'Connor (1997b), *Project Final Report of Research Project No. EV5V-CT94-0363, Methodological Problems in the Calculation of Environmentally Adjusted National Income Figures*, C3ED.

Dasgupta, P. (2001a), 'Valuing objects and evaluating policies in imperfect economies', *Economic Journal*, **111**, C1–C29.

Dasgupta, P. (2001b), *Human Well-Being and the Natural Environment*, Oxford: Oxford University Press.

El Serafy, S. (1981), 'Absorptive capacity, the demand for revenue, and the supply of petroleum', *Journal of Energy and Development*, **7**, 73–88.

El Serafy, S. (1989), 'The proper calculation of income from depletable natural resources', in Y.J. Ahmed, S. El Serafy and E. Lutz (eds), *Environmental Accounting for Sustainable Development: a UNDP–World Bank Symposium*, Washington, DC: World Bank, pp. 10–18.

El Serafy, S. (1991), 'The environment as capital', in R. Costanza (ed.), *Ecological Economics: the Science and Management of Sustainability*, New York: Columbia University Press, pp. 168–75.

Fankhauser, S. (1995), *Valuing Climate Change: the Economics of the Greenhouse*, London: Earthscan Publications.

Ferreira, S. and J.R. Vincent (2003), *Why Genuine Savings?*, San Diego: Department of Economics, University of California, mimeo.

Hamilton, K. (1994), 'Green adjustments to GDP', *Resources Policy*, **20**, 155–68.

Hamilton, K. (1995), *Sustainable Development and Green National Accounts*, London: University College London, unpublished PhD thesis.

Hamilton, K. (2003), 'Sustaining economic welfare: estimating changes in total and per capita wealth', *Environment, Development and Sustainability*, **5**, 419–36.

Hamilton, K. and G. Atkinson (1996), 'Air pollution and green accounts', *Energy Policy*, **24**, 675–84.

Hamilton, K. and M. Clemens (1999), 'Genuine saving rates in developing countries', *World Bank Economic Review*, **13** (February), 333–56.

Hartwick, J.M. (1977), 'Intergenerational equity and the investing of rents of exhaustible resources', *American Economic Review*, **67** (5), 972–4.

Hartwick, J.M. (1990), 'Sustainability and constant consumption paths in open economies with exhaustible resources', *Review of International Economics*, **3**, 275–83.

Hotelling, H. (1931), 'The economics of exhaustible resources', *Journal of Political Economy*, **39** (2), 137–75.

Hueting, R. (1992), 'Correcting national income for environmental losses: a practical solution for a theoretical dilemma', in J.J. Krabbe and W.J.M. Heijman (eds), *National Income and Nature: Externalities, Growth and Steady State*, Dordrecht and Boston, MA: Kluwer, pp. 23–47.

Kunte, A., K. Hamilton, J. Dixon and M. Clemens (1998), *Estimating National Wealth: Methodology and Results*, Washington, DC: World Bank.

Neumayer, E. (1999), *Weak versus Strong Sustainability: Exploring the Limits of Two Opposing Paradigms*, Cheltenham, UK and Northampton, MA, USA: Edward Elgar.

Neumayer, E. (2000), 'Resource accounting in measures of unsustainability: challenging the World Bank's conclusions', *Environmental and Resource Economics*, **15**, 257–78.

Neumayer, E. (2003), *Weak versus Strong Sustainability: Exploring the Limits of Two Opposing Paradigms*, second revised edition, Cheltenham, UK and Northampton, MA, USA: Edward Elgar.

O'Connor, M. and G. Ryan (1999), 'Macroeconomic cost-effectiveness and the use of multi-sectoral dynamic modelling as an environmental valuation tool', *International Journal of Sustainable Development*, **2**, 127–63.

Pandey, K.D., K. Bolt, U. Deichmann, K. Hamilton, B. Ostro and D. Wheeler (2003), *The Human Cost of Air Pollution: New Estimates for Developing Countries*, Washington, DC: Development Research Group and Environment Department, World Bank.

Pearce, D. and G. Atkinson (1993), 'Capital theory and the measurement of sustainable development: an indicator of "weak" sustainability', *Ecological Economics*, **8** (2), 103–8.

Pearce, D.W. and R.K. Turner (1989), *Economics of Natural Resources and the Environment*, Hemel Hempstead: Harvester Wheatsheaf.

Pezzey, J. (2003), *One-sided Unsustainability Tests with Amenities and Shifts in Technology, Trade and Population*, Canberra: CRES, Australian National University.

Pezzey, J. and C. Withagen (1995), 'The rise, fall and sustainability of capital-resource economies', *Scandinavian Journal of Economics*, **100**, 513–27.

Prince, R. and P.L. Gordon (1994), *Greening the National Accounts*, Washington, DC: Congressional Budget Office.

Proops, J., G. Atkinson, B. Frhr. v. Schlotheim and S. Simon (1999), 'International trade and the sustainability footprint: a practical criterion for its assessment', *Ecological Economics*, **28**, 75–97.

Solow, R.M. (1974), 'Intergenerational equity and exhaustible resources', *Review of Economic Studies*, Symposium, 29–46.

US Bureau of Mines (various), *Mineral Commodity Summaries*, Washington, DC: Department of the Interior.

World Bank (1997), *Expanding the Measure of Wealth: Indicators of Environmentally Sustainable Development*, Washington, DC: World Bank.

World Bank (2003), *World Development Indicators*, Washington, DC: World Bank.

World Bank (2004), Adjusted Net Savings Data, Washington, DC: World Bank (http://lnweb18.worldbank.org/ESSD/essdext.nsf/44ByDocName/Green AccoutingWealthEstimates).

PART III

Sustainable development and welfare

7. An assessment of alternative measures of sustainable economic welfare

Philip Lawn

INTRODUCTION

Ecological economists have long believed that the continued growth of macroeconomic systems is both ecologically unsustainable and existentially undesirable.[1] Consistent with this belief, ecological economists have put forward a 'threshold hypothesis' – the notion that when macroeconomic systems expand beyond a certain size, the additional benefits of growth are exceeded by the attendant costs (Max-Neef, 1995; Figure 2.5 in Chapter 2). In order to support their belief, ecological economists have developed a number of indexes to measure and compare the benefits and costs of growth. The first of them, the Index of Sustainable Economic Welfare (ISEW), was originally calculated for the USA by Daly and Cobb (1989). It has since been calculated for the UK, most western European and Scandinavian countries, Canada, Australia, Chile, Japan and Thailand (see Figure 2.7 in Chapter 2, and Figure 8.1 in Chapter 8). Over this time, many of the methods used to calculate the index have been revised. As pointed out in Chapter 2, the ISEW has also been given a variety of different names – for example, a Genuine Progress Indicator or GPI (Redefining Progress, 1995) and a Sustainable Net Benefit Index or SNBI (Lawn and Sanders, 1999; and Lawn, 2000). While there has been a variation in the disparity between GDP and the chosen index calculated for different countries, the trend movement in the ISEW, GPI, and SNBI is very consistent. That is, up to a point, the growth of macroeconomic systems seems to be beneficial to human well-being. Beyond this point, growth appears to have a detrimental impact. On the surface at least, the ISEW, GPI, and SNBI offer solid support for the threshold hypothesis and the need for countries to eventually abandon the growth objective and focus, among other things, on qualitative improvement to achieve sustainable development.

Some recent articles (e.g. Atkinson, 1995; and Neumayer, 1999 and 2000) have called into question the methods used to calculate the ISEW, GPI and SNBI. They also cast doubt over whether such indexes substantiate the threshold hypothesis (e.g. Neumayer, 2000; and Chapter 9). These are very timely contributions since they challenge ecological economists to consider whether their results reflect the trend movement in the sustainable economic welfare of growth or a subconscious desire to design an index to vindicate their own threshold hypothesis. Since, as an advocate of these alternative indexes, this challenge extends to me, I will assess the ISEW and other related measures to determine the extent to which they reflect concrete reality or the prejudices of ecological economists. To do this, three main areas require close attention. They are: (1) the theoretical foundation underlying the indexes; (2) the valuation methods used to construct and calculate the indexes; and (3) the interpretation of the results. I shall deal with each of these separately. Beforehand, I will briefly mention something about each of the relevant indexes.

Gross Domestic Product (GDP)

As explained in Chapter 2, GDP is a monetary measure of the goods and services annually produced by domestically *located* factors of production (i.e. by the natural and human-made capital located in a particular country). GDP can be measured in *nominal* or *real* values. If GDP is measured in nominal values, it is measured in terms of the prices of all goods at the time of production. On the other hand, if GDP is measured in real values, it is measured in terms of the prices of all goods in a particular year – often referred to as the base year. Consequently, annual changes in real GDP reflect the differences in the quantity of goods and services produced from year to year. It is for this reason that, in conventional terms, real GDP is preferred to nominal GDP as a measure of national income.

Most readers will have come across Gross National Product (GNP). GNP is much the same as GDP except that it measures the monetary value of the goods and services annually produced by domestically *owned* rather than domestically located factors of production (i.e. by the natural and human-made capital owned by the citizens of a particular country).

Index of Sustainable Economic Welfare (ISEW) and Genuine Progress Indicator (GPI)

The ISEW and GPI are indicators designed to approximate the sustainable economic welfare or true progress of a nation's citizens. The calculation of both indexes involves the extraction from the national accounts of the various transactions deemed relevant to human well-being (Redefining Progress, 1995). Further adjustments are made to account for aspects of economic activity that GDP ignores. The ISEW and GPI include a number of social and environmental benefits and costs that invariably escape market valuation. The following is a table revealing the typical items used in the calculation of the ISEW and GPI (see Table 7.1).

Table 7.1 includes a range of positive and negative items that are summed to obtain a final index number. All items are valued in monetary terms, as are the ISEW and GPI. The final index number is usually calculated in real

Table 7.1   Items used to calculate the GPI for USA from 1950 to 1995

- private consumption expenditure (+)
- index of distributional inequality (+/−)
- weighted personal consumption expenditure (|)
- cost of consumer durables (−)
- services yielded by consumer durables (+)
- services yielded by roads and highways (+)
- services provided by volunteer work (+)
- services provided by non-paid household work (+)
- public expenditure on health and education counted
  as personal consumption (+)
- cost of noise pollution (−)
- cost of commuting (−)
- cost of crime (−)
- cost of underemployment (−)
- cost of lost leisure time (−)
- the cost of household pollution abatement (−)
- the cost of vehicle accidents (−)
- the cost of family breakdown (−)
- net capital investment (+/−)
- net foreign lending/borrowing (+/−)
- loss of farmland (−)
- cost of resource depletion (−)
- cost of ozone depletion (−)
- cost of air pollution (−)
- cost of water pollution (−)
- cost of long-term environmental damage (−)
- loss of wetlands (−)
- loss of old-growth forests (−)

Notes: Total = sum of all positive and negative items = GPI (valued in dollars);
(+) = positive item; (−) = negative item; (+/−) = item that may be either positive or negative.

Source: Redefining Progress, 1995.

rather than nominal values. The ISEW and GPI basically differ in name
only. It is becoming increasingly common for updated calculations to be
referred to as the GPI. If one compares the original ISEW with recent calculations of the GPI, the list of items used to arrive at the final index
number has varied over time, as have some of the valuation methods. One
also finds a difference in the valuation methods used to calculate the ISEW
and GPI for different countries (see, for instance, Diefenbacher, 1994;
Moffatt and Wilson, 1994; Rosenberg and Oegema, 1995; Jackson and
Stymne, 1996; Jackson et al., 1997; Stockhammer et al., 1997; Guenno and
Tiezzi, 1998; Castañeda, 1999; and Hamilton, 1999). The reasons for these
differences are usually related to the availability of data and the preference
researchers have for specific valuation methods.

It should also be pointed that the ISEW and GPI are not strictly 'green'
measures of GDP. As will be fully explained shortly, both indexes begin
with private consumption expenditure as their foundational item, not GDP
as in the case of Sustainable Net Domestic Product (SNDP).[2] Since the
ISEW and GPI clearly lie outside the conventional national accounting
framework, their calculation does not fall into the output–welfare trap outlined by El Serafy in Chapter 3. Strangely enough, many ISEW and GPI
advocates are unaware of this fact (e.g. Cobb and Cobb, 1994) and have
unknowingly contributed to some of the confusion surrounding measures
of sustainable economic welfare and annual national product.[3]

Sustainable Net Benefit Index (SNBI)

As indicated in Chapter 2, the SNBI is much the same as the ISEW and GPI.
Where the SNBI differs is in the explanation of the rationale for an alternative index and the presentation of the items used in its calculation. The
welfare-related items are sorted into separate 'uncancelled benefit' and
'uncancelled cost' accounts (see Table 7.2). The total of the uncancelled cost
account is subtracted from the uncancelled benefit account to obtain the
SNBI. This approach has the advantage of presenting the results in a manner
consistent with Fisher's (1906) concept of income and capital. It also allows
one to compare the benefits and costs of a growing macroeconomy. In so
doing, it strengthens its own case as well as the case for the ISEW and GPI.

THE THEORETICAL FOUNDATION OF THE ISEW AND GPI

While the development of the ISEW and GPI has been motivated by the
inability of GDP to serve as a measure of sustainable economic welfare,

Table 7.2   Items included in uncancelled benefit (net psychic income) and uncancelled cost (lost natural capital services) accounts – used to calculate the SNBI for Australia from 1966–67 to 1994–95

Uncancelled benefit account	Item value ($)	Account subtotal ($)	Account total ($)	SNBI ($)
Psychic income items				
• private consumption expenditure (+)	X			
• index of distributional inequality (+/–)	X			
• weighted private consumption expenditure (+)	X			
• services yielded by consumer durables (+)	X			
• services yielded by public dwellings (+)	X			
• services yielded by roads and highways (+)	X			
• services provided by volunteer work (+)	X			
• services provided by non-paid household work (+)	X			
• public expenditure on health and education counted as private consumption (+)	X			
• imputed value of leisure time (+)	X			
• net producer goods growth (+/–)	X			
• change in net international position (net foreign lending/borrowing) (+/–)	X			
Total psychic income = Σ psychic income items = XXXX		XXXX		
Psychic outgo items				
• cost of consumer durables (–)	X			
• defensive private health and education expenditure (–)	X			
• cost of private vehicle accidents (–)	X			
• cost of noise pollution (–)	X			

143

Table 7.2 (continued)

	Item value ($)	Account subtotal ($)	Account total ($)	SNBI ($)
Uncancelled benefit account				
• disamenity cost of air pollution (−)	X			
• cost of commuting (−)	X			
• cost of crime (−)	X			
• cost of family breakdown (−)	X			
• cost of underemployment (−)	X			
• cost of unemployment (−)	X			
Total psychic outgo = Σ psychic outgo items = XXX		XXX		
Net psychic income = total psychic income − total psychic outgo = XXXX − XXX = AAA			AAA	
Uncancelled cost account	$	$	$	$
Lost source function items				
• user cost of non-renewable resources (metallic minerals, coal, oil and gas, and non-metallic minerals) (−)	Y			
• loss of agricultural land (−)	Y			
• net change in timber stocks (−/+)	Y			
• net change in fishery stocks (−/+)	Y			
• cost of degraded wetlands, mangroves and saltmarshes (−)	Y			
Total lost source function = Σ lost source function items = YY		YY		

144

Lost sink function items

- cost of water pollution $(-)$ Y
- cost of air pollution $(-)$ Y
- cost of solid waste pollution $(-)$ Y
- cost of ozone depletion $(-)$ Y

Total lost sink function = Σ lost sink function items = YY   YY

Lost life-support services function items

- cost of long-term environmental damage $(-)$ Y
- Ecosystem health index $(+/-)$ Y

Total lost life-support function = Σ lost life-support
function items = YY   YY

Lost natural capital services = lost source function + lost
sink function + lost life-support function = YY + YY + YY = 3BB   BBB

Sustainable Net Benefit Index (SNBI) = net psychic
income − lost natural capital services = AAA − BBB   ZZZ

Notes: $(+)$ = positive item; $(-)$ = negative item; $(+/-)$ = item may be either positive or negative.

145

surprisingly little effort has been devoted towards the establishment of a theoretical foundation to support them.[4] This is why a colleague and I put forward the SNBI (Lawn and Sanders, 1999). Apart from wanting to find out whether Australia had exceeded the welfare-increasing threshold of continuing growth, we wanted to highlight the theoretical foundation underlying the existing ISEW and GPI. In order to demonstrate that the ISEW and GPI have a sound theoretical foundation, I will begin by reiterating the inadequacies of GDP and Sustainable Net Domestic Product (SNDP). I will then show how and in what way the ISEW and GPI are consistent with Fisher's concept of income and capital.

In Chapter 2, it was explained that GDP is a deficient indicator of national income because it fails to measure the maximum amount that a nation can produce and consume over a given period without undermining its capacity to do likewise in the future. To overcome this inadequacy, various subtractions were made from GDP to obtain a measure of SNDP (see equation (2.1) in Chapter 2).

There are, of course, a number weaknesses associated with SNDP. First, there is the issue of whether the SNDP is an appropriate measure of national income. The questionable nature of SNDP arises because, as Fisher (1906) persuasively argued, the annual national dividend does not constitute the goods produced in a particular year, but the services or psychic income enjoyed by the consumers and/or users of the stock of all existing human-made goods. Conceived in this way, this year's income should not include the value of the durable producer and consumer goods manufactured during the current year. Since these goods constitute an addition to the stock of human-made capital, their value should only enter future income calculations once services begin to flow from their eventual use. Only the services rendered this year by non-durable consumer goods and the durable producer and consumer goods manufactured in previous years should be counted as part of this year's income. Since the calculation of the SNDP counts all additions to human-made capital as current income, it falsely conflates the services rendered by capital (income) with the value of the capital that renders them.

Second, since the stock of human-made capital depreciates and wears out through use, its continual maintenance requires the production of new goods that can only occur if there is a continual input of low entropy resources and output of high entropy wastes. This so-called throughput of matter-energy constitutes a cost, not a benefit, which is measured in terms of the natural capital services sacrificed in the process of keeping the stock of human-made capital intact. Thus, as was pointed out in Chapter 2, SNDP is equivalent to an index of sustainable cost, not sustainable economic welfare.

Finally, from a human well-being perspective, SNDP overlooks many welfare-related aspects associated with the socio-economic process. These include the cost of reduced leisure time, the cost of commuting, the cost of crime and family breakdown, the value of volunteer and non-paid household work, and the welfare effect of a change in the distribution of income. Often overlooked, the redistribution of income from the low marginal benefit uses of the rich to the higher marginal benefit uses of the poor can lead to an overall increase in the economic welfare enjoyed by society as a whole (Robinson, 1962; Easterlin, 1974; and Abramowitz, 1979). Hence, while the SNDP of a nation can increase over time, it will not accurately reflect the increase in a nation's economic welfare if the rise in the SNDP is accompanied by a growing income disparity between the rich and the poor.

THE THEORETICAL SUPERIORITY OF THE ISEW AND GPI

Contrary to some opinions, the ISEW and GPI do not lack a theoretical foundation. The ISEW and GPI serve as very good indicators of both income and sustainable economic welfare precisely because they are consistent with Fisher's concept of income and capital. The best way of demonstrating this is to focus on the individual items used to construct the ISEW and GPI.

Private Consumption Expenditure

Unlike the SNDP, which starts with GDP as its initial reference point, the ISEW and GPI begin with private consumption expenditure. This is important because it provides an approximate estimate of what Fisher described as the services or psychic income enjoyed by the ultimate consumers of human-made goods. Using consumption expenditure as the initial reference point does not imply that consumption is itself good – a theoretical failing of the SNDP. It implies that consumption is a 'necessary evil'. That is, it is necessary to consume goods to gain the services they yield. Of course, if the same level of service can be enjoyed from less consumption, this would constitute a societal gain because less production would be required to keep the stock of human-made capital intact. Such a gain, if it were made, would not be reflected in this particular item but would instead be reflected in other items due to a smaller cost of pollution or resource depletion or both. Thus, if a given level of service from consumption was accompanied by a reduction in the rate of production (due, for example, to an increase in the durability of human-made capital), this would lead to a rise in the ISEW and GPI. However, it would lower the SNDP.

Index of Distributional Inequality/Weighting of Private Consumption Expenditure

As I mentioned earlier, the distribution of income can have a significant impact on a nation's economic welfare. If private consumption expenditure does not change from one year to the next but the distribution of income deteriorates, the economic welfare enjoyed by society as a whole is likely to fall because the marginal benefit uses of the rich are less than the marginal benefit uses of the poor. Unless private consumption expenditure is weighted according to changes in the distribution of income, it will inaccurately reflect its true contribution to a nation's economic welfare. This adjustment is made in the calculation of the ISEW and GPI but not so in the case of the SNDP.

The Cost of Consumer Durables

Included in private consumption expenditure is the amount paid in the current year on consumer durables such as cars, refrigerators, and household furniture. This amount constitutes an addition to the stock of human-made capital. It does not constitute current income in the Fisherian sense. In the calculation of the ISEW and GPI, the cost of consumer durables is subtracted from weighted private consumption expenditure. It is not done like this in the calculation of the SNDP.

Services Yielded by Existing Consumer Durables

Not included in private consumption expenditure is the value of the services annually yielded by previously purchased consumer durables. As Fisher argued, these services constitute current income. In the calculation of the ISEW and GPI, the annual value of these services is added to the running total. It is overlooked in the calculation of the SNDP. The service value is usually calculated as a percentage of the total value of the entire stock of consumer durables. Ideally, the percentage rate chosen should reflect the estimated depreciation rate or 'rate of consumption' of consumer durables.

Services Yielded by Publicly Provided Human-made Capital

Consumer durables are not the only form of human-made capital that yields services. Publicly provided human-made capital such as libraries,

museums, roads and highways do likewise. To be consistent with the
Fisherian concept of income and capital, these services are treated as
income and added in the calculation of the ISEW and GPI. They are
again overlooked in the calculation of the SNDP. The service value is
usually calculated in the same way as it is for consumer durables; that is,
as a percentage of the total value of the existing stock of publicly provided human-made capital. Consistent with the Fisherian concept of
income and capital, current expenditure by governments on human-made
capital is not included because it merely constitutes a current addition to
the existing stock.

Services Provided by Volunteer and Non-paid Household Work

Not all benefit-yielding services are provided by market-based economic
activity. The initial reference item of private consumption expenditure
overlooks the services provided by volunteer and non-paid household
work. To obtain a better indicator of the psychic income enjoyed by a
nation's citizens, the ISEW and GPI include these services. The SNDP
does not.

Disservices Generated by Economic Activity

The items so far discussed make a positive contribution to the psychic
income of a nation. However, the socio-economic process involves a range
of irksome activities while it also generates many undesirable side-effects.
To extend the concept of psychic income to that of 'net psychic income',
the cost of irksome and psychic outgo-related aspects must also be
included. The ISEW and GPI do this by deducting the following:

- the cost of noise pollution;
- the cost of commuting;
- the cost of crime;
- the cost of underemployment;
- in some cases, the cost of unemployment;
- the cost of lost leisure time.

Defensive and Rehabilitative Expenditures

A large portion of the human-made capital produced each year does
not contribute to the psychic income of a nation. It is produced to
prevent or minimise the extent to which the undesirable side-effects of the
socio-economic process reduce the psychic income enjoyed in the future.

In calculating the ISEW and GPI, the following defensive and rehabilitative expenditures are subtracted from the running total:

- the cost of household pollution abatement;
- the cost of vehicle accidents;
- the cost of family breakdown;
- in some cases, a certain percentage of private health expenditure
  assumed to constitute a form of defensive expenditure.

Net Capital Investment

The inclusion of this particular item is contentious. One of the key implications of the Fisherian concept of income and capital is that additions
to the stock of human-made capital should not be counted as income.
The ISEW and GPI go a long way towards ensuring this by subtracting
current expenditure on consumer durables and by not adding current government expenditure on human-made capital. However, the calculation of
the ISEW and GPI includes the net investment in the stock of producer
goods (plant, machinery, and equipment). If the calculation of this item
was based on an estimate of the net increase in the total stock of producer
goods, as it is in the calculation of SNDP, the inclusion of this item would
be inconsistent with Fisher's concept of income and capital. It is not,
however, calculated in this manner. Rather, net capital investment is calculated as the increase in the stock of producer goods above the amount
required to keep the quantity of producer goods per worker intact.

As contentious as this item is, there is some justification for its inclusion.
In Chapter 2, it was argued that human-made capital cannot replicate the
critical instrumental services provided by natural capital. As such, natural
capital and its human-made counterpart are complementary forms of
capital. Both natural and human-made capital must be individually maintained to achieve sustainability. In terms of the stock of human-made
capital, complementarity implies that the quantity of producer goods per
worker must not fall. Should the stock of producer goods exceed this
requirement, the difference constitutes an increase in a nation's productive
capacity. This, of course, is a clear benefit and thus added when calculating
the ISEW and GPI.

Net Foreign Lending/Borrowing

This item is included because a nation's long-term capacity to sustain the
psychic income generated by the socio-economic process depends very
much on whether natural and human-made capital is domestically or

foreign owned. Evidence clearly indicates that many countries with large foreign debts have difficulty maintaining the investment levels needed to keep their stock of human-made capital intact (e.g. Argentina in recent times). Furthermore, they are often forced to liquidate natural capital stocks to repay debt (George, 1988).

Cost of Sacrificed Natural Capital Services

As I explained earlier, one of the major implications of Fisher's concept of income and capital is its recognition that the continual maintenance of human-made capital is a cost. The cost emerges by way of the natural capital services lost in obtaining the throughput required to keep the stock of human-made capital intact. To be consistent with the Fisherian concept of income and capital, it is necessary to deduct the cost of the lost source, sink and life-support services provided by natural capital. The ISEW and GPI do this by deducting the following:

- the loss of farmland and the cost of resource depletion (lost *source* services of natural capital);
- the cost of ozone depletion and air and water pollution (lost *sink* services of natural capital);
- the cost of long-term environmental damage and the loss of wetlands and old-growth forests (lost *life-support* services of natural capital).

All up, the ISEW and GPI have a sound theoretical foundation based on Fisher's concept of income and capital. This makes the ISEW and GPI far superior indicators of both income and sustainable economic welfare than GDP and the SNDP. Moreover, provided the benefits and costs of the socio-economic process can be measured with some degree of accuracy, it is reasonable to believe that the ISEW and GPI can serve as a valuable means of assessing whether, at the national level, the additional benefits of growth are being exceeded by the additional costs.

There is, as explained in Chapter 2, a theoretical weakness associated with the ISEW and GPI that also extends to the SNBI. All three indexes merely count the cost of lost natural capital services. Whilst it is important to obtain a better measure of economic welfare by subtracting the cost of environmental damage, it is equally important to know if a nation's stock of natural capital has declined to such an extent that the economic welfare it currently enjoys cannot be sustained in the future. The ISEW, GPI and SNBI do not provide this information. As such, they serve only as a means to ascertaining whether a nation's macroeconomy has surpassed its optimal scale. Since natural capital maintenance is required to achieve sustainability, it is advisable to undertake biophysical assessments of a nation's resource stocks and critical ecosystems and present the information in something akin to a natural capital account. Only then will it be possible to ascertain whether a nation's macroeconomy has also exceeded its maximum sustainable scale. The topic of natural capital accounting is taken up in greater detail in Part IV.

ASSUMPTIONS AND VALUATION METHODS USED TO CALCULATE THE ISEW AND GPI

I believe the validity of the criticism levelled at the ISEW, GPI, and SNBI is greatest in relation to the valuation methods used for their calculation (see Maler, 1991; Atkinson, 1995; Hamilton, 1994, 1996; and Neumayer, 1999, 2000). To assess the valuation methods and assumptions used, I will focus on the more contentious methods. The majority of criticism has been levelled at the valuation of the following items listed in Table 7.1 – private consumption expenditure; the index of distributional inequality and the subsequent weighting of private consumption expenditure; defensive and rehabilitative expenditures; the cost of resource depletion; and, finally, the tendency to deduct the cumulative cost of ozone depletion, long-term environmental damage and lost old-growth forests.

Private Consumption Expenditure

The monetary value of private consumption expenditure is extracted directly from the national income accounts. The criticism here is levelled at the assumption that all private consumption expenditure contributes to human well-being. Since this item includes the consumption of such things as junk food, tobacco products, alcohol and guns, it is unlikely that all consumption expenditure advances the psychic income of a nation's citizens. In response, it may be a valuable exercise to determine which elements of private consumption expenditure should be omitted from the final estimation of the ISEW and GPI. Of course, this requires the researcher to make subjective judgments about the service-yielding qualities of physical goods which, in the end, may lead to greater criticism. Not surprisingly, the issue has been largely avoided by ISEW and GPI advocates.

Another way of dealing with this problem is to conduct a sensitivity analysis by selectively excluding some of the components of private consumption expenditure. For example, private consumption expenditure includes a category for 'cigarettes and tobacco' and another for 'alcoholic drinks'. The full amount of the former could be omitted and half of the latter. There might also be a justification for excluding a small percentage of expenditure on 'food' – say 20 per cent. Given the magnitude of the consumption expenditure item, omissions of this nature could lead to a small variation in the overall index which would then allow analysts to make their own conclusions regarding its impact on sustainable economic welfare.

Conversely, one could argue that junk food and tobacco products should not be omitted given that the ISEW and GPI already include specific items to capture some of the costs of undesirable forms of consumption (e.g. higher health costs and reduced productivity). There is, therefore, the potential to double-count some costs by omitting a certain percentage of all consumption expenditures on the assumption that they provide few if any benefits. Clearly, there is a need for further debate on this issue.

There is another important consideration regarding private consumption expenditure that warrants closer examination (Lawn, 2000). Private consumption expenditure is measured in real rather than nominal money values in order to capture the change in the physical quantity of goods consumed over time. For two reasons, an increase in real private consumption expenditure cannot be directly equated with a proportionate increase in psychic income. The first is due to the law of diminishing marginal utility which suggests that as people increase their consumption of physical goods, the service they enjoy increases at a diminishing rate. The second is due to the fact that an increase in the rate at which some individual goods are consumed may not increase the service one enjoys at all. Consider, for example, the lighting of a room by a single light bulb. Is more service experienced if three light bulbs are worn out or 'consumed' over one year compared to just one light bulb because the latter is more durable? No, because the total service provided by the three fragile light bulbs is the same as that provided by the more durable light bulb.

Despite this, real private consumption expenditure may still prove the best available reference point in the estimation of economic welfare. Why? It is generally recognised that people will pay a higher price for a good embodying superior service-yielding qualities. Consequently, a measure of psychic income can be approximated with the use of market prices. For instance, the rental value of a car, a house, a TV or a refrigerator – i.e. the amount paid to rent durable goods for a one-year period – can be used as a proxy measure of the annual services they yield. In addition, the service yielded by the goods consumed entirely during the accounting period in which they are purchased (non-durables) can be valued at their actual market prices (Daly, 1991).

Of course, variations in the market prices and rental values of physical goods occur for reasons other than changes in their service-yielding qualities. The price of a good can also be affected by: (1) the relative prices of the different forms of resources available to produce it; (2) the actual quantity or supply of the good itself; and (3) changes in taxes, the nominal money supply, and the opportunity cost of holding money. Clearly, for prices to remain a proxy indicator of psychic income, it is necessary to eliminate all price-influencing factors other than those related to a good's service-yielding qualities. Given that this is a near impossible task, there are two choices available. The first option is to leave prices as they are; that is, to rely on current prices. The second is to deflate the nominal annual value of private consumption expenditure by an aggregate price index, such as the Consumer Price Index (CPI). If the former option is chosen, the nominal value of private consumption expenditure will embody unwanted price influences over and above any use value-related influences. If the latter is chosen, one obtains a real value of private consumption expenditure. But, in so doing, one also eliminates the price-influencing effect of a variation in use values – the very influence that one wants to maintain in order for prices to be used as an approximate measure of psychic income.

The most desirable option, and the option chosen by ISEW, GPI and SNBI advocates, is to follow the lead of Daly and Cobb (1989) and use, as a reference point, the real value of private consumption expenditure. This second option is desirable for the following reason. While the law of diminishing marginal utility suggests that an increase in psychic income will be proportionately less than any increase in the quantity of physical goods consumed, the law is based on the assumption that there is no change in their service-yielding qualities. It is reasonable to assume that, through technological progress, the service-yielding qualities of most goods will continue to increase for some time to come. If so, this will largely offset the effect of the law of diminishing marginal utility. To what extent it does so, one cannot ascertain; however, it should be sufficient to ensure that any positive impact on psychic income over time is closely approximated by changes in real private consumption expenditure.

Index of Distributional Inequality/Weighting of Private Consumption Expenditure

In general, the method of adjusting consumption expenditure involves the use of an index of distributional inequality that is constructed from the Gini coefficient of income distribution. The index of distributional inequality is assigned a value of 100.0 for the first year of the study period and adjusted in accordance with changes over time in the Gini coefficient. Private consumption expenditure is then divided by the index value and multiplied by 100. An improvement/deterioration in the distribution of a nation's income results in the upward/downward weighting of private consumption expenditure.

There are two main criticisms of this approach. First, following evidence on the link between income distribution and environmental quality, it has been suggested that a more equal distribution of income can lead to a greater rate of environmental damage. If so, a more equal distribution of income would presumably lower the ISEW and GPI as much as it might increase it. This suggests that no weighting should be applied to private consumption expenditure.

I disagree with this criticism for two reasons. In the first instance, let us assume that a more equal distribution of income increases the present welfare contribution made by private consumption expenditure and also results in deteriorating environmental quality. This does not alter the welfare-related justification for the adjustment to private consumption expenditure since any increase in resource depletion and environmental degradation should be captured by other items used to calculate the ISEW and GPI (e.g. the environmental cost items). Next, the argument put forward linking income distribution and environmental damage is unconvincing. The argument is based on the view that sustainability is positively correlated with current savings, whereby the latter can fall as a consequence of redistributing income from the rich (who have a high marginal propensity to save) to the poor (with a low marginal propensity to save). The overall fall in savings presumably contributes to growing environmental damage. As true as the savings impact of income redistribution might be, it is equally true that a less equal distribution of income leads to environmental deterioration because the poor, usually subsistence farmers in many Third World countries, are forced to live beyond the carrying capacity of their local environments in order to survive. In addition, much of the savings undertaken in industrialised countries takes the form of human-made capital accumulation. This invariably occurs at the expense of natural capital depletion, as evidenced by national measures of genuine savings that include the depreciation of natural as well as human-made capital (Pearce, 1993). Last but not least, the alternative policy option to redistribution – namely, further growth of macroeconomic systems – appears to be the principal factor contributing to environmental damage.

The second criticism lies in the use of the Gini coefficient to establish an index of distributional inequality. Neumayer (2000) claims this technique is very subjective and ad hoc. Neumayer believes the Atkinson index of distributional inequality (Atkinson, 1970) is less subjective because it makes explicit the researcher's assumption regarding a society's aversion to income inequality.

I disagree; indeed, I believe it is the converse. By starting with an index value of 100.0, the Gini coefficient method makes no subjective assumption about the desirability of the distribution of income at the beginning of the study period. It is only assumed that an improvement/deterioration in the distribution of income has a positive/negative impact on the overall welfare of a nation's citizens. This is hardly subjective since, as already mentioned, the welfare impact of a changing distribution of income has empirical support. On the other hand, the Atkinson index approach requires the researcher to make an explicit choice as to what is society's aversion to income inequality at the beginning of the study period. This seems to be far more open to subjectivity.

One final point. Stockhammer et al. (1997) go much further than most and use the index of distributional inequality to weight the final or raw ISEW value. Whether this is justified is debatable. There is certainly good reason for weighting the services provided by consumer durables along with private consumption expenditure. However, while it could be successfully argued that the cost of environmental damage, crime and family break-down is disproportionately borne by the poor, it could also be argued that the poor benefit most from public consumption expenditures. Given what appears to be a clear case of inconsistency and the potential for different methodologies to significantly alter the ISEW, GPI and SNBI, further debate on this issue is required.

Defensive and Rehabilitative Expenditures

The subtraction of defensive expenditures has been widely criticised (Maler, 1991; UNSD, 1993; Hamilton, 1994, 1996; and Neumayer, 1999). It has been suggested that the concept of defensive expenditure is very dubious because it is impossible to draw the line between what does and does not constitute a defensive form of expenditure. For example, as Neumayer (1999, p. 83) argues: 'If health expenditures are defensive expen-ditures against illness, why should food and drinking expenditures not count as defensive expenditures against hunger and thirst? Are holiday and entertainment expenditures defensive expenditures against boredom? Should they all be subtracted from private consumption expenditures?' Furthermore, a United Nations review of national accounting has argued that when the concept of defensive expenditures is pushed to its logical con-clusion, scarcely any consumption expenditure contributes to an improve-ment in human welfare.

There is some degree of truth in the above criticism. Certainly some per-centage of food and drinking expenditure is defensive, as is spending on clothes and housing. However, there is a fundamental difference between necessary expenditure on such things as food and drink and expenditures people feel increasingly required to make to protect themselves against the unwanted side-effects of the socio-economic process. It is safe to say that the latter are defensive in nature and the majority of the former are not. In addition, if private consumption expenditure was confined to defensive measures only, a lot less spending would take place since, for example, expenditure on cosmetic surgery would not occur. Nor would spending on gourmet food at a restaurant. Perhaps there is some justification for counting only half of all money spent on food and drink as welfare enhancing? As it is, where calculations of the ISEW, GPI, and SNBI involve deductions for defensive expenditures (e.g., private health and education expenditure), only a percentage of the total expenditure is deducted.

Whilst not directly criticising the subtraction of defensive expenditures, some observers have stressed the need to attribute the cost of such expenditures to the year in which the injurious activities took place (e.g. Leipert, 1986). As is quite rightly argued, a failure to address this issue will result in the overstatement of the economic welfare of earlier years. Except for the ISEW calculated for Austria by Stockhammer et al. (1997), little has been done in this regard. The lack of any action is due largely to the difficulty in assigning the present cost of defensive expenditures to the years in which the damaging activities took place. To date, the overall impact on the ISEW, GPI and SNBI of subtracting defensive expenditures has been less significant than other costs. This may not, however, continue to be the case. Hence, in order for future calculations of the ISEW, GPI and SNBI to better approximate the economic welfare generated in a given year, it will be necessary for the present cost of damaging activities to be imputed and attributed to past years.

Cost of Sacrificed Natural Capital Services

Perhaps the greatest criticism of the ISEW and GPI has been levelled at the methods used to calculate the cost of resource depletion plus the tendency of researchers to deduct the cumulative cost of ozone depletion, long-term environmental damage, and lost old-growth forests.

In terms of the cost of non-renewable resource depletion, there is, again, little if any consistency in the methods used by the ISEW and GPI proponents. This has attracted criticism in itself. As for the methods used, Neumayer (2000) is particularly critical of the rationale behind the use of a replacement cost approach. Neumayer believes a resource rent approach should be used. This has been done in a number of ISEW and GPI calculations; however, the typical resource rent approach involves a deduction of the total cost of non-renewable resource depletion. In most instances, it also involves the assumption of escalating non-renewable resource prices. Neumayer argues against the deduction of the total cost of non-renewable resource depletion by claiming that El Serafy's (1989) 'user cost' formula is the correct means of calculating resource rents. The significance of El Serafy's user cost formula is that only a portion of the total cost of resource depletion is deducted.

I agree entirely with Neumayer regarding the El Serafy user cost formula, although the interest rate used in the formula (see equation (7.1) below) should be replaced by the regeneration rate of the renewable resource that must be cultivated to keep the total stock of natural capital intact (Lawn, 1998).[5] However, I disagree with Neumayer's argument against the use of a replacement cost approach. Neumayer dislikes the replacement cost approach because he believes there is no reason why non-renewable resources have to be fully replaced in the present when there are adequate reserves available for many years to come. If there is no current requirement to fully replace non-renewable resources then, according to Neumayer, it is wrong to use a replacement cost approach to calculate the cost of depletion. I disagree with Neumayer because the ISEW and related measures are interested in the *sustainability* of, as well as the economic welfare generated by, economic activity. While the present quantity of resources being extracted from non-renewable resource stocks can be sustained for some time without having to find or establish a renewable resource replacement, this does not mean that it can be sustained indefinitely. And while it may not be necessary to think about a replacement resource for some time, for proper accounting purposes, the actual cost of establishing a renewable resource substitute must be attributed to the point in time when the depletion took place. Indeed, this is the basis behind the El Serafy user cost method.

It might be argued that I am being inconsistent here – after all, I am arguing in favour of the replacement cost approach while also promoting the use of El Serafy's user cost formula. The El Serafy user cost formula is regarded as just one of many ways to execute the resource rent approach. However, the beauty of the El Serafy user cost formula is that it can be used to calculate resource rents and replacement costs, and so it is not entirely correct to say it is exclusively a resource rent method. For example, consider the El Serafy user cost formula below:

$$X/R = 1 - \frac{1}{(1+r)^{n+1}} \tag{7.1}$$

where X = true income (resource rent); R = total net receipts (gross receipts less extraction costs); r = the discount rate (or the regeneration rate of renewable resources should a strong sustainability approach be adopted);

n = number of periods over which the resource is to be liquidated; $R - X$ = user cost or the amount of total net receipts that must be set aside to establish a replacement asset to ensure a perpetual income stream.

This user cost approach is a resource rent method in that the portion of the proceeds from resource extraction that does not constitute a user cost is a genuine resource rent (X). It is also a replacement cost method in that the portion of the proceeds from resource extraction that does constitute a user cost is, in fact, the genuine cost of resource asset replacement $(R - X)$. Since it is the user cost that ought to be deducted when calculating the ISEW, GPI and SNBI, the El Serafy formula serves its purpose as a replacement cost means of estimating the cost of resource depletion.

As for the assumed escalation of non-renewable resource prices over time, Neumayer's (2000) observation that most commodity prices have not increased in real terms is entirely correct. Nevertheless, in view of the expected life of many non-renewable resources and the projected rates of depletion, the price of non-renewable resources should be rising to reflect their impending absolute scarcity. That they have not simply reflects the fact that markets, while very good at signalling relative scarcities (e.g. the scarcity of oil relative to coal), are woefully inadequate at signalling the absolute scarcity of the total quantity of all low entropy resources available for current and future production (Howarth and Norgaard, 1990; Norgaard, 1990; Bishop, 1993; Daly, 1996; and Lawn, forthcoming). Should one use the actual market prices of non-renewable resources to assist in the calculation of the ISEW, GPI and SNBI if they fail to reflect their increasing absolute scarcity? I think not. To get an accurate picture of sustainable economic welfare, one should use the best estimate of rising non-renewable resource prices. Many studies have used a 3 per cent escalation factor. In the calculation of the SNBI (Lawn and Sanders, 1999; and Lawn, 2000), a 2 per cent escalation factor was assumed. In all, an assumed escalation of non-renewable resource prices seems justified.

Another highly contentious issue is whether the deduction term for the cost of ozone depletion, long-term environmental damage and lost old-growth forests should, in each case, be a cumulative total. By cumulative I mean that the amount deducted for each year is equal to contribution made to the cost for the year in question plus the accumulated cost from previous years. Neumayer (2000) believes this is wrong since it involves double counting. He believes that only the present cost should be deducted. Neumayer has a very good point here and unless accumulation of past costs can be adequately justified, it should be abandoned.

However, I believe that cost accumulation can be justified because the ISEW, GPI, and SNBI are calculated to approximate the sustainable economic welfare being experienced by a nation's citizens over the course of a particular year. In the case of ozone depletion, long-term environmental damage and lost old-growth forests, the impact on the sustainable economic welfare in any given year depends very much on what has happened in the past. Hence, the total cost in any given year must reflect the amount required to compensate a nation's citizens in that year – in a sense, a compensatory fund – for the cumulative impact of past and present economic activities on the natural environment.

THE NEED FOR A MORE ROBUST AND CONSISTENT SET OF VALUATION METHODS

There is little doubt that the establishment of more robust means of valuation should strengthen the ISEW, GPI and SNBI as well as increase the policy-guiding value they currently possess. However, the most urgently needed refinement concerns the establishment of a consistent set of valuation methods. To date, there have been as many as five different approaches to the calculation of some of the items that make up these alternative indexes. The inconsistency problem also extends to the choice of items. For example, in some studies, the imputed value of leisure time is added (Lawn and Sanders, 1999; and Lawn, 2000); in others, the value of lost leisure time is deducted (Redefining Progress, 1995); and in others, there is no inclusion of leisure at all (Daly and Cobb, 1989; and Stockhammer et al., 1997). Furthermore, the inconsistency problem is compounded by the existence of three different names for essentially the same index.

Most people are aware of the United Nations System of National Accounts (SNA). The SNA sets out the standardised methods by which GDP and other conventional macroeconomic indicators are calculated. A consistent set of valuation methods and procedures, as well as an agreed upon name, is also required for the ISEW, GPI and SNBI. While it is unlikely that many governments would initially acknowledge and certify the new index, professional and academic organisations and societies are much more likely to do so. This is critically important. The eventual acceptance of a new welfare index – including its eventual use as a policy-guiding barometer – is likely to depend heavily upon its recognition by large, reputable organisations.

A Suitable Name for an Alternative Welfare Index

Given the likely benefit of having just one name for an alternative welfare index, which of the three that currently exist is the most appropriate? Alternatively, is there a superior name that has yet to be suggested? It would seem to me that a number of factors should be taken into account when determining an agreed-upon name. First, the name must be relatively short and simple. Second, the name must describe, in a non-technical fashion, what is being measured. Third, the name must avoid alienation. People from whatever background or position in society must feel, from the name alone, that they are an integral, living element of the index – that the index reflects the welfare of the nation in which they live and participate. For these reasons, I lean towards the Genuine Progress Indicator as the best name so far devised.

A Standardised Set of Items and Valuation Methods to Calculate the Indexes

Any move towards the standardisation of items and valuation methods must take into account the availability of the data required to calculate the individual items. After all, if the aim of standardisation is to eliminate inconsistency and facilitate inter-country comparisons, there is little point agreeing on the items if the data needed to calculate certain items is not available in many countries. From my own experience in calculating the SNBI for Australia – a country possessing a wealth of statistical information – I am acutely aware of the difficulty obtaining appropriate data. Data availability will undoubtedly be a more pressing problem in many Third World countries. If, in trying to establish a standardised welfare index, the lack of available data leads to an index with so few items as to render it superfluous, it may be expedient to have two indexes – a more comprehensive index for countries with extensive data sets; an abridged version that can be calculated for all nations to permit inter-country comparisons.

Second, the choice of valuation technique for each particular item should be aimed at minimising the subjectivity required on the part of the researcher. By subjectivity, I mean the extent to which one is left to make his or her own assumptions in order to calculate the individual item in question. Maximising researcher objectivity lends itself to consensus, and consensus is clearly necessary for an alternative welfare index to be broadly accepted by reputable organisations and the wider community.

INTERPRETING THE RESULTS OF PAST STUDIES

To what extent do the ISEW, GPI and SNBI serve as reliable measures of sustainable economic welfare and as empirical support for the threshold hypothesis? Considerably more, it would seem, than GDP or any other macroeconomic indicator. Having said this, a number of things must be kept in mind. First, there is the already discussed issue of whether current valuation methods are sufficiently robust to ensure the final index values are suitably accurate. Second, the ISEW, GPI and SNBI must be supplemented by a satellite account of natural capital to determine whether the changing level of economic welfare is ecologically sustainable. Third, the list of items used to calculate the ISEW, GPI and SNBI is not exhaustive – there are many welfare-related factors unaccounted for (e.g. the disutility of certain forms of work and the existence values of natural capital). Fourth, as Neumayer (1999) has pointed out, some items dominate others such that it is possible for a small variation in dominant items to overwhelm large variations in the remainder. Overcoming this problem may require the decomposition of the dominant items into a number of smaller items and a sensitivity analysis to assess their individual impact on the final index value.

Fifth, while the ISEW, GPI and SNBI convey useful information about the current manifestations and immediate effects of past and present activities, they reveal much less about the future impact of current activities. In line with suggestions put forward by Asheim (1994, 1996), Pezzey (1993) and Pezzey and Wiltage (1998), it may be expedient to employ forecasting techniques that would allow researchers to incorporate into the ISEW, GPI and SNBI the probable benefits and costs of current actions. This, in turn, would strengthen the policy-guiding relevance of these alternative indexes.

Sixth, it is universally recognised that a single index cannot tell us everything about sustainable development although the consistent trend revealed by the ISEW, GPI and SNBI is enough to suggest that the costs of continuing growth are, for many countries, already exceeding the additional benefits. Finally, since monetary-based indicators are far from perfect, the value of the ISEW, GPI and SNBI would be greatly enhanced if the indexes were supplemented by non-monetary welfare and sustainability indicators (e.g. a comparison between a nation's ever-changing ecological footprint and biocapacity. See Wackernagel et al., 1999; and Chapter 11).

CONCLUSION

As imperfect as the ISEW, GPI and SNBI are, I believe the illumination of a sound theoretical foundation and the evolution of more robust valuation methods will unquestionably strengthen the case for these alternative indexes. It should also lead to wider acceptance of the threshold hypothesis and agreement over which countries have exceeded their optimal macroeconomic scale. Above all, the quest for more appropriate indicators of sustainable economic welfare must remain a high priority for ecological economists at a time when all but the world's poorest nations urgently need to make the transition away from growth to that of sustainable qualitative improvement – better known as sustainable development.

NOTES

1. For a background on ecological economics see Lawn (2002).
2. Compare the first item in Table 7.1 (used to calculate the GPI) and the first item on the right-hand side of equation (2.1) in Chapter 2 (used to calculate SNDP).
3. Even in this book, Patterson (Chapter 19) includes the ISEW and GPI in the category of green GDP.
4. Perhaps the one exception is Stockhammer et al. (1997).
5. This is because the regeneration rate of a renewable resource is effectively its interest rate.

REFERENCES

Abramowitz, M. (1979), 'Economic growth and its discontents', in M. Boskin (ed.), *Economics and Human Welfare*, New York: Academic Press.

Asheim, G. (1994), 'Net national product as an indicator of sustainability', *Scandinavian Journal of Economics*, **96**, 257–65.

Asheim, G. (1996), 'Capital gains and net national product in open economies', *Journal of Public Economics*, **59**, 419–34.

Atkinson, A. (1970), 'On the measurement of inequality', *Journal of Economic Theory*, **2**, 244–63.

Atkinson, G. (1995), *Measuring sustainable economic welfare: A critique of the UK ISEW*, working paper GEC 95-08, Centre for Social and Economic Research on the Global Environment, Norwich and London.

Australian Bureau of Statistics (1992), *Unpaid Work and the Australian Economy: Occasional Paper*, Catalogue No. 5240.0, Canberra: AGPS.

Bishop, R. (1993), 'Economic efficiency, sustainability, and biodiversity', *Ambio*, May, 69–73.

Castañeda, B. (1999), 'An index of sustainable economic welfare (ISEW) for Chile', *Ecological Economics*, **28**, 231–44.

Cobb, C. and J. Cobb (1994), *The Green National Product*, New York: University Press of America.

Daly, H. (1991), *Steady-State Economics*, 2nd edn, Washington DC: Island Press.

Daly, H. (1996), *Beyond Growth: The Economics of Sustainable Development*, Boston: Beacon Press.

Daly, H. and J. Cobb (1989), *For the Common Good*, Boston: Beacon Press.

Diefenbacher, H. (1994), 'The index of sustainable economic welfare in Germany', in C. Cobb and J. Cobb (eds), *The Green National Product*, New York: University Press of America.

Easterlin, R. (1974), 'Does economic growth improve the human lot?', in P. David and R. Weber (eds), *Nations and Households in Economic Growth*, New York: Academic Press.

El Serafy, S. (1989), 'The proper calculation of income from depletable natural resources', in Y. Ahmad, S. El Serafy and E. Lutz (eds), *Environmental Accounting for Sustainable Development*, Washington DC: World Bank.

Fisher, I. (1906), *Nature of Capital and Income*, New York: A.M. Kelly.

George, S. (1988), *A Fate Worse than Debt*, New York: Grove.

Guenno, G. and S. Tiezzi (1998), *An Index of Sustainable Economic Welfare for Italy*, Working Paper 5/98, Fondazione Eni Enrico Mattei, Milan.

Hamilton, C. (1999), 'The genuine progress indicator: methodological developments and results from Australia', *Ecological Economics*, **30**, 13–28.

Hamilton, K. (1994), 'Green adjustments to GDP', *Resources Policy*, **20**, 158–68.

Hamilton, K. (1996), 'Pollution and pollution abatement in the national accounts', *Review of Income and Wealth*, **42**, 291–304.

Howarth, R. and R. Norgaard (1990), 'Intergenerational resource rights, efficiency, and social optimality', *Land Economics*, **66**, 1–11.

Jackson, T. and S. Stymne (1996), *Sustainable Economic Welfare in Sweden: A Pilot Index 1950–1992*, Stockholm: Stockholm Environment Institute.

Jackson, T., F. Laing, A. MacGillivray, N. Marks, J. Ralls and S. Styme (1997), *An Index of Sustainable Economic Welfare for the UK, 1950–1996*, Guildford: University of Surrey Centre for Environmental Strategy.

Lawn, P. (1998), 'In defence of the strong sustainability approach to national income accounting', *Environmental Taxation and Accounting*, **3**, 29–47.

Lawn, P. (2000), *Toward Sustainable Development: An Ecological Economics Approach*, Boca Raton: Lewis Publishers.

Lawn, P. (2002), 'Grounding the ecological economics paradigm with ten core principles', *International Journal of Agricultural Resources, Governance, and Ecology*, **2** (1), 1–21.

Lawn, P. (forthcoming), 'How well do resource prices serve as indicators of natural resource scarcity?', *International Journal of Sustainable Development*.

Lawn, P. and R. Sanders (1999), 'Has Australia surpassed its optimal macroeconomic scale: finding out with the aid of "benefit" and "cost" accounts and a sustainable net benefit index', *Ecological Economics*, **28**, 213–29.

Leipert, C. (1986), 'From gross to adjusted national product', in P. Ekins (ed.), *The Living Economy: A New Economics in the Making*, London: Routledge and Kegan Paul.

Maler, K. (1991), 'National accounts and environmental resources', *Environmental and Resource Economics*, **1**, 1–15.

Max-Neef, M. (1995), 'Economic growth and quality of life', *Ecological Economics*, **15**, 115–18.

Moffat, I. and M. Wilson (1994), 'An index of sustainable economic welfare for Scotland, 1980–1991', *International Journal of Sustainable Development and World Ecology*, **1**, 264–91.

Neumayer, E. (1999), 'The ISEW – not an index of sustainable economic welfare', *Social Indicators Research*, **48**, 77–101.

Neumayer, E. (2000), 'On the methodology of the ISEW, GPI, and related measures: Some constructive suggestions and some doubt on the threshold hypothesis', *Ecological Economics*, **34**, 347–61.

Norgaard, R. (1990), 'Economic indicators of resource scarcity: a critical essay', *Journal of Environmental Economics and Management*, **19**, 19–25.

Pearce, D. (1993), *Blueprint 3: Measuring Sustainable Development*, London: Earthscan.

Pezzey, J. (1993), *The Optimal Sustainable Depletion of Non-renewable Resources*, University College, London.

Pezzey, J. and C. Wiltage (1998), 'The rise, fall, and sustainability of capital-resource economies', *Scandinavian Journal of Economics*, **100**, 513–27.

Redefining Progress (1995), 'Gross production vs genuine progress', Excerpt from the *Genuine Progress Indicator: Summary of Data and Methodology*, San Francisco: Redefining Progress.

Robinson, J. (1962), *Economic Philosophy*, London: C.A. Watts.

Rosenberg, K. and T. Oegema (1995), *A Pilot ISEW for The Netherlands 1950–1992*, Amsterdam: Instituut Voor Milieu – En Systeemanalyse.

Stockhammer, E., H. Hochreiter, B. Obermayr and K. Steiner (1997), 'The index of sustainable economic welfare (ISEW) as an alternative to GDP in measuring economic welfare: The results of the Australian (revised) ISEW calculation 1955–1992', *Ecological Economics*, **21**, 19–34.

United Nations Statistical Division (UNSD) (1993), *Integrated Environmental and Economic Accounting*, New York: Handbook of National Accounting, Series F, No. 61.

Wackernagel, M., L. Onisto, P. Bello, A. Callejas Linares, S. Susana Lopez Falfan, J. Mendez Garcia, A.I. Suarez Guerrero and Ma. G. Suarez Guerrero (1999), 'National natural capital accounting with the ecological footprint concept', *Ecological Economics*, **29**, 375–90.

8. Policy implications of the Index of Sustainable Economic Welfare: Thailand as a case study

Matthew Clarke

INTRODUCTION

Thailand has been one of the world's most successful economies over the past three decades. The constant high rates of growth it has achieved have been central in reducing poverty levels (measured in terms of income levels) from nearly one-third of the population in 1975 to less than 10 per cent in 1999 (Warr, 2001). However, in addition to the benefits of economic growth, such as reduced poverty, there are associated costs that can reduce social welfare. Such costs include various forms of pollution, environmental degradation and social instability.

An increasing number of studies reveal that, beyond a certain point, the positive welfare contribution of economic growth can cease to exist and eventually lead to its diminution – a consequence of the hidden and traditionally unreported costs of economic growth (Daly and Cobb, 1990; Diefenbacher, 1994; Hamilton, 1998; Jackson and Marks, 1994; Lawn and Sanders, 1999; Rosenberg and Oegema, 1995; Stockhammer et al., 1997). These studies involve the estimation of a new measure of welfare commonly referred to as an Index of Sustainable Economic Welfare (ISEW). The ISEW is an attempt at calculating the relevant benefits and costs of growth – namely, economic, social, political, environmental and spiritual benefits and costs – to ascertain a more accurate measure of the sustainable economic welfare associated with a nation's economic activity. The ISEW is being widely accepted as a useful indicator of sustainable development at the national level.

This chapter estimates an ISEW for Thailand over a 25-year period, 1975–99. As Thailand is often presented as a model for other developing countries to imitate, it is a worthwhile country to review (Watkins, 1998). Indeed, it should be of interest to development planners to apply this new approach to measuring welfare to developing countries to investigate whether it is possible for low-income countries prematurely to reach the point at which economic growth no longer increases economic welfare but, instead, reduces it. Moreover, development planners can utilise the ISEW to ascertain which social and economic development policies have been detrimental to economic welfare and those that are likely to boost economic welfare in future years.

This chapter concludes that Thailand, which is a low-middle income country, is approaching the point at which economic growth produces both diminishing and, at times, negative welfare returns as the costs of achieving growth begin to outweigh the associated benefits. This conclusion is significant for policy makers and highlights the importance of considering development prescriptions that offer alternatives to the current orthodoxy of giving primacy to achieving economic growth.

THAILAND'S INDEX FOR SUSTAINABLE ECONOMIC WELFARE

The findings of previous ISEW studies are summarised in Castañeda (1999). Apart from the work by Castañeda on Chile, all previous ISEW studies have focused on developed countries. The results across these studies are very consistent: welfare increased in line with economic growth until the late 1970s or early 1980s (though at a slower rate), at which time the ISEW began to fall despite continuing increases in economic growth. These studies reveal that, beyond a certain point, the costs of achieving economic growth begin to outweigh the associated benefits. The resultant decline in welfare reflects a possible failure on the part of national governments to achieve sustainable development. The point at which marginal increases in economic growth result in negative returns has been labelled the 'threshold point' (Max-Neef, 1991, 1995). Such a concept is not new within the literature (Hicks, 1940; Pigou, 1962; Ng and Ng, 2004). Over the past three decades, the possible crossing of this point by developed countries has been widely discussed (see Daly, 1971, 2000; Barkley and Seckler, 1972; Zolatas, 1981).

Serious policy implications flow from these results for development planners. The major implication is that the primary goal of economic and social policy should not be the attainment of economic growth without consideration of its associated costs. For developing countries, this implication is significant as it challenges the underlying tenants of mainstream development economics (Clarke and Islam, 2004).

Developing countries are characterised by low income levels, unstable employment, political instability and poor social capital. Orthodox development prescriptions hold that economic growth will remedy these ills. Yet,

if a threshold point can be reached by a country with low national income
levels, and economic growth causes diminishing and negative welfare
returns, a whole new approach to development economics is required.

Application of the ISEW

A society is a system comprised of hierarchical and interconnected subsystems (Capra, 1982; Dopfer, 1979; Clayton and Radcliffe, 1996; Islam and
Clarke, 2001; Islam et al., 2004) (see also Chapters 2 and 18). The subsystems relevant to human welfare include the economic, social, political,
environmental and spiritual domains. Each of these subsystems interacts
to form part of a larger ecological parent system (see Figure 8.1 below). The
interrelatedness of these subsystems means that achieving economic
growth may occur at the direct expense of one or more subsystems. This is
invariably expressed in terms of undesirable feedback effects that not only

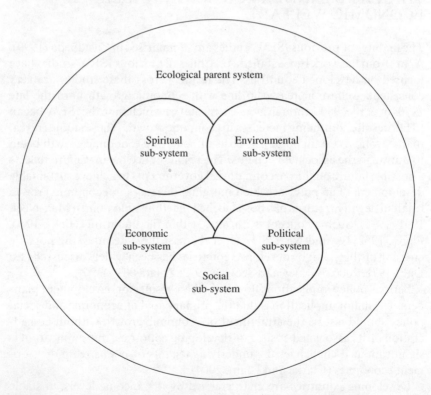

*Figure 8.1   Representation of hierarchical and interconnected systems
                analysis*

have an immediate welfare impact, but influence future economic outcomes. Clearly, measures of economic welfare must take all impacts, both direct and indirect, into account.

One of the strengths of the ISEW is that these various subsystems and their relationships and impacts on welfare are explicitly considered and accounted for in some way (Clarke and Islam, 2004). How? Consider the following factors that are estimated to calculate the ISEW for Thailand (other adjustments might be necessary for other countries) (Islam and Clarke, 2001; Clarke and Islam, 2004):

Economic domain
- Personal consumption adjusted for changes in income inequality;
- Benefits derived from consumer durables;
- Cost of commuting.

Social domain
- Public expenditure on education;
- Public expenditure on health;
- Private expenditure on health;
- Cost of increasing urbanization.

Political domain
- Benefits of government provided streets and highways;
- Cost of corruption;
- Public debt.

Environmental domain
- Air pollution;
- Water pollution;
- Noise pollution;
- Loss of forests;
- Non-renewable resource depletion;
- Long-term environmental damages.

Spiritual domain
- Cost of commercial sex work.

Consider, also, Table 8.1 that lists the items used to calculate the ISEW for Thailand along with the rationale for their inclusion. While the various forms of consumption account for the direct impact of economic activity on welfare (e.g. personal consumption and public expenditure on health, education and roads), the various defensive expenditures and environmental costs reflect the undesirable feedback effects of past activities on the economic, social, and environmental subsystems. The inclusion of commercial sex work is as an example of how increasing urbanisation, dislocation, and declining moral capital can impact deleteriously on the spiritual domain.

Table 8.1 ISEW per capita and GDP per capita for Thailand, 1975–99 (1988 prices in baht)

Year	Economic (millions of baht)	Social (millions of baht)	Political (millions of baht)	Environmental (millions of baht)	Spiritual (millions of baht)	ISEW (millions of baht)	ISEW per capita	GDP per capita
1975	289 271	−14 226	−3336	−81 373	−18 646	171 690	4050	14 662
1976	309 968	−14 380	−2771	−80 580	−20 371	191 866	4440	15 754
1977	333 312	−17 629	−5263	−137 464	−22 430	150 526	3400	16 942
1978	348 689	−17 828	−4460	−145 862	−24 558	155 981	3449	18 237
1979	368 041	−17 613	−5865	−70 782	−25 744	248 037	5379	18 819
1980	386 847	−16 607	−7034	−75 363	−27 190	260 653	5550	19 458
1981	405 849	−20 549	−8540	−79 451	−28 562	268 747	5614	20 206
1982	408 616	−17 597	−10 231	−83 773	−30 133	266 882	5464	20 883
1983	432 608	−17 658	−11 473	−83 698	−32 043	287 736	5811	21 729
1984	438 488	−21 985	−13 914	−87 772	−33 754	281 063	5556	22 504
1985	439 241	−25 719	−15 881	−90 177	−35 137	272 327	5258	22 996
1986	447 554	−28 279	−18 989	−74 774	−36 950	288 562	5448	23 722
1987	483 945	−35 342	−17 922	−78 871	−40 599	311 211	5777	25 561
1988	521 801	−43 117	−17 445	−85 397	−46 051	329 791	6000	28 380
1989	552 434	−48 866	−16 382	−91 478	−51 838	343 870	6153	31 316
1990	603 071	−54 663	−10 593	−113 112	−57 650	367 053	6519	34 565
1991	622 392	−60 523	−7050	−120 985	−62 420	371 414	6520	37 073
1992	655 585	−63 159	−2937	−126 737	−66 967	395 785	6849	39 506
1993	719 644	−57 618	781	−134 028	−72 808	455 971	7816	42 765
1994	785 056	−57 295	3409	−141 474	−79 645	510 051	8631	45 174

1995	853 737	−59 299	8 159	−150 382	−86 771	565 444	9 510	48 511
1996	929 336	−66 005	10 343	−158 653	−91 513	623 508	10 372	51 489
1997	932 210	−65 835	2 765	−163 368	−89 590	616 182	10 132	49 691
1998	830 688	−55 185	−292	−163 192	−79 414	532 605	8 665	45 348
1999	832 001	−70 019	−7 335	−148 076	−82 165	524 406	8 505	45 789

Source: Compiled from Clarke and Islam, 2004.

Due to a lack of space, a full explanation of the methodology used for estimating these separate costs and benefits is not provided here. It can be found elsewhere in Clarke and Islam (2004). In general, though, the methodology follows that set out previously in Daly and Cobb (1990) and Cobb and Cobb (1994). There is also a lengthy discussion on valuation methods in Chapter 7 of this book.

Results of the Thai ISEW

As both Table 8.2 and Figure 8.2 show, the trend movement of economic welfare for Thailand, when measured by the ISEW for the period 1975 to

Table 8.2   Summary of Adjustments for Thai ISEW

Item	Positive/ negative	Rationale	Methodology
Personal consumption		Basis of ISEW	From Thai National Statistics Office (NSO) (1997, 1999)
Income inequality		Accounting for inequality	Equally distributed equivalent level of income Atkinson's (1970)
Public expenditure on education	Positive	Adding in non-defensive expenses	75% of public expenditure on education due to low base (NSO 1997, 1999).
Public expenditure on health	Positive	Adding in non-defensive expenses	75% of public expenditure on health due to low base (NSO 1997, 1999).
Commuting	Negative	Subtracting costs for time lost	US$219 per car calculated in 1990 extrapolated to cover all years (Tanaboorboon et al., 1990)
Urbanisation	Negative	Subtracted for defensive private expenditure	18% of Bangkok personal income is spent for access to clean water and air (World Bank 1999)
Private expenditure on health	Negative	Subtracted for defensive private expenditure	50% of all private health expenditure (Cobb and Cobb 1994; NSO 1997, 1999)
Public expenditure on roads	Positive	Accounting for services not included in public expenditure	50% of all public expenditure on roads (Daly and Cobb 1990; NSO 1997, 1999)

Table 8.2   (continued)

Item	Positive/ negative	Rationale	Methodology
Consumer durables	Positive	Accounting for services not included in public expenditure	10% of expenditure on private consumer durables (Daly and Cobb 1990; NSO 1997, 1999.
Corruption	Negative	Subtracting for unaccounted political costs to society	0.0088% of GDP (1975–81), 0.0074% of GDP (1982–88), 0.007% of GDP (1989–99) based on Phongpaichit and Piriyarangsan (1994)
Debt	Negative	Subtracting for unaccounted political costs to society	50% of interest paid on public Debt (NSO 1997, 1999)
Air pollution	Negative	Subtracting costs of environmental damage	Costs of pollution abatement for CO_2, CO, NOX, SOX, SPM (Guenno and Tiezzi 1998, Dept. of EDP 1990).
Water pollution	Negative	Subtracting costs of environmental damage	Costs of cleaning water is 7.5 baht per kilogram of Biochemical Oxygen Demand (BOD) (Phansawas 1987; TESCO 1993; Dept. of IW 1986)
Noise pollution	Negative	Subtracting costs of environmental damage	1% of GNP (Daly and Cobb 1990; NSO 1997, 1999)
Deforestation	Negative	Subtracting costs of environmental damage	886 baht per hectare of forest lost to soil erosion (Panayotou and Parasuk 1990)
Long-term environmental damage	Negative	Subtracting costs of environmental damage	Estimated damage for each tonne of carbon emissions is 21.59 baht (Nordhaus 1991; Dixon 1999)
Commercial sex work	Negative	Unaccounted costs to spiritual system	3% of GNP (Phongpaichit et al., 1998; NSO 1997, 1999)

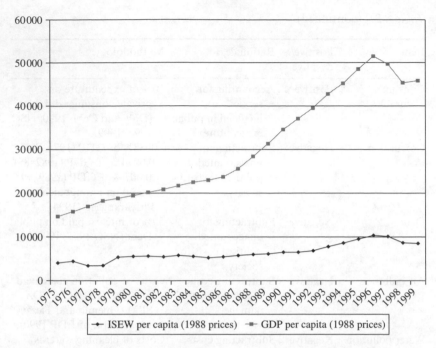

Figure 8.2   *Comparison of ISEW per capita and GDP per capita*
             measures of welfare for Thailand, 1975–99 (1988 prices in
             baht)

1999, was vastly different to that of economic welfare when conventionally
measured by economic growth. The changing influences and feedbacks
from the various subsystems severely impacted on human welfare. This has
been captured by the ISEW in terms of the significant rise in social, environmental and spiritual costs. Not only did the ISEW per capita increase
at a slower rate than per capita GDP, it also decreased at times when per
capita GDP was increasing. The ISEW per capita rose and fell throughout
the 1980s, effectively being unchanged in 1986 from the 1979 figure. In comparison, per capita GDP rose by more than 25 per cent over the same
period. During the 1990s, both the ISEW per capita and per capita GDP
increased. However, they rose at significantly different rates – ISEW per
capita rising at a much slower rate than per capita GDP. It was during the
1990s that the divergence between the two indices became quite apparent.

  Interestingly, the peak of both indices occurred in 1996, just prior to the
Asian financial crisis of 1997. While Thailand's per capita GDP recovered
very rapidly, the ISEW failed to rally as quickly. Until further evidence and
data becomes available, it is too early to confirm whether this is a newly

established trend or a crisis-specific fluctuation. However, by drawing on the results of other studies (see Castañeda, 1999, for a survey), this new divergence might well have been expected, if not have been a predictable outcome.

It is important to realise that although both indices are money-metric, they are not cardinal in nature. Having said this, it is possible to infer from these two time series a distinct variation and divergence in the two trend lines. Thus, the welfare experienced by the Thai population between 1975 and 1999 is, in this instance, dependent on the shape of these two trend lines, rather than the magnitude of each and the distance between them.

As Figure 8.2 illustrates, the trend line for per capita GDP has three main phases; the initial steady rise to 1986, the accelerated growth to 1997, and the final dip and recovery to 1999. The pattern for ISEW per capita is quite different. The initial rise is slower – there is not an accelerated period of growth – nor is there an indication of a recovery in the final year following the decline in the index in 1997. Perhaps, of greater importance, is the growing divergence between the two indices. This increasing disparity suggests that the relationship or correlation between per capita GDP per capita and the per capita ISEW is weakening over time. Such a weakening casts doubts over the long-term desirability of both achieving economic growth and positioning economic growth as the main development policy objective.

The weakening relationship between economic growth and economic welfare is better illustrated in Figure 8.3 by normalising both indices and starting both per capita GDP and ISEW per capita with an index of 100.0 in 1975.

Up to the mid 1980s, both GDP per capita and ISEW per capita tracked each other quite closely with a slow increase. While both indices continued to grow from the 1980s, growth in per capita GDP was certainly more accelerated. This resulted in the divergence between the two indices becoming more prominent over the study period. Again, this suggests that the positive relationship between economic growth and welfare is becoming weaker over time as the increasing associated costs of economic growth begin to outweigh (or at least match) the additional welfare benefits.

POLICY IMPLICATIONS OF THE THAI ISEW

Since the middle of the last century, the central tenet of public policy in most economies has been the achievement of economic growth (Nordhaus and Tobin, 1973; Manning, 2001). This policy emphasis occurred in both developed and developing countries. Its emphasis has been justified on the assumption that economic growth automatically increases welfare (Samuelson et al., 1978; Kaosa-ard, 2000). The major question underlying

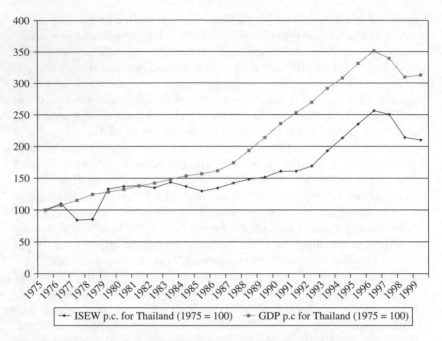

Figure 8.3   Comparison of ISEW per capita and GDP per capita for Thailand (1975 = 100)

the ISEW approach is whether an increase in economic growth 'really reflects the true changes in welfare' (Brekke, 1997, p. 158). The results discussed above suggest this is not always the case.

Achieving economic growth in the manner that occurred in Thailand has caused social, political, and environmental pressures such as pollution, urbanisation, increased levels of stress, etc., which has caused reduced levels of welfare. Therefore, expectations for improving society's welfare through continuous economic growth need to be re-examined, as do the economic and social policies for achieving this outcome.

Hagerty et al. (2001) have shown that basing development policies on the results of welfare indices, such as the ISEW, is entirely legitimate if the results are: (1) judged to be reliable; (2) have established time series measures; and (3) can be disaggregated to analyse the index's subcomponents. Hagerty et al. do note, however, that policies based on welfare indices are largely dependent on how welfare is defined within these indices. Nevertheless, and despite the potential policy value of alternative welfare indices, policy prescriptions based on the analysis of the ISEW are rare within the literature, especially for developing countries.

Three policies guidelines are set out below based on the results found in this empirical exercise for Thailand. It is reasonable to expect that the same policies would also be valid for other developing countries exhibiting similar characteristics to Thailand. The purpose of these guidelines is to encourage a widening of current development policy prescriptions.

Reduced Emphasis on Economic Growth

Economic growth generates both costs and benefits. It is undeniable that economic growth can lift income levels, reduce absolute poverty and increase material standards of living. But, of course, economic growth can also increase environmental, social and political stress. The desirability of economic growth should be determined by its net benefits on social welfare. A balanced approach to achieving economic growth must be encouraged. Economic growth is certainly an important ingredient for increasing social welfare, but it is not sufficient in itself. If the net benefits of economic growth are negative, welfare-enhancing policies that are not growth focused must be embraced.

Economic growth should not be the only priority of government policy. Economic growth aimed at specific sectoral areas (Warr, 2001) and for specific purposes would be better 'than pursuing economic growth for its own sake and hoping that the benefits will be spread widely enough that the poor derive some gains' (Fields, 1995, p. 76).

Increased Emphasis on Pro-poor Policies

The aim of pro-poor policies should be one of ensuring that those living in absolute poverty receive a greater share of the benefits of any future economic growth plus the residual benefits from previous growth. The northeast region of Thailand is one of the kingdom's poorest regions with poverty rates similar to parts of sub-Saharan Africa (Watkins, 1998). The welfare benefits of the economic growth experienced in Thailand over the past three decades have largely bypassed this part of the country whose population remains largely rural. However, the welfare costs of economic growth, such as environmental pressure resulting from increased industrial activity, have been disproportionately borne by these poor people (Dixon, 1999; Warr, 2001).

A pro-poor policy that ought to be given greater attention is that of income redistribution. Various public policy instruments exist in this regard, the most common being taxation. It is possible to redistribute income through increased (or enforced) taxation on wealth, property, inheritance, foreign currency transactions and the consumption of luxury goods. Other valuable redistribution options include taxation credits and improved provision of welfare services in the form of a social security safety net.

Whilst there are attendant costs with redistribution (Pigou, 1962), it is more likely to reduce income inequality than economic growth. The reduction of inequality can also reduce the poverty elasticity of national income so that future growth has a greater impact on reducing poverty levels (World Bank 2000; Deolalikar 2002). The reduction of inequality also encourages social inclusion which, itself, has potential welfare benefits (Killock 2002; Maxwell 2001, 2003; McKay 2002; White 2001).

Increased Emphasis on Other Subsystems

Public policies that enhance the social, political, environmental or spiritual subsystems will have positive effects on social welfare. It is possible that policies of this nature might compromise efforts to achieve economic growth (e.g. tighter control over environmental resource depletion and improved labour market conditions can impede the rate of economic growth in the short run). However, the beneficial welfare impact may outweigh any costs of foregone or lost economic growth.

Adjusted income measures of welfare were initially developed on the implicit understanding that society is systems-based and the interrelationships between the various subsystems have a significant impact on social welfare. By adopting this approach – made explicit in the application of the ISEW to Thailand – the importance of non-economic subsystems in determining welfare becomes apparent.

POLICY IMPLICATION ROBUSTNESS

The suggested policy frameworks based on the ISEW results above have three strengths and one obvious weakness. This section will briefly review each of them before drawing the conclusion that policy implications based upon ISEW results are valuable and can increase the likelihood of sustainable development being achieved in developing countries.

Strength 1: Systems Analysis

The original development of income-adjusted measures of welfare (Sametz, 1968; Nordhaus and Tobin, 1973; Daly and Cobb, 1990) contained an implicit acknowledgement that the economy is part of a larger interrelating system. This general approach highlights the positive and negative consequences that achieving economic growth has on other subsystems within society. This recognition is an important tenet of this framework.

Systems analysis must also be considered when drawing policy implications from ISEW results. It should be recognised that, just as economic growth impacts upon other domains, a focus on the environmental domain, for example, will also impinge upon other domains once feedback effects begin to manifest themselves throughout the total system. It should also be recognised that these interrelating consequences can be either positive or negative. While the ISEW attempts to account for systems-based feedback effects, it clearly performs this function in an imperfect manner. Thus, before policies based upon ISEW results are adopted and implemented, a more thorough systems analysis of their impact must be undertaken.

Strength 2: Capturing Sustainability Paths

Ecological sustainability cannot be adequately reflected by a single index number, such as GDP. However, as Atkinson et al. (1997, p. 62) have argued, 'sustainability is a property of the path the economy is on and not of the state of the system at any given time'. Given that the ISEW can reveal the trend movement in economic welfare that, itself, incorporates a range of environmental costs, it can provide insights into the 'sustainability' path of a particular nation. Enhancing a nation's sustainability path is a distinct strength of the policies emanating from ISEW results and analysis. Such policies can improve a nation's likelihood of achieving sustainable development.

Strength 3: Encouraging Alternative Development Prescriptions

In much in the same manner as the Human Development Index (UNDP, 1995), the ISEW is an alternative measure of development to traditional representative indicators, such as per capita GDP. By defining development more widely than simply income, the value of the ISEW in terms of its policy implications lies in its questioning of development orthodoxy and the creation of a space in which alternative development prescriptions are encouraged. Given the current predilection with economic growth, it is unlikely that the policy implications suggested by the ISEW results will be fully implemented in the near future. However, by proposing wider development prescriptions, the ISEW, like the Human Development Index, should impact on the policy debate by encouraging dissent from the orthodoxy. Over the long term, its impact on policy prescriptions may be quite significant.

Weakness 1: Construction and Uncertainty

As with all economic measures, the ISEW is a constructed number. Starting with personal income, the ISEW is calculated by making certain adjustments that reflect both the costs and benefits of pursuing a policy of economic growth. These adjustments are based on value judgments. Whilst these value judgments are explicit (and more explicit than the value judgments that underpin the standard national accounts, such as GDP), the final ISEW estimate is highly dependent upon the analyst's arbitrary values, choices, and preferences for: (1) the methodologies used to estimate the various costs and benefits, and (2) what costs and benefits are included or excluded from the ISEW (Clarke and Islam, 2004). See Table 8.1 which sets out the methodologies used to estimate the ISEW.

Given the different methodologies available to the researcher, different results can be obtained depending on the choice of assumptions and valuation techniques used. This can, of course, lead to a different development interpretation of a country and different policy implications. While a standard set of costs and benefits have evolved over time (starting with Nordhaus and Tobin, 1973, and Daly and Cobb, 1990), most ISEW studies involve slight variations in the items used and the valuation methods employed to estimate their value (cf. Daly and Cobb, 1990; Diefenbacher, 1994; Hamilton, 1998; Jackson and Marks, 1994; Lawn and Sanders, 1999; Rosenberg and Oegema, 1995; Stockhammer et al., 1997). In the case of the ISEW for Thailand, the costs of corruption and commercial sex work have been included. These were seen to be specific to the Thai development experience. While excluding these two adjustments would not significantly affect the final ISEW, different policy implications may follow (see Figure 8.4). Further, due to the methodology selected, other adjustments might be particularly large and overwhelm the remaining adjustments. For instance, in the case of the Thai ISEW, the environmental costs are twice as significant as any other subsystem adjustment, and may be solely responsible for driving the divergence between the GDP per capita and ISEW per capita indices.

Likewise, the selection of what is included in the ISEW is also central to the final analysis. This is a significant criticism of the ISEW (Neumayer, 1999). The decision to exclude or include an adjustment to income is often reliant on the analyst's opinion as to whether an activity associated with achieving economic growth can be considered a regrettable form of expenditure. Criticism of this approach centres on the exclusions of regrettables and whether many consumption goods could be also labelled regrettable, such as food, clothing, transport, driver education and insurance. According to Lebergott (1993, p. 8), 'Regret is a word of seismic potency. It can be applied to a thousand facets of the real world'. Extending the

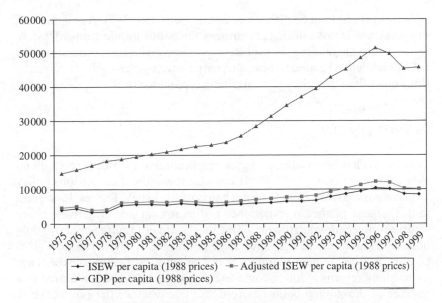

*Figure 8.4   Comparison of GDP per capita, ISEW per capita and
            adjusted ISEW per capita for Thailand, 1975–99 (1988
            prices in baht)*

work of Sen (1993) in which food does not provide utility, but the functioning of food does, it may be legitimate to argue that expenditure on food
is regrettable since it must be purchased to facilitate its functioning. In a
similar manner, commuting is necessary to acquire income. Indeed, if the
argument is extended to incorporate the Second Law of Thermodynamics,
all consumption ultimately leads, not to utility or functioning, but to
waste.

Clearly, the ISEW results upon which policy implications are based are
heavily indebted to the value judgments of the analyst. As an uncertain and
constructed number, a level of hesitancy should accompany consideration of
the development policies it suggests. However, whilst the seriousness of this
weakness should not be underestimated, it is not enough to condemn the
ISEW to redundancy. Many of the problems associated with this weakness
would be overcome if a standard set of methodologies and adjustments were
uniformly undertaken when estimating ISEW for different countries.
Perhaps a consistent and agreed-upon set of adjustments and methodologies
should be developed so that the assumptions of the compiling analyst can be
reduced or excluded altogether. As all ISEW studies undertaken reasonably
approximate each other in terms of adjustments and methodologies, this

agreement should not be difficult to obtain (see Chapter 7). As mentioned, this weakness is not sufficient to dismiss the policy implications of ISEW results. Notwithstanding the problems associated with their estimation, the ISEW highlights the need to base alternative development policies on something other than the primacy of attaining economic growth.

CONCLUSION

This chapter has involved an empirical application of the ISEW to Thailand over a 25-year period, 1975–99. It has also highlighted the various policy implications that flow from the calculation of the ISEW. The results suggest that Thailand is already experiencing diminishing and negative welfare returns from economic growth. These results are not unique but have only been previously found for developed countries. It should be of great concern to development planners that Thailand has begun to experience diminishing returns at low income levels. Additional work is required in a number of developing countries to determine whether the experience of Thailand is unique or common to the developing world. If diminishing and negative welfare returns from economic growth can be reached prematurely, alternative theories of development must be found. Development policies should include a reduced focus on achieving economic growth, an increased emphasis on reducing poverty rates through income redistribution and a heightened emphasis on the impact that all interrelated subsystems have on economic welfare. Further work is also required to establish a common set of methodologies and adjustments so that the assumptions made by the individual analyst do not unduly bias the estimation of the ISEW.

ACKNOWLEDGEMENTS

This chapter is a substantially revised version of 'Widening development prescriptions: policy implications of an Index of Sustainable Economic Welfare (ISEW) for Thailand', *International Journal for Environment and Sustainable Development*, Volume 3 (3/4), pp. 262–75 (2004). The author would like to thank Dr Sardar Islam (Victoria University) for his participation in the research program leading to this paper. He would also like to thank Dr Adis Israngakurn (Thai Development Research Institute, Thailand) for his assistance in calculating the estimates for environmental damage and Dr Phil Lawn (Flinders University) for his helpful comments. Finally, the author gratefully acknowledges the financial support of the Australian Research Council (grant LP0348013) in partnership with the

Victoria Department of Premier and Cabinet, Australia, and World Vision Australia.

REFERENCES

Atkinson, A. (1970), 'On the Measurement of Inequality', *The Journal of Economic Theory*, **2**, 244–63.
Barkley, P. and D. Seckler (1972), *Economic Growth and Environmental Decay: The Solution Becomes the Problem*, New York: Harcourt Brace Jovanovich.
Brekke, K. (1997), *Economic Growth and the Environment*, Cheltenham, UK and Lyme, USA: Edward Elgar.
Capra, F. (1982), *The Turning Point*, London: Fontana.
Castañeda, B. (1999), 'An Index of Sustainable Economic Welfare (ISEW) for Chile', *Ecological Economics*, **28** (2), 231–44.
Clarke, M. and S. Islam (2004), *Economic Growth and Social Welfare: Operationalising Normative Social Choice Theory*, Amsterdam: North Holland.
Clayton, A. and N. Radcliffe (1996), *Sustainability: A Systems Approach*, London: Earthscan.
Cobb, C. and J. Cobb (1994), *The Green National Product*, Lanham: University Press of America.
Daly, H. (1971), 'Towards a New Economics – Questioning Growth', in W. Johnson and J. Hardesty (eds), *Economic Growth Verses the Environment*, Belmont: Wadsworth Publishing.
Daly, H. (2000), *Ecological Economics and the Ecology of Economics*, Cheltenham, UK and Northampton, MA, USA: Edward Elgar.
Daly, H. and J. Cobb (1990), *For the Common Good*, Boston: Beacon Press.
Deolalikar, A. (2002), *Poverty, Growth, and Inequality in Thailand*, ERD Working Paper Series No. 8, Manila: Asia Development Bank.
Department of Energy Development and Promotion (1990), *Industry Survey*, Bangkok: DEDP (in Thai).
Department of Industrial Works (1986), *Industry Survey – 1985*, Bangkok: DIW (in Thai).
Diefenbacher, H. (1994), 'The Index of Sustainable Economic Welfare', in J. Cobb and C. Cobb (eds), *The Green National Product*, Lanham: University Press of America.
Dixon, C. (1999), *The Thai Economy: Uneven Development and Internationalism*, London: Routledge.
Dopfer, K. (1979), *The New Political Economy of Development: Integrated Theory and Asian Experiment*, Melbourne: Macmillian.
Fields, G. (1995), 'Income Distribution in Developing Economies: Conceptual, Data, and Policy Issues in Broad-Based Growth', in M. Quibira and M. Dowling (eds), *Current Issues in Economic Development*, Hong Kong: Oxford University Press.
Guenno, G. and S. Tiezzi (1998), 'The Index of Sustainable Economic Welfare (ISEW) for Italy', *Nota Di Lavoro*, **5** (98).
Hamilton, C. (1998), 'Measuring Changes in Economic Welfare', in R. Eckersley (ed.), *Measuring Progress*, Melbourne: CSIRO Publishing.
Hicks, J. (1940), 'The Valuation of Social Income', *Economica*, **7**, 104–24.

Islam, S. and M. Clarke (2001), 'Measuring the quality of life: a new approach empirically applied to Thailand', paper presented at *INDEX2001 Quality of Life Indicators Conference*, Rome, 2–5 October.

Islam, S., M. Munasinghe and M. Clarke (2004), 'Making Long-term Economic Growth More Sustainable? Evaluating the costs and benefits', *Ecological Economics*, **47**, 149–66.

Jackson, T. and N. Marks (1994), *Measuring Sustainable Economic Welfare*, Stockholm: Stockholm Environment Institute in cooperation with The New Economics Foundation.

Kaosa-ard, M. (2000), *Social Impact Assessment: Synthesis Report*, Bangkok: TDRI.

Killock, T. (2002), *Responding to Inequality*, Inequality Briefing Paper No. 3, London: DFID.

Lawn, P. and R. Sanders (1999), 'Has Australia surpassed its optimal macroeconomic scale? Finding out with the aid of benefit and cost accounts and a sustainable net benefit index', *Ecological Economics*, **28** (2), 213–29.

Lebergott, S. (1993), *Pursuing Happiness*, Princeton: Princeton University Press.

Manning, I. (2001), 'Equity and Growth', in J. Niewenhuysen, P. Lloyd and M. Mead (eds), *Reshaping Australia's Economy*, Cambridge: Cambridge University Press.

Max-Neef, M. (1991), *Human Scale Development*, New York: Apex Press.

Max-Neef, M. (1995), 'Economic Growth and Quality of Life: A Threshold Hypothesis', *Ecological Economics*, **15** (2), 115–18.

Maxwell, S. (2001), 'Innovative and Important. Yes, but also Instrumental and Incomplete: The Treatment of Redistribution in the "New Poverty Agenda"', *Journal of International Development*, **13** (3), 331–41.

Maxwell, S. (2003), 'Heaven or Hubris: Reflections on the New "New Poverty Agenda"', *Development Policy Review*, **21** (1), 5–25.

McKay, A. (2002), *Defining and Measuring Inequaliy*, Inequality Briefing Paper No. 1, London: DFIS.

National Statistical Office (NSO) (1997), *National Income of Thailand, 1951–1996 Edition*, Bangkok: NESDB.

National Statistical Office (NSO) (1999), *Statistical Yearbook Thailand, 1998*, No. 45, Bangkok: NESDB.

Neumayer, E. (1999), 'The ISEW – Not an Index of Sustainable Economic Welfare', *Social Indicators Research*, **40**, 77–101.

Ng, S. and Y. Ng (2004), 'Welfare-reducing Growth Despite Individual and Government Optimalisation', *Social Choice and Welfare*, **18**, 497–506.

Nordhaus, W. (1991), 'To Slow or Not to Slow: The Economics of the Greenhouse Effect', *Economic Journal*, **101**, 920–37.

Nordhaus, W. and J. Tobin (1973), 'Is Growth Obsolete?', in M. Moss (ed.), *The Measurement of Economic and Social Planning*, New York: National Bureau of Economic Research.

Panayotou, T. and C. Parasuk (1990), *Land and Forest: Projecting Demand and Managing Encroachment*, Bangkok: TDRI.

Phansawas, T. (1987), *Community Wastewater Pollution in The Bangkok Metropolitan Area*, Bangkok: ONED (in Thai).

Phongpaichit, P. and S. Piriyarangsan (1994), *Corruption and Democracy in Thailand*, Chiang Mai: Silkworm Books.

Phongpaichit, P., S. Piriyarangsan and N. Treerat (1998), *Guns, Girls, Gambling, Ganja: Thailand's Illegal Economy and Public Policy*, Chiang Mai: Silkworm Books.

Pigou, A. (1962), *The Economics of Welfare*, 4th edn, London: Macmillian.

Rosenberg, D. and T. Oegema (1995), *A Pilot Index of Sustainable Economic Welfare for the Netherlands, 1952 to 1992*, Amsterdam: Institute for Environment and Systems Analysis.

Sametz, A. (1968), 'Production of goods and services: the measurements of economic growth', in E. Sheldon and W. Moore (eds), *Indicators of Social Change*, New York: Russell Sage Foundation.

Samuelson, P., R. Hancock and R. Wallace (1978), *Economics*, 2nd Australian edition, Sydney: McGraw-Hill.

Sen, A. (1993), 'Capability and Well-being', in M. Nussbaum and A. Sen (eds), *The Quality of Life*, Oxford: Clarendon Press.

Stockhammer, L., F. Hochrieter, B. Obermayer and K. Steiner (1997), 'The Index of Sustainable Economic Welfare. The Results of the Austrian (revised) ISEW Calculations 1955–1992', *Ecological Economics*, **21**, 19–34.

Tanaborrboon, Y. (1990), 'Recommendations for relieving traffic problems in Bangkok', in *Proceedings of the First Conference on Environment and Natural Resources Conservation in Thailand*, Bangkok: TDRI.

TESCO (1993), *Environment Plan for Development in Bangkok and Central Areas*, Bangkok: Ministry of Science, Technology and Environment (in Thai).

Warr, P. (2001), 'Poverty reduction and sectoral growth: evidence from southeast Asia', paper presented for the WIDER Development Conference, *Growth and Development*, Helsinki, 5–6 May.

White, H. (2001), 'National and International Redistribution as Tools for Poverty Reduction', *Journal of International Development*, **13** (3), 343–52.

Watkins, K. (1998), *Economic Growth with Equity: Lessons from Asia*, Oxford: Oxfam.

World Bank (1999), *Thailand: Building Partnerships for Environmental and Natural Resources Management*, Bangkok: World Bank.

World Bank (2000), *World Development Report 2000/2001: Attacking Poverty*, New York: Oxford University Press.

Zolotas, X. (1981), *Economic Growth and Declining Welfare*, New York: New York University Press.

9. Some constructive criticisms of the Index of Sustainable Economic Welfare

Simon Dietz and Eric Neumayer

INTRODUCTION

The Index of Sustainable Economic Welfare (ISEW) was first calculated for the United States by Daly and Cobb (1989). It draws upon an earlier tradition of attempts to build a comprehensive indicator of economic welfare, beginning with Nordhaus and Tobin (1972). Since then it has been applied to a handful of other countries, including several in Western Europe as well as Australia, Chile and Thailand (see Table 9.1). As Table 9.1 shows, some practitioners have chosen to change its name. It has appeared as the Genuine Progress Indicator (GPI), the Sustainable Net Benefit Index (SNBI) and most recently as the Measure of Domestic Progress (MDP).[1] It would be fair to say that these linguistic turns reflect the degree of confidence different practitioners have placed in the ISEW's ability to measure welfare, sustainability and 'genuine' progress. Different practitioners have also made incremental but significant changes to the methodology for calculating some of the index's component parts. In general, no two studies are quite the same. We shall have much more to say on this point below.

Fundamentally, what the original proponents of the ISEW were trying to do was create a combined indicator of welfare and sustainability.[2] They understood welfare to be the satisfaction of human preferences, whereby the emphasis was placed on a comprehensive notion of preferences including much more than just income and consumer products. What they understood by sustainability is not as easy to explain. Almost certainly they supported the notion of *strong* sustainability, according to which at least a portion of a nation's natural capital resources (including sinks such as the atmosphere) must be preserved for all time. However, it is possible to show that by adding and subtracting different forms of capital in calculating the ISEW (see below), it is technically an expression of the notion of *weak* sustainability, according to which the task is only to preserve the

Table 9.1   ISEW and derivative studies in chronological order

Authors	Country	Name
Daly et al. (1989)	USA	ISEW
Cobb and Cobb (1994)	USA	ISEW
Diefenbacher (1994)	West Germany	ISEW
Jackson and Marks (1994)	UK	ISEW
Moffatt and Wilson (1994)	Scotland	ISEW
Rosenberg et al. (1995)	Netherlands	ISEW
Jackson and Stymne (1996)	Sweden	ISEW
Castañeda (1997)	Chile	ISEW
Jackson et al. (1997)	UK	ISEW
Stockhammer et al. (1997)	Austria	ISEW
Guenno and Tiezzi (1998)	Italy	ISEW
Hamilton (1999)	Australia	GPI
Lawn and Sanders (1999)	Australia	SNBI
Redefining Progress (ongoing, beginning in 1999)	USA	GPI
Clarke and Islam (2003)	Thailand	ISEW
Jackson (2004)	UK	MDP

total capital stock, not necessarily natural capital *per se* (see Neumayer, 1999a, 2003).

The ISEW has perhaps two prime motivations. The first is the obvious flaws that the traditional indicators of macroeconomic activity, gross domestic product (GDP) and gross national product (GNP), have in measuring welfare and sustainability. In Chapter 6, we made the point that, although GDP and GNP were not intended to be measures of welfare (see Neumayer, 1999a), in practice they have often been construed in that way. Secondly, proponents of the ISEW were confident that it would give expression to a notion commonly held by ecological economists: that continued growth of the economy would at some point in time cease to be sustained by the global ecosystem.

CONCEPTUAL ISSUES

What has until recently been missing from the ISEW literature has been a substantial theoretical foundation, something that has not escaped the notice of its detractors in the past (e.g. Atkinson, 1995; contributors in Cobb and Cobb, 1994; Neumayer, 1999a, 1999b). Lawn (2003) has gone some way towards filling this hole. He shows that the index gives a degree of expression to a concept of income and capital first developed by Fisher (1906) in which it is the services that give final consumers utility that count, not the products that yield the services.

Though different authors have calculated the ISEW in different ways, the core components of the index can be generalised follows:

ISEW = Personal consumption weighted by income inequality
         + domestic labour
         + non-defensive public expenditure
         − defensive private expenditure
         − difference between expenditure on consumer durables
             and service flow from consumer durables
         − costs of environmental degradation
         − depreciation of natural resources
         + capital adjustments   (9.1)

The basic building block of the index is personal consumption expenditure, which is weighted with an index of income inequality in order to embrace the notion that extra money could be of greater marginal utility to the poor than to the rich. From here, it is easiest to understand the additions and deductions made in terms of Fisher's (1906) notion of flows of services. It follows that some service flows providing utility are not included in personal consumption expenditure and thus need to be added. These include non-defensive public expenditure on, for example, health, education and roads and an estimate of the value of domestic labour services from housework and parenting. One also adds growth in capital and net foreign lending/borrowing. This sits rather awkwardly with our explanation in terms of consumer welfare. In fact, these components are added, because the ISEW is concerned not only with welfare but also with sustainability. For instance, consumer expenditure financed by international debt is unlikely to be sustainable.

Other service flows are included in personal consumption expenditure but should not be, because they are not associated (directly) with consumer utility. Hence one deducts defensive private expenditures on such things as health, education, commuting and personal pollution control and the difference between expenditure on consumer durables and the flow of services they provide, which is estimated as the depreciated value of the total stock of consumer durables. Other deductions that have from time to time been made include the cost of national advertising[3] (Cobb and Cobb, 1994) and the costs of crime and family breakdown (Jackson, 2004). Other components are not included in personal consumption but need to be deducted, because they reduce the welfare of consumers either now or in the future.

These include, firstly, the costs of environmental degradation. This typically includes such things as air pollution, water pollution, ozone depletion and the long-term environmental damage resulting from climate change. Secondly, one deducts the depreciation of natural resources, including non-renewable mineral and fossil fuel resources, the loss of natural habitats such as wetlands and the loss of farmland.

In almost all ISEW and derivative studies undertaken thus far, a striking pattern has emerged. Until around the 1970s or early 1980s, the ISEW grows in line with GNP. However, around this time it apparently reaches a turning point and either levels off or in some cases falls. In reviewing the earlier empirical evidence, Max-Neef (1995) describes this trend as the 'threshold hypothesis'. In his own words, 'for every society there seems to be a period in which economic growth brings about an improvement in the quality of life, but only up to a point – the threshold point – beyond which, if there is more economic growth, quality of life may begin to deteriorate' (Max-Neef, 1995, p. 117). This does indeed appear to reinforce the suspicions of Daly and others.

Yet, it is worth asking whether the persistence of the threshold hypothesis is in fact a true reflection of welfare growth and decline, or whether this strong result is an artefact of some methodological flaws. In this chapter, we show that the existence of a threshold is virtually inevitable as soon as one makes some questionable assumptions regarding the growth of the costs of non-renewable resource depletion and long-term environmental damage. In addition, we offer some cautionary notes on the way in which private consumer expenditure is adjusted for income inequality and on which expenditures, if any, should properly be regarded as defensive. In summary, we take issue with the calculation of four components of the ISEW:

1. the valuation of the depletion of non-renewable resources;
2. the cumulative cost of long-term environmental damage;
3. the adjustment of private consumer expenditure for income inequality;
4. the deduction of defensive expenditures.

Elsewhere, critics of the ISEW have asked some very important conceptual questions. In particular, Neumayer (2004a, p. 4) argues that it is not possible to combine an indicator of current welfare with an indicator of sustainability, Indeed, 'what affects current well-being need not affect sustainability and vice versa'. For example, the depletion of non-renewable resources is a key determinant of sustainability, because the available stock of natural capital is diminished for future generations. On the other hand, it makes little difference to current welfare. We have already seen the problems that this causes the ISEW: the inclusion of capital adjustments do not seem to fit with the post hoc theoretical framework offered by Fisherian income. Since our remit is to focus on practical rather than conceptual problems, we will not persevere with this argument: suffice to say it is important and the interested reader is directed to Neumayer (2004a). For all that, the ISEW's focus on comprehensive current welfare is laudable. Indeed, the emerging sustainable consumption discourse gives the ISEW renewed salience, because, according to some, the task of making society consume more sustainably is in large part a question of separating out those things that we consume that make us 'happier' and those that do not or even make us less happy (see Levett, 2003).

DEPLETION OF NON-RENEWABLE RESOURCES

In Chapter 6, we pointed out that the way in which the depletion of non-renewable resources was valued had an important bearing on the magnitude of genuine saving rates and therefore, to some extent, on cross-national patterns through time. It turns out that the same is true of ISEW estimates. In this case, there are three points of debate. Firstly, there is the question of whether it should be the resources extracted within a nation's borders or the resources consumed there that are valued. Secondly, there is the question of whether to use replacement costs or resource rents to value each unit of resource depleted. Thirdly, if one elects to use resource rents, there is the question of whether one calculates total resource rents or user costs – the so-called El Serafy method. We deal with each of these questions in turn.

Resource Production or Resource Consumption?

ISEW studies have not been consistent in which of these they have used as the basis for valuing non-renewable resource depletion. All studies that use resource rents to value each unit of depletion value resource extraction rather than consumption. These are: Daly and Cobb (1989) for the United States; Diefenbacher (1994) for Germany; Guenno and Tiezzi (1998) for Italy; Lawn and Sanders (1999) for Australia; and Stockhammer et al. (1997) for Austria. On the other hand, those studies using replacement costs to value each unit of depletion have been divided between valuing extraction and consumption. Cobb and Cobb (1994) and Redefining Progress (1999) use resource extraction. In contrast, those using consumption are: Hamilton (1999) for Australia; Castañeda (1999) for Chile; Jackson and Marks (1994), Jackson et al. (1997) and Jackson (2004) for the UK; Jackson and Stymne (1996) for Sweden; Moffat and Wilson (1994) for Scotland; and Rosenberg et al. (1995) for the Netherlands.

Those studies applying the resource rent method to value each unit of depletion are correct to value resource extraction rather than consumption, because resource rents from extraction, not consumption, are an addition to the national accounts. To subtract the value of consumption instead would be subtracting something that was not there in the first place. However, the opposite is true for those studies applying the replacement cost method. The rationale behind the replacement cost method, which we will elaborate below, is that non-renewable resources will eventually run out and will have to be replaced, at some point in full, by renewable resources. On this basis it becomes irrelevant whether resources are sourced domestically or imported: it is the cost of replacing all the non-renewable resources consumed that matters. Therefore Cobb and Cobb (1994) and Redefining Progress (1999) are wrong to use resource extraction when they use the replacement cost method. But which method should one choose: the resource rent or the replacement cost method? We turn to this question now.

Resource Rents or Replacement Costs?

In Daly and Cobb's (1989) original ISEW for the United States, each unit of non-renewable resource extracted is valued using the resource rent method. With this method, non-renewable resource depletion is equal to the income that accrues from extracting and selling the resource stock. In fact, it can equal either all of the income that accrues or only a part of it, depending on whether one calculates total resource rents or user costs – the so-called 'El Serafy' method. We will discuss this issue below. There is an obvious and accepted rationale for using resource rents to value depletion. Since non-renewable resources are by definition irreversibly lost in the process of extraction, some if not all of the income accruing should be considered unsustainable.

When Cobb and Cobb (1994) recalculated the US ISEW five years later, they opted for the replacement cost method instead. This method constitutes a clean theoretical break from the resource rent method. Here, the value of non-renewable resource depletion should be derived from the cost of substituting all the non-renewable resources used with renewable resources (this explanation reinforces the point made above that it is resource *consumption* rather than production that is the appropriate subject of per-unit valuation with the replacement cost method). This follows from the assumption that non-renewable resources will eventually have to be fully substituted by renewable resources.

There are two chief difficulties with the replacement cost method. The first concerns the assumption that non-renewable resources will have to be fully substituted by renewable resources. Of course, in the long run this must be true. The problem is that in calculating the ISEW it is assumed all non-renewable resources consumed have to be replaced straightaway. There is no reason why this should be the case when, even now, there are large remaining reserves of many non-renewable resources. The assumption becomes even less tenable when we retrospectively calculate the ISEW as far back as the 1950s and 1960s: one ends up assuming that in, say 1950, all oil used in that year has to be fully replaced by renewables at once! In the present-day climate, renewable resources continue to offer in many cases a marginally expensive option compared to non-renewable resources and thus the profit-maximising consumer (intermediate industrial user or final consumer) will in most cases continue to opt for non-renewables. Why not wait until renewable resources are relatively cheap? They are unlikely to be so expensive in the future, which brings us to the second weakness of the replacement cost method.

In Cobb and Cobb (1994), the replacement cost of every barrel of oil equivalent was escalated by 3 per cent per annum throughout the entire 1950 to 1990 period and anchored around an assumed cost of $75 per barrel in 1988. All the other replacement cost-based studies to date (see above) have followed suit. Cobb and Cobb justify their escalator by pointing to the costs per foot of oil drilling in the 1970s, a period in which high prices made it economically viable to explore more marginal oil reserves. In this period, they report that drilling costs increased by 6 per cent per annum. One would expect to see extraction costs spiral as the resource becomes increasingly scarce, but Cobb and Cobb stretch the principle rather too far when they argue that the same will be true of renewable fuels, 'though not as dramatically' (Cobb and Cobb, 1994, p. 267). Therefore they arrive at an annual cost escalator of 3 per cent. The problem with extending their reasoning to renewable resources is that, as well as scarcity, the unit cost of renewable resources will be influenced by technology costs. In the long run, we will most likely have to rely on solar energy to replace the bulk of non-renewable energy used. In line with many new technologies, solar power is currently marginally expensive because the technology is in the early stages of development. Costs will fall in time as the technology improves (Lenssen and Flavin, 1996). Furthermore, the influx of solar energy currently exceeds total world energy demand by at least an order of magnitude (Norgaard, 1996). Ergo, it is not scarce. All in all, it may be more appropriate to assume falling annual replacement costs.

Escalating replacement costs in this way contributes to the threshold hypothesis. Neumayer (2000) showed that, as a consequence of the way in which non-renewable resource depletion is calculated using replacement costs, the deduction term will grow over time provided resource use does not fall by more than the 3 per cent factor used in escalating costs. Furthermore, it will grow at a rate faster than GNP if GNP growth is smaller than 3 per cent plus the growth rate of resource use. In other words, if resource use is non-decreasing, as indeed it tends to be, and GNP grows at less than 3 per cent, which is not uncommon either, then the escalated costs of non-renewable resource depletion will cause an increasing gap between GNP and the ISEW, *ceteris paribus*. Figure 9.1 makes this point clear. It shows the rate of growth of GNP versus the rate of growth of non-renewable resource depletion costs, escalated by 3 per cent per annum, for four ISEW country studies: the Netherlands, Sweden, the UK and the USA. In all four cases, the escalated replacement costs of non-renewable resource depletion are growing faster than GNP. Not only that, they constitute a significant proportion of all deductions made to arrive at ISEW estimates. Neumayer (1999a) calculates that it makes up 37 per cent of all deductions taken from the US ISEW in 1990, 31 per cent of those taken from the UK ISEW in 1996, 21 per cent of those taken from the Swedish ISEW in 1992 and 36 per cent of those taken from the Dutch ISEW in 1992. If, instead of escalating replacement costs by 3 per cent per annum, we assume them to be constant, Figure 9.1 illustrates that we no longer the see the marked divergence between non-renewable resource depletion costs and GNP growth. Indeed, in the UK and US indices, they actually grow more slowly than GNP. This casts some considerable doubt on the threshold hypothesis.

Total Resource Rents or User Costs According to the El Serafy Method?

If one opts to value non-renewable resource extraction using resource rents, as indeed we have argued one should, then there is some debate over whether it is better to calculate total resource rents or user costs. One can calculate the latter using the El Serafy method (El Serafy, 1989). This is a debate that we have already visited in Chapter 6 in the context of genuine saving. Of the ISEW studies that have used the resource rent method, Lawn and Sanders (1999) computed their SNBI for Australia with user costs, while all other studies have used total resource rents.

In Chapter 6, we explained the theory behind these different measures of resource rents and the practice of computing them. From a theoretical perspective, total resource rents assume that none of the income derived from extracting a non-renewable resource is sustainable. On the other hand, the El Serafy method in effect partitions the income stream generated into an unsustainable part: the user cost, and a sustainable part: Hicksian income. So there is some lower income generated by non-renewable resource extraction that can indeed be sustained into the future. This makes a degree of sense, because some of the proceeds of extraction can be invested in other forms of capital – fixed and human – that might at least partly substitute

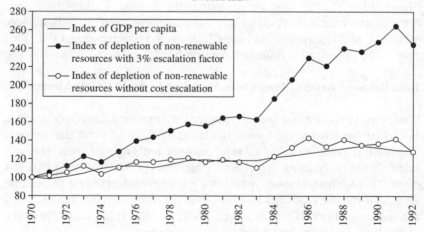

Figure 9.1   *GDP/GNP per capita and the value of non-renewable resource*
depletion with and without escalating replacement costs.
Examples from the Netherlands, Sweden, the UK and the USA

for the depleted natural capital stock. There can also be shortcomings with
the computation of total resource rents in practice. Most importantly, the
total resource rent method depends on the assumption of inter-temporally
efficient markets that naturally lead to optimal prices. There is no reason
to presume resource pricing is optimal though, not least because of the

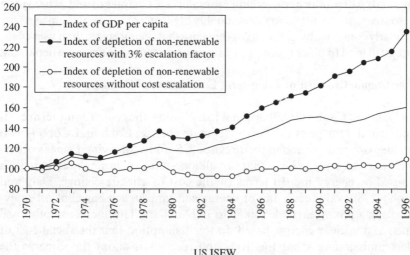

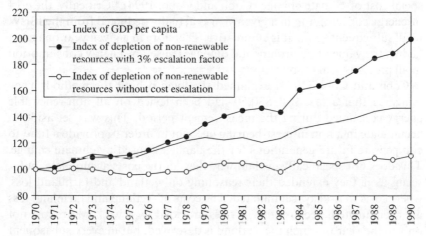

Figure 9.1 (continued)

external costs of extraction. The El Serafy method does not depend on the optimality assumption.

In addition, although total resource rents should in theory be computed as price minus the marginal cost of extraction multiplied by the volume of the resource that is extracted, it is generally necessary to substitute average costs for marginal costs. To the extent that marginal costs are increasing (thus squeezing profits) whereas average costs are not, average costs will tend to overestimate resource depletion. That said, when the discount rate and the number of remaining years of the resource stock are both low, the two methods will produce converging estimates (see Chapter 6) and, where total resource rents do not seem unreasonably high, one can look at them as a particularly conservative estimate, in the sense that, being larger than user costs, they will tend to place more emphasis on non-renewable resource depletion.

The Cumulative Cost of Long-term Environmental Damage

In Daly and Cobb's (1989) original ISEW study, the cost of long-term environmental damage is the cost of climate change. Cobb and Cobb (1994) include ozone depletion in their revised US study, following Eisner's observation in the same volume that not all long-term environmental damage is caused by energy use. In terms of the cost of climate change, Daly and Cobb (1989) value each unit of energy consumed (each barrel of oil equivalent) in a given year at US$0.50 in 1972 dollars. This includes both fossil fuels and nuclear energy, based on the assumption that the social cost of decommissioning spent fuel rods and reactors is about the same as the social cost of climate change (Cobb and Cobb, 1994).[4] Critically, the cost of energy consumption in a given year is actually deducted from the ISEW in all subsequent years: it is cumulative. Therefore in a given year one must deduct the value of environmental damage caused by energy consumption in all previous years too.

Cobb and Cobb (1994) explained the logic behind the method. They imagined that a tax of US$0.50 had been levied on all non-renewable energy consumed during the measurement period. This was set aside to accumulate in a non interest-bearing account in order to provide a fund to compensate future generations for the damage caused by climate change. This does not specifically explain why they let the costs accumulate, but it seems as if they extended their reasoning on wetland and farmland loss, where costs were also accumulated. The costs of wetland and farmland loss are accumulated, because the services provided by a wetland are lost not only in the year in which the wetland is destroyed, but in every subsequent year too. Alternatively, they may have reasoned that the proceeds of a non-accumulated tax would not have provided compensation to future generations for emissions prior to the introduction of the tax. Cobb and Cobb (1994) value the cost of ozone depletion in a very similar way, being US$15 per unit production of CFC-11 and CFC-12 in 1972 prices, accumulated year-on-year after the year of production.

Cobb and Cobb (1994) conceded that they set the unit cost of energy consumption at US$0.50 arbitrarily. In Jackson et al.'s (1997) ISEW and Jackson's (2004) MDP, both for the UK, and Stockhammer et al.'s (1997) ISEW for Austria, each tonne of greenhouse gas emissions is valued at its marginal social cost. Jackson et al. (1997) and Jackson (2004) derive their unit cost estimate from Fankhauser (1995), which is generally considered to be a consensus estimate. The marginal social cost of a tonne of greenhouse gas emissions is the total discounted value of all future damage arising from that tonne of emissions. But instead of deducting the marginal social cost of a given year's emissions for that year only, both studies allow the costs to accumulate over time by making deductions in all following years.

Whichever theoretical underpinning one chooses – and the notion of marginal social cost is more rigorous – allowing the costs of long-term environmental damage to accumulate is problematic (Atkinson, 1995; Neumayer, 2000). In valuing each tonne of greenhouse gas emissions at its marginal social cost, the future cost of a tonne of emissions is already included in terms of its discounted value over all time. Letting the costs accumulate annually amounts to multiple counting. Hamilton (1999) recognises this problem and does not accumulate costs in his GPI computations for Australia. On the other hand, Cobb and Cobb (1994) are explicitly accumulating *undiscounted* costs. To recap, they do so apparently because they are valuing the annual loss in climate services resulting from greenhouse gas emissions. But it is not possible to simply extend the notion of lost services from the wetland scenario to that of climate change, because we have barely begun to feel the impacts of climate change. Up until now, the lost services associated with greenhouse gas emissions have been negligible. Furthermore, it is very difficult to establish, let alone come close to quantifying, the relationship between greenhouse gas emissions arising from energy consumption and the loss of elements of a habitable climate. Indeed, climate change is a fundamentally complex process. On a practical note, Cobb and Cobb imagined that tax proceeds in any year are set aside to compensate future generations. This is fine, but according to the logic of accumulation one needs to make the same deposit in the following year, the year after that and so on, and must find from somewhere the revenue to cover all previous years' emissions. This is surely not what they had in mind.

Choosing to accumulate the cost of long-term environmental damage turns out to be a 'big' decision in terms of calculating the ISEW in the same way as escalating the costs of non-renewable resource depletion is. In the US ISEW the cumulative cost of climate change constitutes 33 per cent of all deductions made in 1990. In the UK ISEW the cumulative cost of climate change and ozone depletion amounts to 32 per cent of all deductions made in 1996 and in Sweden it amounts to 23 per cent of all deductions made in 1992. Figure 9.2 demonstrates that such estimates of long-term environmental damage contribute a great deal to the threshold hypothesis. The similarities with the case of non-renewable resource depletion are once again striking. The rate of growth of the accumulated costs

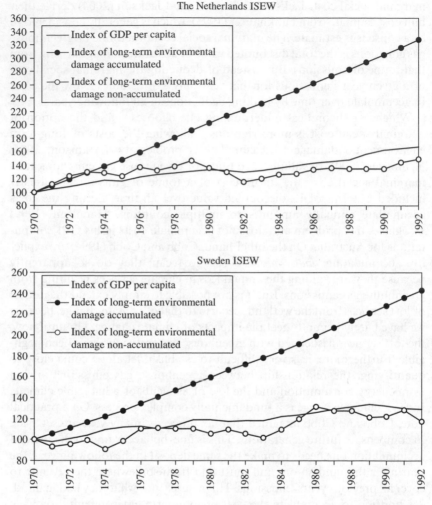

*Figure 9.2   GDP/GNP per capita and the value of long-term environmental
damage with and without accumulation costs. Examples from
the Netherlands, Sweden, the UK and the USA*

of climate change outstrips that of GDP/GNP in all four countries, with
the gap widening year by year. *Ceteris paribus*, this will magnify any
genuine threshold effect that might possibly exist.

If the costs of climate change are not accumulated, then Figure 9.2 shows
that this divergence is no longer apparent. In the Netherlands and Sweden,
the rate of growth of long-term environmental damage is about the same as

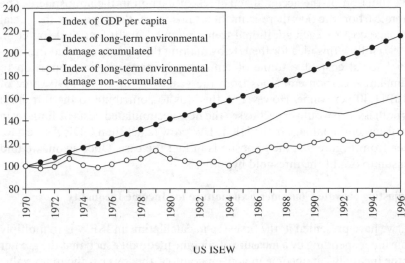

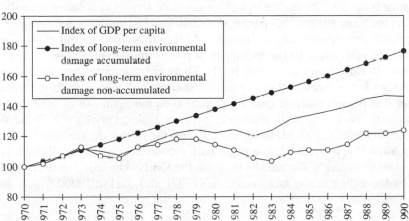

Figure 9.2 (continued)

GDP/GNP throughout the measurement period and, in particular, is lower than GDP/GNP for most of the 1980s and early 1990s. In the UK and the USA, the growth rate of long-term environmental damage is in fact lower than that of GDP/GNP for the whole period, and the difference between the two trends widens year on year, such that long-term environmental damage is virtually an ever decreasing proportion of gross production.

Even if the marginal social cost of greenhouse gas emissions is not accumulated, it is still appropriate to allow costs to increase from one year to the next, as the marginal social cost of each tonne of emissions is a positive function of the accumulated stock of carbon in the atmosphere. The more carbon dioxide there is in the atmosphere, the greater is the social damage cost of each additional tonne pumped in. In fact, Jackson et al. (1997) follow this idea for the UK by making the assumption that the marginal social cost of a tonne of emissions is increasing in proportion to cumulative carbon emissions from the year 1900 up to its 1990 value of GBP11.40 per tonne. However, if this was to contribute to the threshold hypothesis, we would expect to see the non-accumulated costs of long-term environmental damage in the UK ISEW grow faster than GDP. As we have seen from Figure 9.2, the opposite is in fact the case. Once again, we find reason to doubt the threshold hypothesis.

Adjusting Private Consumer Expenditure for Income Inequality

As we have presented it, the first step in calculating an ISEW is to multiply consumer spending by a measure of income inequality such that the greater is the inequality in income in a given country, the lower is the index value and the more the product term is scaled down. The motivating assumption behind this adjustment is that an 'additional [say] thousand dollars in income adds more to the welfare of a poor family than it does to a rich family' (Cobb and Cobb, 1994, p. 31). There are differences between ISEW studies in the method they use to adjust consumer spending. One reason for this is that available data on income inequality vary from country to country. We focus on the difference between Jackson et al.'s (1997) ISEW and Jackson's (2004) MDP for the UK and the rest of the studies.

Most ISEW studies use an index of income inequality to adjust consumer spending and generally they use the Gini coefficient or a derivative. On the other hand, Jackson et al. (1997) and Jackson (2004) use the so-called Atkinson index:

$$\text{Atkinson index} = 1 - \exp\left[\sum (Y_i / \bar{Y})^{1(1-\varepsilon)} f_i\right]^{1(1-\varepsilon)} \qquad (9.2)$$

where Y_i = the mean income of all individuals in the ith income group (out of a total of n groups); $\bar{Y}$ = mean income for the whole population; f_i = the proportion of the population with incomes in the ith group; and ε = a parameter estimating the weight attached by society to income inequality that must be chosen by the researcher.[5]

Importantly, ε can be either positive, which implies society is averse to an unequal distribution of income (with larger values implying greater aversion), zero, which implies society is indifferent, or in principle at least negative, which implies society has a positive preference for income inequality.

The advantage of the Atkinson index lies in ε: it forces the researcher to be explicit in his/her assumption about how averse society is to income inequality. A thousand dollars may indeed be worth more in welfare terms to the poor than it is to the rich, but, even if this is the case (and some would disagree), by how much? Therefore we can either make an assumption about society's aversion to income inequality, or we can resort to empirical estimates from attitudinal surveys on the level of well-being associated with different income levels. Pearce and Ulph (1995) estimate ε lies between 0.7 and 1.5, with a best estimate of around 0.8. This is the value used by Jackson et al.

If one uses the Gini coefficient, then the first step is normally to select a year as the base year and index all other years relative to this. Then unadjusted consumer spending is divided by this index and multiplied by 100. This is problematic, because the approach has no clear welfare-theoretic interpretation. In other words, it does not make explicit its assumption as to how averse society is to income inequality. Instead, it makes a rough and ready adjustment to consumer spending that is at best relative to the base year of the index in any case (Jackson et al., 1997).

Even if one does choose to adjust consumer spending with the Atkinson index, which we recommend, one needs to take care in interpreting the resulting ISEW. In particular, one needs to exercise caution in interpreting ISEW results in absolute terms. Indexing consumer spending makes the ISEW an index, and as such one can either restrict oneself to interpreting changes in the ISEW over time, or one must explicitly state what the base year was chosen in indexing income inequality.

Deduction of Defensive Expenditures

Leipert provides a useful definition of defensive expenditures: 'expenditures . . . made to eliminate, mitigate, neutralize, or anticipate and avoid damages and deterioration that industrial society's process of growth has caused to living, working, and environmental conditions' (Leipert, 1989, p. 28). Put another way, if, in Fisher's (1906) terms, we want to measure the psychic income consumers gain when they enjoy the services provided by commodities, then defensive expenditures should embrace what we spend on insulating ourselves from the 'psychic outgo' of the economic process (Lawn, 2003, p. 111). The question of what, if any, defensive expenditures to deduct in calculating the ISEW is in fact a subset of a debate in national accounting that has been 'live' for as long as national accounting itself: whether all commodities currently produced are a source of final satisfaction to consumers or whether they might properly be regarded as 'intermediate inputs regrettably required to produce other useful goods' (England, 1998, p. 3).

But the major problem with deducting defensive expenditures is where to draw the line. One might agree that consumer spending on commuting to work is not so much psychic income as psychic outgo (though by no means everyone would choose to live next to their workplace even if they did have the choice), but some ISEW estimates have gone as far as considering spending on health and education defensive. In Cobb and Cobb's (1994) US GPI, for instance, they effectively deduct half of all public and private spending on health and education on the grounds that it is defensive. Vis-à-vis education, they deduct spending on primary and secondary education as 'people attend school because others are in school and the failure to attend would mean falling behind in the competition for diplomas or degrees that confer higher incomes on their recipients' (Cobb and Cobb, 1994, p. 54). Similarly, they rather arbitrarily deduct half of all spending on health, because they assume that this half is simply spent in order to compensate people for 'growing health risks due to urbanization and industrialization' (Cobb and Cobb, 1994, p. 55). But if this is the case one can classify most spending as defensive. Neumayer (2004b, p. 154) asks, 'why should food and drinking expenditures not count as defensive expenditures against hunger and thirst?' Even if one accepts Daly and Cobb's defence that they only deduct defensive expenditures beyond the baseline environmental conditions, one could still argue that some portion of all spending is forced by undesirable modes of modern living. As the Commission of the European Communities et al. has argued (1993, p. 1), 'pushed to its logical conclusion, scarcely any consumption improves welfare in this line of argument'.

Certainly in the case of education, Cobb and Cobb are at odds with most economists, who would suggest that education expenditures (even at primary and secondary levels) are productive and welfare-improving. With regard to their health expenditure deductions, they would presumably concede the choice of deducting half of all spending is arbitrary. We would advise greater caution in classifying expenditure as defensive.

CONCLUSION

In this chapter, we have sought to make some constructive criticisms of the ISEW methodology. We encourage practitioners in the field to question certain assumptions that may give a false impression of the threshold in the growth of sustainable welfare. In doing so, we acknowledge that some recent studies, especially Hamilton's (1999) GPI for Australia, are themselves doing so and improving their accounts as a result. We do not exclude the existence of thresholds altogether. We have simply demonstrated that two key deductions made in calculating the ISEW – the cost of non-renewable resource depletion and the cost of long-term environmental damage – are highly influential in creating the threshold, but are much less important given what we consider to be more reasonable assumptions.

In summary, we recommend the following to ISEW practitioners. Firstly, in valuing non-renewable resource depletion, those who choose to apply the resource rent method should base their calculations on national extraction, while those who choose to use replacement costs need to use estimates of national consumption. We also recommend that those using resource rents consider the implications of calculating user costs according to El Serafy rather than total resource rents. Most importantly, we caution against using a 3 per cent cost escalation factor in calculating replacement costs: there does not seem to be a reasonable theoretical basis for escalating replacement costs and its effect on the cost of non-renewable resource depletion over time is manifest. Given some frequently observed trends in resource use and GDP/GNP growth, we have shown that it is inevitable that the ISEW will diverge from GDP/GNP, *ceteris paribus*. Second, practitioners should not, in our view, let the costs of climate change and ozone depletion accumulate yearly. Again, we see no reasonable theoretical basis for doing so and the effect this has on the cost of long-term environmental damage is very large indeed. Third, in adjusting consumer expenditure for income inequality, we recommend using the Atkinson index rather than a more crude method of adjustment based on Gini coefficients. Doing so ensures one adopts a transparent position on just how much more utility extra consumption gives the poor compared to the rich. Fourth, and finally, we urge caution in classifying expenditures as defensive. It is always rather difficult to argue a form of expenditure is fully defensive, and some, such as education, do not seem to accord with the notion at all.

NOTES

1. Osberg and Sharp (2002a, 2002b) have also produced the Index of Economic Well-Being, which they compute for a selection of OECD countries. This is similar in its aims to the ISEW, but makes a much less comprehensive set of adjustments for environmental degradation and none at all for resource depletion (Neumayer, 2004a).
2. It is worth noting that not all ISEW practitioners believe that increases in the ISEW truly indicate increasing sustainability and progress (Jackson, 2004; Lawn, 2003).
3. Cobb and Cobb's contestable rationale is that national advertising does not offer information of value but instead 'tends to be aimed at creating demand for products and brand name loyalty through the use of images that have little to do with the actual product' (Cobb and Cobb, 1994, p. 55).
4. Cobb and Cobb (1994, p. 73) provide no evidence to support this assumption. In their view, '[t]he cost of keeping radioactive elements with long half-lives out of the environment for thousands of years is anybody's guess'.

5. Atkinson (1983) suggested that ε can be thought of as the amount of income that could be transferred from a rich person to a poor person such that the net benefit of doing so remains positive. In other words, the gain enjoyed by the poor person is greater than the loss felt by the rich person plus transfer costs.

REFERENCES

Atkinson, A. (1983), *The Economics of Inequality*, Oxford: Oxford University Press.

Atkinson, G. (1995), Measuring sustainable economic welfare: a critique of the UK ISEW, *Working Paper GEC 95-08*, Norwich; London: Centre for Social and Economic Research on the Global Environment.

Castañeda, B. (1999), 'An index of sustainable economic welfare (ISEW) for Chile', *Ecological Economics*, **28**, 231–44.

Clarke, M. and S.M.N. Islam (2003), *Diminishing and negative returns of economic growth: an index of sustainable economic welfare (ISEW) for Thailand*, Melbourne: Victoria University, Mimeo.

Cobb, C.W. and J.B. Cobb (eds) (1994), *The Green National Product: a Proposed Index of Sustainable Economic Welfare*, Lanham, MD; Mankato, MN: University Press of America; Human Economy Center.

Commission of the European Communities, Eurostat, International Monetary Fund, OECD, United Nations and the World Bank (1993), *System of National Accounts 1993*, Brussels, Luxembourg, New York, Paris, Washington, DC.

Daly, H.E. (1977), *Steady-state Economics: the Economics of Biophysical Equilibrium and Moral Growth*, San Francisco: W.H. Freeman.

Daly, H.E. and J.B. Cobb (1989), *For the Common Good: Redirecting the Economy towards Community, the Environment, and a Sustainable Future*, Boston: Beacon Press.

Diefenbacher, H. (1994), 'The Index of Sustainable Economic Welfare: a Case Study of the Federal Republic of Germany', in C.W. Cobb and J.B. Cobb (eds) (1994), *The Green National Product: a Proposed Index of Sustainable Economic Welfare*, Lanham, MD; Mankato, MN: University Press of America; Human Economy Center, pp. 215–45.

El Serafy, S. (1989), 'The Proper Calculation of Income from Depletable Natural Resources', in Y.J. Ahmed, S. El Serafy and E. Lutz (eds), *Environmental Accounting for Sustainable Development: a UNDP–World Bank Symposium*, Washington, DC: World Bank, pp. 10–18.

England, R.W. (1998), 'Measurement of social well-being: alternatives to gross domestic product', *Ecological Economics*, **25**, 89–103.

Fankhauser, S. (1995), *Valuing Climate Change: the Economics of the Greenhouse*, London: Earthscan Publications.

Fisher, I. (1906), *Nature of Capital and Income*, New York: A.M. Kelly.

Guenno, G. and S. Tiezzi (1998), An index of sustainable economic welfare for Italy, *Working Paper 5/98*, Milan: Fondazione Enrico Mattei.

Hamilton, C. (1999), 'The genuine progress indicator: methodological developments and results from Australia', *Ecological Economics*, **30**, 13–28.

Jackson, T. (2004), *Chasing Progress: Beyond Measuring Economic Growth*, London: New Economics Foundation.

Jackson, T., F. Laing, A. MacGillivray, N. Marks, J. Ralls and S. Stymne (1997), *An Index of Sustainable Economic Welfare for the UK 1950–1996*, Guildford: University of Surrey, Centre for Environmental Strategy.

Jackson, T. and N. Marks (1994), *Measuring Sustainable Economic Welfare: a Pilot Index for the UK 1950–1990*, Stockholm; London: Stockholm Environnment Institute; New Economics Foundation.

Jackson, T. and S. Stymne (1996), *Sustainable Economic Welfare in Sweden: a Pilot Index 1950–1992*, Stockholm: Stockholm Environment Institute.

Lawn, P.A. (2003), 'A theoretical foundation to support the index of sustainable economic welfare (ISEW), genuine progress indicator (GPI) and other related indexes', *Ecological Economics*, **44**, 105–18.

Lawn, P.A. and R.D. Sanders (1999), 'Has Australia surpassed its optimal macro-economic scale? Finding out with the benefit of "benefit" and "cost" accounts and a sustainable net benefit index', *Ecological Economics*, **28**, 213–29.

Leipert, C. (1989), 'Social costs of the economic process and national accounts: the example of defensive expenditures', *Journal of Interdisciplinary Economics*, **3**, 27–46.

Lenssen, N. and C. Flavin (1996), 'Sustainable energy for tomorrow's world – the case for an optimistic view of the future', *Energy Policy*, **24**, 769–81.

Levett, R. (2003), *A Better Choice of Choice: Quality of Life, Consumption and Economic Growth*, London: Fabian Society.

Max-Neef, M. (1995), 'Economic growth and the quality of life', *Ecological Economics*, **15**, 115–18.

Moffatt, I. and M.C. Wilson (1994), 'An index of sustainable economic welfare for Scotland, 1980–1991', *International Journal of Sustainable Development and World Ecology*, **1**, 264–91.

Neumayer, E. (1999a), *Weak versus Strong Sustainability: Exploring the Limits of Two Opposing Paradigms*, Cheltenham, UK and Northampton, MA, USA: Edward Elgar.

Neumayer, E. (1999b), 'The ISEW: not an index of sustainable economic welfare', *Social Indicators Research*, **48**, 77–101.

Neumayer, E. (2000), 'On the methodology of ISEW, GPI and related measures: some constructive suggestions and some doubt on the "threshold hypothesis"', *Ecological Economics*, **34**, 347–61.

Neumayer, E. (2003), *Weak versus Strong Sustainability: Exploring the Limits of Two Opposing Paradigms*, Cheltenham, UK and Northampton, MA, USA: Edward Elgar.

Neumayer, E. (2004a), Sustainability and well-being indicators, *Research Paper 23/2004*, United Nations University, World Institute for Development Economics Research.

Neumayer, E. (2004b), 'Indicators of Sustainability', in T. Tietenberg and H. Folmer (eds), *Yearbook of Environmental and Resource Economics 2004/05*, Cheltenham, UK and Northampton, MA, USA: Edward Elgar, pp. 139–88.

Nordhaus, W.D. and J. Tobin (1972), 'Is growth obsolete?', *Economic Growth, Research General Series 96F*, New York: National Bureau of Economic Research, Columbia University Press.

Norgaard, R.B. (1986), 'Thermodynamic and economic concepts as related to resource-use policies: synthesis', *Land Economics*, **62**, 325–7.

Osberg, L. and A. Sharpe (2002a), 'An index of economic well-being for selected OECD countries', *Review of Income and Wealth*, **48**, 291–316.

Osberg, L. and A. Sharpe (2002b), 'International comparisons of trends in economic well-being', *Social Indicators Research*, **58**, 349–82.

Pearce, D.W. and A. Ulph (1995), A social discount rate for the United Kingdom, *Working Paper GEC 95-01*, Norwich; London: Centre for Social and Economic Research on the Global Environment.

Redefining Progress (1999), *The 1998 US Genuine Progress Indicator: Methodology Handbook*, San Fransisco: Redefining Progress.

Redefining Progress (various years), Genuine Progress Indicator, San Fransisco: Redefining Progress, last viewed at http://www.rprogress.org/projects/gpi/, June 2004.

Rosenberg, D., P. Oegema and M. Bovy (1995), *ISEW for the Netherlands: Preliminary Results and some Proposals for Future Research*, Amsterdam: IMSA.

Stockhammer, E., H. Hochreiter, B. Obermayr and K. Steiner (1997), 'The index of sustainable economic welfare (ISEW) as an alternative to GDP in measuring economic welfare: the results of the Austrian (revised) ISEW calculation 1955–1992', *Ecological Economics*, **21**, 19–34.

PART IV

Sustainable development and natural capital
accounting

10. Measurement of the natural capital stock: conceptual foundations and preliminary empirics

Richard W. England

INTRODUCTION

> What really is capital and what does it mean for value, growth, and distribution? Is it a pile of produced means of production? Is it dated labor? Is it waiting? Is it roundaboutness? Is it an accumulated pile of finance? Is it a social relation? Is it an independent source of value? The answers to these questions are probably matters of belief. (Rosser, 1991, p. 125)

With this agnostic set of questions, Rosser simultaneously summarised the history of capital theory and also alerted us to the danger of reducing the capital concept to a simple formula. As those familiar with the history of economics are aware, economists have faced a series of controversies concerning the definition and meaning of capital. These disputes date back at least to the era of Adam Smith. Ecological economics will certainly encounter similar controversies as it develops and matures.

In this chapter, I first survey some of the definitions of 'natural capital' that one can find in the literature. Using some ideas of Georgescu-Roegen, I then suggest how to put the natural capital concept into sharper theoretical focus. In light of this conceptual revision, my chapter closes by assessing several preliminary efforts to measure natural capital.

NATURAL CAPITAL: A CRITICAL SURVEY

During recent years, ecological economists have cited numerous concrete examples of what they mean by 'natural capital'. Daly (1994) mentions fossil fuel reserves and populations of fish and trees. Cleveland (1994) points to climate, soil and mineral deposits. Ayres (1996), in turn, refers to such items as aquifers and stratospheric ozone. Perhaps the most frequently cited example is biodiversity, a particular facet of ecosystems (Jannson and

Jannson, 1994; Ehrlich, 1994; and Cleveland, 1994). Some authors also mention what seem to be 'processes'. Cleveland (1994), for instance, offers operation of the hydrologic cycle as an example of natural capital. Recycling of nutrients and pollination of crops have also been cited by Berkes and Folke (1994).

All of these specific examples of natural capital are persuasive and instructive. At the same time, however, the sheer diversity of these examples is worrisome. One wonders whether the concept of natural capital can cover simple objects or things, states of affairs, complex systems or structures and dynamic processes all at the same time.

Instead of trying to derive a concept of natural capital inductively from a diversity of particular examples, one can, alternatively, offer a formal definition of its content. Several authors have followed this path. Natural capital, according to Daly (1994), is the stock that yields a flow of natural services and tangible natural resources. Berkes and Folke (1994) go a step further. For them, natural capital consists of three major components:

1.   non-renewable resources extracted from ecosystems;
2.   renewable resources produced and maintained by ecosystems;
3.   environmental services.

Although these formal definitions provide valuable guideposts as we explore the paths linking humanity and nature, they are imperfect. How, exactly, can one tell whether a particular asset is natural or not? Is it proper to conceptualise services generated by ecosystems, materials extracted from those ecosystems and the ecosystems themselves as various forms of natural capital? Doesn't that formulation risk confusion between assets and income flows?

GEORGESCU-ROEGEN ON PRODUCTION THEORY

In an effort to focus and refine the concept of natural capital, I propose that we tap one of the classics of modern economics, the discussion of production theory by Georgescu-Roegen (1971). In that chapter, Roegen distinguished between two very different elements of the production process: 'fund elements, which represent the agents of the process, and the flow elements, which are used or acted upon by the agents' (Georgescu-Roegen, 1971, p. 230). That is, there are the active subjects of production which physically shape and transport, chemically alter, and in various other ways transform materials and energy. These fund elements cannot play their

Table 10.1 Dimensionality of funds and flows

	Input or output flow	Services of fund element
Amount	Kilograms	Machine-hours
	Joules	Cattle-hours
Rate	Kilograms per hour	Machines
	Joules per hour	Cattle

transformative role, however, without access to the passive objects of production, input flows of low-entropy materials and energy.

During the course of production, fund elements maintain their physical identity and integrity while input flows are typically transformed into output flows of qualitatively different character. The fundamental distinction between fund and flow elements of production is suggested by their separate dimensionality (see Table 10.1). Although the same physical item will occasionally appear as both fund and also flow within the same production process (e.g. the use of hammers to hammer hammers), that is typically not the case.

What about the connection between flows and stocks in the production process? The response of Georgescu-Roegen (1971, pp. 223–7) was both insightful and also emphatic:

1. A flow does not necessarily represent either a decrease or an increase in an actual stock of the same substance. For example, the output flow of melted glass from a furnace does not diminish the stock of melted glass within the furnace, nor does that flow accumulate as a stock of molten glass in a warehouse.
2. There are occasional cases in which some sort of material flows from one stock to another. For most cases, however, the connection is between one stock and one flow. That is, a flow is an analytical or actual stock spread over some time interval. For example, one can measure the notional stock of fossil fuels extracted from the Earth's crust since the industrial revolution or the actual stock of plutonium which has accumulated on Earth since the dawn of the nuclear age.
3. The provision of services by a fund requires a duration, and the quantity of service a fund can provide during a time period is *rigidly* determined by its structure. On the other hand, the decumulation of a stock is highly *variable* and constrained only by the availability of transformative funds. For example, an oil refinery can process only so many barrels of oil daily whereas the annual flow of oil extracted from nature

could triple if sufficient resources were invested in oil rigs and other appropriate funds.

Roegen's contribution to production theory, grounded as it was in classical thermodynamics, is not a complete foundation for conceptualising natural capital. One also needs to draw upon the lessons offered by ecological research. As Faber et al. (1995, pp. 44 and 48) have noted:

> [O]rganisms . . . interact with each other as part of their mutual maintenance . . . We term these interactions as services, and the organisms as funds . . . [A]ll organisms are funds, necessarily rendering services to other organisms.

Thus, the transformative activity of funds should be theorised at the scale of populations interacting within an ecosystem, not at the scale of an individual organism.[1]

REVISING THE NATURAL CAPITAL CONCEPT

Putting these methodological dicta to work, let us first identify the fund elements of the global system:

1. $(B_1, \ldots, B_m)$ the populations of non-produced organisms, each population representing a particular biological species;
2. $(K_1, \ldots, K_n)$ the populations of durable, produced means of production (capital goods);
3. L, the population of human producers and their dependents; and
4. A, the Earth's surface area, which serves as a site for other funds' activity and as a solar energy collector.

What distinguishes the produced capital goods (the K_j) from the non-produced biological populations (the B_i)? One might be tempted to say that the capital goods are nonliving machines whereas the non-produced funds are living populations. That notion is incorrect, however, and reflects a narrowly industrial point of view. In fact, produced capital goods include domesticated plants and animals as well as various types of tools, equipment and structures.[2] As Perrings (1987) has implied, the crucial distinction is whether humans exercise a substantial degree of control over another fund or not. Capital goods, then, are the mechanical or biological slaves of humanity. Non-produced organisms, on the other hand, reproduce, develop and evolve without a significant degree of conscious human intervention.

It is commonly argued that humans and their slaves, both biological and mechanical, occupy 'developed' land areas (A_H) whereas non-produced species live on 'undeveloped' land (A_B). This distinction has a great deal of merit, but cannot avoid a certain degree of ambiguity. Rats and viruses largely outside human control thrive in New York and New Delhi, whereas indigenous peoples inhabit the 'wilderness' of the Amazon. Let us assume, however, that particular parcels of land can be classified as either 'settled' or 'wild', but not both, so that $A = A_B + A_H$ (Schröder, 1995).

Upon what does the activity of the various funds depend? Each, in its own distinctive way, requires input flows of energy and of appropriate materials at the appropriate moments.[3] As Georgescu-Roegen (1971, p. 303) insisted, there are two and only two sources of these input flows:

> [M]ankind disposes of two sources of wealth: first, the finite stocks of mineral resources in the Earth's crust which within certain limits we can decumulate into a flow almost at will, and second, a flow of solar radiation the rate of which is not subject to our control.

Each fund also requires information and purpose, as recorded in its genetic code, consciousness and memory, or engineering design (Boulding, 1978; Georgescu-Roegen, 1971; Faber et al., 1995).

Let us denote the solar energy flow by φ and the input flows from inert terrestrial stocks as $x_k \geq 0$, $k = 1, 2, \ldots, p$. Since the activity of funds does not physically consume or annihilate matter or energy, we must expect output flows as well, call them $w_k \geq 0$, $k = 1, 2, \ldots, p$. The non-living stocks from which flows are extracted and into which materials are emitted are denoted by $S_k > 0$, $k = 1, 2, \ldots, p$. For some purposes (such as tracking entropic dissipation of materials), it would be desirable to disaggregate each global stock into a matrix of physically homogeneous, but spatially-specific, stocks.[4] That refinement is not pursued here.

Thermodynamic principles teach us that these connections among funds, flows and stocks are both cyclic and also entropic. With minor exceptions, the physical masses of particular chemical elements remain unchanged as these substances change location, combine chemically with other substances, and migrate between inert stocks and active funds. This conservation of physical masses gives rise to the carbon cycle and other material cycles within the global system. Energy flows, on the other hand, are linear and irreversible from a state of low to high entropy. Hence, we need to take account of an outflow of degraded energy into outer space (Smil, 1991), denoted here by e. These considerations lead us to the picture of our global system presented in Figure 10.1.

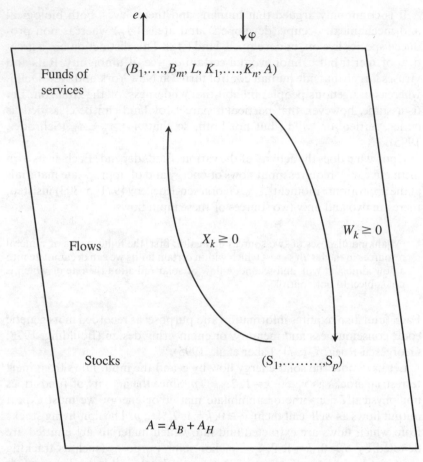

Figure 10.1   The global system

A variety of trends during the modern era can be displayed within this simple framework. These trends include:

1. human population growth ($\Delta L > 0$);
2. human settlement of new territories ($\Delta A_H > 0$);
3. loss of habitats for non-domesticated species ($\Delta A_B < 0$);
4. loss of biodiversity ($\Delta m < 0$);
5. increased specialization within the economic subsystem ($\Delta n > 0$);
6. technological innovation and obsolescence ($\Delta K_j < 0$ for some j; $\Delta K_j > 0$ for other j);

7.   human synthesis of new materials ($\Delta p > 0$)
8.   combustion of fossil fuels ($\Delta e > 0$).

A list of this length and importance suggests that Figure 10.1 provides an effective conceptual framework for thinking about economy–environment interactions.

What, then, are the components of natural capital? Our analytical map of the global system (Figure 10.1) suggests an amazingly diverse list of candidates: (1) the Earth's non-depreciating surface; (2) the solar flux, or perhaps the sun itself; (3) the interacting set of non-produced, but biologically reproducible, populations in various ecosystems; and (4) the physically diverse set of material stocks in the Earth's crust and atmosphere.

By 'amazingly diverse', I mean two very different things. First, the sheer number of non-produced biological populations and inert physical stocks is immense. Millions of species have evolved biologically on this planet, and only a few have been domesticated. There are hundreds of thousands of chemical compounds, many the products of biological evolution but an increasing number the creation of industrial society.

Our list of candidates for inclusion as natural capital is also incredibly diverse for another, more subtle reason: the dimensionality of the candidates. The rate of solar flux is measured in joules per second. The rate of services by natural funds is measured simply by km^2, bees, trees, etc. The rate of input flow from geochemical stocks is measured in kilograms per second. The stocks themselves are measured in kilograms. Hence, issues of both physical diversity and also temporality arise as one seeks to define and measure natural capital.[5]

It seems, therefore, that we face several options as we try to define natural capital:

* Definition 1 (**D1**): (A, B_1, . . ., B_m), or
* Definition 2 (**D2**): **D1** + (S_1, . . ., S_n), or
* Definition 3 (**D3**): **D2** + the capitalised value of φ.

The first definition accepts only non-produced funds as natural capital. Although still physically and biologically diverse, this narrow version avoids the dimensionality issue and focuses attention on the active agency of nature. D1 also theorises natural capital as durable 'fixed assets' and reflects an ecological perspective.

The second and third definitions, on the other hand, acknowledge that funds cannot play their productive roles without access to inventories of 'working capital' (i.e. low-entropy materials and energy). These broader, thermodynamically-informed conceptions of natural capital carry a significant methodological price, however: dimensional as well as numerical complexity.

Note that these three definitions do not distinguish between 'critical' and 'non-critical' forms of natural capital, a topic addressed in Chapter 11. Given the complexity of biogeochemical systems (thresholds, nonlinearities, irreversibilities, mutations and so on), it is difficult to know in advance which particular forms of natural capital are critical to preserve if we are to achieve sustainability. Perhaps the lowly inhabitants of English hedgerows will ultimately turn out to be more significant than stratospheric ozone.

EFFORTS TO MEASURE NATURAL CAPITAL

Several efforts to measure the planet's stock of natural capital have already been undertaken. Dixon and Hamilton (1996), for example, have tried to estimate the instrumental value of several forms of natural wealth. These categories include proved and probable reserves of minerals and fossil fuels, crop and pasturelands and the present value of timber and non-timber benefits of forests. Although these categories do not include all of the physical forms of natural capital and also do not correspond exactly to any one of its three possible definitions, the authors provide some empirical evidence that natural capital is indeed a significant portion of humanity's wealth, especially in the developing nations.

Costanza et al. (1997) have provided empirical estimates of the annual service flow from a substantial portion of the natural capital stock. For most (but not all) of the globe's terrestrial and marine ecosystems, the authors have estimated willingness-to-pay (WTP) at the margin for 17 categories of ecosystem services. Because of its emphasis on living ecosystems, this study did not include the value of nonrenewable fuels, minerals, or the atmosphere in its estimates. Hence, its findings appear to be consistent with D1, my narrowest definition of natural capital.[6]

Because markets for ecosystem services are either imperfect or absent, Costanza et al. found it difficult to estimate marginal WTP for each type of ecosystem service. Their mean flow estimate for an incomplete listing of services equalled $33 trillion per year. This flow estimate, of course, is not the same thing as a capital value. In order to convert this annual service flow into an estimated value for the global stock of natural capital, one first needs to specify a time horizon and then decide whether to discount the values of future ecosystem services and, if so, by how much per annum.

Correcting an error that I committed in an earlier paper on this topic

Table 10.2   Discount rates and uncertainty

Future period	Years hence	Discount rate within period (% per year)
Immediate	1–5	4
Near	6–25	3
Medium	26–75	2
Distant	76–300	1
Far distant	Over 300	0

Source: Weitzman (2001, p. 270).

(England, 1998), I now argue that our time horizon should be a very long, but finite, one. After all, our sun will expire in several million years and all biological species (including our own) are likely to become extinct at some time in the future. For the purposes of this chapter, I will adopt a fairly conservative time horizon of 10 000 years, a period equal in length to the one since settled agriculture emerged in the Middle East.

What annual discount rate should apply during this future of ten millennia? If one were to heed the recommendations of the US Office of Management and Budget, then one would use an annual rate of 7 per cent to capitalise the values of future ecosystem services (Portney and Weyant, 1999, p. 5). Taking this path, one would arrive at a capital value slightly greater than 5.0×10^{15}, an impressive figure indeed. Most of this total represents the discounted values of ecosystem services during the next half century.

Recent theoretical research suggests, however, that it is inappropriate to use the same annual discount rate into the distant future.[7] Weitzman (2001) has argued that serious uncertainties about future economic magnitudes imply smaller discount rates as one imagines years deeper into the future. His argument is persuasive and implies a schedule of discount rates like that in Table 10.2. If one uses this table of discount rates to calculate the present value of global ecosystem services for the next ten thousand years, one arrives at an even more impressive result, 7.3×10^{15}.

CONCLUSIONS

Let me end this chapter with a pair of observations. First, natural capital has become a foundational concept of ecological economics during the past decade or more. Unfortunately, authors have not agreed on the meanings that they give to this concept. These disagreements could result in analytical confusion and costly debates. Utilizing principles from thermodynamics and ecology, I have attempted to demonstrate that natural capital can be given a precise, theoretically-grounded meaning.

Having defined natural capital, one can then try to gauge its magnitude. This effort to measure the stock of natural capital cannot avoid questions of time horizon and discounting of future economic values. Utilizing the value of ecosystem services estimates of Costanza et al. (1997), a time horizon of 10 000 years and the gamma discounting approach of Weitzman (2001), I estimate that the world's stock of natural capital exceeds 7.3×10^{15}. The sheer magnitude of this estimate implies that depleting the stock of natural capital would have monumentally tragic consequences for humanity.

But, of course, the estimate is highly problematic. Frederick et al. (2002), for example, have published a survey of empirical evidence that tends to undermine time discounting altogether. From the standpoint of research strategy, it is preferable that ecological economists refine their measurements of the Index of Sustainable Economic Welfare (ISEW) instead of debating whether precise measurements of the natural capital stock can be achieved.

NOTES

1. For a similar approach, see Boulding (1978, Chapter 4) and Clark and Munro (1994).
2. A proposal to reform the US national income accounts incorporates this assumption. See Bureau of Economic Analysis (1994, Table 1).
3. On the crucial importance of the timing of the inputs to funds, see Georgescu-Roegen (1971, Chapter 9). Note the similarities to Faber and Proops (1990, Chapter 8).
4. Hence, there is a stock of ozone at ground level in Manhattan and a stock of ozone over Antarctica at tropospheric altitudes. Same substance, different consequences for humanity.
5. This complexity of the natural capital concept has been acknowledged by several authors, for example, Berkes and Folke (1994) and Victor (1991). For a valuable discussion of the heterogeneity of a system's elements and the implications for aggregation, see Martel (1996).
6. It is important to note that some nonliving stocks (S_k) are also a source of service flows. The stock of stratospheric ozone, for example, protects humans and other living species from ultraviolet solar radiation.
7. See the essays in Portney and Weyant (1999), for example. Also, refer to Heal (2000, Chapter 9) and Newell and Pizer (2003).

REFERENCES

Ayres, R.U. (1996), 'Statistical measures of unsustainability', *Ecological Economics*, **16**, 239–55.

Berkes, F. and C. Folke (1994), 'Investing in cultural capital for sustainable use of natural capital', in A. Jansson, M. Hammer, C. Folke and R. Costanza (eds), *Investing in Natural Capital*, Washington DC: Island Press, pp. 128–49.

Boulding, K.E. (1978), Ecodynamics, Beverly Hills: Sage.

Bureau of Economic Analysis (1994), 'Integrated economic and environmental satellite accounts', *Survey Current Business*, **74**, 33–49.

Clark, C.W. and G.R. Munro (1994), 'Renewable resources as natural capital: the fishery', in A. Jansson, M. Hammer, C. Folke and R. Costanza (eds), *Investing in Natural Capital*, Washington DC: Island Press, pp. 343–61.

Cleveland, C.J. (1994), 'Re-allocating work between human and natural capital in agriculture: examples from India and the United States', in A. Jansson, M. Hammer, C. Folke and R. Costanza (eds), *Investing in Natural Capital*, Washington DC: Island Press, pp. 179–99.

Costanza, R., R. d'Arge, R. de Groot, S. Farber, M. Grasso, B. Hannon, K. Limburg, S. Naeem, R. O'Neill, J. Parvelo, R. Raskin, P. Sutton and M. van den Belt (1997), 'The value of the world's ecosystem services and natural capital', *Nature*, 15 May 1997, 253–60.

Daly, H. (1994), 'Operationalizing sustainable development by investing in natural capital', in A. Jansson, M. Hammer, C. Folke and R. Costanza (eds), *Investing in Natural Capital*, Washington DC: Island Press, pp. 22–37.

Dixon, J. and K. Hamilton (1996), 'Expanding the measure of wealth', *Finance and Development*, December, 15–18.

Ehrlich, P.R. (1994), 'Ecological economics and the carrying capacity of earth', in A. Jansson, M. Hammer, C. Folke and R. Costanza (eds), *Investing in Natural Capital*, Washington DC: Island Press, pp. 38–56.

England, R.W. (1998), 'Should we pursue measurement of the natural capital stock?', *Ecological Economics*, **27**, 257–66.

Faber, M. and J.L.R Proops (1990), *Evolution, Time, Production and the Environment*, Berlin: Springer-Verlag.

Faber, M., R. Manstetten and J.L.R. Proops (1995), 'On the conceptual foundations of ecological economics: a teleological approach', *Ecological Economics*, **12**, 41–54.

Frederick, S., G. Loewenstein and T. O'Donoghue (2002), 'Time discounting and time preference: a critical review', *Journal of Economic Literature*, **40**, 351–401.

Georgescu-Roegen, N. (1971), *The Entropy Law and the Economic Process*, Cambridge: Harvard University Press.

Heal, G. (2000), *Nature and the Marketplace*, Washington DC: Island Press.

Jannson, A. and B. Jansson (1994), 'Ecosystem properties as a basis for sustainability', in A. Jansson, M. Hammer, C. Folke and R. Costanza (eds), *Investing in Natural Capital*, Washington DC: Island Press, pp. 74–91.

Martel, R.J. (1996), 'Heterogeneity, aggregation, and a meaningful macroeconomics', in D. Colander (ed.), *Beyond Microfoundations: Post Walrasian Macroeconomics*, Cambridge: Cambridge University Press.

Newell, R.G. and W.A. Pizer (2003), ' Discounting the distant future: how much do uncertain rates increase valuations?', *Journal of Environmental Economics and Management*, **46**, 52–71.

Perrings, C. (1987), *Economy and Environment*, Cambridge: Cambridge University Press.

Portney, P.R. and J.P. Weyant (1999), 'Introduction', in P.R. Portney and J.P. Weyant (eds), *Discounting and Intergenerational Equity*, Washington DC: Resources for the Future.

Rosser, J.B., Jr. (1991), *From Catastrophe to Chaos: A General Theory of Economic Discontinuities*, Boston: Kluwer.

Schröder, T. (1995), 'Daly's optimal scale of economic activity', *Ecological Economics*, **14**, 163–4.

Smil, V. (1991), *General Energetics*, New York: John Wiley & Sons.

Victor, P.A. (1991), 'Indicators of sustainable development: some lessons from capital theory', *Ecological Economics*, **4**, 191–213.

Weitzman, M.L. (2001), 'Gamma discounting', *American Economic Review*, **91**, 260–71.

11. Indicators and measures of critical natural capital

Rudolf de Groot, Lars Hein, Carolien Kroeze, Rik Leemans and David Niemeijer

INTRODUCTION

Natural ecosystems contribute to human well-being by providing a multitude of services which have many ecological, economic, and cultural values. Yet, the full value and critical importance of natural ecosystems continues to be underestimated leading to continued loss and degradation of our remaining natural capital. An important issue in environmental policy-making is the problem of determining the extent to which natural ecosystems, and their services, can be considered 'critical' (de Groot et al., 2003).

In the literature, several definitions of critical natural capital have been given. Some examples include the following:

- 'That set of environmental resources which performs important environmental functions and for which no substitutes in terms of human, manufactured, or other natural capital currently exist' (Ekins et al., 2003).
- 'Vital parts of the environment that contribute to life support systems, biodiversity, and other necessary functions denoted as keystone species and processes' (Turner, 1993).
- 'Critical natural capital consists of assets, stock levels, or quality levels that are: (1) highly valued; and either (2) essential to human health, or (3) essential to the efficient functioning of life support systems, or (4) irreplaceable or non-substitutable for all practical purposes (e.g. because of antiquity, complexity, specialization, or location)' (English Nature, 1994).

The above definitions all focus on the interpretation of criticalness of natural capital as natural capital that is 'important' (i.e. crucial or vital). There is, however, another aspect to criticality that relates to the degree to which natural capital is threatened or vulnerable. Thus, certain ecosystems can be considered critical because they are threatened or because they are important or both. The problem for decision-makers is that both importance and threat have many different dimensions and are measured by many different indicators. This leads to decisions based on incomplete information regarding the degree to which the criticality of natural capital can be affected by development decisions. As a result, many development projects lead to undesirable external effects (e.g. the degradation and loss of ecosystems and their services) which can only be repaired or compensated at a very high cost, if at all.

This chapter therefore presents a framework to select indicators that can be used to systematically assess the criticality of ecosystems in terms of their ecological, economic, and cultural importance. It also reveals, in the second major section of the chapter, a range of indicators to describe the changing pressures, state, and impacts of development decisions on natural capital.

In the next four major sections, a series of short case studies is presented describing some examples of sustainability indicators and thresholds for four types of ecosystems:

- a nitrogen-based pressure-index for rivers;
- water quality (state) indicators for wetlands;
- vegetation productivity as an integrative state-indicator for agro-ecosystems in drylands; and
- services and threats associated with forest systems.

The final major section of the chapter draws some conclusions regarding the means by which our integrated approach to critical natural capital indicators can be used as an environmental policy and decision-making tool.

AN INDICATOR FRAMEWORK TO DETERMINE CRITICALITY OF NATURAL CAPITAL

As mentioned in the introduction, the criticality of natural capital has many dimensions. This major section presents a framework to select indicators that can be used to assess the ecological, economic, and cultural importance of ecosystems. Also revealed are a range of indicators to describe the criticality of natural capital in terms of changing pressures, state and impacts on natural capital.

When one considers the many possible dimensions to the criticality of natural capital, it is clearly not easy to measure the effects of certain interventions on the sustainability of natural ecosystems. This measurement problem is made doubly difficult by the many interactions between the various indicators used to reveal the criticality of natural capital. As a result, changes to natural capital that separately might not lead to critical situations – e.g. because individual sustainability thresholds have not been exceeded – might, in combination, jeopardise the integrity and health of the ecosystem in question.

To facilitate decision-making, attempts have been made to find common denominators for the various sets of indicators that describe: (1) the *threat* to natural capital (pressures–state–impact), and (2) the *importance* of remaining natural capital in terms of ecosystem services and values. These attempts are illustratively summarised in Figure 11.1. The figure shows that changes in state variables can lead to changes in the supply of ecosystem services which, in turn, can affect the ecological, economic, and cultural values or importance of the natural capital under consideration.

Natural Capital Threat Assessment

To assess the threats to natural capital, Ten Brink (2000) has developed a natural capital index (NCI) which is defined as the product of ecosystem quantity and quality. For simplicity, ecosystem *quantity* is defined by Brink as the size of the ecosystem or the percentage of area of a country or region covered by ecosystems. Ecosystem *quality*, on the other hand, is defined as the ratio between the current state of the ecosystem and the baseline state, whereby the postulated baseline is the estimated pre-industrial condition of the ecosystem.

As a test-case, Brink applied the NCI concept to the whole of Europe. Based on the CORINE land cover database (http//dataservice.cea.eu.int/ dataservice), the amount and location of natural areas in Europe was determined. Unfortunately, information on ecosystem quality is relatively scarce at the European scale. As a substitute, Ten Brink applied seven ecosystem pressures on the assumption that the lower the ecosystem pressure, the greater the probability of high ecosystem quality, and vice versa. He used geographically explicit data to generate the following biologically relevant pressures:

1.　rate of climate change;
2.　human population density;
3.　consumption and production levels;
4.　isolation/fragmentation of the ecosystem;
5.　acidification;
6.　eutrophication; and
7.　exposure to high ozone concentration.

To arrive at an aggregate percentage figure for ecosystem quality, each pressure variable was preliminary graded on a linear scale from pressure

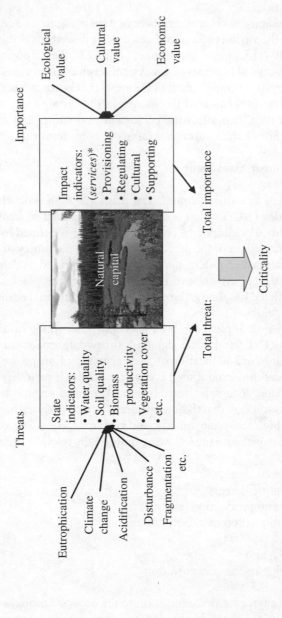

(*) Changes in state indicators lead to changes in supply of ecosystem services which in turn affects the value (importance) of the natural capital in question.

Figure 11.1 Indicator framework to determine criticality of natural capital

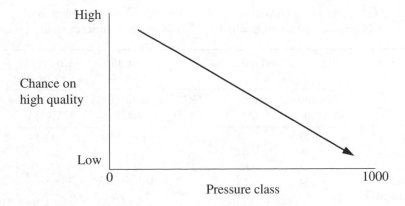

Source: Ten Brink, 2000.

Figure 11.2 Relation between quality and pressure

class 0 (no pressure) to pressure class 1000 (very high pressure) (see Figure 11.2).

To indicate the probability of high ecosystem quality or, alternatively, the total threat to biodiversity, the seven pressure indicators for each 1km^2 grid cell were added to obtain a single pressure index that could range anywhere from 0 to 7000. It was arbitrarily assumed that the chance of high ecosystem quality existing in natural areas with a pressure index greater than 2500 was low.

From column (1) in Table 11.1 below, it is clear that the remaining quantity of natural areas in many European countries constitutes a small percentage of the total land area. In addition, the quality of the natural areas shown in column (2) is very poor. As a consequence, the NCI revealed in column (3) ranges from a low of 0 in the Netherlands, Belgium–Luxembourg, and Germany to a high of 63 in Finland.

Brink (2000) openly admits that this NCI method has many shortcomings and requires further improvement. However, since the underlying assumptions are used consistently, the NCI approach is very useful at revealing the variations between different regions and periods. Indeed, so much so, this NCI method is adopted by the United Nations Convention on Biological Diversity as a key indicator in the assessment of changing biodiversity levels.

Assessment of Natural Capital Importance

To aggregate the economic importance of natural capital, one can monetarily evaluate the services provided by natural ecosystems. The Millennium

Table 11.1   *Towards a critical natural capital index based on* threat *and* importance: *an example of 14 European Union countries*

Country	Threat index (3)			Importance index (4)		Criticalness index (5)
	Quantity × (%) (1)	Quality = (%) (2)	NCI (%) (3)	$billions per year	(%)	[(100 − NCI) × IMP%]/100
Finland	97	65	63	54	38	14.1
Sweden	88	64	56	–	–	–
Greece	48	68	32	–	–	–
Spain	54	54	29	10	7	5
Portugal	57	51	29	2.4	1.7	1.2
EU Average	49	45	22			
United Kingdom	33	50	17	15.3	10.7	8.9
Ireland	22	72	16	22	15.4	12.9
Austria	68	14	9	2.1	1.5	1.4
Italy	42	16	7	7	4.9	4.6
France	35	18	6	12	8.4	7.9
Denmark	13	16	2	2.3	1.6	1.6
Germany	33	0	0	10	7	7
Belgium– Luxembourg	21	0	0	0.65	0.5	0.5
Netherlands	12	0	0	5.2	3.6	3.6

Notes: (1): This column gives the percentage of remaining natural habitat in a given country based on CORINE data base (http//dataservice.eea.eu.int/dataservice).

(2): Based on combination of environmental pressures. A quality of 0 means that the mean pressure index for that country is so high that the chance of a high ecosystem quality is considered very low (see text for further explanation).

(3): The Natural Capital Index designed by ten Brink (2000) can be interpreted as the inverse of the threat to the natural capital in a given country: i.e. a high NCI-value corresponds with a low threat-index.

(4): Ideally, the importance-index should consist of three columns: ecological, economic and cultural importance of the (remaining) natural capital. For simplicity, the importance index uses the average monetary value for the combined services provided by each ecosystem type (see Figure 11.3), multiplied by the total coverage in each country (based on the CORINE land cover data base). No data was found for Sweden on Greece.

Column (5): By multiplying the threat index (i.e. 100 − NCI) with the importance index (%), the (relative) criticality of natural capital in the listed countries is listed in the last column.

Ecosystem Assessment (2003) identified four main types of ecosystem services: (1) provisioning services; (2) regulating services; (3) cultural services; and (4) life-supporting services (see Figure 11.3).

Various authors have attempted to assign monetary values to these four services. Table 11.2 provides a list of aggregated values of the main

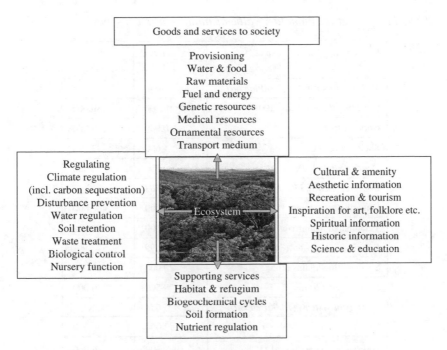

Sources: de Groot et al., 2002 and Millennium Ecosystem Assessment, 2003.

Figure 11.3   Goods and services provided by natural ecosystems

ecosystem types identified by Costanza et al. (1997) based on more than one-hundred individual case studies. While there are several methodological problems that would need to be overcome to increase the accuracy of these aggregations (e.g. scaling issues and dynamic aspects), they nonetheless provide vital information on the relative importance of particular ecosystems to the national or global economy.

Column (4) in Table 11.1 shows the monetary value of the natural capital belonging to 12 European countries (data for Sweden and Greece were not available). These values are used as a proxy for the relative importance of the natural ecosystems in each country. The importance index is calculated by multiplying the average monetary value of the combined services provided by each ecosystem type (see Figure 11.3) with the total coverage of ecosystems in each country (based on the CORINE land cover data base).

Ideally, the different approaches to measuring threat and importance would be combined to determine the criticality of, and thresholds for, sustainable use of ecosystems at a given geographical location. Of course,

Table 11.2　Average monetary value of main ecosystem types

Ecosystem ('Natural Capital')	US$/ha/year (*)	US$/ha (#)
Marine systems (36.122 million ha)	430	
Sea grass & algae beds (200)	19.000	380.000
Coral reefs (62)	6.000	120.000
Shelf sea (2.660)	1.600	32.000
Open ocean (33.200)	250	5.000
Coastal systems (345 e6 Ha)	16.783	
Estuarine ecosytems (180)	23.000	460.000
Tidal marsh/mangroves (165)	10.000	200.000
Riverine/Freshwater (365 e6 Ha)	13.699	
Swamps/floodplains (165)	20.000	400.000
Lakes/rivers (200)	8.500	170.000
Terrestrial systems (13.061 e6 Ha)	638	
Forest – tropical (1.900)	2.000	40.000
Forest – temperate/boreal (2.955)	300	6.000
Grass-/rangelands (3.898)	230	4.600
Tundra (743)	–	–
Ice/rock (1.640)	–	–
Sand desert (1925)	–	–

Notes:
(*) Values calibrated for 1994, based on Costanza et al. (1997).
(#) In case of total loss of an ecosystem, a so-called capital or net present value should be calculated which is the present value of the stream of future benefits that an ecosystem will generate under a particular management regime. Present values are typically obtained by discounting future benefits and costs; the appropriate rates of discount are often a contested issue, particularly in the context of natural resources (Millennium Ecosystem Assessment, 2003). Another way of looking at this is to see the annual benefits as the interest on the Natural Capital providing the goods and services that generate these benefits. At an interest rate of 5% the capital value is 20 × the interest (i.e. annual value).

at the planetary scale, criticalness is infinite because we only have one planet. However, at the national and local scale, trade-offs have to be made based on different gradations of criticality of the natural capital involved.

Overall, Table 11.1 shows that, based on threat alone (i.e. the NCI in column (3)), natural capital is least critical and, thus, least threatened in

Finland, Sweden and Greece. Conversely, it is most critical in the Netherlands, Belgium–Luxembourg and Germany. If we combine the NCI with the importance-criterion, the most critical situations occur where the criticalness index in column (5) is very high. Circumstances of this nature exist in Finland (14.1), Ireland (12.9), the UK (8.9), and France (7.9). Of course, these are very rough approximations, but the approach can help to identify critical situations, especially at more local scales.

In the following sections, four case studies are described that summarise the findings on sustainability indicators, thresholds and the criticality of natural capital for four types of ecosystems: rivers, wetlands, agro-ecosystems in drylands and forests.

SUSTAINABILITY INDICATORS AND THRESHOLDS FOR AQUATIC SYSTEMS: EXAMPLE OF NITROGEN

As previously discussed, the NCI is the product of ecosystem quantity and quality. For aquatic systems, the ecosystem quantity can be considered the total area of water located within a certain region. This information is usually readily available. However, ecosystem quality is more difficult to assess. Several indicators for sustainability can be identified. These can be selected at the level of environmental pressure (e.g. input of a pollutant to a river); the state of the environment (e.g. concentrations of the pollutant in the water); or in terms of its impact on the system (e.g. the number of fish dying from pollution in rivers and coastal waters).

One of the most important threats to many aquatic systems is eutrophication which is caused by excess nutrient levels in rivers. Nitrogen (N) inputs from land are among the most important reasons why eutrophication occurs. Here we discuss the possibility of developing an N-based NCI for rivers and coastal waters. More specifically, we discuss the usefulness of nitrogen as an indicator for ecosystem quality.

Nitrogen in Rivers as an Indicator of Sustainability

Nitrogen is one of the natural compounds found in rivers. There are, nevertheless, three different forms of nitrogen: (1) dissolved inorganic nitrogen which is mainly nitrate and ammonium (DIN); (2) dissolved organic nitrogen (DON); and (3) particulate nitrogen (PN). Of these, DIN is the most relevant form of nitrogen with respect to the environmental impact on rivers, largely because of its complete and direct bio-availability. We therefore focus our attention on DIN in this section.

It is not a simple exercise to determine the extent to which DIN levels in rivers and coastal waters are exceeding natural or desirable levels. Model calculations that indicate current DIN fluxes from world river basins have increased six-fold relative to pre-industrial times (Green et al., 2004). One could easily argue that virtually all world rivers are affected by human activities. Therefore, natural DIN levels cannot be deducted from current measurements. Nevertheless, measurements in relatively unaffected river systems may provide some indication of what natural levels once were. Meybeck (1982) has analysed a number of relatively unpolluted rivers and has shown that there is a wide range of nitrogen levels in rivers of this type. However, on average, the DIN yield in relatively undisturbed rivers is about 40 kg N/km^2 of watershed per year. We have taken this DIN yield as a useful level of comparison.

Figure 11.4 presents calculated DIN yields for 176 of the world's rivers that are included in the N-model. The results indicate that, in 1990, about 60 per cent of these world rivers had DIN yields exceeding the 'natural' level of 40 kg N/km^2 of watershed per year. These rivers cover about 55 per cent of the exoreic surface of the Earth (exoreic meaning 'draining into seas'). By 2050, it is estimated that these percentage will have increased to 75 per cent of the rivers and 75 per cent of the exoreic surface area. Among the rivers with relatively low DIN yields (i.e. less than 40 kg N/km^2 watershed per year in 1990) are the Back, Kazan, Yukon, Mackenzie, Colorado, Lena, Murray-Darling, Rio Grande, Nile, Niger and Euphrates Rivers. The rivers with extremely high DIN yields are, for instance, the Yangtze (961 kg N/km^2 in 1990) while the following rivers have DIN yields exceeding 1000 kg N/km^2 per year: the Hudson, Rhone, Elbe, Ganges, Damra and Pearl. The highest yield was calculated for the River Rhine (1564 kg N/km^2 in 1990).

Critical Loads

So far, we have compared actual or envisaged DIN yields to what could be considered the natural level. Although this is an indication of eutrophication, it does not necessarily reflect the severity of the problem. Many ecosystems can handle some additional N inputs without great difficulty. It would, therefore, be more interesting to compare actual or envisaged DIN yields to some critical loads, reflecting the level that could be added to rivers without ecosystem damage. So far, studies on critical loads for nitrogen inputs have mainly focused on terrestrial systems. For instance, critical loads for N inputs to terrestrial systems have been identified for Europe as part of the so-called RAINS model (Posch et al., 1997; Alcamo et al., 1990). These include maximum inputs of nitrogen

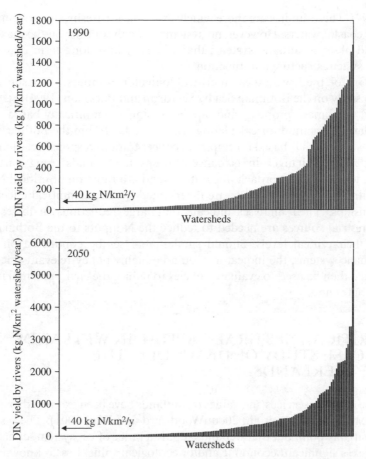

Sources: Seitzinger and Kroeze, 1998; Kroeze and Seitzinger, 1998.

*Figure 11.4   Modelled DIN yields of 176 of the world's rivers in 1990
and 2050*

and sulphur, and take into account their acidifying and eutrophying effects. These critical loads are typically based on mass balances, assuming that part of the nitrogen that enters the system is lost as gaseous dinitrogen (N_2) through denitrification and as nitrate through leaching and runoff.

For river systems and coastal waters, there is a wide variety of studies available on the impact of enhanced N concentrations on the ecosystem, and on the relation between N concentrations and indicators such as oxygen and chlorophyll levels. For individual systems, relations between target levels and N loads have been analysed (e.g. Sverdrup and Barkman,

1994). These studies are more widely available for freshwater systems than for coastal waters. However, no systematic analyses exist on the maximum load of N to aquatic systems that will not cause long term damage to ecosystem structure and function.

One of the few studies on critical loads for N inputs to coastal waters is a study on the Bothnian Sea by Sevrdrup and Barkman (1994). Sevrdrup and Barkman propose and apply a simple empirically-based mass-balancing method for calculating critical loads of N in the Bothnean Sea. This approach is based on empirical concentration–response relationships, and relates changes in N concentrations to N loads using particular models. In their approach, the critical load is a function of critical N concentrations which, in turn, are determined by local empirical effect relationships. Their analyses indicate that large reductions in losses from terrestrial sources are needed to reduce the N inputs to the Bothnian Sea to their critical levels. Should similar analyses be conducted on other aquatic systems, the indicators would be highly policy-relevant since they could then be used to evaluate policies to reduce the environmental impact of nutrients.

CRITICAL NATURAL CAPITAL IN WETLANDS: A CASE STUDY OF DE WIEDEN, THE NETHERLANDS

The multiple services and values of wetlands have been examined in a range of studies (Turner et al., 2000; Woodward and Wui, 2001). These studies invariably point out that wetlands supply a range of ecosystem services that possess significant economic and/or ecological value. Less is known about the amount of critical natural capital that is required to maintain the various services supplied by wetlands. In this major section, we analyse four main services of the De Wieden wetland in the Netherlands and examine to what extent we can define the critical natural capital of this wetland. In this case study, critical natural capital is defined in relation to water quality, since water quality is the main indicator for the capacity of the system to supply the four services. De Wieden is one of the most extensive lowland peatlands in north-western Europe and it includes a large range of different waterbodies (lakes, canals, marshlands), reedlands, extensive agricultural lands and forests. For this study, a case study area has been selected that comprises the central part of De Wieden – in total around 5200 hectares. It includes the four biggest lakes of De Wieden and the surrounding marshlands (see Figure 11.5).

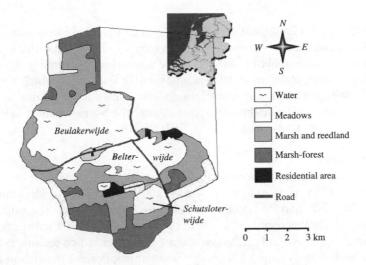

Figure 11.5   Map and location of De Wieden

Services Supplied by De Wieden

The four main ecosystem services supplied by De Wieden are reed cutting, fisheries, recreation and habitat service. These are briefly discussed below.

Reed cutting

The reed of De Wieden has been cut for several centuries and is used mainly for thatched roofs. Reed cutting is practiced on some 1400 hectares (Natuurmonumenten, 2000) and is locally an important industry, employing around 220 people (De Bruin et al., 2001). Most of the reed cutting is done in combination with farming and/or fisheries – a suitable combination given that most of the reed cutting takes place between October and March which follows the April to September period when most farming and fishing activities are conducted.

Fisheries

Professional fishermen fish each of the four lakes of the case study area, which comprises, in total, around 1600 hectares of open water. There are 11 professional fishermen working in the area (Hein, 2004). The most important species is eel, which is fished with hoop nets. Fishermen also collect the whitefish that ends up in the nets, in particular, bream and roach, although the prices of these fish are relatively low (Klinge, 1999).

Natural capital accounting

Recreation
De Wieden is an important area for recreation, attracting visitors on short holidays as well as day-trippers. Visitors enjoy a range of activities including boating, sailing, hiking, fishing, canoeing, surfing, swimming and sunbathing. Every year, some 172 000 people visit De Wieden, of which 100 000 people engage in water sports (Hein, 2004). The benefits of this service accrue to both visitors (who come from all over the Netherlands) and locals employed in the tourism sector.

Habitat service
De Wieden is highly important for biodiversity conservation. It provides a habitat to a wide range of water- and meadow-birds, dragonflies, butterflies, fish and so on, and it contains, together with the adjacent wetland of De Weerribben, the world's only population of a subspecies of the large copper butterfly (*Lyacena dispar*). The otter, which became extinct in the Netherlands some 12 years ago, was reintroduced to the area in June 2002. The area is protected under national laws, is included in the EU habitat and birds directives, and was recently appointed a Ramsar site (November 2002).

Linking the Services to Water Quality

Up to the 1960s, the lakes of De Wieden were oligotrophic. The transparency of the lakes exceeded two metres, which was sufficient to see the lake bottom in most of the area. Since then, however, population pressures in the region have increased and the agricultural production around the lakes has intensified. This has resulted in a rapid increase in the input of nutrients in the area which has caused major ecological changes in the lakes – in particular, a shift to a turbid ecosystem dominated by bream (*Abramis brama*). Since the mid 1970s, nutrient influxes have decreased and the water quality has gradually improved (Van Berkum, 2000). In the four lakes, phosphorus (P) is the main limiting nutrient (Van Berkum, 2000; Waterboard Groot Salland, 2000). Currently, the summer averages for total P are around 0.1 mg/litre, and average transparency has increased to some 40 centimetres (Waterboard Reest en Wieden, 2004). Nevertheless, the water is still eutrophic, turbid, and the fish community remains dominated by bream.

Defining Critical Natural Capital

Defining critical natural capital requires the supply of ecosystem services to be linked to the state of the ecosystem (Ekins et al., 2003). In this case study, two state indicators are considered: phosphorus level and transparency of the lake. These indicators are connected through a process of hysteresis – that is, low phosphorus levels result in high transparency and high phosphorus in low transparency. At intermediate phosphorus levels, the system may exist in either a turbid or clear water state (Scheffer, 1998). If, at the intermediate levels, the total phosphorus concentration is sufficiently low, clear water may also be reached through biomanipulation – for example, changing the species composition of the lake by removing at least 75 per cent of the benthivorous fish. This, in turn, can initiate a shift to clear water (see, for details, Scheffer, 1998). Below, we discuss their relevance for the four services supplied by De Wieden.

Reed cutting
Reed cutting does not depend upon the lake being transparent. It is also relatively insensitive to changes in the phosphorus levels in the water column since reed plants are able to access the substantial amounts of phosphorus stored in the peat layer (Clevering, 1998; Romero et al., 1999).

Fisheries
Regarding fisheries, the main commercial fish, eel, is not sensitive to water transparency because it is essentially nocturnal. It is also relatively insensitive to phosphorus levels (Svedang et al., 1996). To the contrary, the whitefish, and in particular the bream, are dependent upon turbid water. Furthermore, the recent improvement in water quality has resulted in a strong decrease in the supply of one commercially important fish. Pikeperch, an important income earner during the 1970s and 1980s, requires a high turbidity level in the lakes. At present, the phosphorus levels are too low and the water transparency too high for this fish to thrive.

Recreation
Recreation is strongly influenced by both transparency and phosphorus levels. A high transparency provides better quality swimming water and is also more attractive for boaters (Van der Veeren, 2002). Low phosphorus concentrations are required to avoid blooms of blue-green algae during warm summer days.

Habitat service
As for nature conservation, water transparency is particularly important because it strongly influences the capacity of different species to forage in the water. Around 24 threatened species would benefit from a switch to clear water, and there are no rare or threatened species that can be expected to decline from such a shift (Hein, 2004).

Defining Critical Natural Capital in Terms of Water Quality

As mentioned at the beginning of this chapter, critical natural capital can be defined as natural capital which is responsible for important environmental functions that cannot be provided by manufactured capital (Ekins et al., 2003). The aim of this section was to examine the critical water quality required to sustain the four services supplied by the De Wieden wetlands. Several lessons can be obtained from the De Wieden case study. First, the various services depend upon different water quality levels. Whereas recreation and nature conservation benefit from low nutrient levels and clear water, the fisheries sector does not. Reed cutting is not much dependent upon water transparency or phosphorus concentrations. Hence, thresholds for critical natural capital may vary for each service supplied by a system. A change in the system that is beneficial for the supply of one service may impact negatively on other services. This complicates the use of critical natural capital indicators. For De Wieden, it is only possible to define critical natural capital values related to particular management objectives. For instance, if the management objective is to maximise the benefits from recreation and nature conservation – which currently provide some 80 per cent of the economic value of the wetland (Hein, 2004) – a critical natural capital level may be defined in relation to the threshold at which the ecosystem switches from a clear to a turbid water state. This critical natural capital level corresponds to a total phosphorus level in the water of the lakes of 0.03 mg/litre (without the application of bio-manipulation), or 0.09 mg/litre in cases where reductions in nutrient inputs are combined with bio-manipulation techniques in order to achieve clearer water (Hein, 2004).

SUSTAINABILITY INDICATORS AND THRESHOLDS FOR AGRO-ECOSYSTEMS IN DRYLANDS

Drylands cover some 41 per cent of the Earth's land surface and contain a wide range of ecosystems ranging from hyper-arid deserts to semi-arid savannas and dry-subhumid woodlands. Arable farming and livestock herding are the most important sources of livelihood for the majority of the dryland inhabitants, with livestock dominating the drier areas and arable farming dominating the less dry areas (Millennium Ecosystem Assessment, 2003).

A large proportion of all drylands is located in the developing countries of Latin America, Africa and Asia. In these countries, a strong distinction between natural and man-made ecosystems is often hard to draw since farmers do not cut down all trees and shrubs on their fields. They also regularly leave their land as fallow. Herders typically do not enclose their stock on fenced fields but move their animals from one grazing area to another. As a consequence, it is difficult to establish 'natural' or base line values for key environmental sustainability indicators. It is more useful to look at the relative performance of indicators for areas with similar soils, geomorphology and average rainfall.

Threats and Indicators

Unlike wetlands and rivers, eutrophication is not a major issue in most drylands. To the contrary, loss of soil fertility is perhaps the single most important factor that can negatively affect the ability of drylands to deliver ecosystem goods and services. Soil fertility loss, often expressed in terms of declining levels of carbon, nitrogen, phosphorus and potassium in the topsoil, is caused by soil erosion, the removal of crops and crop residues that have taken up soil nutrients and reduced vegetation cover. The latter reduces nutrient cycling and increases the vulnerability of soil to erosion.

A critical indicator of the condition of drylands is soil organic matter. It is directly related to the chemical and physical fertility (and stability) of the soil and indirectly related to the condition of the vegetation. Low soil organic matter goes hand-in-hand with low nitrogen levels and reduced availability of other soil nutrients. Moreover, it increases the soil's vulnerability to erosion and soil crusting. The resulting poor soils also retain less soil moisture, thereby further affecting the ability of the soil to provide ecosystem services. Finally, if vegetation cover is also reduced, soil organic matter further declines since what is forgone is the input of decaying organic material from leaves, stems and roots.

Technically, soil organic matter is an ideal indicator to measure dryland sustainability. While this may not be the case in absolute terms, because the natural levels of organic matter vary with soil type, rainfall regime and geomorphology, it is certainly the case in relative terms if one is comparing the situation in similar areas. However, in practice, measurement of soil organic matter for larger areas in poor countries is impracticable. This implies that we need to seek other proxy indicators to measure sustainability in dryland agro-ecosystems.

A good candidate for a proxy indicator is vegetation productivity. Unlike soil organic matter, vegetation productivity is regularly monitored through remote sensing (natural vegetation and crops) and agricultural statistics (crops only). Vegetation productivity is only a proxy indicator for sustainability because it is affected by a range of factors. For example, natural vegetation productivity is affected by fluctuations in rainfall, grazing and bush fire. Crop productivity, on the other hand, is affected by fluctuations in rainfall, labour availability, market prices, and the use of manure and mineral fertilizer. Not all changes in vegetation productivity can thus be attributed to declining or improving environmental sustainability and care must be taken when interpreting spatial and temporal trends of vegetation productivity.

A natural capital index (NCI) for drylands can thus be operationalised in terms of the relative vegetation productivity of areas with similar socio-economic and environmental characteristics. This can take the form of a spatial comparison of neighbouring areas or a temporal comparison of one and the same area. In either case, averages or running means rather than individual observations must be compared to eliminate the shorter-term effects of factors such as rainfall fluctuations.

Vegetation Productivity as a Sustainability Indicator in the Sahel

Vegetation productivity analyses have been conducted for the African Sahel region. This region has long been considered a prime example of poverty- and overpopulation-induced land degradation, leading some authors to speak of a Sahel Syndrome (Lüdeke et al., 1999). In the Sahel context, overexploitation of natural resources has led to a serious decline in natural capital (for example by loss of fertile topsoil through erosion and loss of biodiversity through overgrazing and deforestation) that was further exacerbated by the droughts of the early 1970s and mid-1980s.

Several recent remote sensing studies have attempted to measure the degradation of natural capital in Sahel by using vegetation productivity as a proxy (Nicholson et al. 1998; Prince et al. 1998; Eklundh and Olsson 2003). These studies, which involve an examination of long-term trends in satellite-based vegetation indices, have, without exception, revealed a strong recovery of vegetation productivity following the major droughts of the 1970s and 1980s. In other words, what was initially interpreted as a permanent decline in natural capital now appears to have been primarily a temporary setback that is part of the normal fluctuations in primary productivity typical of drylands.

Remote sensing studies of this type cover both natural vegetation and crops. In a recent study of the Sahelian country of Burkina Faso, the spatial and temporal characteristics of crop productivity were closely examined. The study led to findings similar to those in relation to natural vegetation productivity (Niemeijer and Mazzucato, 2002).

The findings of these studies highlight several important points. Drylands are characterised by highly dynamic natural and social environments (see Niemeijer, 1996). This makes it difficult to distinguish between tempo-rary changes in the provision of ecosystem goods and services and a more permanent decline in natural capital. Casual observation or measurement can lead to very misleading results that underestimate the resilience of the natural vegetation and land users to cope with drought and other adverse trends. Only long-term measurements, ideally combining remote sensing, crop and livestock statistics and ground-truthing can reveal the true insight into the complex array of factors affecting: (1) the ability of the environment to provide goods and services, and (2) whether this ability has been reduced on a temporary or more permanent basis. In some cases, a spatial analogy can be used whereby areas with similar natural endowments are compared to determine if different forms of land use lead to different productivity levels that, in turn, could be indicative of the effect of land use on natural capital.

Conclusions

The dynamic character of drylands and the large spatial variations in natural endowments make it difficult to define absolute thresholds beyond which natural capital is critically impaired – and leads to lasting negative effects on the provision of goods and services. This, together with the role of technology, is one of the reasons carrying capacity is a problematic concept in drylands. Irrigated agriculture carried out by a small population can lead to serious salinisation problems, whereas a much larger population can carry out sustainable rainfed farming. In all, what works in one area may not work in another.

SUSTAINABILITY INDICATORS AND THRESHOLDS FOR FOREST SYSTEMS

The total area of forests comprises 5322 million hectares or approximately 41 per cent of the Earth's land surface. Forested ecosystems are very diverse and range from the dense rainforests of the tropics to open deciduous woodlands in semi-arid climates, and from evergreen to deciduous, and coniferous to broadleaved. The geographical distribution of the different forests is strongly determined by climate (Cramer and Leemans, 1993). In high latitudes and altitudes, forest boundaries and tree lines are determined by extreme temperatures. Elsewhere, moisture availability largely determines if trees can establish and survive.

According to most definitions, a forest is defined as land that is intended to be used as forested land (i.e. a definition based on use) or as land with a tree canopy cover above some minimum threshold (i.e. a definition based on cover). In the tropics, the minimum threshold is low. The Food and Agricultural Organization (FAO), for example, uses a minimum of 30 per cent cover to define forests in the tropics, while many forest agencies in developed countries use 80 per cent. Forested land that has been harvested but is yet to re-grow is often still categorised as forest in many databases (Watson et al. 2000). These differences in definition make it extremely difficult to develop comprehensive forest assessments.

Importance

In total, over 3.3 billion cubic metres of timber and pulp is delivered yearly by forests. Forests therefore have a significant economic value. There are, however, many other services and functions provided by forests. These include fuel, biodiversity, carbon sequestration, water supply, slope stabilisation and cultural services and functions.

Fuel wood
Wood fuels are the sole source of energy for millions of people. Generally, fuel wood is collected individually and not traded in markets. Additionally, some of the rapidly growing mega-cities in developing countries rely heavily on fuel wood as their main energy source. At the local level, the consequent high demand for fuel wood constitutes a major driver of deforestation but, simultaneously, an important source of income for poor rural people.

Biodiversity
Forested ecosystems provide habitat for half or more of the world's known plant and animal species (Heywood and Watson, 1995). More than 12 per cent of the world's known plant species and about 75 per cent of its mammals are threatened by forest decline. The diversity of tree species is highest in the tropics, while boreal forests in the north contain high levels of unique moss and lichen communities.

Carbon sequestration
Forested ecosystems play a major role in the global carbon cycle and improved management, afforestation, and reduced rates of deforestation could well sequester additional carbon and help to slow the build-up of atmospheric CO_2 concentrations. This could consequently reduce the rate of climate warming (Watson et al., 2000). Forests contribute over two-thirds of global terrestrial Net Primary Production and over three-quarters of global terrestrial Net Biome Production (Cramer et al., 1999).

Water supply
More than three-quarters of the world's freshwater comes from forest catchments. Forest soils capture and store water and, through such buffers, guarantee a supply of water in dryer seasons. Water quality noticeably declines as forest condition and cover decreases. Furthermore, natural hazards such as floods and soil erosion increase.

Slope stabilisation
Forests in mountain areas are an important form of protection against snow avalanches and landslides.

Cultural values
Forests and woodlands constitute the single source of life for millions of indigenous people who live in them. They also provide cultural services in the form of recreational pursuits and spiritual and artistic inspiration.

Numerous non-wood forest services and functions are thus also important. The combined economic value of non-market services may exceed the economic value of direct use of timber and pulp. In many instances, these values are not considered in the determination of forest utility.

Threats

The vigour and extent of forest has been steadily declining throughout human history. Over the last millennium, global forest area has been reduced by half (FAO, 2001). Three-quarters of this loss occurred during the last two centuries. Continuous forests have completely disappeared in 25 countries and another 29 countries have lost more than 90 per cent of these forests. Although forest cover and biomass in Europe and North America is currently increasing, deforestation in the tropics continues at the rate of ten million hectares per year.

Over the longer term, climate change will undoubtedly alter forested ecosystems (McCarthy et al., 2001). Leemans and Eickhout (2004), for example, have calculated that with an increase of 3ºC in the global mean surface temperature, 40 per cent of all forest will depauperate. In addition, the altered climatic conditions will be unsuitable for many forest species in their current locations. This is doubly concerning given that more than 60 per cent of these species are unable to migrate towards more suitable conditions – a consequence of limited dispersal mechanisms and the fragmentation of modern landscapes. Even where sustainable integrated forest management is implemented effectively over the next decades, climate change will further increase the vulnerability of forested ecosystems. Forests are generally resilient ecosystems but this resilience will be rapidly jeopardised.

Major drivers of forest degradation and deforestation include (Lambin et al., 2001; Geist and Lambin, 2002):

- the low political and societal profile of forest in many countries;
- competitive land use;
- slow change of traditional wood production-oriented forest management paradigms;

- the lack of integrated forest management to secure the integrity of the forest ecosystem;
- pollution and climate change;
- an acceleration of natural and human-induced disturbance regimes (especially fire and pests);
- illegal harvesting of forest resources.

In some instance, these drivers amplify the impact of other drivers. For example, the El Niño-induced droughts in 1996–97 allowed much Indonesian forest to be burnt by illegal deforestation practices. These fires affected the air quality of large regions and were even visible in the global atmospheric CO_2 concentrations (Page et al., 2002).

Generally, private forest owners have a better record for sustainable management than governments and larger companies. However, many conditions, such as access to market information, the capacity to manage and cooperation between smallholders to ensure economies of scale and long-term tenure rights, are required for private owners to be effective forest managers.

Indicators and Thresholds

The status of sustainable forests has many dimensions and can be assessed by many criteria and indicators. The most commonly used indicators are the extent of forests, deforestation rates, and forest vitality. Many of these indicators are difficult to measure because the state of forests is the result of many, often opposing, processes. Also, many of the indicators are not able to indicate thresholds beyond which forests rapidly decline. Forests are generally seen as rather resilient ecosystems that can cope with many different stresses.

CONCLUSIONS

From the case studies provided in this chapter, it is clear that determining the criticality of natural capital is not an easy task. Criticality is the result of many factors affecting both the threats to (pressure–state–impact indicators) and the importance of natural capital. Criticality is also based on different value perspectives (ecological, economic and cultural) all of which interact in different ways. As such, a simple and definite answer to the criticality of natural capital is unlikely to be found.

In addition to this, measuring sustainability poses very different problems for different ecosystems. Indeed, the amount of critical capital required to sustain the particular environmental functions within one ecosystem may differ, as was illustrated in the case of the De Wieden wetland.

Yet decisions have to be made about the allocation of resources for the conservation and sustainable use of ecosystems. Finding an appropriate set of indicators therefore remains an important challenge. Incorporation of the notion of critical natural capital and associated indicators in decision support systems is potentially an important innovation. The use of so-called 'causal networks' that allow the selection of a limited number of indicators to be tailored to the research or policy question at hand might well improve the efficiency of selection and use of critical natural capital indicators (Niemeijer and de Groot, in preparation). Such indicators need to be defined having borne in mind the most important environmental functions (goods and services) provided by an ecosystem as well as their dependence on the condition of the critical natural capital that provides them.

REFERENCES

Alcamo J., R. Shaw and L. Hordijk (eds) (1990), *The RAINS Model of Acidification: Science and Strategies in Europe*, Dordrecht, the Netherlands: Kluwer.

Clevering, O.A. (1998), 'An investigation into the effects on growth and morphology of stable and die-back populations of Phragmites australis', *Aquatic Botany*, **60**, 11–25.

Costanza, R., R. d'Arge, R. de Groot, S. Farber, M. Grasso, B. Hannon, K. Limburg, S. Naeem, R. O'Neill, J. Paruelo, R.G. Raskin, P. Sutton and M. van den Belt (1997), 'The value of the world's ecosystem services and natural capital', *Nature*, **387**, 253–60.

Cramer, W., D.W. Kicklighter, A. Bondeau, B. Moore, C. Churkina, B. Nemry, A. Ruimy and A.I. Schloss (1999), 'Comparing global models of terrestrial net primary productivity (NPP): overview and key results', *Global Change Biology*, **5**, 1–15.

Cramer, W.P. and R. Leemans (1993), 'Assessing impacts of climate change on vegetation using climate classification systems', in A.M. Solomon and H.H. Shugart (eds), *Vegetation Dynamics Modelling and Global Change*, New York: Chapman-Hall, pp. 190–217.

De Bruin, R., H. Oostindie and J. Meindertsma (2001), *Strategical Economic Analysis of De Wieden* (in Dutch: *Strategische bedrijfsanalyse in De Wieden*), Wageningen, the Netherlands: Streekwijzer.

De Groot, R.S., M. Wilson and R. Boumans (2002), 'A typology for the description, classification and valuation of ecosystem functions, goods and services', *Ecological Economics*, **41** (3), 393–408.

De Groot, R.S., J.P. van der Perk, A. Chiesura and A.J.H. van Vliet (2003), 'Importance and threat as determining factors for criticality of natural capital', *Ecological Economics*, **44** (2/3), 187–204.

Ekins, P., S. Simon, L. Deutsch, C. Folke and R.S. de Groot (2003), 'A framework for the practical application of the concepts of critical natural capital and strong sustainability', *Ecological Economics*, **44** (2/3), 165–85.

Eklundh, L. and L. Olsson (2003), 'Vegetation index trends for the African Sahel 1982–1999', *Geophysical Research Letters*, **30** (8), 1430.

English Nature (1994), 'Sustainability in practice', *Planning for Environmental Sustainability: Issue Number 1*, Peterborough, UK: English Nature.

FAO (2001), 'Global forest resources assessment 2000: Main report', *FAO Forestry Paper 140*, Rome: Food and Agriculture Organization of the United Nations.

Geist, H.J. and E.F. Lambin (2002), 'Proximate causes and underlying driving forces of tropical deforestation', *Bioscience*, **52**, 143–50.

Green P.A., C.J. Vörösmarty, M. Meybeck, J.N. Galloway, B.J. Peterson and E.W. Boyer (2004), 'Pre-industrial and contemporary fluxes of nitrogen through rivers: a global assessment based on typology', *Biogeochemistry*, **68**, 71–105.

Heywood, V.H. and R.T. Watson (eds) (1995), *Global Biodiversity Assessment*, Cambridge: Cambridge University Press.

Hein, L.G. (2004), 'Optimising the management of complex dynamic ecosystems: an ecological-economic modelling approach', PhD Thesis, Wageningen University.

Klinge, M. (1999), *Fish Management Plan in Northwest Overijssel* (in Dutch: *Visstandbeheersplan Noordwest Overijssel*), Rotterdam, the Netherlands: Witteveen en Bos.

Kroeze C. and S. Seitzinger (1998), 'Nitrogen inputs to rivers, estuaries and continental shelves and related nitrous oxide emissions in 1990 and 2050: a global model', *Nutrient Cycling in Agroecosystems*, **52**, 195–212.

Lambin, E.F., B.L. Turner II, H.J. Geist, S.B. Agbola, A. Angelsen, J.W. Bruce, O. Coomes, R. Dirzo, G. Fischer, C. Folke, P.S. George, K. Homewood, J. Imbernon, R. Leemans, X. Li, E.F. Moran, M. Mortimore, P.S. Ramakrishnan, J.F. Richards, H. Skånes, W.L. Steffen, G.D. Stone, U. Svedin, T.A. Veldkamp, C. Vogel and J. Xu (2001), 'The causes of land-use and land-cover change: moving beyond the myths', *Global Environmental Change – Human and Policy Dimensions*, **11**, 261–9.

Leemans, R. and B. Eickhout (2004), 'Another reason for concern: regional and global impacts on ecosystems for different levels of climate change', *Global Environmental Change*, **14**, 219–28.

Lüdeke, M.K.B., O. Moldenhauer and G. Petschel-Held (1999), 'Rural poverty driven soil degradation under climate change: the sensitivity of the disposition towards the Sahel Syndrome with respect to climate', *Environmental Modeling and Assessment*, **4**, 315–26.

McCarthy, J.J., O.F. Canziani, N. Leary, D.J. Dokken and K.S. White (eds) (2001), *Climate Change 2001: Impacts, Adaptation and Vulnerability*, Cambridge: Cambridge University Press.

Millennium Ecosystem Assessment (2003), *Assessment: Ecosystems and Human Well-being: A Framework for Assessment*, Washington DC: Island Press.

Meybeck M. (1982), 'Carbon, nitrogen and phosphorus transport by world rivers', *American Journal of Sciences*, **282**, 401–50.

Natuurmonumenten (2000), *Nature Vision De Wieden* (in Dutch: *Natuurvisie De Wieden*), 's-Graveland, the Netherlands: Vereniging Natuurmonumenten.

Nicholson, S.E., C.J. Tucker and M.B. Ba (1998), 'Desertification, drought, and surface vegetation: An example from the West African Sahel', *Bulletin of the American Meteorological Society*, **79** (5), 815–29.

Niemeijer, D. (1996), 'The dynamics of African agricultural history: is it time for a new development paradigm?', *Development and Change*, **27** (1), 87–110.

Niemeijer, D. and V. Mazzucato (2002), 'Soil degradation in the West African Sahel: How serious is it?', *Environment*, **44** (2), 20–31.

Niemeijer, D. and R.S. de Groot (in preparation), 'Framing environmental indicators: Moving from causal chains to causal networks'.

Page, S.E., F. Siegert, J.O. Rieley, H.-D.V. Boehm, A. Jayak and S. Limink (2002), 'The amount of carbon released from peat and forest fires in Indonesia during 1997', *Nature*, **420**, 61–5.

Posch M., J.-P. Hettelingh, P.A.M. de Smet and R.J. Downing (eds) (1997), *Calculation and mapping of critical thresholds in Europe: Status Report 1997*, Coordination Center for Effects, RIVM Report 259101007, ISBN No. 90-6960-069-2, Bilthoven, the Netherlands: National Institute for Public Health and the Environment.

Prince, S.D., E. Brown de Colstoun and L.L. Kravitz (1998), 'Evidence from rain-usee efficiencies does not indicate extensive Sahelian desertification', *Global Change Biology*, **4** (4), 359–74.

Romero, J.A., H. Brix and F.A. Comín (1999), 'Interactive effects of N and P growth, nutrient allocation and NH_4 uptake kinetics by Phragmites australis', *Aquatic Botany*, **64**, 369–80.

Scheffer, M. (1998), *Ecology of Shallow Lakes*, Dordrecht, the Netherlands: Kluwer.

Seitzinger, S. and C. Kroeze (1998), 'Global distribution of nitrous oxide production and N inputs in freshwater and coastal marine ecosystems', *Global Biogoechemical Cycles*, **12** (1), 93–113.

Svedang, H., E. Neuman and H. Wiskstrom (1996), 'Maturation patterns in female European eel: age and size at the silver eel stage', *Journal of Fish Biology*, **48**, 342–51.

Sverdrup, H. and A. Barkman (1994), *Critical Loads of Nitrogen for Marine Ecosystems: Suggesting and Applying a Simple Method to the Bothnian Sea*, proceedings of the Grange-over-Sands Workshop, 24–6 October, 1994.

Ten Brink, B.J.E. (2000), *Biodiversity indicators for the OECD Environmental Outlook and Strategy*, RIVM Rapport 402001014, Globo Report Series 25.

Turner, R.K. (ed.) (1993), *Sustainable Environmental Economics and Management. Principles and Practice*, London: Belhaven Press.

Turner, R.K., C.J.M. van den Bergh, T. Soderqvist, A. Barendregt, J. van der Straaten, E. Maltby and E.C. van Ierland (2000), 'Ecological–economic analysis of wetlands: scientific integration for management and policy', *Ecological Economics*, **35**, 7–23.

Van Berkum, J.A. (2000), *Waterplants and De Wieden: Rehabilitation of the Water Quality* (In Dutch: *Waterplant en Wieden: herstel van helder water*), Zwolle, the Netherlands: Waterboard Groot Salland.

Van der Veeren, R.J.H.M. (2002), 'Economic analyses of nutrient abatement policies in the Rhine basin', Ph.D. Thesis Free University Amsterdam, the Netherlands.

Waterboard Reest and Wieden (2004), *Database with Water Quality Monitoring Data Period 1970–2004*, Meppel, The Netherlands: Waterboard Reest en Wieden.

Waterboard Groot Salland (2000), *Watershed Analysis Northwest Overijssel* (in Dutch: *Stroomgebiedsanalyse Noordwest Overijssel*), Zwolle, the Netherlands, Waterboard Groot Salland.

Watson, R.T., I.R. Noble, B. Bolin, N.H. Ravindranath, D.J. Verardo and D.J. Dokken (eds) (2000), *Land Use, Land-Use Change and Forestry*, Cambridge: Cambridge University Press.

Woodward, R.T. and Y. Wui (2001), 'The economic value of wetland services: a meta analysis', *Ecological Economics*, **37**, 257–70.

12. Ecological Footprint accounts for advancing sustainability: measuring human demands on nature

Mathis Wackernagel, Dan Moran, Sahm White and Michael Murray

SUSTAINABILITY IS SPECIFIC

The Problem: Human Demand is Eroding the Planet's Natural Assets[1]

While much discussion of global resources over the last few decades has focused on the depletion of non-renewable resources such as minerals, ores and petroleum, it is increasingly evident that renewable resources, and the ecological services they provide, are also at great or even greater risk (UNEP, Stockholm Environment Institute, 1999; WRI, UNDP, UNEP and World Bank, 2000; Millenium Ecosystem Assessment, 2004). Examples include collapsing fisheries, carbon-induced climate change, stratospheric ozone depletion, species extinction, deforestation, desert-ification and the loss of groundwater in much of the world. The depletion of these assets is serious since people are a part of nature and depend on its steady supply of the basic requirements for life (Krautkraemer, 1998): food, water, energy, fibres, waste sinks and other life-support services. The depletion is particularly serious since the human demand for these resources is still growing, thereby accelerating the liquidation of natural assets.

Out of this concern, the sustainability proposition emerges. Sustainability is a simple idea. It is based on the recognition that when resources are con-sumed faster than they are produced or renewed, the resource is depleted and eventually used up. The elimination of essential resources is fundamen-tally problematic; substitution can be expensive or impossible, especially when considering global ecological resources. Worsening ecological condi-tions threaten people's well-being. When humanity's ecological demands in terms of resource consumption and waste absorption exceed what nature can supply, we move into what is termed 'ecological overshoot' (Meadows et al., 2004). Just as constant erosion of business capital weakens an enterprise, overshoot erodes the planet's 'natural capital', and reduces humanity's ecological resources, our ultimate means of livelihood.[2] Thus, the goal of sustainability implies a commitment to creating satisfying lives for all within the means of nature.

Defining core requirements for sustainability is fairly straightforward. By defining them in specific, observable terms, these requirements become measurable and hence potentially manageable. However, there are numerous practical difficulties associated with attempts at reaching sustainability. One barrier lies in current economic incentives that reward 'unsustainability'. Trying to make the world sustainable is at times frustrating and confusing in our current economic environment, and the task can appear overwhelming. It can also be ominous, since recognising ecological limits challenges how, according to conventional economic development, we organise our lives – even though the purpose of sustainability is to secure our well-being.

At the core of this quest for sustainability is the desire to secure well-being for all people, over the long term. One necessary condition for universal well-being is to be able to live within ecological limits. These limits are not like a rigid wall that brings a speeding car to a halt. In fact, ecological limits can be transgressed easily. More timber can be harvested than re-grows, more fish can be caught than are spawned, more CO_2 can be emitted than nature can reabsorb, and topsoil can be eroded while crops grow. Initially, most of these transgressions go unnoticed.

The importance of avoiding overshoot is still routinely ignored not only in general conversations but also in many public policy discussions of sustainability. In fact, our ability to transgress ecological limits without perceptible consequences has created influential misconceptions in the sustainability debate. For example, there is a perception, often voiced in the business press, that because there are no apparent shortages of raw materials, the concept of limits has been overstated. This confusion is caused by the seeming elasticity of ecological limits, and new technologies that enable rapid resource extraction and easier access to remote locations. But, like in a car low on fuel, accelerating to 90 miles per hour does not disprove the fuel gauge. Similarly, pumping water out of an aquifer more quickly does not change its ultimate capacity or recharge rate.

Once humanity reaches the biological limits or carrying capacity of the planet, further expansion in this direction impoverishes us, since the requirements of human life are not met with the 'interest' of regenerative nature, but by liquidating natural productive capital. This is why systematic resource accounting – documenting the cumulative effect of humanity's consumption of natural capital and generation of waste – is core to achieving sustainability. As long as our society, and particularly governments and business leaders, remain unaware of nature's capacity or how resource use compares to the existing stocks, overshoot may go undetected, increasing the ecological deficit and reducing the biological capacity available for society. The depletion of ecological assets systematically undermines the well-being of people. Livelihoods disappear; irreconcilable conflicts emerge; families are hurt; land becomes barren; and resources become more costly before eventually running out.

Continued overshoot is not inevitable. Humankind can choose to reduce its overall demand through collective action; this is even possible without immediate hardship if we exercise foresight (Brown, 2003; Ehrlich and Ehrlich, 2004; Meadows et al., 2004; Speth, 2004). If humanity does not react in time, we will face the prospect of collapse. No matter the exact circumstances of such a global decline, returning from a state of overshoot necessarily implies a significantly lower level of resource availability compared to previous conditions.

The Goal: Satisfying Human Needs

We need development that enhances people's possibility of having healthy and secure lives, and that is fair to people alive today and in the future, while at the same time maintaining the integrity of our ecological assets. That's what we mean by 'rewarding lives for all within the means of nature'.

Rewarding lives for all is, first of all, possible. But, more importantly, it might be an enabling ingredient for sustainability; that is, universal well-being may not be an attribute of a sustainable society as much as a prerequisite. There are three reasons why this may be the case. First, social and economic inequities threaten political stability and international security. How can one expect constructive cooperation in an increasingly interdependent and fragile world if large social or geographical sectors of humanity do not have access to basic amenities for healthy and secure lives? Recent disputes over issues such as the privatisation of public services, the World Trade Organization's meeting in Cancun, and international acceptance of the Kyoto Protocol have each been fuelled by the moral belief in the equitable use of natural resources. Increasing ecological scarcity and competition for ecological capacity will probably fuel destructive social conflict and degrade our social fabric.

Second, once humanity is in ecological overshoot, development based on expansion of resource consumption becomes a negative-sum game.

If the planet is 'full' of people who are depleting its natural capital, making more stuff cannot make humanity better off. Such development not only appropriates nature's income, but also erodes nature's capacity to provide present and future services. As a consequence, addressing standards of living and equity through increasing resource use becomes a physically impossible strategy that only accentuates the conflict over resources. A genuine approach to sustainability must include more realistic strategies that recognise the implications of ecological limits and their consequences for social equity, rather than just promising more production.

Third, development needs to take advantage of people's desires, rather than ignoring or combating them. Essentially, people want fulfilling lives – an aspiration that can become a positive engine for sustainable development. After all, successful programs for a sustainable society cannot be built on martyrdom and suffering. To make sustainability a reality, we must find ways for people to thrive in all senses without overtaxing the ecosystems that support us.

Most science-based definitions of sustainability recognise these as pillars of sustainability. For example, in *Caring for the Earth*, the World Conservation Union (IUCN), together with the United Nations Environment Programme (UNEP) and the World Wide Fund for Nature (WWF), defined sustainable development as 'improving the quality of human life while living within the [regenerative] capacity of supporting ecosystems' (WCN et al., 1991, p. 10).

Similarly, in their publication, 'Action for global sustainability', the Union of Concerned Scientists argues that 'humanity must learn to live within the limits of natural systems while ensuring an adequate living standard for all people'. The 'four system conditions' of sustainability developed by the Natural Step, under the leadership of Karl-Henrik Robèrt, build on the dual sustainability imperatives: one system condition explains the human imperative while the remaining three detail what living within the means of nature involves.[3]

All of these approaches agree that these two imperatives – staying within the capacity of our ultimate means (our 'natural capital') and reaching our ultimate ends (rewarding lives for everybody) – lie at the centre of the sustainability challenge.

Framing sustainability with these two core requirements makes the concept more tangible and effective. Some may object that this approach leaves out an often-mentioned 'third element' – the economy. But it does not. The economy is the domain where all the action happens. While economic performance is not a goal in itself, it is a means by which to achieve the goal: meeting the human imperative without violating the ecological imperative.

Present Obstacles to Sustainable Resource Management

While simple to spell out, sustainability is hard to implement. Some initiatives have successfully reduced human pressure on distinct ecosystems, but on the whole, humanity has not lived up to the challenge to reduce, or even stabilise human pressure. There are many reasons why this is the case. The most prominent one may be that the challenge seems too daunting. It is daunting for the population of the developed nations, the 'golden billion' that is blessed with unprecedented personal wealth and material abundance, since the current situation provides them with comfortable lives and their privileges might be called into question if the world adopts a sustainable path. It is also daunting for the other six billion-plus members of humanity, since they lack resources for mobilising development that does not liquidate natural and social assets. Many are caught in daily survival struggles that make it nearly impossible to allocate resources for redirecting our common course.

Too few of the institutions serving the developed nations have taken an active stand on sustainability, giving teeth to their policies or making progress toward measuring sustainability. These institutions have a propensity to keep the debate fuzzy, which conveniently diffuses the pressure to address the challenge, thereby maintaining the status quo. This allows such institutions to express their concerns about the future in vague discussion, while not risking accountability for their actions or having to abandon the system that maintains their privileges.

Vagueness is also advanced by a few misconceptions of core concepts. For example, ecological limits are considered to be visible and obvious. But they are not visible. The most influential decision-makers in the world, including most professionals, live urban industrial lives where scarcity is not present in their daily routines. Urban shoppers enjoy an explosion of diverse and refined products, taking for granted the basic supply of energy, clean water and resources that sustain them.

Nor are the limits obvious. As explained above, due to the possibility of overshoot, resource use can increase even after ecological limits have been transgressed. Humanity can, for a while, take more than nature can regenerate. This overshoot eats up nature's reserves and weakens its capacity to regenerate. Without balancing our ecological books, we do not know whether humanity draws on nature's income or nature's capital.

Also, society does not easily perceive ecological limits through a monetary lens. For wealthy people, resource prices have decreased over the years, as pointed out by a litany of economic studies (e.g. Barnett and Morse, 1963; Simon, 1996; Krautkraemer, 1998). Prices only signal availability of a resource on the market, not its availability in the biosphere (Rees and

Wackernagel, 1999). In other words, price is much more a reflection of extractive capability than remaining supply of unextracted resources.

Finally, many have claimed that it is impossible to assess with certainty the remaining stocks of resources. While this cannot be interpreted as a reason for assuming resources to be unlimited, this argument hardly applies to the most critical renewable resources. Many of them are above ground and therefore visible and measurable.

For all these reasons, sustainable resource management is only possible if sustainability is defined in a way that is accountable and consistent with ecological realities. This chapter argues in the following sections that the sustainability approach outlined above can serve as such a consistent and specific accounting framework for meeting the challenge of sustainable resource management.

MEASURING SUSTAINABILITY AND OVERSHOOT

Keeping Track of Humanity's Use of Nature with the Ecological Footprint

As simple and generic as 'living within the means of nature' sounds, the ecological bottom-line condition for sustainability turns out to be a specific, measurable criterion. It is measured by determining how much nature, or, more specifically, regenerative biological capacity, is available and comparing this supply with human demand. Only if annual human demand does not exceed nature's annual supply can we claim to meet the criterion.

The Ecological Footprint methodology provides a natural capital account that can determine at each scale, from the global down to the household, how much of nature's services are appropriated for supporting various activities.

The supply side of the equation is the most straightforward part of the resource assessment. The amount of nature (bioproductive capacity or 'biological capacity') that humanity has available worldwide is given by the size of the planet's areas that are biologically productive.[4] To determine the per capita supply of biological capacity, the biologically productive land and sea that exists in a given year is divided by that year's population. For the year 2001, this resulted in an average of 1.8 hectares per person, while in 1991 it was 2.1 hectares (see Table 12.1).[5]

These hectares we call global hectares since they are hectares of biologically productive space with world-average productivity. Global hectares allow us to standardise Footprints around the world according to their biological potential. One hectare of marginal land would be counted as less than an average global hectare, while a hectare of productive rainforest would appear as more than one global hectare.

Expressed in global hectares, of these 1.8 hectares of available land per person, 0.81 are forests, 0.53 crop land, 0.27 grazing land and 0.13 biologically productive ocean areas, most of which are located on continental shelves. The remainder corresponds to the biological capacity occupied or compromised by built-up areas.

Humanity may want to choose not to use all of the 1.8 global hectares per capita since the human species is not alone on this planet. People share this planet with over 10 million other species – most of which are excluded from the spaces occupied so intensively for human purposes such as industrial agriculture and urban areas.

There is a great range of opinion about how much bioproductive area should be kept relatively untouched for other species, even for the merely utilitarian reason of maintaining species that are necessary for basic life-support services. Some conservation biologists suggest setting aside at least one-quarter for bio-preservation, and in some areas up to 75 per cent. The highest conservation targets in policy documents are far smaller. The authors of the Brundtland Report *Our Common Future* (WCED, 1987) invited the world community to protect 12 per cent of all the biologically productive space, which is politically courageous, but still may be ecologically insufficient.[6] In contrast, leading Harvard biologist, E.O. Wilson, proposes setting aside 50 per cent of the Earth's biological capacity (Wilson, 2002). Still, using the smaller conservation goal put forward in the Brundtland Report, the bioproductive space available per person today shrinks from 1.9 to 1.7 global hectares.

This availability can now be compared to human demand for biological capacity, which is calculated by adding up the areas from all over the world that are occupied to produce the resources they consume and to absorb the waste they generate. This total represents a population's Ecological Footprint, which is proportional to the level of consumption and population size and inversely proportional to the efficiency of the prevailing technology. Non-renewable resources, such as metals, are reflected in the accounts only to the extent that their use damages the biosphere, for instance through mining, processing and consumption. We currently account only for the embodied energy (the total energy used to produce the product and all the resources it is composed of) associated with the use of non-renewable resources.

The Footprint approach we have developed over the decade builds on publicly available statistics from United Nations agencies and aims to provide robust underestimates of human demand on nature in order to avoid exaggerating the severity of the present ecological condition.

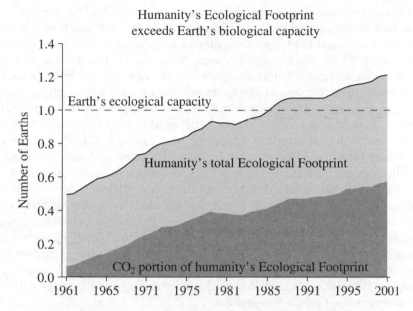

Humanity's Ecological Footprint
exceeds Earth's biological capacity

Note: The Ecological Footprint compares human demand with the regenerative capacity of the biosphere (or the planet's 'biological capacity'). Over the last 40 years, humanity's draw on nature has grown from using 50 per cent of the biosphere's capacity to using 120 per cent – the equivalent of 1.2 Earth's capacity (Wackernagel et al., 2002). With a population of over six billion people, and an average Ecological Footprint of 2.2 global hectares per person, the world is currently operating with an ecological debt of 0.4 global hectares per person. This overuse is possible because resources can be harvested more rapidly than the ecosystem can regenerate them – in other words, by liquidating natural capital rather than living off of interest. Examples of liquidating natural capital include overfishing, overharvesting of timber, and depletion of groundwater.

This overshoot is the globe's ecological deficit. It represents the amount by which the Ecological Footprint of humanity exceeds the biological capacity available to humanity. Individual nations can also run ecological deficits if their Ecological Footprint exceeds the biological capacity of the country. To compensate the deficit, nations can either import resources or liquidate their natural capital stock. For the planet as a whole, the only way to exceed biocapacity is through depletion of natural capital since there is no inter-planetary resource trade.

Figure 12.1 Ecological overshoot

We do this by leaving out aspects that are not conclusively documented. Examples include the use of freshwater with very locally specific impacts, or the emission of a variety of pollutants.

On the flip side of the Footprint equation – that is, the side dealing with biological resources – we have tried to consistently make overestimates. For example, if an area performs multiple functions, it is only counted once in a Footprint assessment. This means that none of the services or resource flows in the Ecological Footprint accounts are provided on the same piece of land or sea space, thereby ensuring that all areas are added only once to the Ecological Footprint. Contrary to some misinterpretations of the ecological footprint, this does not imply that areas are unable to provide a number of services simultaneously, or that the accounts are built on such an assumption. Ecological Footprint accounts merely document to what extent one human use of nature excludes other human uses of nature. For example, if an area provides timber but also, as a secondary function, collects water for agricultural irrigation, the Ecological Footprint only includes timber use, the primary function. In cases of double cropping, both crops are included, but only at their percentage share of the crop area.

Finally, if there is uncertainty about the yields of a given bioproductive space, we use an optimistic figure to provide a conservative estimate of human demand. To make Footprints internationally comparable, we express them in standardised global hectares, as defined above. Hence, each nation's or region's actual productive area is multiplied by the relative productivity ratio of each type of terrain such that global hectares credited to regions with large areas of low productivity are adjusted for comparison with other more productive regions.

Similar to static GDP accounts that document economic performance, Ecological Footprint accounts describe ecological outcomes by documenting human dependence on ecological flows. They do this by using static accounts that add up resource flows as captured by national statistics, and therefore do not depend on extrapolation or an understanding of causal relations. As in the case of GDP accounts, Footprints also provide a myriad of other indicators and subcomponents that can be extracted from the overall accounts. In other words, Footprints offer not just a single result, but a comprehensive accounting system that allows for a variety of additional analyses.[7]

Our latest and most complete estimates, based on 2001 data (WWF, Global Footprint Network and UNEP World Conservation Monitoring Centre, 2004),[8] are revealed in Table 12.1 below. The table compares the Ecological Footprint and the biological capacity of 22 selected countries. This alphabetic list shows the Ecological Footprint and the biological capacity per person as well as the country's population. Of particular note is that the average American required approximately 10 global hectares to provide for his or her consumption. This Ecological Footprint is over five times more than is available per person worldwide. In comparison, the average German's Footprint was half that size (4.8 global hectares per person). To calculate a nation's total Footprint, simply multiply the population by the per capita Footprint. The results for 150 countries are available at www.footprintnetwork.org and www.panda.org/livingplanet.

Table 12.1   Comparison of the Ecological Footprint and the biological capacity of 22 selected countries

	Population	Ecological Footprint	Biological capacity	Ecological deficit (−) or reserve (+)
	[millions]	[global ha/cap]	[global ha/cap]	[global ha/cap]
World	6148	2.2	1.8	−0.4
Argentina	38	2.6	6.7	4.2
Australia	19	7.7	19.2	11.5
Brazil	174	2.2	10.2	8.0
Canada	31	6.4	14.4	8.0
China	1293	1.5	0.8	−0.8
Egypt	69	1.5	0.5	−1.0
France	60	5.8	3.1	−2.8
Germany	82	4.8	1.9	−2.9
India	1033	0.8	0.4	−0.4
Indonesia	214	1.2	1.0	−0.2
Italy	58	3.8	1.1	−2.7
Japan	127	4.3	0.8	−3.6
Korea Republic	47	3.4	0.6	−2.8
Mexico	101	2.5	1.7	−0.8
Netherlands	16	4.7	0.8	−4.0
Pakistan	146	0.7	0.4	−0.3
Philippines	77	1.2	0.6	−0.6
Russia	145	4.4	6.9	2.6
Sweden	9	7.0	9.8	2.7
Thailand	62	1.6	1.0	−0.6
United Kingdom	59	5.4	1.5	−3.9
USA	288	9.5	4.9	−4.7
Combined	*4148*	*2.4*	*1.9*	*−0.5*

Notes: In the last column, negative numbers indicate an ecological *deficit*, positive numbers an ecological *reserve*. All results are expressed in global hectares, hectares of biologically productive space with world-average productivity.

Note that numbers may not always add up due to rounding. These Ecological Footprint results are based on 2001 data (WWF, Living Planet Report 2004)

In addition to using optimistic yield figures and leaving out impacts documented with insufficient data, Ecological Footprint figures are conservative estimates of human demand on nature because they do not include substances and activities that are categorically at odds with sustainability. For example, bio-accumulative toxins such as plutonium, mercury, CFCs, DDT, and PCBs are persistent compounds whose concentration will only rise with continued use. Footprint results point out only how much biological capacity is necessary to maintain the *potentially* sustainable activities of humanity, and say nothing of the activities that are inherently unsustainable.

In spite of these underestimates, the accounts show that global overshoot is occurring. Even though the average Footprint in 2001 of all 6.15 billion people on Earth was 2.2 global hectares per person, significantly smaller than the average of most industrialised nations, humanity's Footprint overall still exceeded the biologically productive capacity that existed worldwide by over 20 per cent. If we set aside 12 per cent of the globe's biological capacity for other species and ban all consumptive human uses in these areas, then overshoot amounts to over 30 per cent of available biocapacity. In other words, it would take nearly 1.3 years to regenerate what humanity consumed during 2001.

The global North–South divide becomes powerfully evident from looking at Footprint results. While the one billion people living in high-income countries (primarily OECD countries)[9] have an average Footprint of 6.4 global hectares per person, the 2 billion people living in lowest income countries use 0.8 global hectares per person. OECD countries' Footprints exceed their own biocapacities by an average of 3.3 global hectares per person (WWF, 2004). This is what we term an 'ecological deficit'. All non-OECD countries put together barely run an ecological deficit since their collective Footprint is about equal to the combined biological capacity available in these countries.

Worldwide distribution of people's Footprints and country's biological capacity has changed over time, too. Countries with rapid population growth lose with equal rapidity their per capita biological capacity. In fact, if increasing pressure on resources leads to a decline of the biological productivity of their ecosystems, this decline proceeds at an even faster rate. Consider Table 12.2 below, that compares the Ecological Footprint and biological capacity of high income, middle income, and low income countries.

Overall, the trend of the last ten-year period of our data, roughly the ten years after the UNCED Rio conference in 1992, shows that per capita Footprints in the wealthy countries increased by 8 per cent per person, while in the rest of the world the per capita Footprint declined by about 8 per cent on average. At the same time, biological capacity per person shrank 12 per cent over that ten-year time period (WWF, 2004).

Table 12.2 Comparison of the Ecological Footprint and the biological capacity of high income, middle income and low income countries

(2001 data)	Population	Ecological Footprint	Biological capacity	Ecological deficit	Per capita Ecological Footprint change 1991–2001	Per capita biocapacity change 1991–2001
	(millions)	(global ha/person)			(% change since 1991)	
High income countries	920	6.4	3.3	3.1	8%	−7%
Middle income countries	2971	1.9	2.0	−0.1	−5%	−10%
Low income countries	2226	0.8	0.7	0.1	−11%	−16%
World	6148	2.2	1.8	0.4	−2%	−12%

Note: While the Ecological Footprint per capita in wealthy countries continued to increase from 1991 to 2001, it decreased on average in the rest of the world. Loss of per capita biological capacity was even more dramatic in poorer countries, mainly driven by population expansion (see: WWF's *Living Planet Report 2004* at www.panda.org/livingplanet).

Limitations of Ecological Footprint Analysis

The Footprint accounts do not attempt to provide the full picture for managing resources sustainably. Since the bias is towards not exaggerating human demand on nature, many significant impacts or resource uses are understated or neglected. Most prominently, the accounts undercount the waste side of the human economy, as well as its dependence on freshwater. Footprint analyses also say nothing about quality of life. They merely reflect the gross, quantifiable draw on nature from a given way of life.

There are many aspects of Footprint accounts that could be enhanced to make them more robust, versatile and sensitive (Wackernagel and Yount, 2000). But these imperfections do not make Footprint accounts 'useless for policy analysis', as van Kooten and Bulte (2000) have claimed. In fact, these authors and others seem caught in a few misconceptions about carrying capacity and Footprint analyses (e.g. van den Bergh and Verbruggen, 1999; VROM Council, 1999; Pearce, 2000). For example, they made the following claims:[10]

- Carrying capacity accounts are questionable since 'the evidence from exercises involving crops and food, and from fuel wood availability, suggests that quite a few African countries have gone well beyond carrying capacity. But this means that they must be steadily dying or starving (independently of any crisis droughts, etc.), or that the numbers are wrong, or that they have found other strategies for coping with physical scarcity' (Pearce, 2000). Our point is that a country with an ecological deficit can cope with the deficit for a limited period of time in two ways. Either it can still afford to import biological capacity from abroad (as in the case of Egypt), or the country overshoots its own biological capacity through the liquidation of natural capital, which is possible for some time. The effect of overshoot is natural capital stock depletion – and, indeed, that is what we are witnessing in many parts of the world, and for the Earth as a whole. Prime examples are loss of forests, arable land, fish stocks and water sources due to over fishing, over harvesting, over grazing and aquifer depletion, each of which temporarily support unsustainable levels of consumption.
- 'Carrying capacity indicators imply zero substitutability between assets' (van Kooten and Bulte, 2000, p. 265). On the contrary, Footprint accounts document how much capacity can be used without depleting the natural capital stock. Since Footprint accounts aggregate a number of ecological services, they imply plenty of substitutability among various natural capital services, possibly exaggerating substitutability

among various land-types. The bottom-line conclusion of Footprint assessment is merely that the overall or aggregate use of natural services must not exceed nature's regeneration rate if overshoot is to be avoided. Focusing on avoiding overshoot may be interpreted as limiting the footprint's utility to strong sustainability – i.e. the credo that securing people's well-being depends on maintaining natural capital. This would be limiting since some argue that 'strong sustainability' is too stringent because other assets such as technology and knowledge can compensate for lost ecological assets. Whether this is the case or not, managing for 'weak sustainability' also needs reliable records of assets. For instance, if Ecological Footprints become larger than the available biological capacity, policy analysts still need measures to track natural capital in order to determine whether the loss is compensated by other kinds of capital gains.

- 'Carrying capacity is irrelevant since resource yields can be increased in the case of renewable resources, and depletion profiles can be extended by technology in the case of non-renewable resources' (Pearce, 2000). Indeed, carrying capacity or biological capacity, as we call it, can be altered. It can be eroded as in the case of desertification, and enhanced as in the case of careful management schemes. That's why Ecological Footprints are always compared to the biological capacity of a given year. Footprints merely document what happened, not what could happen. In fact, as Footprint accounts point out, technological efficiency is one possible strategy to reduce humanity's draw on nature (as long as the efficiency gains are not outpaced by an increase in consumption).

- 'Carrying capacity calculations have limited relevance when trade is possible since the scarce resource can be imported in exchange for another asset in which the exporting nation has a comparative advantage' (Pearce, 2000). Footprint accounts do not argue against trade or for self-sufficiency. They point out that not all countries can be net importers of biological capacity if global overshoot is to be avoided. Footprint accounts make ecological trade imbalance visible and show to what extent nations depend on net imports of ecological services. Further, Pearce's interpretation that shifting to imports from high-yield areas will reduce a country's overall Footprint is incorrect. From a global perspective, the change of ecological burden from such a shift would be a zero-sum game. And, in fact a shift to imports from higher-yield areas does not reduce the importer's Footprint. Also, it is not our point to claim that 'certain economies that are highly urbanised (e.g. Netherlands, Singapore, Hong Kong) can never be sustainable since they can never meet their ecological demands from their own land' (Pearce, 2000). Rather, we point out the ecological impossibility of *all* countries following the Dutch example – or, as pointed out above, that of OECD as a whole.

● 'Carrying capacity is a *survivability* concept not a *sustainability* concept. Survivability is about maximizing the time available on Earth for human species, independently of the quality of that existence' (Pearce, 2000). We agree. Living within carrying capacity is a minimum requirement for sustainability. In other words, living within global carrying capacity is necessary but not sufficient for sustainability. Currently, humanity does not even meet Pearce's survivability criterion. This points to the need to reduce overall human demand and the need for robust carrying capacity accounts to track progress.

● Calculating the fossil fuel Footprints in terms of area needed to absorb the corresponding CO_2 is inadequate according to some critics (van den Bergh and Verbruggen, 1999; Pearce, 2000). We argue that this approach is the prevailing way of dealing (or rather not dealing) with atmospheric CO_2 accumulation. This space represents the degree by which the planet would need to be larger in order to cope with anthropogenic CO_2 output. Finding other ways to combat atmospheric CO_2 accumulation would open dramatic possibilities for reducing humanity's Footprint. Another method of calculating the fossil fuel Footprint is to assess the biological area necessary to produce a substitute. This would lead to even larger Footprints.

In summary, in spite of possibilities for improvement, current Footprint accounts are reasonably robust underestimates of the extent to which nations' (or the world's) ecological demands are exceeding nature's regeneration rate.

Interpreting Ecological Footprint Results

Ecological Footprints and ecological deficits provide us with a number of critical insights. The case for the globe as a whole is simple: most fundamentally, the minimum requirement for global sustainability is that humanity's Footprint must be smaller than the biosphere's biological capacity. In contrast, the implications for nations are less straightforward. For example, is Sweden, with a large Footprint per person but even larger biological capacity per person, ecologically sustainable? What about Egypt, which has a per capita Footprint smaller than the global average biological capacity, yet larger than its domestic biological capacity? Clearly, if everyone in the world led the same lifestyle as the average Swede, the Earth would not be able to sustain its human population for very long. Nor would humanity be sustainable if all countries ran an ecological deficit like Egypt.

While Footprint analyses do not answer the question of whether a given country should live within the world's average biological capacity, or within its national biological capacity, they offer a quantitative measure of the ecological challenges and conflicts humanity needs to resolve if it wants to achieve global sustainability.

Apart from scrutinizing the ecological performance of countries from a number of angles, Ecological Footprints also provide a context for analysing, exposing, and counteracting overshoot.[11] They make a case against running ecological deficits, an issue even more serious than accumulating economic deficits. With an ecological deficit, there is no collateral securing the debt, no intention to pay back future generations, and, without solid Ecological Footprint accounts, no mechanism to document how much we owe. We are writing cheques without balancing the (ecological) books. More specifically, these analyses help to:

- manage common assets more effectively;
- serve as a warning device for economic and military long-term security, and to recognise emerging scarcities and overall global trends;
- recognise (decreasing) options by analysing the compound effect of a number of ecological pressures such as climate change, fisheries collapse, agriculture, forestry conflicts and urban sprawl;
- identify local and global possibilities for climate change mitigation and the competition between domestic sinks, joint implementation and domestic CO_2 reduction; and
- test policy options for future viability and possible unintended consequences.

But there is another benefit to establishing Footprint accounts. A nation profits from analysing its ecological deficit, because reducing it could increase a country's competitiveness. That's what we concluded in *Winners and Losers in Global Competition* (Sturm et al., 2000), a study sponsored by a Swiss bank. For this study, we analysed to what extent national competitiveness as defined by the World Economic Forum correlates with the ecological sustainability and ecological performance of nations. In a more recent piece (Wackernagel et al., 2004b), we compared ecological performance to countries' credit ratings.

Obviously, there are countries that are competitive while still living with an ecological deficit. Examples are Switzerland, Holland, Singapore and Japan. These are all countries that were lucky to enjoy an early head start and accumulate financial assets in a time when expansion was easy. With this financial advantage, they are still able to access resources.

However, in the future, for those countries with ecological deficits that are still competitive, it may be increasingly difficult to maintain or gain competitiveness as the global ecological deficit increases and resources become scarcer. These countries will be wise to reduce their ecological deficit in order to decrease their risk exposure and secure future well-being. Also, countries without ecological deficits will be enticed to become more protective about, and give more care to, their strategic ecological reserves as they become ever more valuable assets. At the same time, both of these strategies strengthen global sustainability.

Non-competitive countries living beyond their biological capacity will have great difficulty keeping afloat. Their ecological deficits may play out as ever larger liabilities. In these countries, sustainability requires a structural change in the economy that will be difficult to achieve with their poor competitive position and their lack of financial assets to pay for such a transition. These countries are faced with the daunting challenge of eliminating their lagging competitiveness, resulting from weak infrastructure and a scarcity of financial resources and training, while at the same time dealing with the liability of an ecological deficit.

This is particularly significant in global terms, since the world economy's ecological deficit is increasing. As this ecological debt builds, ecological productivity is reduced. Because this depletion of natural capital will make it more difficult for countries to cover their ecological debt, it is in the self-interest of nations with an ecological deficit to reduce it. In an ecologically indebted world, it will also become more difficult for every country to cover its ecological deficit by foreign purchasing. In the short term, this predicament can be circumnavigated with strong currencies, improved access to less-exploited resources and cheaper and more efficient extraction methods. In the long term, however, ecological scarcity will be a major brake on the economy. And not only because of resources: waste sinks, currently used almost free of charge, will become a cost factor because of international agreements such as the Kyoto Protocol (carbon dioxide), Montreal (stratospheric ozone-depleting gases), and Basel (the export of industrial wastes). It will therefore be critical for all to reduce ecological deficits with an eye toward creating economic stability and ensuring each nation's quality of life.

For those countries with abundant ecological endowments such as Finland or Sweden, it is easier to remain competitive. They have greater room to manoeuvre. For them, too, it makes strategic sense to restrict their resource consumption and waste production since, as ecological creditors, they are in a position to enhance their current and future competitive advantage. Using up their ecological reserves or even reducing them would jeopardise their future economic advantage, thus making them more vulnerable to economic downturns. It is therefore in the interest of each nation – both creditors and debtors – to reduce their nation's Ecological Footprints.

This insight could serve as an incentive for all countries to reduce their national Footprints and more effectively manage and protect their ecological resources as they increasingly become a strategically significant part of national wealth. If individual countries act in their long-term self-interest, the result will be global sustainability.

CONCLUSION: CHANGE IN FAVOUR OF SUSTAINABILITY IS POSSIBLE

To achieve sustainable resource management, it is essential to abandon fuzzy sustainability concepts and become specific about the core requirements of sustainability. These requirements can be spelled out in explicit terms, the most paramount being to avoid ecological overshoot.

From the perspective of resource management, overshoot may be the most central sustainability concern. The good news is that it can be measured – the bad news is that it is no longer merely a possibility: in many regions and even for the planet as a whole, we are already in ecological overshoot. As pointed out, OECD countries generate not only a disproportionate share of human pressure on the biosphere, but also represent the segment of humanity that exceeds its own biological capacity by the greatest proportions.

While these trends can still be ignored today as long as diminishing reserves of natural capital remain, as the biosphere accumulates an ecological debt, impending costs point clearly to the ultimately overriding undesirability of continuing ecological overshoot on social, economic and security grounds.

Nations can protect themselves from the fallout of overshoot first and foremost by developing ecological accounts that are able to track it. Accounts lead to accountability and eventually appropriate action. Also, governments may want to run effective social marketing campaigns that gather popular support for reducing human pressure. Without his groundwork, it is unlikely that policy reforms for building a sustainable society will be successful.

NOTES

1. The early part of the chapter builds on Hawken and Wackernagel (2000). Later sections expand on Wackernagel (2001) (europa.eu.int/comm/environment/enveco/studies 2. htm#26). An earlier version of this paper was published as Wackernagel et al. (2004a).
2. This approach is consistent with the notion of 'strong sustainability'. Strong sustainability refers to the criterion of not depleting natural capital. Weak sustainability, in contrast, implies no depletion of total capital, i.e. natural as well as human-made capital. This means that natural capital could be diminished as long as it is compensated by a commensurate increase of human-made capital. Apart from the lack of adequate methods to compare the value of human-made and natural capital, such weak sustainability would assume that there is substitutability between human-made and natural capital. While there is some substitutability among different aspects of natural capital (e.g. fuelwood versus bio-fuel from corn), and even some marginal substitutability between natural capital and human-made capital (e.g. fuel-wood versus windmills), there is no absolute substitutability, since human and non-human life depend on the functioning of the biosphere. In the past, weak sustainability may have been a sufficient criterion for beneficial development. But this is no longer the case in a time of global overshoot. Since humanity is using the biosphere's capacity more rapidly than it can regenerate, further trade-offs of building human-made capital at the expense of natural capital undermine the well-being of future generations. Nevertheless, strong sustainability does not condemn humanity into stagnation. On the contrary: stagnation is more likely with weak sustainability policies since they could continue to liquidate natural capital. In contrast, societies adopting strong sustainability could continue to flourish. For example, human-made technology can become more effective in providing services to people without increasing its draw on natural capital, or costs of expanding human infrastructure can be saved by stabilizing or even reducing human population.
3. For more information on the Natural Step, see www.naturalstep.org.
4. We define the biologically productive space on the planet as the area that contain the productive ecosystems. Deserts and highly marginal lands (both of which contain life and significant biodiversity) are excluded. Our rough estimates suggest that this 'biologically productive space' may harbour over 90 per cent of the biosphere's biomass production.
5. One hectare corresponds to 10 000 m^2 or 2.47 acres. One hectare is roughly the size of a soccer field.
6. Today, about 3 per cent of biologically productive space is set aside as protected reserves, worldwide. However, conservation biologists believe that, independent of interspecies fairness, it may require far more merely for the utilitarian goal of biodiversity preservation. Wildlife ecologist and scientific director of the Wildlands Project, Reed Noss, along with Allen Cooperrider, conclude that most regions will need protection of some 25 to 75 per cent of their total land area in core reserves and inner buffer zones. These projections all assume that this acreage is distributed optimally with regard to representation of biodiversity and viability of species, and is well connected within the region and to other reserve networks in neighbouring regions (Noss and Cooperrider, 1994).
7. For more details, visit www.footprintnetwork.org with links to key references. One of the most recent discussion of the national accounts is available in Monfreda et al. (2004).
8. The first study of national Footprints was by Wackernagel et al. (1997). The methods are also described in Wackernagel et al. (1999) and most recently in Wackernagel et al. (2005), online at www.footprintnetwork.org/download.php?id=5.
9. The member countries of the Organization for Economic Co-operation and Development include: Australia, Austria, Belgium, Canada, Czech Republic, Denmark, Finland, France, Germany, Greece, Hungary, Iceland, Ireland, Italy, Japan, Korea, Luxembourg, Mexico, the Netherlands, New Zealand, Norway, Poland, Portugal, Spain, Sweden, Switzerland, Turkey, the United States and the United Kingdom.

10. In view of the limited space, the following list and responses are merely a succinct summary of the arguments. See also Wackernagel and Silverstein (2000).
11. Ecological Footprint accounts provide a variety of tools and indicators for countries, such as the production Footprint, impacts of different sectors, dependencies on particular resources, and so on that can provide a richer picture of the ecological performance of a country. Wackernagel and Yount (2000) give an overview of possible uses of the tool.

REFERENCES

Barnett H. and C. Morse (1963), *Scarcity and Growth*, Baltimore: Johns Hopkins Press.

Brown, L.R. (2003), *Plan B: Rescuing a Planet under Stress and a Civilization in Trouble*, Norton.

Ehrlich, P. and A. Ehrlich (2004), *One With Nineveh: Politics, Consumption, and the Human Future*, Washington, DC: Island Press.

Hawken, P., A. Lovins and L.H. Lovins (1999), *Natural Capitalism*, Boston: Little, Brown.

Hawken, P. and M. Wackernagel (2000), 'Satisfying lives for all within the means of nature: how a honed GRI could advance true sustainability', Boston: GRI/CERES. (http://globalreporting.org/PilotFeedback/ CommissionedFeedback /CommissionedFeedback.htm).

Krautkraemer, J. (1998), 'Nonrenewable resource scarcity', *Journal of Economic Literature*, **36**, 2065–107.

Meadows, D.H., J. Randers and D.L. Meadows (2004), *Limits to Growth: The 30 Year Update*, White River, VT: Chelsea Green.

Monfreda, C., M. Wackernagel and D. Deumling (2004), 'Establishing national natural capital accounts based on detailed ecological footprint and biological capacity accounts', *Land Use Policy*, **21**, 231–46.

Noss, Reed F. and Allen Y. Cooperrider (1994), *Saving Nature's Legacy – Protecting and Restoring Biodiversity*, Washington, DC: Island Press.

Pearce, D. (2000), *Public Policy and Natural Resources Management*, draft paper for DGXI, European Commission.

Pearce, D., E. Barbier and A. Makandya (1989), *Blueprint for a Green Economy*, London: Earthscan.

Pearce, D. and E. Barbier (2000), *Blueprint for a Sustainable Economy*, London: Earthscan.

Rees, W. and M. Wackernagel (1999), 'Monetary analysis: turning a blind eye on sustainability', *Ecological Economics*, **29** (1), 47–52.

Robèrt, K.H. (2000), 'Tools and concepts for sustainable development', *The Journal for Cleaner Production*, **8** (3), 243–54.

Simon, J. (1996), *The Ultimate Resource 2*, Princeton, NJ: Princeton University Press.

Speth, J.G. (2004), *Red Sky at Morning: America and the Crisis of the Global Environment*, Yale, CT: Yale University Press.

Sturm, A., M. Wackernagel and K. Muller (2000), *The Winners and Losers in Global Competition*, Chur/Zurich: Verlag Ruegger.

United Nations Environment Programme (UNEP), Stockholm Environment Institute (1999), *Global Environment Outlook 2000*, New York: Oxford University Press.

van den Bergh, J. and H. Verbruggen (1999), 'Spatial sustainability, trade and indicators: an evaluation of the ecological footprint', *Ecological Economics*, **29** (1), 61–72.

van Kooten, G.C. and E.H. Bulte (2000), *The Economics of Nature: Managing Biological Assets*, Oxford: Blackwell.

VROM Council (1999), *Global Sustainability and the Ecological Footprint*, Advice 016E, The Hague: Council for Housing, Spatial Planning and the Environment.

Wackernagel, M. (2001), 'Advancing sustainable resource management: using ecological footprint analysis for problem formulation, policy development, and communication', prepared for DGXI, European Commission, Redefining Progress, Oakland (europa.eu.int/comm/environment/enveco/studies 2.htm#26).

Wackernagel, M., Larry Onisto, Alejandro Callejas Linares, Ina Susana López Falfán, Jesus Méndez García, Ana Isabel Suárez Guerrero and Ma. Guadalupe Suárez Guerrero (1997), *Ecological Footprints of Nations: How Much Nature Do They Use? How Much Nature Do They Have?*, Commissioned by the Earth Council for the Rio+5 Forum, International Council for Local Environmental Initiatives, Toronto.

Wackernagel, M., Larry Onisto, Patricia Bello, Alejandro Callejas Linares, Ina Susana López Falfán, Jesus Méndez García, Ana Isabel Suárez Guerrero and Ma. Guadalupe Suárez Guerrero (1999), 'National natural capital accounting with the ecological footprint concept', *Ecological Economics*, **29** (3), 375–90.

Wackernagel, M. and J. Silverstein (2000), 'Big things first: focusing on the scale imperative with the ecological footprint', *Ecological Economics*, **32** (3), 391–4.

Wackernagel, M. and J. David Yount (2000), 'Footprints for sustainability: the next steps', *Environment, Development and Sustainability*, **1** (2), 21–42.

Wackernagel, M., S. White and D. Moran (2004a), 'Using ecological footprint accounts: from analysis to applications', *International Journal of Environment and Sustainable Development*, **3** (3/4), 293–315.

Wackernagel, M., Chris Martiniak, Fred Wellington, Chad Monfreda and Steve Goldfinger (2004b), 'Does a nation's ecological performance affect its economic stability? The potential for enhancing sovereign credit risk assessments with ecological resource accounts', in S. Schaltegger and M. Wagner (eds), *Sustainability Performance and Competitiveness* (forthcoming).

Wackernagel, M., Chad Monfreda, Dan Moran, Paul Wermer, Steve Goldfinger, Diand Deumling and Michael Murray (2005), 'National footprint and biocapacity accounts 2005: the underlying calculation method', Oakland, California, (www.footprintnetwork.org/download.php?id=5).

Wilson, E.O. (2002), *The Future of Life*, New York: Alfred A. Knopf.

World Commission on Environment and Development (WCED) (1987), *Our Common Future* (aka: The Brundtland Report), Oxford: Oxford University Press.

World Conservation Union (WCN), United Nations Environment Programme (UNEP), and World Wide Fund for Nature (WWF) (1991), *Caring for the Earth*, World Conservation Union (IUCN), Gland, Switzerland.

World Resources Institute (WRI), United Nations Development Programme (UNDP), UNEP and World Bank (2000), *World Resources 2000–2001, People and Ecosystems: The Fraying Web of Life*, New York: Oxford University Press.

World-Wide Fund for Nature International (WWF), Global Footprint Network, UNEP World Conservation Monitoring Centre, Norwegian School of Management, Centre for Sustainability and the Global Environment (SAGE) –

University of Wisconsin-Madison and WWF-UK, 2004, *Living Planet Report 2004*, WWF, Gland, Switzerland.

World-Wide Fund for Nature International (WWF), Global Footprint Network, UNEP World Conservation Monitoring Centre (2002), *Living Planet Report 2004*, WWF, Gland, Switzerland.

World-Wide Fund for Nature International (WWF) (2004), *Living Planet Report 2004*, at www.panda.org/livingplanet.

13. Managing for sustainability: ecological footprints, ecosystem health and the Forest Capital Index

David Rapport and Ola Ullsten

ECOSYSTEM CHANGE

We may define ecosystems most simply as the interactions of plants and animals with their abiotic environment. As such, we may identify their ecological character in terms of species dominance (plant or animal), energy flux, nutrient flows and the like. Humans are part of these systems, and we may thus also identify ecosystems in terms of their socio-cultural characteristics. Indeed, increasingly, humans have so modified nature, that the socio-economic (and hence culturally determined) impacts are now the dominant force in ecosystem dynamics (Vitousek et al., 1997). Further, increasingly the landscape has been transformed by wholly human-constructed and maintained ecosystems: e.g. agro-ecosystems, agro-forestry, aquaculture, dams (creating mammoth lakes), diversions for rivers (for irrigation, and/or energy) and so forth.

Even without human influence, in the time before *Homosapiens* and our immediate progenitors, two to three million years ago, ecosystems were anything but static. Over various time scales, from geological to ecological, ecosystems undergo change, owing to geological, ecological and evolutionary forces. Large inland seas, which once covered two-thirds of what is now North America, transformed into fertile plains and grasslands. Continents have formed, and migrated over the Earth's surface – propelled by the geological forces of plate tectonics. In these migrations, tropical ecosystems have become arctic, or sub-arctic. Forests have been gained and lost, lakes appear and disappear, and sometimes connect with and disconnect from the sea – as is the history of the great expanse of waters now known as the Baltic Sea.

Today, there is no evidence that these 'larger forces' have been quieted. No doubt they continue to come into play, at gigantic spatial and temporal scales. However, it is evident that at infinitely smaller ecological time scales, humans have become the major influence (and some might say, the major scourge) of the planet's near-term history. It is also evident that the process of human transformation of the Earth's ecosystems is fraught with risks for the future of humanity. There is accumulating evidence that as human populations are swelling to historic highs, the vitality and health of the Earth's ecosystems is sinking to historic lows (Rapport et al., 2003). We are most likely in the early phase of the sixth mass extinction of life on Earth – this one largely triggered by the rapacious use of planetary resources by humans. Healthy ecosystems, which are the very basis of subsistence for rural populations (*World Conservation*, 2004) are not only at risk, but many, including very large ecosystems such as the Mesopotamian Wetlands, are virtually dead. Many others (including the Aral Sea, tropical forests and coral reefs) appear to be in increasingly dire straits.

COGNITION AND HUMAN VALUES

It would seem a natural response in view of these unfolding transformations, to take corrective action as a society, globally, regionally and locally. Indeed, that is the goal of public policy on the environment. And progress has been registered. The Montreal Protocol appears as the Gold Standard for effective international action – resulting in a strong and sustained commitment by the global community to stem the thinning of the Earth's protective troposphere ozone layer by phasing out the use of sources of chlorofluorocarbons, the primary cause of the deterioration in the ozone layer. The Kyoto Accord has, after long delays, been ratified and constitutes a commitment by a majority of nations to stem the release of so-called 'greenhouse' emissions (particularly carbon dioxide). Add to these the Ramsar Convention, Agenda 21, the Law of the Sea, and the work of various regulatory bodies at national and international levels, and there is at our disposal a virtual armada of policies and control mechanisms designed to modify and alleviate human pressures on the Earth's ecosystems.

At the same time, we remain cognisant that these policies, while mostly pointing in the right direction, are thus far insufficient to stem the global tide of ecosystem collapse. It is not the lack of knowledge, per se, that is the issue: there are any number of authoritative reports that document the changing state of the environment and clearly give cause for concern. Rather, it is the lack of political will that appears to be the major barrier to a more concerted effort to bring humankind into balance with their ecosystems. At root, it is human values that need massive transformation – to be an effective counter-balance to the ongoing transformation and degradation of the Earth's ecosystems.

While information on the state of the environment is ever more abundant, very little is in a form readily communicated to the public and decision makers. What is needed is the development of summary trends on the state of the Earth's ecosystems, much as we have summary trends on the state of health of the economy.

This is also the principal motivation behind the proposed Forest Capital Index (FCI). The FCI would assess the environmental sustainability of forest ecosystems. The development of an index, as a summary of trends in the health and vitality of forest ecosystems, has been recommended by the World Commission on Forests and Sustainable Development (Salim and Ullsten, 1999). The FCI is to serve as a composite measurement of the quality of stewardship of the forest capital, and signal its progress or lack thereof to policymakers and the public at large. Since monitoring conditions in the forest and woodland ecosystems are well established, the development of an FCI represents a unique opportunity to communicate, in a synthetic manner, the results of forest monitoring to both decision makers and the public. Before turning to the description of the FCI, we discuss two complementary concepts, namely that of 'ecological footprint', and that of 'ecosystem health'. These notions provide a conceptual underpinning for the choice of indicators of the FCI.

ECOLOGICAL FOOTPRINTS AND ECOSYSTEM HEALTH

Ever since the publication of *An Essay on the Principle of Population* by Thomas Malthus (Malthus, 1803) there have been concerns that the human population might increase beyond the Earth's carrying capacity (Hardin, 1968; Catton, 1982). While it has long been recognized that humans are part of the ecology of nature (Hawley, 1950), far too little attention has been given to the fact that humans are fully dependent on the well-functioning of the Earth's ecosystems, and thus that, in order to achieve a reasonable quality of life, it is as essential to protect the health of ecosystems as it is to achieve economic viability.

There are various ways to portray pressures on and changes in the environment. Pressures can be measured in terms of the 'ecological footprint', a concept that measures the per capita dependence on natural resources. The response of ecosystems to these pressures can be measured in terms of the degree of 'ecological integrity' – the degree to which ecosystems are transformed from a 'pristine' state, or in terms of ecosystem health – that is in terms of the ecosystem's capacity to maintain its structure and function. These three concepts are closely interrelated (Rapport, 2000). Yet each has its unique focus and its particular strengths and weaknesses. All three, however, reach common ground in drawing attention in various ways to the growing loss of harmony between humans and the ecosystems in which they live.

The notion of 'ecological footprint' (EF) adds a special contribution in efforts to come to grips with the Earth's carrying capacity by drawing attention to the land area required per capita to support current consumption levels. In most cases, populations require for more land to sustain their consumption than they physically occupy.

The EF can be measured in a variety of ways: e.g. in terms of the net carbon released for a per capita increase in population in a particular area (Rees, 1999), or in terms of the hectares of land required to sustain a given geographical unit. In essence, the EF is an '. . . accounting tool that enables us to estimate the resource consumption and waste assimilation requirements of a defined human population or economy in terms of a corresponding productive land area' (Wackernagel and Rees, 1996).

Thus the EF portrays the degree to which human societies are parasitic on nature (Peacock, 1999). For example, the ecological support for the human population in the geographical unit of the city of Vancouver (British Columbia, Canada), which is contained in an area of 11 420 hectares, draws upon a productive land area of 2 360 600 hectares (Rees, 1999). Thus the ecological footprint of Vancouver is 207 times the area occupied by its citizens. Rees terms this ratio the 'overshoot factor'. For the lower Fraser Basin as a whole (the ecological region in which Vancouver is situated), the land area occupied is 830 000 hectares, while the ecological footprint is estimated to be 10 000 000 hectares, or an overshoot factor of 12. At the very least, such calculations provide a picture of the relative degree of exploitation amongst different communities and regions.

The ecological footprint of North America is at least an order of magnitude greater than the footprint of India. There is no iron-clad rule that this need be the case, since with wealth comes the capacity to design 'smart' systems that conserve resources while furthering economic objectives. And to some degree, this has taken place (for example, hybrid cars, harnessing wind power, 'smart' houses, and so on) but overall, any gains made in this respect have been overridden by increased per capita consumption. In fact, very few nations have a footprint small enough to ensure sustainability (Wackernagel and Rees, 1996; Chapter 12). Further, the EF calculations suggest that if all countries were to live at the level of consumption of North Americans (as many aspire), it would take 3 or 4 Planet Earths to accommodate this on a sustainable basis.

Calculations on a nation-wide basis are equally revealing of vast inequalities. The economically privileged nations have a far larger ecological footprint than economically disadvantaged nations do. The rich nations can only sustain their lavish life-styles (relative to the rest of the world) by drawing down the natural capital of the poor countries.

The concept of 'ecological integrity' is another means to reflect the degree of harmony or balance between humans and their ecosystems. Instead of focusing on resource consumption per capita, this concept focuses on the degree to which any given ecosystem can said to be in its 'natural' state – a state taken as that which would exist in the absence of humans, or human influences. Given that humans are part of ecosystems, the notion of a 'natural state' as one only existing with the exclusion of humans, constructs an artificial reality. Yet the purpose of such a construct is clear enough. The issue is, essentially, how far has the condition of nature been transformed by humans and, in the process, deformed through human activity? Indices of ecological integrity have been constructed, particularly for aquatic ecosystems, based upon a dozen or so metrics, each of which relates to some aspect of the structure or function of these complex systems (Karr and Chu, 1999). Commonly used metrics include biodiversity, nutrients, toxic substances, community structure, disease prevalence and the health of key species. An index of biotic integrity allows policy makers to assess the degree to which aquatic and terrestrial ecosystems have been altered through human use.

This works best in those cases where one may safely presume that the more the system departs from 'natural' the less suitable it is for human occupation. In essence this perspective measures any departure from 'natural conditions' as degradation. While this may be useful in monitoring wilderness reserves or other protected areas, it is less relevant to human-dominated ecosystems, which by their very nature are generally greatly transformed from their condition before human colonization. For these situations, which in fact now envelope most of the Earth's ecosystems, the key environmental question is not the degree to which these systems have departed from a 'natural' state, but rather the degree to which these systems maintain their full capacity to function. Such considerations lead us directly to the notion of ecosystem health.

It has been recently reaffirmed by many international organizations (for example the World Bank, the World Resources Institute and the United Nations Environment Programme) that the vitality of the Earth's ecosystems ought to be a key priority for the 21st century (United Nations Development Programme et al., 2001), and further, that healthy ecosystems are essential to ensure food security for rural peoples (World Conservation, 2004). The notion of ecosystem health forms the third underlying concept that has stimulated the development of the forest capital index.

Healthy ecosystems may be defined as those that are free from ecosystem 'distress syndrome' (Rapport et al., 1985) and maintain their resilience, organization, and vitality (Rapport et al., 1998a, 1998b; Rapport and Whitford, 1999). Ecosystem distress syndrome is characterized by declines in biodiversity, declines in long-lived native species, the leaching of nutrients from terrestrial ecosystems, the accumulation of nutrients in aquatic ecosystems, reduced counter-active capacity (or resilience) that is, the capacity to recover from disturbance, and increased disease susceptibility (in both humans and other biotic components of the system).

The notion of 'resilience' is particularly important, as it measures the capacity of ecosystems to recover from perturbations such as fire, flood, drought and so on. Such perturbations are a key mechanism by which ecosystems adapt to changing environments (Whitford et al., 1999). However, ecosystems altered by anthropogenic stress invariably exhibit the loss of resilience (Whitford et al., 1999) and this loss results in a permanent loss of ecosystem function. The loss of ecosystem functions has negative consequences for human well-being in terms of human health, sustainable livelihoods and socio-cultural well-being (Rapport et al., 1998a, 1998b; Costanza et al., 1997; Maffi 2001).

In short, ecosystem health can be broadly defined as the 'capacity for maintaining biological and social organization on the one hand and the ability to achieve reasonable and sustainable human goals on the other' (Nielsen, 1999, p. 66). Quantitative measures may be found, not only in the biophysical attributes, but as well in social, economic, cultural and human health indicators (Rapport, 1995; Rapport et al., 2003).

With respect to human health, degraded ecosystems often increase health vulnerabilities (Rapport and Lee, 2003). For example, outbreaks of cholera in coastal communities, have been associated with eutrophication of coastal marine waters. Eutrophication favours the proliferation of the pathogen, *Vibrio cholerae*, commonly found in coastal marine systems associated with phytoplankton and zooplankton communities (Huq and Colwell, 1996). In nutrient enriched waters (for example, as a result of fertilizer run-off from agricultural practices) and under suitable temperature and salinity conditions, non-virulent (dormant) forms of the bacteria become virulent (actively reproductive). Thus, as coastal marine ecosystems become nutrient-enriched as a result of agricultural runoff as well as from urban and industrial inputs, conditions become more favourable for the transformation of *Vibrio cholerae* to a virulent reproductive state, which in turn increases the likelihood of contracting the disease due to more humans coming into contact with the pathogen through contaminated water and/or food supplies. Many other human pathogens are similarly traceable to ecological imbalances. These include outbreaks of Lyme disease, dengue fever and swine flu (McMichael, 1997; Patz, 1996; Rapport and Lee, 2003).

SUSTAINING HUMAN FUTURES

Once ecosystem health has become severely compromised, recovery may become impossible, at least in ecological time, even if the initial causes of ecosystem pathology have been removed (Rapport and Whitford, 1999). Overgrazing by cattle transformed a once healthy arid grassland in SW New Mexico (USA) into a shrub land dominated by creosote bush and mesquite (Whitford, 1995). Once these shrubs become dominant they cause further depletion of soil nutrients and thus entrain a process of desertification.

Thus information on conditions and trends within ecosystems ought to take into account not only indicators of the per capita utilization of the Earth's resources (the ecological footprint), but also indicators of the viability of human-dominated ecosystems (i.e. indicators of ecological integrity and ecosystem health). Thus, there appears to be a dual policy challenge: both to reduce the size of the ecological footprint and to improve the health of ecosystems. These twin objectives appear to be complementary and interdependent. To meet this challenge requires public information that summarizes in some reasonable way, the overall situation with respect to the changes in the viability of the world's ecosystems. One ambitious plan to do just that for one of the world's most prominent and threatened ecosystems, namely forest ecosystems, is the construction of an index of forest sustainability, known as the Forest Capital Index.

THE FOREST CAPITAL INDEX

The Forest Capital Index (FCI) was proposed as a broad measure of the sustainability and health of forest-dominated ecosystems. In recommending the development of such an index, the World Commission on Forests and Sustainable Development (WCFSD) took into account the many complex manifestations of change, from the biophysical to the socio-economic and cultural (Salim and Ullsten, 1999). The Commission recognized that, for policy purposes, it would be highly desirable to condense these various indicators into an index that represents trends in the state of the global and regional forest ecosystems. Here we present an abbreviated description of the FCI, adapted from Ullsten et al. (2004).

In economic discourse, 'capital' refers to a stock of productive resources. Thus a literal translation of the term 'capital' in the forest context might refer to the stock of standing timber, or biomass, or some such equivalent. However the WCFSD, as indicated above, adopted a broader perspective. They not only included a measure of the stock of standing timber (or forest cover) but also took account of the degree to which the functions of forest ecosystems are maintained. This requires the assessment of productivity, nutrient cycling, the maintenance of cultural values, practices and uses and so on.

A major challenge is how to incorporate all of these dimensions in a way in which policy makers and the public will readily understand the changes in conditions and trends in the health of forest ecosystems. One way of meeting this challenge is to construct an index, i.e. the FCI, by which a single number would take into account ecological, socio-economic, and cultural aspects of forest ecosystems.

There are many potential ways to do this, but all run into one fundamental problem – namely, that the various indicators that comprise the FCI lack a common denominator.

However this remains an issue for the construction of most indices in which disparate information is brought together. The key here is that whatever index is produced, there is a need for transparency – that is, the calculation of the index based on various indicators needs to be explicit and the trends in the individual metrics that go into the index should also be displayed.

For many decades, a growing number of experts, policy makers, NGOs, and intergovernmental organizations have called for the sustainable use of natural resources including forests, and ways to measure the components of sustainability (ITTO, 1992; UNCED, 1992; Anonymous, 1994, 1995; Salim and Ullsten, 1999; Rapport et al., 2003). In 1987, the World Commission on Environment and Development (WCED) popularized the term 'sustainable development', which means satisfying needs for livelihoods without eroding the natural capital. In economic terms, this translates as living off the 'interest', not the 'capital'.

In 1992, the United Nations Conference on Environment and Development (UNCED, the Earth Summit) called for development of indicators of sustainable development, as means for monitoring progress (UNCED, 1992). The Intergovernmental Forum on Forests (IFF), established in 1994, and its successor, the UN Forest Forum (UNFF), discussed the need for the systematic evaluation of global forests.

Many agencies and programs carry out the monitoring of the extent and incremental gain or loss of forests, and publish periodic measures of the extent of the world's forest cover. The Helsinki Processes (Anonymous, 1994) and Montreal Processes (Anonymous, 1995) have identified a number of indicators of forest condition based on prior work by the UNCED (1992) and ITTO (1992). A number of other initiatives related to forests and forestry indicators have arisen – notably, UNEP's Global Environment Outlook program (UNEP, 2003), the Food and Agriculture Organization's

State of the World's Forests (FAO, 2003), the Canadian Forest Service's Criteria and Indicators program, the World Resource Institute's Pilot Analysis of Global Ecosystems (Matthews et al., 2000), NASA, the USEPA forest monitoring programs, and State of the Environment reporting in a number of countries. Agencies such as the World Bank, FAO, OECD and NASA also compile and list hundreds of indicators on forest condition and associated socio-economic variables. A number of initiatives in forest certification have emerged to encourage sustainable use of forest resources, such as the Forest Stewardship Council (http://www.fscoax.org) and the Pan European Forest Certification (http://www.pefc.org).

The construction of a Forest Capital Index (FCI) is a logical next step in support of sustainable utilization and conservation of the world's forest resources. The FCI is a way of combining relevant but complicated data related to the trends and condition of forest ecosystems composed of individual indicators which, when considered individually, provide only partial answers to forest sustainability questions. Large sets of indicators, while they may be of enormous benefit to scientific research, generally confuse the public and decision makers. What they need to know is simply whether forests are moving towards or away from sustainability. An FCI designed as a performance index based on sub-indices ought to be capable of providing this assessment. The FCI captures aggregate or overall trends understandable to both decision makers and the public.

The FCI is thus directed towards aggregating and communicating important information on the state of the world's forest-dominated ecosystems. The FCI provides a single number, based upon selected indicators that measure various aspects of forested landscapes. Trends in the FCI will reveal the degree to which the health of forested ecosystems is being compromised or improved through human activity. Ideally, the FCI would apply to all forests, natural and managed, regardless of size and type, and go beyond giving guidance for forestry practices alone.

Andreasen et al. (2001) discuss the general criteria for a useful index of integrity (and health) of terrestrial ecosystems: it must be multi-scaled, grounded in natural history, relevant and helpful, flexible, measurable and comprehensive (i.e. it must incorporate components of ecosystem composition, structure and function). The FCI takes these same considerations into account and might proceed by:

1. selecting a limited number of indicators that measure the status of forest resources and services of forest-dominated ecosystems;
2. aggregating the chosen indicators and targets into a regularly updated Index;

3. applying the chosen FCI methodology in a series of pilot studies in countries with different types of forest dominated landscapes and phases in the development of the use and exploitation of forests, using the same measurement protocol at all sites;
4. studying the institutional arrangements needed for gathering, keeping and updating data over time and facilitating their application in national forest policies; and
5. assessing changes in the FCI over time.

Selecting Indicators

The development of the FCI would build upon a range of existing forest ecosystem monitoring and measurement efforts and make use of indicators that have been developed from processes such as the Criteria and Indicators (C&I) reporting developed under the Montreal and Helsinki Processes (Anonymous, 1994, 1995), which serve as measures of sustainable forestry.

The individual components ought to satisfy the following conditions: they should be sensitive to change; respond to stress in a predictable and unambiguous manner; be supported by precise, accurate, reliable and, if possible, readily available data for all nations; be verifiable and reproducible; and be understood and accepted by intended users. A good indicator will have a direct link from environmental measurement to practical policy options (Dale and Beyeler, 2001). The indicator data must also be objectively collected, and representative of a wide range of forest types.

Aggregating Indicators into a Forest Capital Index

Once selected, the indicators need to be aggregated into an index reflecting the overall health of forest dominated ecosystems (Rapport et al., 1985, 1998a, 1998b; Rapport and Whitford, 1999). This FCI, when regularly updated, should permit evaluation of progress, or lack thereof, in sustaining the health of forest dominated ecosystems.

Aggregation of indicators into an index involves the construction of a mathematical model that defines the relationships of the component indicators. Aggregation can be complicated, partly because different indicators are reported in different units of measure on different time and spatial scales. Also, various components may be given different relative weights (e.g. would forest cover changes have the same significance (weight) as changes in diversity of trees or bird species or overall biodiversity?). Further, one must account for non-linear behaviour, in that changes in some components of the index, beyond a threshold, may have a more dramatic impact on ecosystem health than changes in other components.

Thus weighting the importance of the indicators is a significant issue. Weighting the index, as well as indicator choice, is ultimately a subjective decision and open to criticism (Andreasen et al., 2001). However, if the process of aggregation and weighting of the index is carried out by means of a careful, scientific, and thorough consultation process, the index will be accepted by a reasonable majority of stakeholders. Whatever system is chosen, it should be constructed such that it can apply equally across all regions, ensuring the validity of making comparisons between countries.

One of the dangers in any weighting scheme is that there is the potential for eclipsing the value of a particularly critical component of an index (Ott, 1978). For example, suppose that in constructing the FCI, particular soil ions, such as calcium ($Ca+$), are taken into account. $Ca+$ is a critical indicator of forest health and its decline may signal the onset of a potentially serious risk to forest ecosystems. Yet if the concentration of this particular ion is only one small component of the FCI, this decline could easily be overlooked. This is especially likely if other indicators of forest ecosystem health, such as productivity, have not yet responded to this change. In cases like this it is likely that the value of an FCI would fail to signal an important change in the health of the forests since the impact on the FCI, owing to declining levels of soil Ca, would be buried or 'eclipsed' by the lack of change in other variables.

Another example of 'eclipsing' would be the sudden disappearance of a 'sentinel' species, for example, an interior forest bird species, while other indicators of forest health, such as primary productivity, forest cover, soil nutrients and so on remain unchanged. Here too, an FCI would fail to register the loss of a potential 'miner's canary' of the health of forested ecosystems.

The only way to avoid such pitfalls, which are inherent in any index of 'health' status, would be to also examine the trends in the various indicators comprising the index, in order to be sure that such vital information is not overlooked. In essence, both the index and its constituent indicators must be examined simultaneously, as part of the same information system. For decision makers, this might be accomplished by using a diagrammatic approach, such as taken in the 2002 Environmental Sustainability Index (World Economic Forum et al., 2002). This approach would serve to highlight worrisome changes in any critical component of an index. At the same time, the index provides the overall trends in forest health in a format that is more readily understood by decision makers and the public at large.

To clarify this further, we draw an analogy to commonly used environmental indices such as air pollution or water quality. The public (and decision makers) are of course interested mainly in the general trends, and in particular, whether critical thresholds which might endanger public health have been reached. With air pollution, for example, certain levels of pollution trigger public response such as reducing industrial activity that emits significant amounts of air pollution, or restricting the use of automobiles in the impacted areas. At the same time it is understood that an overall air quality index does not fully reflect all risks. For example, if there was a surge in 'small particulates', which can be a serious respiratory health risk, this might be eclipsed by the broad spectrum of other indicators that comprise the air pollution index. In such a case, it would be essential to provide the public and policy makers with supplementary information to the effect that a particularly worrisome component of air quality has been observed to be on the increase, even if the overall index has been little changed.

Studying Institutional Arrangements for Collection and Upkeep of Data

An important prerequisite for implementing the FCI is an understanding of the institutional arrangements needed for gathering, keeping and updating data over time and thus making the index operational for the adoption of appropriate policies and as a tool for informing the public. A clear understanding is required of who will produce the FCI, and how, and who will use it. Governmental, business, and NGO and community audiences have different needs, capacities and perspectives that may need to be considered. They may also be wedded to particular performance measurement tools and systems into which the FCI might need to be integrated. Should the FCI be calculated by independent parties in various parts of the world, it would need to conform to certain criteria. One would need to understand the type of capacities needed, capacity gaps, and offer strategies for addressing them. A key purpose for the FCI is to improve forest ecosystem-related decision making. Use of the FCI under different institutional conditions must be demonstrated so that actual benefits can occur.

Calculating the index will be computation-intensive and require specialized software. The software will be needed to perform the required calculations, to serve as a data storage facility and to present the results of the index in a visually attractive format. Because the FCI is likely to use spatially referenced data, a platform with Geographic Information System capabilities should be used.

Assessing Changes in the Forest Capital Index Over Time

A key function of the FCI would be to assess changes over time in the sustainable use of forest resources. Changes in forest ecosystem conditions and use will be measured against some initial period – ideally that period should be chosen as one in which forest ecosystems were minimally impacted by human activity (Woodwell, 2002). However the question remains, for forest ecosystems, should the standard (or benchmark period) be the condition and forest cover that pertained 8,000 years ago – a period prior to significant human influences on forest ecosystems? If this benchmark were to be chosen, the value of the index today for many regions of the world would be rather low (on average less than 50 per cent of the benchmark value). Even if a more recent period were taken to be the benchmark, for example, the condition of forests at the beginning of the 20th century, the current value in many areas would also be rather depressed as large scale clearing of forests have taken place in the 20th century. Some argue on pragmatic grounds, that for policy purposes, one could adopt the value of the index in the first year of calculation as the standard (Matthews et al., 2000).

Since the policy implication of the FCI is to portray trends, it may well be that the year of the first calculation is as suitable as any to show the direction of change. However, at the same time, some historical reference points would be useful to indicate the recent history of forest transformation and serve to motivate policies to restore forest health to its full potential.

DISCUSSION

The construction of overall measures of ecosystem health designed to inform decision makers and the public on overall conditions and trends poses a great many challenges. The proposed FCI is an attempt to meet these challenges for one of the world's most critical ecosystems. Currently, in the monitoring of conditions and trends in forest ecosystems there are myriad indicators, often motivated more by what can be measured, than by the utility of the measurements in informing decision makers and the public about the sustainability of forested ecosystems. In proposing the construction of an FCI, we recognize both the dangers of oversimplifying the available information as well as the dangers of having a bewildering number of indicators from which no clear picture emerges.

In effect, the FCI seeks middle ground between the two extremes: complexity which fails to communicate, and simplicity which devolves into being overly simplistic. Ultimately, what is sought is a measure with a solid footing in our understanding of the complex dynamics of the forest–human interactions, and with a strong capacity to communicate that understanding to decision makers and the public.

Potential Audiences and Users of the FCI

There is a wide range of important audiences, including governments, corporations, non-governmental organizations, academe, think tanks and research organizations, intergovernmental organizations (including the UN system), financial institutions from national to global and the news media. It is also vital to reach the public – the benefactors of services provided by healthy forest ecosystems – in order to build support for such a measuring system. Public support is essential to build political will and to encourage business to use the index. The development of an FCI will take into consideration that different actors have different needs in terms of level of detail of information. An FCI should be seen as an information system, and the FCI and the components it builds on should be published simultaneously, so that both the larger picture and the details are available to index users with full transparency.

The development of an FCI is likely to provide benefits to society in many different ways. It will permit evaluation of progress in sustaining forest capital in a country, serve as a benchmark for assessing whether forest capital is increasing or declining and create a global framework for valuation of forest ecosystem services. The introduction and use of an FCI would make available a kind of 'score card' or 'report card' that attributes a numerical value to various forest functions, including a 'GDP-like' one-dimensional index of the total (Salim and Ullsten, 1999). This may serve as a helpful tool in debt-for-nature swap agreements, and in designing tradable permits involving forests within the Kyoto Protocol and otherwise.

Human activities have eroded global forest capital and other natural resources over many centuries, and are undermining the ability of future generations to meet their own needs from the natural resource base (Dasgupta, 1982; Pearse, 1990). This applies not only to forests, but also to other major global ecosystems (for example, coral reefs, wetlands, grasslands, fresh water bodies (lakes, rivers), as well as marine systems). Current indices, such as the GDP, do not take into account the necessity for the sustainability of nature (Tietenberg, 1992). By expressing the values of forests, which often lie outside the domain of routine economic calculus, the FCI would increase awareness about the degree to which current use of the world's resources is taking account of future generations by safeguarding the natural capital of forests. The same sort of consideration would apply to all of the world's major ecosystems.

Information Gaps Concerning the Natural Capital

The very process of formulating an FCI would identify gaps in our knowledge of forests and would lead to additional research focused on filling those gaps. Data gaps should be analysed with regard to their significance for creating a robust and reliable index. Other data gaps may become apparent in the course of development of the index. The programme of activities to formulate an FCI will necessitate a pooling of resources, expertise, resources and outputs from established monitoring activities that could lead to far more incremental value than if researchers were to continue to operate independently of and sometimes at cross purposes with one another.

Spatial Scales for the Forest Capital Index

An important consideration for construction of an FCI is the spatial scale to which is applies. Are we thinking of the global picture, a country level perspective, a particular region (say a watershed or biome), or some other defined area? In principle, the FCI could be applied to any defined region, provided the data are obtained that relate to that particular domain. The concept of biomes, eco-zones, regions, districts and sites, as well as basins, watersheds and sub-watersheds have found various applications in reporting on the changing state of environments (e.g. Bird and Rapport, 1986). We envision a nested hierarchy of such regions for purposes of constructing an FCI. Ideally, there will be ways of aggregating such eco-logically-based constructs to merge with political boundaries at state and federal levels. Within the European Community, the EC Water Framework Directive provides strong support for such an approach.

The FCI can be viewed as a 'top down' approach to management of the forest. However, it is not intended to be biased in that direction. It should equally serve 'bottom-up' processes – that is, community-driven processes to change the management of local forests which are the ecosystem in which that community thrives. This would particularly be the case if it were the community that suggested the parameters which are most meaningful to the health of their forest ecosystems, including not only the bio-physical aspects, but as well the socio-economic and cultural dimensions. The main goal of the FCI is to provide information as to the changes in the health/condition of forest-dominated ecosystems. That information should be of equal value to local communities and the various levels of governance.

Linking the Forest Capital Index to Economic and Social Indices

During the last decades of the twentieth century, environmental issues have gained increasing prominence. Indeed, sustainable development has become one of the core organising concepts of environmental policy and can be defined as the maintenance of important environmental functions into the indefinite future (Ekins and Simon, 2001). However, sustainability is also an inherently vague concept whose scientific definition and meas-urement still lacks wide acceptance. If measurement methods indicating both short- and long-term targets are developed (Mills and Clark, 2001), the concept can be made much more concrete, and it should become possible to assess needs in order to achieve healthy ecosystems at various spatial scales.

To become policy relevant the FCI must have the potential of being linked to existing and planned broader indices for sustainable development at the national and international level if it is to be widely used. Two prominent examples of forest-based criteria and indicator sets are the Montreal Process (Anonymous, 1995; used by the United States and 13 other temperate and boreal forest countries) and the Helsinki Process used by European countries. These sets of criteria and indicators allow for standardized measurements of agreed-upon variables including biodiversity, productive capacity of forests, protection of soil and water, contributions to the global carbon cycles, economic factors and contributions and legal and institutional issues pertinent to forest management. These well-established systems offer us two helpful assets. First, the rich data sets they provide give us starting points for the selection of indicators and yield useful data to populate them. Second, because these sets of indicators have already been agreed upon by large constituencies, we can capitalize on the investment of time, money and other resources that have moved diverse stakeholder sets from dispute to dialogue to data. This will be important, as the FCI will be subject to scrutiny by many groups.

CONCLUSION

Managing sustainability is about trying to reduce the ecological footprint of humans that has, over time, resulted in a serious erosion of the viability of the world's major ecosystems. Indeed, as a consequence of human domination of most of the Earth's ecosystems, their vitality and health is now at a historic low. Thus far, policy responses triggered by observations that the environment has become seriously compromised have failed to stem the continued degradation.

There are many reasons why that is the case. One of them is the inability of political systems to handle issues that are, by definition, long-term in character and involve the perspective of planetary survival. This, however, does not mitigate the role and responsibility of science to provide better and more comprehensible information about the unfolding transformation of the Earth's ecosystems. Concepts such as the ecological footprint, ecological integrity and ecosystem health have an important role to play in structuring new and comprehensive information systems on the environment.

The increasing availability of indicator data on a broad scale (particularly from the use of remote sensing technologies) makes comprehensive assessments of the vitality of the Earth's ecosystems more feasible than ever before. In many cases, however, improved technologies for monitoring conditions and trends in the Earth's ecosystems have only led to 'information overload'. With intergovernmental agencies and other institutions reporting hundreds of indicators, scientists, decision makers, and the public, are hard pressed to answer the simple question: what are the trends in the health, viability, sustainability of ecosystems for particular regions or countries as a whole?

In the forest sector, the situation motivated the proposal for constructing an index of forest capital. The FCI is intended to serve as a vehicle for communicating to decision makers and the general public, the overall trends of forest ecosystem health. Its focus is on ecosystem viability, including (at least eventually), the socio-economic, cultural, governance and human health aspects, as well as the biophysical aspects of forest-dominated ecosystems.

Much attention has been rightly placed on the size of our ecological footprint. But this alone is insufficient. Information on footprints suggests the degree of stress to which regional ecosystems are subjected. But, by itself, this information does not tell us whether or not the regional ecosystem can sustain these levels of stress. To address this question, and to provide an overall picture of whether forests are improving or declining, one needs an overall measure of ecosystem health and its changes over time. This is the central motivation governing the construction of the FCI. While there is certainly no unanimous agreement among scientists or decision makers on indicators for use in indices of sustainability, or on methods of aggregation or weighting, there is agreement that one needs, urgently, a mechanism for making sense of large amounts of conflicting data.

A transparent protocol for constructing an FCI would represent an important step in this direction. It also represents an opportunity, based on this approach, to develop indices for communicating the status and trend of all of the world's ecosystems, as efforts to ensure their viability intensifies in the 21st century.

ACKNOWLEDGEMENTS

The development of a conceptual basis for a forest capital index has been very much enhanced by discussions that took place at the international workshop on the Forest Capital Index co-convened by the authors at the University of Guelph, Canada, in 2002. A more extensive discussion of this topic is to be found in a jointly authored paper by workshop participants (Ullsten et al., 2004). The authors are indepted to Luisa Maffi for her editorial scrutiny.

REFERENCES

Andreasen, J.K., R.V. O'Neill, R. Noss and N.C. Slosser (2001), 'Considerations for the development of a terrestrial index of ecological integrity', *Ecological Indicators*, **1**, 21–35.

Anonymous (1994), 'European criteria and most suitable quantitative indicators for sustainable forest management', adopted by the first expert level follow-up meeting of the Helsinki conference, Geneva.

Anonymous (1995), 'Criteria and indicators for the conservation and sustainable management of temperate and boreal forests', The Montreal Process, Canadian Forest Service, Hull, Quebec.

Bird, P.M. and D.J. Rapport (1986), *State of the Environment Report for Canada*, Ottawa: Canadian Government Publishing Centre.

Catton, W.R., Jr. (1982), *Overshoot: The Ecological Basis of Revolutionary Change*, Urbana: University of Illinois Press.

Costanza, R., R. d'Agre, R. de Groot, S. Farber, M. Grasso, B. Hannon, S. Naeem, K. Limburg, J. Paruelo, R.V. O'Neill, R. Raskin, P. Sutton and M. van den Belt (1997), 'The value of the world's ecosystems services and natural capital', *Nature*, **387**, 253–60.

Dale, V.H. and S.C. Beyeler (2001), 'Challenges in the development and use of ecological indicators', *Ecological Indicators*, **1**, 3–10.

Dasgupta, P. (1982), *The Control of Resources*, Oxford, UK: Blackwell.

Ekins, P. and S. Simon (2001), 'Estimating sustainability gaps: methods and preliminary applications for the UK and the Netherlands', *Ecological Economics*, **37**, 5–22.

FAO (2003), *The State of the World's Forests 2003*, Rome: Food and Agriculture Organization.

Hardin, G. (1968), 'The tragedy of the commons', *Science*, **162**, 1243–8.

Hawley, A.H. (1950), *Human Ecology: A Theory of Community Structure*, New York: Roland Press.

Huq, A. and R.R. Colwell (1996), 'Vibrios in the marine and estuarine environment: Tracking *Vibrio Cholerae*', *Ecosystem Health*, **2**, 198–214.

ITTO (International Tropical Timber Organization) (1992), *Criteria for the Management of Sustainable Tropical Forest Management*, Yokohama: ITTO.

Karr, J.R. and E.W. Chu (1999), *Restoring Life in Running Waters: Better Biological Monitoring*, Washington, DC: Island Press.

Maffi, L. (ed.) (2001), *On Biocultural Diversity: Linking Language, Knowledge, and the Environment*, Washington, DC: Smithsonian Institution Press.

Malthus, T.R. (1803), *An Essay on the Principle of Population*, 2nd edn (ed.) J. Johnson, London: Routledge.

Matthews, E., R. Payne, M. Rohweder and S. Murray (2000), *Pilot Analysis of Global Ecosystems (PAGE): Forest Ecosystems*, Washington, DC: World Resources Institute.

McMichael, A.J. (1997), 'Global environmental change and human health: impact assessment, population vulnerability, research priorities', *Ecosystem Health*, **3**, 200–210.

Mills, T.J. and R.N. Clark (2001), 'Roles of research scientists in natural resource decision-making', *Forest Ecology and Management*, **153**, 189–98.

Nielsen, N.O. (1999), 'The meaning of health', *Ecosystem Health*, **5**, 65–6.

Ott, W.R. (1978), *Environmental Indices – Theory and Practice*, Ann Arbor: Ann Arbor Science.

Patz, J.A. (1996), 'Global climate change and emerging infectious diseases', *Journal of the American Medical Association*, **275**, 217–23.

Peacock, K. (1999), 'Staying out of the lifeboat: Sustainability, culture and the thermodynamics of symbiosis', *Ecosystem Health*, **5**, 91–103.

Pearse, P. (1990), *Introduction to Forestry Economics*, Oxford, UK: Blackwell.

Rapport, D.J. (1989), 'What constitutes ecosystem health?', *Perspectives in Biology and Medicine*, **33**, 1120–32.

Rapport, D.J. (1995), 'Ecosystem health: exploring the territory', *Ecosystem Health*, **1**, 5–13.

Rapport, D.J. (2000), 'Ecological footprints and ecosystem health: complementary approaches to a sustainable future', *Ecological Economics*, **32**, 367–70.

Rapport, D.J. and V. Lee (2003), 'Ecosystem approaches to human health: some observations on North/South experiences', *Environmental Health*, **3** (2), 26–39.

Rapport, D.J. and W. Whitford (1999), 'How ecosystems respond to stress: Common properties of arid and aquatic systems', *BioScience*, **49** (3), 193–203.

Rapport, D.J., H.A. Regier and T.C. Hutchinson (1985), 'Ecosystem behaviour under stress', *The American Naturalist*, **125**, 617–40.

Rapport, D.J., R. Costanza, P. Epstein, C. Gaudet and R. Levins (eds) (1998a), *Ecosystem Health*, Oxford, UK: Blackwell Science.

Rapport, D.J., R. Costanza and A. McMichael (1998b), 'Assessing ecosystem health: Challenges at the interface of social, natural, and health sciences', *Trends in Ecology and Evolution*, **13** (10), 397–402.

Rapport, D.J., W. Lasley, D.E. Rolston, N.O. Nielsen, C.O. Qualset and A.B. Damania (eds) (2003), *Managing for Healthy Ecosystems*, Boca Raton: CRC Press.

Rees, W.E. (1999), 'Consuming the earth: the biophysics of sustainability', *Ecological Economics*, **29**, 23–7.

Salim, E. and O. Ullsten (1999), *Our Forests . . . Our Future: Report of the World Commission on Forests and Sustainable Development*, Cambridge: Cambridge University Press.

Tietenberg, T. (1992), *Environmental and Natural Resource Economics*, New York: Harper Collins.

Ullsten, O., P. Angelstam, A. Patel, D.J. Rapport, A. Cropper, L. Pinter and M. Washburn (2004), 'Towards the assessment of environmental sustainability in forest ecosystems: measuring the natural capital', *Ecological Bulletin*, **51**, 471–86.

United Nations Development Programme, United Nations Environment Programme, The World Bank, World Resources Institute (2001), *World Resources 2000–2001: People and Ecosystems: The Fraying Web of Life*, Washington, DC: World Resources Institute.

UNCED (1992), United Nations Conference on Environment and Development, *Agenda 21: Program of Action for Sustainable Development*, New York: UN Department of Public Information.

United Nations Environment Program (UNEP) (2003), *Global Environmental Outlook Program*, at http://www.grid.unep.ch/geo/geo3.

Vitousek, P.M., H.A. Mooney, J. Lubchenco and J.M. Melillo (1997), 'Human domination of the Earth's ecosystems', *Science*, **277**, 494–9.

Wackernagel M. and W.E. Rees (1996), *Our Ecological Footprint: Reducing Human Impact on the Earth*, Gabriola Island, BC: New Society Publishers.

Whitford, W. (1995), 'Desertification: Implications and limitations of the Ecosystem Health Metaphor', in D.J. Rapport, R. Costanza, P. Epstein, C. Gaudet and R. Levins (eds), *Ecosystem Health*, Malden: Blackwell Science, pp. 273–94.

Whitford, W., D.J. Rapport and A. deSoyza (1999), 'Using resistance and resilience measurement for "fitness" tests in ecosystem health', *Journal of Environmental Management*, **57**, 21–9.

Woodwell, G.M. (2002), 'The functional integrity of normally forested landscapes: A proposal for an index of environmental capital', *Proceedings of the National Academy of Sciences USA*, **99**, 13 600–605.

World Conservation (2004), 'World conservation voices of Asia', *IUCN Bulletin*, 7.

World Economic Forum (Global Leaders of Tomorrow Environment Task Force), Yale University (Yale Center for Environmental Law and Policy), Columbia University (Center for International Earth Science Information Network) (2002), *2002 Environmental Sustainability Index*, New Haven: Yale Center for Environmental Law and Policy, at http://www.ciesin.org/indicators/ESI/ESI2002_21MAR02tot.pdf.

PART V

Sustainable development and indicators of human–environment interaction

14. Sustainability scenarios as interpretive frameworks for indicators of human–environment interaction

Janne Hukkinen

INTRODUCTION

This chapter highlights the necessity, significance and benefits of alternative sustainability scenarios as interpretive frameworks for indicators of human–environment interaction. Alternative sustainability scenarios make explicit the fact that there are many interpretations of what the path toward sustainability might look like. Scenarios of the future provide a series of reference points against which to assess the significance of specific indicator values. Incorporation of alternative scenarios into the indicator framework also helps policy makers to design adaptive policies with which to encounter surprising events.

Indicators make a lot of sense to us because they reflect a fundamental characteristic of human beings. Around one year of age, a human child begins to display a cognitive feature that differentiates her from other primates: she understands that other persons are intentional agents like the self (Tomasello, 1999). This understanding ensures the cultural evolution of human beings, because it locks an individual's cognitive development with that of her fellow human beings. Indicator systems are one reflection of this lock-in between the individual and her social environment. The much-applied pressure–state–response (PSR) indicator system, for example, enables an individual or a group of individuals to communicate to other individuals a causally rooted intent to action. There exists some identifiable pressure (P) which is likely to induce a change in the state (S) of affairs which, in turn, calls for an intentional response (R) from human beings. PSR is simply an efficient way for individuals to convince others of the need for intentional action.

The PSR framework is also a scenario of future development, composed of anthropogenic pressure on the environment, the state of the system of human–environment interaction resulting from such pressure, and the societal response to ease the pressure (OECD, 1993). Scenarios, that is, plausible causal descriptions of future trends and events, are not new to indicator systems. A recent US National Research Council volume on sustainability recommends combining the PSR measurement data with a scenario so as to capture a fundamental idea of sustainable development – namely, that humans can not only impair nature's life support systems but also respond by protecting environmental quality (National Research Council, 1999).

In practice, however, the role of scenarios in indicator systems often goes unrecognized. Indicator systems tend to assume the existence of just one scenario, rather than several alternative ones, and often pay no attention to explaining what exactly this one scenario is. Indicators are included in an indicator system more on the basis of the ease and availability of measurements than their relationship with a scenario (Baltic 21 Secretariat, 2000; Maa- ja metsätalousministeriö, 1999).

The fact that sustainability indicators today make reference to only one, often implicit, scenario is problematic from several perspectives. First, recent ecosystem studies have shown that in many ecosystems, even those relatively undisturbed by human activity, smooth change can be interrupted by sudden drastic switches to a contrasting state. There may exist several alternative locally stable states for the ecosystem (Scheffer et al., 2001; Holling and Sanderson, 1996). From the sustainability perspective, this means that there is no single ecologically sustainable state, but many such states. An indicator system rooted in just one sustainability scenario is incapable of illustrating shifts between alternative ecologically sustainable states. Second, numerous social scientific studies of environmental issues emphasize that sustainability, when understood to include not just ecological but socio-cultural dimensions as well, is inherently socially constructed (Dietz et al., 2003; Dryzek, 1997; Flyvbjerg, 2001; Hajer, 1995; Hukkinen, 1999; Lee, 1993; Redclift, 1992). Different social groups, stakeholders and communities in the society perceive differently what a sustainable future might be. Each group has its own well-reasoned rationale for holding the view of sustainability that it does, and it is impossible to justify any single sustainability scenario as the 'correct' or 'optimal' one. Policy makers who assess the values of sustainability indicators with reference to a single sustainability scenario in fact commit themselves to partisanship in the political contest over sustainability. Finally, as many case studies by environmental and biodiversity management analysts point out, policies meeting socio-ecological sustainability criteria for local areas and shorter time scales often fail to do so for larger areas and longer time scales (Dovers, 1995; Groombridge, 1992; Wolf and Allen, 1995). Alternative scenarios are therefore needed to illustrate the possible contradictions between different spatial and temporal scales of sustainability.

As intentional social beings, we have no good reason to throw away the PSR indicator system as a framework for improving our understanding of sustainability, despite the considerable challenges involved. It is worthwhile to take a closer look at the implications for the use of the PSR framework of the fact that there are several alternative possibilities for a sustainable future. In the following, I will first elaborate the rationale for developing sustainability scenarios by showing that all indicator systems assume the existence of reference scenarios. Empirical material supporting the argument comes from a case remarkably loaded with scenarios of the future, namely, an ongoing debate over the future of a mega-harbour in the metropolitan Helsinki region in Finland. I will then explain how indicator systems can be improved by developing them in conjunction with reference scenarios of sustainability. Empirical material here comes from a case study of natural resource management in northern Finland. Existing sustainability indicators developed by government officials assume one scenario of sustainability for the northern regions. An alternative sustainability scenario, developed by local management experts during a 3-year EU project on sustainable reindeer management in northern Fennoscandia and north-west Russia, would require a significant broadening of the rationale and scope of the existing indicator system. I will conclude with some of the practical challenges and policy benefits of developing an indicator system anchored in alternative sustainability scenarios.

THE MEANINGS OF AN INDICATOR

The PSR framework assumes a scenario of human–environment interaction in three important ways. First, it assumes the *existence* of a scenario in which a given phenomenon (P) constitutes a pressure, a phenomenon (S) a state, and a phenomenon (R) a response. Second, it assumes that P, S and R each exist to a *degree* which justifies calling them a pressure, state and response, respectively. Finally, in assuming a scenario, the PSR also commits itself to a sustainability *policy*. Recent developments surrounding the planning and construction of a new harbour in Finland allow us to investigate these aspects of the PSR scenario.

In May 2003, the Vuosaari harbour project just east of Helsinki, Finland, faced the highest hurdle yet on its already painstaking track. Since the early 1990s, the project, which aims to build a container traffic harbour with an annual capacity of twelve million metric tons of cargo, had survived severe public criticism and several court cases relating to its location next to an EU Natura 2000 nature protection area, its impact on the rapidly growing suburb of Vuosaari nearby and the construction of its transportation arteries through the communities of the larger Helsinki region (Helsingin satamahanke, 1995; VUOPE-työryhmä, 1996; Pyykkönen, 2002). When dredging under the future harbour began, very high concentrations of tri-butyl tin (TBT) were discovered in the bottom sediments (Laitinen, 2003a). The likely source of the TBT, which has adverse reproductive impacts on aquatic organisms, was a shipyard that had operated on the site over several decades.

The TBT took virtually everybody by surprise. The harbour constructors did not know how to handle the material (Laitinen, 2003b; Vuosaaren satamauutiset; 2003). The regulators did not have standards for it (Erkkilä, 2003; Laitinen, 2003c). The environmentalists could only tell horror stories of its adverse impacts elsewhere in the world (Laitinen, 2003d; Kaikkonen, 2004). By June 2004, however, the regulators had given permission to dredge and dispose in the Baltic Sea material from areas where the TBT concentration was below 200 micrograms per kilogram (g/kg) (Vuosaaren satamauutiset, 2004). Many environmental organizations and scientists argued that the TBT concentration designated by the regulators was arbitrary, that there was no guarantee that the TBTs that would be released as a result of the permitted dredging would not harm the aquatic organisms of the fragile Baltic ecosystem, and that the safest solution would have been not to dredge at all and seal off the material at the bottom of the sea (Laitinen, 2003d; Kaikkonen, 2004).

The dispute over TBTs reflects the existence, degree and policy issues of scenarios and indicators. First the existence issue. To argue that a phenomenon P is a pressure to the system of human–environment interaction assumes knowledge of what the system of human–environment interaction is (that is, its boundaries, objects and relations) and why P can indeed be considered a pressure on that system. In the Vuosaari harbour case, the discovery of TBTs forced a reconsideration of what was considered in public policy to be the focal area of human–environment interaction. Before TBTs, the debate focused on the terrestrial ecosystem enclosed in the Natura 2000 nature protection area. After TBTs, the debate shifted to the bottom sediments of the aquatic ecosystem around the future harbour.

Furthermore, to say that TBTs are a pressure to the aquatic system is also to argue that securing the reproductive capacity of aquatic organisms in the long run is one of the key elements of a sustainability scenario for the future harbour-environment system. The problem, however, is that things could change unexpectedly. What if five years from now a marine ecologist discovers that the minute concentrations of TBT that were accumulated in the bottom sediments over the decades have in fact already reduced the viability of aquatic life in the region for centuries to come? This is not a far-fetched scenario given the dearth of studies over the long-term impact of TBTs in the aquatic ecosystem surrounding the Vuosaari harbour (Laitinen, 2003a). Such a discovery might well reduce the relative significance of TBTs as a pressure on human–environment interaction and increase the relative significance of some other indicator of pressure. Since the viability of the aquatic ecosystem is reduced for the foreseeable future, why not focus on, say, securing the recreational value of the archipelago surrounding the harbour as the key element of a sustainability scenario? Less of a concern to human health, TBTs would surely not be an indicator in a scenario constructed around the maintenance of recreation value. Similarly altered would be the indicators of state and response.

The issues raised by the PSR framework relate not only to the existence of an indicator but also to its degree. To argue that a phenomenon which exists at a quantity Q constitutes a pressure P on the system of human–environment interaction assumes detailed quantitative knowledge of the relationships governing the future behaviour of the system. Often such knowledge is difficult to come by, as the behaviour of the system can have several pathways that are contingent upon unexpected events. Two challenges ensue. First, it may be difficult to know what exact quantity constitutes a pressure on the system. Second, even if that quantity were known, it is likely to be pertinent to one scenario alone, but not other scenarios.

The Vuosaari case again reflects these challenges. While the regulators have taken the position that dredging wastes from bottom sediments with a TBT concentration below 200 g/kg can be disposed of in the sea, some environmental scientists and environmental groups think there is inadequate scientific evidence to reach such a conclusion (Vuosaaren satamauutiset, 2004; Sykkö, 2004). Furthermore, it is not difficult to imagine a credible scenario where the currently regulated 'safe' TBT concentration level would be either too low or too high. The level would be too low if ecological investigations showed that significant adverse impacts had already occurred in aquatic ecosystems of large regions surrounding the Helsinki peninsula as a result of long-term exposure to TBTs. In fact, studies conducted by the regulators during 2004 revealed high levels of TBT in the bottom sediments of waters around Helsinki, suggesting this scenario is a real possibility (Erkkilä, 2004). In this case, the game would have been lost in terms of saving the viability of aquatic ecosystems, and the focus of future policies would shift to other themes (such as recreation, as envisioned in the previous paragraph). On the other hand, the 'safe' TBT level would be too high if ecosystem studies showed that adverse impacts had taken place precisely in those bottom sediments where TBT concentration was higher than the permissible level. Applying a margin of safety, the regulators would probably be inclined to lower the TBT level deemed safe for sea disposal.

The irony in the Vuosaari case is that sea disposal of dredged material with TBT concentration below 200 g/kg already started in 2004. This reality brings us to the third issue of the PSR framework, namely, that assessing the value of an indicator on the basis of a single scenario also commits policy makers to a single policy. The regulatory framework for TBTs was articulated in terms of two absolute limits, with sea disposal of dredged material allowed at a TBT concentration below 3 g/kg, allowed also but with a permit at concentrations between 3 and 200 g/kg, and prohibited at a concentration above 200 g/kg (Erkkilä, 2004). Such a framework essentially fixes future policy options along a single scenario which rather resembles a one-way road with traffic lights: you may either go, or wait for a while for a permit to let you go, or you must stop altogether. Policy preparation for alternatives such as those described in the above paragraphs is effectively closed out. Yet, as I will argue in a later section, consideration of the wider range of policy options is not just reasonable, it has several policy benefits.

IMPROVING THE INDICATORS

I will now compare two sets of indicators and scenarios to show that indicators are strongly connected to scenarios and that this connectivity can be used to improve indicators. I will start with a set of governmental indicators of sustainable reindeer management in Finland. Dissecting this set into pressure, state and response indicators, I can present the PSR scenario assumed by the government's sustainability indicators. Thereafter, I will do the same analysis in reverse on an alternative set of indicators and a scenario. Starting from a scenario of sustainable reindeer management which was developed by reindeer herders, officials and researchers in a collaborative EU project on sustainable reindeer management in northern Fennoscandia and Russia, I will infer a set of sustainability indicators assumed by the collaboratively developed scenario. Comparison of the governmental sustainability scenario with that developed during the collaborative EU project forms the basis for the revised sustainability indicators, which are considerably broader in rationale and scope than the original governmental indicators.

From Indicators to Scenario

Reindeer have been hailed as an icon representing northern people and environment. Whereas the Sámi, the aboriginal people of northernmost Europe, see it as their thread of life both in cultural and economic terms, the neighbouring Finns to the south have integrated this animal as another additional element into their agricultural cycles. Today, reindeer management in Finland faces considerable internal and external pressures for change as a result of the complex processes of modernization and globalization (Forbes et al., 2004). The top governmental regulator of reindeer management is the Ministry of Agriculture and Forestry (MoAF), assisted by their research arm, the Finnish Game and Fisheries Research Institute (GFRI). At the local level, reindeer management is administered by 56 reindeer herding co-operatives (RHC) (see Figures 14.1 and 14.2).

To meet the challenges of modernization and globalization in a sustainable way, MoAF maintains a set of indicators of sustainable reindeer management (Table 14.1). The indicators measure the productivity of reindeer population, the ecological carrying capacity of reindeer herding region, the significance of reindeer management for the regional economy, the profitability of reindeer management, and the quality of reindeer-related products. In Table 14.1, these indicators have been categorized into pressure, state and response indicators.

The categorization into PSR indicators in Table 14.1 can be used to construct the sustainability scenario underlying the indicators. As was explained in the first section of this chapter, the PSR indicator framework always assumes a scenario expressing an intent to action. The scenario that is described below begins with a statement of the vision of sustainable reindeer management. This vision originates in the introductory sections of the MoAF's reports on indicators of sustainable use of natural resources in Finland (Maa- ja metsätalousministeriö 1999, 2004). The scenario description then progresses chronologically. First, it assembles the P indicators in Table 14.1 and describes their content in brief narrative statements, with the assumption that the items measured by the P indicators are posing a threat (a pressure) to the vision. Thereafter, the scenario description assembles the S indicators and narrates their content with the assumption that, despite the pressures, movement toward the vision has taken place as a result of the policy and management actions.

What these actions to achieve the vision are, is articulated in the response stage of the scenario narrative on the basis of the R indicators of Table 14.1. In light of the discussion in the second major section of this chapter, it should be noted that the MoAF scenario is based on the existence of indicators but not their degree, since the MoAF reports give no target quantities for the indicators. The resulting scenario of sustainable reindeer management as inferred from the MoAF indicators for sustainable reindeer management is as follows:

- *Vision of sustainable reindeer management*: Reindeer management is based on natural pastures and feeding is minimized so as to maintain

Source: Hukkinen et al., 2003c.

Figure 14.1   Municipalities in northern Finland (Hukkinen et al., 2003c)

the image, legal framework, ecological sustainability, and economic
profitability of the livelihood.

- *Pressure*: Very large numbers of reindeer threaten the ecological and
  economic viability of the livelihood. Too many reindeer also pose
  threats to other land uses, such as agriculture and tourism. Pressure
  on the carrying capacity of the ecosystem is indicated by the high
  densities of live reindeer.

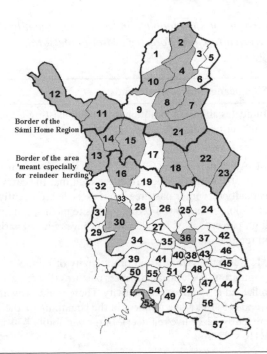

No	RHC	No	RHC	No	RHC
1	Paistunturi	20	(recent RHC fusion)	39	Isosydänmaa
2	Kaldoaivi	21	Lappi	40	Mäntyjärvi
3	Näätämö	22	Kemin-Sompio	41	Kuukas
4	Muddusjärvi	23	Pohjois-Salla	42	Alakitka
5	Vätsäri	24	Salla	43	Akanlahti
6	Paatsjoki	25	Hirvasniemi	44	Hossa-Irni
7	Ivalo	26	Pyhä-Kallio	45	Kallioluoma
8	Hammastunturi	27	Vanttaus	46	Oivanki
9	Sallivaara	28	Poikajärvi	47	Jokijärvi
10	Muotkatunturi	29	Lohijärvi	48	Taivalkoski
11	Näkkälä	30	Palojärvi	49	Pudasjärvi
12	Käsivarsi	31	Orajärvi	50	Oijärvi
13	Muonio	32	Kolari	51	Pudasjärven-Livo
14	Kyrö	33	Jääskö	52	Pintamo
15	Kuivasalmi	34	Narkaus	53	Kiiminki
16	Alakylä	35	Niemelä	54	Kollaja
17	Sattasniemi	36	Timisjärvi	55	Ikonen
18	Oraniemi	37	Tolva	56	Näljänkä
19	Syväjärvi	38	Posion-Livo	57	Halla

Note: Shading indicates the home RHC of herders participating in the RENMAN-WP 1 workshops (2001–3). The three zones seperated by thick lines correspond approximately with the three zones indentified in the RENMAN scenarios in the next minor section 3.2. (Hukkinen et al., 2003c)

Figure 14.2 Reindeer herding co-operatives (RHC) in Finland

Table 14.1 *Indicators of sustainable reindeer management by Ministry of Agriculture and Forestry (Maa-ja metsätalousministeriö, 1999 and 2004)*

Indicator	Significance and current trends	PSR*
1. Productivity of reindeer population	Indicates ability to maintain or expand existing reindeer population.	
1.1 Number of reindeer	MoAF** (advised by GFRI***) sets the maximum allowable number of live reindeer such that the carrying capacity of winter pastures is not exceeded (currently 203 700, set in 2000). Feeding, parasite medication and high percentage of female reindeer have reduced variation in reindeer numbers.	P
1.2 Meat production per live reindeer	Measures the viability and productivity of reindeer population. Deteriorated winter pastures (lichen) are reflected in reindeer productivity. There is a downward trend (15–18 kg/live reindeer in the beginning of the 1990s, currently 12 kg/live reindeer). Large variability between RHCs****.	S
1.3 Calf percent	Number of calves per 100 female reindeer counted during culling. Indicates productivity, because 70% of slaughtered reindeer are calves.	S
2. Ecological carrying capacity of reindeer herding region	Reindeer management is based on reindeer's ability to get its food from nature (implied by law, which permits reindeer grazing regardless of land ownership). Increased reindeer population, lack of pasture rotation and other land uses have contributed to deterioration of winter pastures.	
2.1 Density of live reindeer	Average is 2 live reindeer per sq km, with a variation of 0.7–3.2 live reindeer per sq km. Calculated also in terms of number of reindeer per land area covered with lichen.	P
2.2 Area and condition of winter and summer pastures, pasture rotation	Tree lichen is vital in central and southern RHCs during the critical spring season. Tree lichen area has diminished due to forestry. Percentage of summer pastures is the largest in the south; percentage of winter pastures is largest in the north. Good quality summer pastures are needed to maintain pasture rotation.	S

Table 14.1 (continued)

Indicator	Significance and current trends	PSR*
3. Significance of reindeer management for the regional economy	Significance: 1) meat, side products from slaughtering, souvenirs; 2) services (safaris, races, demonstration of reindeer herding practices); 3) northern image. Trends: 1) diminishing number of reindeer owners (1999/2000 nearly 5900 owners, now 5500); 2) increasing herd sizes; 3) aging herders. Turnover of reindeer management 60 million euros, mostly meat production.	R
4. Profitability of reindeer management	Components: producer price of meat, cost of feeding, reindeer damage compensation for reindeer owners, compensation paid by RHCs for damage caused by reindeer. Uses of feeding: harsh winter emergency, pasture control, stabilization of management.	S
5. Quality of products	Objective is to control the production chain, with a focus on meat quality.	R

Notes:
* PSR: P = pressure, S = state, R = response;
** MoAF – Ministry of Agriculture and Forestry;
*** GFRI = Finnish Game and Fisheries Research Institute;
**** RHC = Reindeer Herding Co-operative.

- *State*: The carrying capacity of the ecosystem is indicated by the condition of pastures and particularly the availability of lichen. Stringent application of maximum allowable number of reindeer per RHC has improved pastures, increased lichen coverage, minimized feeding, improved profitability and reduced the negative impact of reindeer herding on other land uses. Regulations encouraging entrepreneurship and the benefits of scale have made the population of reindeer herders much younger and fewer than today.
- *Response*: MoAF has reduced the maximum allowable numbers for reindeer for the reindeer herding region as a whole, and for individual RHCs, on the basis of ecological monitoring data and studies by the GFRI. Economic support systems for reindeer herding encourage larger herd sizes to reap the benefits of scale. Reindeer meat quality is monitored and managed throughout the production cycle, from pastures to the consumer.

The scenario inferred from the MoAF indicators of sustainable reindeer management raises several issues. First, legislation on reindeer management in Finland states that, within the reindeer herding area, other land uses may not present significant harm to reindeer herding. Yet the MoAF indicators fail to measure or monitor the presence of any such harm. Second, while the indicator reports introduce reindeer management as a socio-culturally significant livelihood, the indicators make no attempt to monitor such significance. Third, regional variability of reindeer management is mentioned but not recognized as a characteristic to be measured with indicators. Finally, decreased productivity and lichen cover are presented as the key indicators of pasture degradation. In reality, decreased productivity tells more about the gradually constraining impact of other land uses on reindeer management, and lichen cover is only one of many indicators of the ecological condition of pastures. These issues lay the groundwork for the participatory scenarios, to which we now turn.

From Scenario to Indicators

The task in this section is to identify the deficiencies of current MoAF indicators for sustainable reindeer management by comparing them with the indicators that would be needed to monitor sustainable reindeer management as articulated by the stakeholders in the RENMAN project. The procedure is reverse in order to that of the previous minor section. I will first present the participatory scenarios developed by the stakeholders of Finnish reindeer management and then infer the set of indicators that these scenarios assume. As a synthesis, I will compare the inferred indicators with the MoAF indicators and propose a new set of sustainability indicators for reindeer management in Finland.

The participatory scenarios were developed during a 3-year EU-funded research project entitled RENMAN ('The challenges of modernity for reindeer management: integration and sustainable development in Europe's subarctic and boreal regions'). The overall thrust of the RENMAN project was to 'integrate the indigenous people in an integrative study between politics and science', with the specific objectives of 'participatory assessment and systems analysis of different reindeer management regimes', and the development of 'integrative scenarios and management plans for future sustainability' (Forbes et al., 2004, pp. 7–9). Work package 1 (WP1), one of ten RENMAN WPs, focused on the development of participatory institutions for reindeer management in Finland, and conducted all research activities in a participatory research mode. Researchers and reindeer herders became expert partners in WP1. The research questions set forth by WP1 were formulated in collaboration between researchers and reindeer herders. The research itself consisted of joint fieldwork, discussions, communications, meetings, writings, translations and reviews. Three participatory workshops were organized during the three-year project and led to final recommendations developed in intensive deliberations among researchers, herders and government officials (Hukkinen et al., 2002, 2003a; Heikkinen et al., 2003a). The scenario of sustainable reindeer management developed in participatory workshops is as follows:

- *Vision of sustainable reindeer management*: Reindeer management is a socio-ecological innovation and national brand of Finland because it has the proven capacity to enhance long-term resilience and sustainability of northern communities with various local reindeer management traditions.
- *Pressure*: Uniform administration and regulation across the entire reindeer herding region is insensitive to the local strengths of reindeer management. Other land uses (hydropower, forestry, tourism) have diminished and deteriorated reindeer pastures and continue to do so. Regulation based on productivity and profitability alone is insensitive to the cultural aspects of reindeer management, which secure the existence of small northern communities.
- *State*: The state of the pastures and their interaction with the surrounding communities is measured with several indicators, of which lichen cover is only one. Indicators aim to provide an overview of the health and resilience of human–environment interaction in reindeer management. Each indicator has several target values, expressed as bandwidths. Bandwidths are the set of limits that define the range of solutions available for the different actors involved in reindeer management in a particular region without exceeding that region's carrying capacity. Management options are considered under different carrying capacities that depend on alternative scenarios of the desired social and ecological context of reindeer management. Three regions of reindeer management can be identified on the basis of differences in ecosystems, culture and management practice: the Sámi Home Region in the north, the forest zone in central Lapland and the Arctic agriculture zone in the south (Figures 14.1 and 14.2).
- *Response*: Administrative reforms clarify responsibility for reindeer management and push it to the local level. MoAF delegates significant administrative and regulatory responsibilities over land use to local co-operative councils. Regulatory reforms include restrictions on tourism and forestry in the reindeer herding area, labelling of reindeer management and its products as normal (with fencing, feeding and parasite medication) and organic (with free range pastures and no medication), and local level participation in

the determination of reindeer quotas. Economic support encourages the young to enter the livelihood.

To infer a set of sustainability indicators from the scenario described above, I will rely on a categorization of sustainability indicators that I developed in an interdisciplinary analysis of the theoretical foundations of human–environment indicators. In that work, I identified the deficiencies of current sustainability indicators by comparing and synthesizing different theories of change in human–environment interaction, including population ecology, neo-classical economics, systems ecology and institutional economics (Hukkinen, 2003a). The empirically based deficiencies identified here are similar to those found in the theoretical analysis. The deficiencies, or fields of future development of indicators, are (1) scale dependence of indicators; (2) indicators for measuring the ecological impacts of industrial production; (3) indicators of bounded carrying capacity; (4) indicators for measuring the congruence between ecosystems, institutions and reindeer management; and (5) indicators for technological, institutional and ecological path dependence.

The first difference between the MoAF indicators and the indicators that would be needed to monitor the RENMAN scenario is in what could be termed the *scale dependence* of indicators. This refers both to the spatial and temporal range of applicability of a particular indicator and the interdependencies between indicators. The MoAF indicators are assumed to be applicable across the reindeer herding area with no distinctions between the different sub-regions. Furthermore, the MoAF indicators monitor reindeer management in terms of reindeer densities, lichen cover and the productivity and profitability of the livelihood. In contrast, the RENMAN indicators would look considerably more complex. The indicators would be regionally specific, at least at the level of the three regions identified in the scenario (Sámi Home Region, forest zone, arctic agriculture). They would also expand the narrow focus of the MoAF indicators to broader socio-ecological and cultural dimensions of reindeer management. The regionally specific sets of indicators would strive to monitor the health and resilience of human–environment interactions in terms of permissible bandwidths.

Second, the RENMAN indicators would provide a much more comprehensive picture than the MoAF indicators of the *ecological impacts of anthropogenic production systems*. The most striking example of this is the position of reindeer management in the two PSR scenarios. In the MoAF scenario, reindeer density is seen as a pressure with negative impacts on other land uses. In the RENMAN scenario, this is only one of many chains of impact, since other land uses also constitute a pressure with negative impacts on reindeer management. Studies conducted under the RENMAN project revealed a complex web of interactions in the utilization of northern resources, the outcome of which is reflected in the state of today's reindeer management system (Heikkinen et al., 2003b). Reindeer management is so comprehensively embedded in northern ecosystems that it is an effective proxy indicator of large-scale and long-term environmental impacts caused by hydropower development, forestry and tourism. Obviously, these environmental impacts have changed reindeer management practices in ways that have induced further environmental changes, such as increased reindeer densities and reduced lichen cover, but the driver of massive environmental change is nonetheless the industrial utilization of natural resources (Massa, 1983).

Third, the RENMAN scenario points toward a need to develop more refined indicators of ecological carrying capacity, something I will here refer to as *bounded carrying capacity*. The MoAF indicators assume that there exists a single ecological carrying capacity for the ecosystem in Lapland, measurable in terms of lichen cover. The RENMAN scenario presents a more complex picture. While ecological carrying capacities do exist, they are specific to particular ecosystems, policies, and management practices. These locally specific boundary conditions can be expressed in scenarios, such as that expressed in the RENMAN project. The Sámi Home region, for example, is characterized by open tundra, large herd sizes, free range grazing, feeding only in emergencies and conflicts with tourism. Reindeer management in the forest zone takes place in pastures severely affected by hydropower development, intensive forestry and tourism, and uses a mixture of free range grazing and feeding. In the Arctic agriculture zone of the south, reindeer management is closely tied with hay growing and other agriculture, reindeer are fenced in and fed during the winter and herds are relatively small (Hukkinen et al., 2003b). Clearly, lichen cover as an indicator of ecological carrying capacity is more relevant in the Sámi Home region of the north than in the Arctic agriculture zone of the south, where intensive forestry has destroyed significant areas of ground and tree lichen, and feeding has, as a result, become an integral part of viable reindeer management. In the south, the MoAF vision of free ranging reindeer on 'natural' pastures is nothing short of wilderness romanticism. But also in the open tundra region, the RENMAN studies advise a more qualified approach to lichen cover as an indicator of carrying capacity. In the Näkkälä RHC in northernmost Finland and adjacent sites in Norway, intensive grazing and trampling result in a different vegetation pattern from that of a less intensive reindeer management regime, but the intensity does not threaten the carrying capacity of the system as a whole. In fact, the RENMAN modelling studies indicate that even if reindeer numbers were at their socially and economically sustainable maximum in Finnish Lapland, the ecological carrying capacity of the system would not be threatened as long as herd movement is actively managed (Forbes et al., 2004).

Fourth, indicators capable of describing the *congruence between ecosystems, institutions, and reindeer management* are required to monitor the success of the policy measures described in the RENMAN scenarios, such as the devolution of administrative and regulatory responsibility over land use to local councils, and the crafting of solutions sensitive to local actors, conditions and culture. Recent evolution of reindeer slaughtering in Lapland illustrates how the current regulatory and policy context is blind to such considerations. Before Finland joined the EU in 1995, reindeer were traditionally slaughtered outside at the culling site in the freezing winter temperatures. Under MoAF's interpretation of EU hygiene regulations, the RHCs were required to build central slaughterhouses. The new system illustrates a mismatch between the ecosystem functions and the institutions governing the use of the ecosystem, when MoAF demands a slaughterhouse although the ecosystem itself would function as a superior 'slaughterhouse'. There is also a mismatch between production inputs and the institutions, when MoAF forces an economically unviable change from low-capital and labour-intensive slaughtering to industrialized, low-labour, and capital-intensive slaughtering. Finally, there is a mismatch between formal and informal institutions when the socially significant and traditional slaughtering at the culling site has been disrupted by formal EU rules (Hukkinen et al., 2002).

Finally, the MoAF indicators overlook the *path dependent history* of today's reindeer management, whereas the RENMAN indicators would draw from that history. The MoAF vision of reindeer management essentially puts reindeer herders in a bizarre double bind. On the one hand, their reindeer should graze freely on 'natural' pastures. On the other hand, their livelihood is equated with any other modern livelihood facing the global market, with consequent demands for productivity, profitability and benefits of scale. Both aspects of the vision are unrealistic. The supposedly natural pastures have been significantly ravaged over the past five decades by large scale hydropower development, forestry and tourism. Government policies have encouraged larger herd sizes by increasing the minimum herd size requirement for subsidies which, in turn, has forced herders out of the livelihood. There are fewer herders with larger herds whose livelihoods are diminished as the increased income that might have been achieved by increasing the scale of activities has been lost to the costs of mechanization (machines, gasoline, fences and so on) and wages to helping-hands during calf marking and culling. The long-term chairman of the Lapland RHC, Hannu Magga, estimates that the number of full-time reindeer herders in the Lapland RHC dropped from 60 in 1970 to 15 today, and that pasture losses during the same period were about 49 per cent as a result of forest cutting, hydropower reservoirs and tourism (Heikkinen et al., 2003b, pp. 61–3). To understand developments such as these, indicators are needed to measure the technological, institutional and ecological path dependence of conditions influencing reindeer management.

The new set of indicators is presented in Table 14.2 as a synthesis of the MoAF and the RENMAN indicators. Table 14.2 clearly adds complexity

Table 14.2   Revised indicators for sustainable reindeer management in Finland

Indicator	Link with MoAF indicator
1. Ecological impacts of industrial production on reindeer management	
1.1 Impacts of hydropower development	
1.2 Impacts of forestry	
1.3 Impacts of tourism	
2. Bounded carrying capacity of reindeer herding area	A
2.1 Sámi Home Region	A
2.2 Forest zone	A
2.3 Arctic agriculture zone	A
3. Congruence between ecosystems, institutions and reindeer management	B
3.1 Fit between ecosystems and institutions	B
3.2 Fit between ecosystems and reindeer management	B
3.3. Fit between institutions and reindeer management	B
4. Path dependence of reindeer management	
4.1 Technological path dependence	
4.2. Institutional path dependence	
4.3 Ecological path dependence	
5. Productivity of reindeer population	C
5.1 Number of reindeer	C
5.2 Meat production per live reindeer	C
5.3 Calf percent	C
6. Profitability of reindeer management	C
7. Quality of products	C

Notes:
Link with MoAF indicators (for complete list of MoAF indicators, see Table 14.1):
A = replaces MoAF indicator 2. Ecological carrying capacity of reindeer herding region;
B = replaces MoAF indicator 3. Significance of reindeer management for the regional economy;
C = original MoAF indicator.

to the sustainability indicator system. At the same time, a comparison of the indicators in Table 14.2 with the scenarios described by the reindeer herders, officials and researchers shows that the new set of sustainability indicators reflects the relevant issues of current reindeer management policy much more closely than the MoAF indicators. It is to these policy-guiding questions of the new indicators that we turn to in the next section.

POLICY-GUIDING VALUE OF SCENARIO-FRAMED INDICATORS

Considering the indicators in Table 14.2 with the participatory RENMAN scenario presented in the previous minor section highlights several aspects in which the new indicators can help policy making. First of all, scenario-framed indicators are likely to improve the *legitimacy of sustainability policies*. One of the criticisms of environmental indicators, in general, is that they hide the values upon which they are based (Koskinen, 2001). When developed in collaboration with the stakeholders in a policy issue, alternative scenarios make explicit the value assumptions underlying the indicators. As such, scenario-framed indicators can be seen as an effort to broaden the field of co-management from the realm of management proper into the development of the knowledge base required in management. The RENMAN experience speaks to these points. First of all, the RENMAN project was initially welcomed by the reindeer herding community and received positive feedback during and after the project (Lerner, 2003; Lessing, 2003). Furthermore, the Finnish reindeer herding administration embraced the RENMAN approach. For example, the Reindeer Husbandry Research Programme 2003–7, which was published by the governmental GFRI in 2003, was developed collaboratively by a group consisting of researchers, officials, reindeer herders and other experts (Kemppainen et al., 2003). In 2004, the GFRI also began a series of participatory workshops with the aim of developing reindeer management and planning at the local level. The significance of these actions by the GFRI goes beyond research and planning, because of the institute's governmental status and consequent power in shaping national reindeer policy. Among other things, the GFRI plays a key role in determining the maximum allowable reindeer numbers per RHC.

The stakeholder participation required by the development of credible scenarios also improves the *quality of sustainability indicators*. Broad inclusion of expertise results in wider and more relevant knowledge base for indicators (Flyvbjerg, 2001). In the RENMAN case, this was achieved by hiring professional reindeer herders as expert analysts in the project. Three reindeer herders wrote case studies of the recent evolution of reindeer management practices in their own RHCs during the latter part of the twentieth century (Heikkinen et al., 2003b). The case studies provided valuable experiential evidence of the impacts of large scale social and environmental changes at the local RHC level.

Scenario-framing guides policy makers to *apply indicators at the appropriate scale*. For scenarios and the related indicators to make sense, they have to be articulated for particular spatial and temporal scales. One of the most remarkable features of the RENMAN policy and management recommendations, for example, was their spatial specification to three zones: the Sámi Home region, the forest zone and the Arctic agriculture zone. That reindeer management has fundamentally different cultural underpinnings and management practices in different parts of Finnish Lapland is no news to the reindeer herders themselves. The RENMAN project, however, was the first study to point out to government officials that this regional variation should also be reflected in government policies (Hukkinen et al., 2003b; Forbes et al., 2004).

Scenario-framed indicators can also provide *knowledge of the extent to which today's choices determine future policy options*. Path dependence has been identified within many fields of inquiry relevant to sustainability issues, such as technological systems (Hughes, 1987), institutions, cognition and decisions (Hukkinen, 1999; North, 1992), and biological evolution (Gould, 1990; Ehrlich, 2000). It has, however, also been criticized (see Liebowitz and Margolis, 1990). The history of reindeer management in Finnish Lapland is full of path dependence, as described in the previous minor section. Given this history, monitoring the path dependence of today's policies would be warranted, based on indicators of, say, the extent to which economic subsidies and zoning decisions shape the future options for reindeer management.

Finally, I would tentatively propose that scenario-framed indicators, when considered together, may help policy makers *deal with contingencies*, because they can signal vulnerability (systemic capacity for a sudden departure from the sustainability scenario) and resilience (systemic capacity to resist a sudden departure from the sustainability scenario) (Bruun et al., 2002; Hukkinen 2003b). In organizational reliability studies, the coincidence of tight coupling with complexity contributes to the vulnerability of technological systems to accidents (Perrow, 1999; Rochlin et al., 1987).

It is reasonable to apply this message from technological systems to systems of human–environmental interaction more generally, since all ecosystems are dominated by the technology applied by human beings (Vitousek et al., 1997; van Eeten and Roe, 2002). Tightly coupled systems have little slack and permit only limited substitutions in resources and personnel; their buffers and redundancies are rare and deliberate; they have only one method to achieve a goal; they contain invariant sequences; and they permit no delays. Complex systems have many interactions in an unexpected sequence (Perrow, 1999). Both tight coupling and complexity have their counterparts in the indicators described in the previous minor section. Tight coupling can be measured with path dependence indicators, whereas complexity can be measured with indicators of ecological impacts of production and indicators of congruence between ecosystems and management.

Furthermore, recent ecosystem studies suggest that a predictive theory of catastrophic shifts in ecosystems should focus on the scale-dependent feedbacks between consumers and resources. Consumers are positively associated with resource abundance at short spatial range, but negatively at long spatial range, because consumers harvest resources from their surroundings and spread relatively slowly in comparison with the resource flow. The resulting patchiness in the spatial distribution of consumers and resources may signal an imminent catastrophic shift in situations of decreasing resource input (Rietkerk et al., 2004). This explanation of catastrophic shifts also has its counterpart in the indicators described in the last minor section – namely, the necessity to interpret simultaneously the readings of indicators from different spatial scales. When considered together across scales, the indicators of path dependence, production impact, and management congruence can function as an early warning system of catastrophic shifts in human–environment interactions. But resilience, too, has a counterpart in the indicators described in the previous minor section. Resilience here refers to the extent to which the ecosystem can tolerate perturbation without shifting to an alternative stable state (Scheffer et al., 2001). The indicators of bounded carrying capacity attempt to dissect the resilience of a given sustainability scenario into a set of crucial variables with permissible bandwidths. As long as the indicator values remain within the bandwidths, the system described by the scenario is likely to be resilient.

The policy benefits of scenario-framed indicators can be reaped not just in an existing system of human–environment interaction, such as reindeer management, but also in the process of constructing a new one, such as the Vuosaari harbour. Unfortunately, some of the benefits may already have been lost. To begin with, the exclusion of the 'what-if' scenarios in Vuosaari has effectively defined the aquatic ecosystem as the concern overriding all other sustainability concerns, thus potentially eroding the project's legitimacy. Second, the absence of alternative scenarios hides the fact that the Vuosaari harbour brings considerable short-term benefits to the Helsinki region locally, but at the same time, runs in the face of concurrent political demands for long-term regional equity in Finland – demands that have all the more weight as the country already has adequate harbour capacity (Hukkinen, 1996). Third, a key path dependence that alternative scenarios would have been able to articulate is that all future dredging around former docks and harbours in Finland will surely involve meticulous search for TBTs and related materials. Finally, the TBTs came out of the blue, but the construction of scenarios with surprising events and unconventional perspectives would surely prepare the project officials for reliable management (Bruun et al., 2002).

EPILOGUE: WORKING WITH SCENARIO-FRAMED INDICATORS

The indicators proposed in Table 14.2 are sketchy. So are the scientific grounds for anticipating contingencies by simultaneously considering such indicators. Reindeer herders, however, struggling to maintain a livelihood under the pressures of modernization, benefit from an intuitive use of a broad range of heuristic 'indicators' on a daily basis. And their indicators are always presented in the context of a management scenario. After a RENMAN workshop, a reindeer herder from one of the small, southernmost RHCs pointed out to me that he did not think herding would continue long where he came from. When I asked him why he thought so, he gave an answer which I have freely translated below into the language of indicators of sudden shifts in the system of human–environment interaction.

Intensive forestry over the past several decades has forced reindeer management in southern regions onto an increasingly restrictive path, where pastures diminished by forestry require intensive feeding which, in turn, leads to economic hardship. The path shaped by forestry is made more strenuous by a complex of other issues, such as regulatory pressure in the form of minimum herd size requirements for individual herders and maximum permissible quotas for the RHC as a whole, and demographic pressure in the form of fewer and fewer reindeer herders who are getting closer and closer to retirement age. Key pressures on the livelihood are functionally linked and take place simultaneously at different scales. For example, the typically small scale reindeer management operations concentrate resources on reindeer herding farms in the form of hay and other fodder. Large scale forestry, on the other hand, induces overall resource scarcity when natural lichen pastures are destroyed. The result is a patchy system of consumers and resources, viable only with the influx of fodder which, in turn, is extremely vulnerable to external market forces. The system is not very resilient because vital bandwidths are narrow: there are few herders, all of them close to retirement; there are even fewer prospective young herders; pastures are diminishing and, as a result, increasingly vulnerable to climate variation; during winters, the reindeer depend entirely on feeding, the economics of which is very sensitive to price fluctuations; cheap Russian reindeer meat is threatening the profitability of the livelihood; and increasing the scale of operations is too risky.

But there were more optimistic scenarios as well from herders from the forest and tundra zones. While recognizing the path dependent encroachment on pastures by forestry and tourism, they nonetheless take pride in what they consider to be an inherent capacity of reindeer herders to deal with disasters. This professional ethos enables them to widen the bandwidths of the critical aspects of management, usually with the aid of technology. When winters turn harsh, they resort to feeding; when pastures are overgrazed, they turn to active herding with fences, snow mobiles, and four wheelers; when exact timing is required during calf marking and culling as a result of the tight schedules of part-time herders, veterinary inspectors and central slaughterhouses, they resort to airplane and helicopter assistance to observe and guide the herds in the field (Heikkinen et al., 2003b). During such times, reindeer management is no different from modern just-in-time management. The ability to read and interpret multiple indicators simultaneously becomes a prerequisite for success.

ACKNOWLEDGEMENT

Financial support from the Academy of Finland project no. 201223 (Analog) and EUFP5 project no. QLK5-CT-2000-00745 (RENMAN) is gratefully acknowledged.

REFERENCES

Baltic 21 Secretariat (2000), *Development in the Baltic Sea region towards the Baltic 21 goals – an indicator based assessment*, Baltic 21 Series No. 2/2000, Stockholm: Ministry of the Environment.
Bruun, H., J. Hukkinen and E. Eklund (2002), 'Scenarios for coping with contingency: The case of aquaculture in the Finnish Archipelago Sea', *Technological Forecasting and Social Change*, **69** (2), 107–27.
Dietz, T., E. Ostrom and P.C. Stern (2003), 'The struggle to govern the commons', *Science*, **302**, 1907–12.
Dovers, S.R. (1995), 'A framework for scaling and framing policy problems in sustainability', *Ecological Economics*, **12** (2), 93–106.
Dryzek, J.S. (1997), *The Politics of the Earth: Environmental Discourses*, Oxford: Oxford University Press.

van Eeten, M.J.G. and E. Roe (2002), *Ecology, Engineering, and Management: Reconciling Ecosystem Rehabilitation and Service Reliability*, Oxford: Oxford University Press.

Ehrlich, P. (2000), *Human Natures: Genes, Cultures, and the Human Prospect*, Washington, DC: Island Press.

Erkkilä, J. (2003), 'Ympäristökeskus tutkii vielä Vuosaaren ruoppauslupaa' ('Environment Centre continues to investigate Vuosaari dredging permit'), *Helsingin Sanomat*, 23 May, p. B2.

Erkkilä, J. (2004), 'Helsingin vesissä runsaasti TBT:tä' ('Plenty of TBT in waters around Helsinki'), *Helsingin Sanomat*, 17 September, p. C2.

Flyvbjerg, B. (2001), *Making Social Science Matter: Why Social Inquiry Fails and How It Can Succeed Again*, Cambridge: Cambridge University Press.

Forbes, B.C., P. Aikio, T. Arttijeff, H. Beach, M. Bölter, B. Burkhard, O. Furmark, H. Grape, N. Gunslay, L. Heikkilä, H. Heikkinen, T. Helle, R. Horn, C. Höller, J. Hukkinen, P.G. Idivuoma, J.-L. Jernsletten, O. Jääskö, S. Kankaanpää, J. Kantola, N. Kemper, H. Kitti, Y. Konstantinov, T. Kumpula, R. Kyrö, A.M. Laakso, A. Magga, H. Magga, J. Magga, R. Möller, F. Müller, L. Müller-Wille, S. Nevalainen, A. Näkkälä, S. Peth, O. Pokuri, K. Raitio, H. Ranta, M. Sainmaa, P. Soppela, T. Thuen, J. Mathis Turi, M. Turunen, C. Uhlig, M. Vehkaoja, V. Vladimirova and N. West (2004), *RENMAN – Final Report. The Challenges of Modernity for Reindeer Management: Integration and Sustainable Development in Europe's Subarctic and Boreal Regions*, Arctic Centre Reports 41, Rovaniemi: University of Lapland, Arctic Centre and EU FP5 QLK5-CT-2000-00745.

Gould, S.J. (1990), *Wonderful Life: The Burgess Shale and the Nature of History*, New York, NY: W.W. Norton.

Groombridge, B. (ed.) (1992), *Global Biodiversity: Status of the Earth's Living Resources*, Compiled by World Conservation Monitoring Centre, London: Chapman and Hall.

Hajer, M.A. (1995), *The Politics of Environmental Discourse: Ecological Modernization and the Policy Process*, Oxford: Oxford University Press.

Heikkinen, H., J. Hukkinen, O. Jääskö, A. Laakso, L. Müller-Wille, S. Nevalainen, K. Raitio and N. West (eds) (2003a), *Poronhoidon tulevaisuus: Raportti EU: n RENMAN-hankkeen Kittilän työpajasta 13–15.8.2003 (The Future of Reindeer Management: Report of the EU RENMAN Project Workshop in Kittilä 13–15 August 2003)*, in Finnish, Technology, Society, Environment 7/2003, Espoo: Helsinki University of Technology Laboratory of Environmental Protection.

Heikkinen, H., H. Magga, S. Nevalainen and O. Jääskö (2003b), *Kuuluuko sääsken ääni taivaaseen? Poromiesten analyysi poronhoidon murroksista Suomen Lapissa 1900-luvulla (Can the mosquito be heard in heaven? Reindeer herders' analysis of changes in reindeer herding in Finland's Lapland during the 20th century)*, in Finnish, Technology, Society, Environment 3/2003, Espoo: Helsinki University of Technology Laboratory of Environmental Protection.

Helsingin satamahanke – ympäristövaikutusten arviointiselostus (Helsinki Harbour Project – Environmental Impact Statement) (1995), Helsinki: Helsingin kaupunki.

Holling, C.S. and S. Sanderson (1996), 'Dynamics of (dis)harmony in ecological and social systems', in S.S. Hanna, C. Folke and K.-G. Mäler (eds), *Rights to Nature*, Washington, DC: Island Press, pp. 57–85.

Hughes, T.P. (1987), 'The evolution of large technological systems', in W.E. Bijker, T.P. Hughes and T. Pinch (eds), *The Social Construction of Technological Systems*, Cambridge, MA: MIT Press, pp. 51–82.

Hukkinen, J. (1996), 'Ympäristövaikutusten merkittävyys on arvostuskysymys' ('The significance of environmental impact is a judgment issue'), in Finnish, *Impakti*, **2**, 16–17.

Hukkinen, J. (1999), *Institutions in Environmental Management: Constructing Mental Models and Sustainability*, London: Routledge.

Hukkinen, J. (2003a), 'From groundless universalism to grounded generalism: Improving ecological economic indicators of human–environmental interaction', *Ecological Economics*, **44**, 11–27.

Hukkinen, J. (2003b), 'Sustainability indicators for anticipating the fickleness of human–environmental interaction', *Clean Technologies and Environmental Policy*, **5** (3–4), 200–208.

Hukkinen, J., O. Jääskö, A. Laakso, L. Müller-Wille and K. Raitio (eds) (2002), *Poromiehet puhuvat: Poronhoidon ongelmat, ratkaisumahdollisuudet ja tutkimustarpeet Suomen Lapissa poromiesten näkökulmasta (Reindeer herders speak: problems, potential solutions and research needs of reindeer herding in Finnish Lapland from the viewpoint of reindeer herders)*, Technology, Society, Environment 1/2002, Espoo: Helsinki University of Technology Laboratory of Environmental Protection.

Hukkinen, J., O. Jääskö, A. Laakso, L. Müller-Wille, S. Nevalainen and K. Raitio (eds) (2003a), *Poronhoitokulttuurin arvo Suomessa: Haasteet hallinnolle, ohjaukselle ja valvonnalle (The value of reindeer herding culture in Finland. Challenges for administration, management and control)*, in Finnish, Technology, Society, Environment 1/2003, Espoo: Helsinki University of Technology Laboratory of Environmental Protection.

Hukkinen, J., L. Müller-Wille and H. Heikkinen (eds) (2003b), *Development of Participatory Institutions for Reindeer Management in Northern Finland: Preliminary Synthesis and Report*, Technology, Society, Environment 6/2003, Espoo: Helsinki University of Technology Laboratory of Environmental Protection.

Kaikkonen, R. (2004), 'Kumoava päätös ei yllättänyt valittajia' ('Overturning decision did not surprise the plaintiffs'), *Helsingin Sanomat*, 9 July, p. C1.

Kemppainen, J., J. Kettunen and M. Nieminen (2003), *Porotalouden taloustutkimusohjelma 2003–7 (Reindeer Husbandry Research Programme 2003–7)*, in Finnish with English abstract, Fish and Game Reports 281, Helsinki: Finnish Game and Fisheries Research Institute.

Koskinen, H. (2001), *MIPS ja ekologinen selkäreppu tuotteiden potentiaalisten ympäristövaikutusten vertailun menetelminä – ongelmakohtien tarkastelu (MIPS and ecological rucksack as methods for comparing the potential environmental impacts of products – an investigation of problem areas)*, in Finnish, thesis submitted in partial satisfaction of the requirements for the degree of Master of Science. Helsinki: Department of Limnology and Environmental Protection Science, Faculty of Agriculture and Forestry, University of Helsinki.

Laitinen, J. (2003a), 'Vuosaaren sataman ruoppaus keskeytyi' ('Dredging at the Vuosaari harbour halted'), *Helsingin Sanomat*, 13 May, p. B1.

Laitinen, J. (2003b), 'Helsinki jatkaa luvattomia ruoppauksia Vuosaaressa' ('Helsinki continues dredging at Vuosaari without permit'), *Helsingin Sanomat*, 15 May, p. B1.

Laitinen, J. (2003c), 'Vuosaaren sataman ruoppauksiin tarvitaan uusi vesilupa' ('New water permit required for Vuosaari dredging'), *Helsingin Sanomat*, 3 June, p. B1.

Laitinen, J. (2003d), 'Vuosaaresta löytyi odotettua enemmän TBT-yhdisteitä' ('Discoveries of TBT compounds more than expected at Vuosaari'), *Helsingin Sanomat*, 20 June, p. B14.

Lee, K.N. (1993), *Compass and Gyroscope: Integrating Science and Politics for the Environment*, Washington, DC: Island Press.

Lerner, L. (2003), 'Renman-tutkimusprojekti suosittelee parannuksia – maankäyttömuodot poronhoidon keskeisimpiä ongelmia' ('Renman research project recommends improvements – land use practices key problems'), in Finnish, *Lapin Kansa*, 29 November.

Lessing, H. (2003), 'Renman-tutkijat suosittelevat – poro Pohjoismaiden brändiksi' ('Renman researchers recommend – reindeer should be a Nordic brand'), in Finnish, *Pohjolan Sanomat*, 29 November, p. 4.

Liebowitz, S.J. and S.E. Margolis (1990), 'The Fable of the Keys', *Journal of Law and Economics*, **33**, 1–26.

Maa- ja metsätalousministeriö (2004), *Mittarityön tausta ja mittareiden käyttö – porotalous (Background of indicator work and use of indicators – reindeer management)* (www.mmm.fi/mittarit/updated 4 May 2004).

Maa- ja metsätalousministeriö (1999), *Uusiutuvien luonnonvarojen kestävän käytön yleismittarit (General indicators for sustainable utilization of renewable resources)*, in Finnish, MMM Publications 3/1999, Helsinki: Ministry of Agriculture and Forestry.

Massa, I. (1983), *Ihminen ja Lapin luonto – Lapin luonnonkäytön historiaa (Man and the Nature of Lapland – History of the Utilization of Nature in Lapland)*, in Finnish, Suomen Antropologisen Seuran toimituksia 12, Helsinki: Suomen Antropologinen Seura.

National Research Council (1999), *Our Common Journey: A Transition Toward Sustainability*, Washington, DC: National Academy Press.

North, D.C. (1992), *Institutions, Institutional Change and Economic Performance*, Cambridge, MA: Cambridge University Press.

OECD (1993), *OECD Core Set of Indicators for Environmental Performance Reviews*, OECD/DG(93)179, Environment monographs no. 83, Paris: OECD (http://www.oecd.org/env/docs/gd93179.pdf).

Perrow, C. (1999), *Normal Accidents*, Princeton, NJ: Princeton University Press.

Pyykkönen, A.-L. (2002), 'Vuosaaren sataman lähin naapuri on golfkenttä' ('Golf course the closed neighbour to the Vuosaari harbour'), *Helsingin Sanomat*, 8 February, p. B3.

RENMAN (2001), 'The challenges of modernity for reindeer management: integration and sustainable development in Europe's subarctic and boreal regions' (http://europa.eu.int/comm/research/quality-of-life/ka5/en/projects/qlrt_1999_30745_en.htm).

Rietkerk, M., S.C. Dekker, P.C. de Ruiter and J. van de Koppel (2004), 'Self-organized patchiness and catastrophic shifts in ecosystems', *Science*, **305**, 1926–9.

Redclift, M. (1992), *Sustainable Development: Exploring the Contradictions*, London: Routledge.

Rochlin, G.I., T.R. La Porte and K.H. Roberts (1987), 'The self-designing high-reliability organization: aircraft carrier flight operations at sea', *Naval War College Review*, Autumn, 76–90.

Scheffer, M., S. Carpenter, J.A. Foley, C. Folke and B. Walker (2001), 'Catastrophic shifts in ecosystems', *Nature*, **413**, 591–6.
Sykkö, S. (2004), 'Vuosikymmenen valitus' ('Complaint of the decade'), *Helsingin Sanomat*, 17 October, p. D6.
Tomasello, M. (1999), *The Cultural Origins of Human Cognition*, Cambridge, MA: Harvard University Press.
Vitousek, P.M., H.A. Mooney, J. Lubchenco and J.M. Melillo (1997), 'Human domination of Earth's ecosystems', *Science*, **277**, 494–9.
VUOPE-työryhmä (1996), *Vuosaaren satama – perustamissuunnitelma*, 20 March 1996, Helsinki: Helsingin kaupunki.
Vuosaaren satamauutiset (2003), 'Vuosaaren sataman ruoppaus jatkuu alueen itäosassa' ('Vuosaari harbour dredging continues in the eastern part of the area'), No. 1, p. 1.
Vuosaaren satamauutiset (2004), 'Ensimmäinen vaihe TBT: n poistamiseksi sai luvan' ('First stage of TBT removal permitted'), No. 2, p. 1.
Wolf, S.A. and T.F.H. Allen (1995), 'Recasting alternative agriculture as a management model: the value of adept scaling', *Ecological Economics*, **12** (1), 5–12.

15. Getting the most out of eco-efficiency indicators for policy

Nigel Jollands

INTRODUCTION

The search for sustainable development indicators continues unabated. In 1992 the United Nations Conference on Environment and Development (UNCED) posed the challenge 'to develop a concept of indicators of sustainable development in order to identify such indicators' (United Nations Conference on Environment and Development, 1992). This call by UNCED, and others, has led to what Dahl (2000) refers to as a 'new wave' of international action in the development of indicators. Indicators are now a pervasive feature of all aspects of sustainability policy.

This growing interest in sustainable development indicators has extended to indicators for eco-efficiency. Many authors now advocate eco-efficiency indicators as one approach for translating sustainable development goals into tangible measures (Friend, 1998; OECD, 1998; Schmidheiny, 1992). For example, the OECD (1998, p. 13) suggests the need for 'the identification or development of transparent, comprehensive indicators of eco-efficiency as part of a broader set of sustainable development indicators'.

Examples of eco-efficiency indicators developed on Dahl's 'new wave' are numerous, including the Roche eco-efficiency rate (EER) (Glauser and Muller, 1997) and the MIPS (material input per unit of service) indicator developed by the Wuppertal Institute (Hinterberger and Stiller, 1998). Also, several analyses specifically use eco-efficiency indicators for national policy purposes (see, for example, Energy Efficiency and Conservation Authority, 2000; Lawn, 2003; Organisation for Economic Co-operation and Development, 1998; Randla et al., 2002).

Several important observations can be made about the eco-efficiency indicator literature. First, one issue that is notable by its absence is a critical analysis of the meaning of eco-efficiency. Despite many authors attempting to define it, there is a lack of agreement about what 'eco-efficiency' actually means.

A second, related issue is the lack of attention paid to defining an eco-efficiency indicator. Indicators have been defined as 'values', 'parameters', 'measures', 'pieces of information' and 'signs'. This confusion has flowed over to eco-efficiency indicators. This is a concern because a poor understanding of what an eco-efficiency indicator is can limit a policy maker's ability to take advantage of such measurement tools.

A third observation is that the eco-efficiency indicator literature has not focused on identifying the characteristics of ideal eco-efficiency indicators. The general indicators literature is replete with discussions on criteria for ideal indicators. However, little attempt has been made to give some order to these criteria or to apply them to eco-efficiency.

The fourth issue to emerge is the lack of critical debate over the limitations and strengths of eco-efficiency indicators for policy making. A poor understanding of the strengths and limits of eco-efficiency indicators suggests there is a danger they may be used in inappropriate situations (Chatterjee and Finger, 1994).

It is essential that these theoretical issues be ironed out before eco-efficiency indicators can adequately aid decision makers. The purpose of this chapter is to address these issues and thus improve the value of eco-efficiency indicators for policy.

WHAT IS ECO-EFFICIENCY?

The first issue this chapter addresses relates to the meaning of eco-efficiency. The term first entered academic literature in an article by Schaltegger and Sturm in 1990 (Schaltegger and Burritt, 2000). However, Schmidheiny (1992) popularized the term, and the concept of eco-efficiency has subsequently gained in popularity and spread throughout the business world.

Since 1992, the notion of eco-efficiency has also taken hold in wider circles than just business. Scientific, government, and international organizations as well as businesses regard eco-efficiency as 'an essential answer to the global ecological challenge' (Hinterberger and Stiller, 1998, p. 275).

Despite widespread adoption of the eco-efficiency concept, there is 'less unanimity when it comes to the detailed definition of eco-efficiency' (Hinterberger and Stiller, 1998, p. 275). Indeed, the literature includes various authors questioning the strength of current definitions of the term. Even eco-efficiency proponents, such as DeSimone et al. (2000, p. xix), acknowledge that 'the concept of eco-efficiency needs further refinement'. Welford (1997, p. 30) is more forceful: 'I have never found a very clear definition of what this [eco-efficiency] really means and that in itself reflects the confused and often contradictory thinking of eco-modernists'. This lack of a clear interpretation leads to what could be described as a 'chaos of terminology'.

Part of the reason for the lack of unanimity on the meaning of the eco-efficiency concept is the absence of a detailed definition in Schmidheiny's (1992) seminal work. This lack led to the concept having rather vacuous beginnings. Interpretations of eco-efficiency tend to be restricted to business management-related literature and range from the relatively simple to the more detailed, such as the definition developed by the World Business Council for Sustainable Development (WBCSD) (DeSimone et al., 2000).

Simple interpretations of eco-efficiency are, not surprisingly, more common. They tend to appear as off-hand comments in business management-related magazine articles. For example, Williams (1999, p. 37) defines eco-efficiency as 'endeavouring to get more from less for longer'. Similarly, DeSimone et al. (2000, p. xix) comment that eco-efficiency is used to 'describe activities that create economic value while continuously reducing ecological impact and the use of resources'. While these simple interpretations may be appropriate for the magazine audience, they do belie several leitmotifs inherent in this body of literature. In addition to these definitions, Glauser and Muller (1997, p. 201) introduce the notion of opti-mality into their interpretation of eco-efficiency. They state eco-efficiency is 'the optimal use of material, energy, human resources, and capital to supply innovative products to the market'.

A more detailed definition of eco-efficiency comes from the WBCSD. The WBCSD and its predecessors developed the definition through a series of publications and workshops (for example, Business Council for Sustainable Development, 1993; World Business Council for Sustainable Development, 1995 and 2000). The full definition to emerge from the work is:

> Eco-efficiency is reached by the delivery of competitively-priced goods and services that satisfy human needs and bring quality of life, while progressively reducing environmental impacts and resource intensity throughout the life cycle, to a level at least in line with the Earth's estimated carrying capacity (DeSimone et al., 2000, p. 47).

This definition has five core themes: (1) an emphasis on service; (2) a focus on needs and quality of life; (3) consideration of the entire product life cycle; (4) a recognition of limits to carrying capacity; and (5) a process view (DeSimone et al., 2000, p. 47).

Notwithstanding the plethora of interpretations, Hinterberger and Stiller (1998, p. 275) note that all interpretations have an obvious theme in common: 'All concepts call for a more efficient use of natural resources'.

A closer examination reveals several common assumptions that underlie these interpretations. As Welford (2003, p. 164) states, the contemporary approach to eco-efficiency brings with it 'a clear set of values . . . aimed at promulgating business as usual'.

Other assumptions underlie these interpretations, including the following (Jollands, 2003):

1. the desirability of business as usual development (Welford, 2003);
2. placing ultimate faith in unfettered markets and economic growth;
3. making inappropriate assumptions about the controllability of the production process;
4. seeing technology as a fix for environmental problems;
5. relying on questionable assumptions about the independence of the production and environmental processes.

Interpretations of eco-efficiency, based on these assumptions, are limited and can undermine the credibility of the concept; limit the ken of eco-efficiency; lead to inappropriate policy prescriptions; and limit the ability of resource users to address eco-efficiency in a 'holistic' sense.

This is not a call to abandon the concept. Rather, it lays down the challenge to take a broader perspective of eco-efficiency. Other interpretations of the term are possible. In order to build a richer understanding of eco-efficiency, we need to draw on Schaltegger and Burritt's (2000) suggestion that a distinction can be made between eco-efficiency as a concept and as a ratio. To shed light on both of these aspects, we investigate the etymological origins of the term and how it is used in the core theoretical disciplines from which it emerged. The intent here is to frame the discussion of eco-efficiency in a theoretical analysis of its meaning. This theoretical foundation has largely been ignored in the modern day eco-efficiency literature, which has tended to have a practical and empirical focus.

Etymological Origins of the Eco-efficiency Term

The English word 'efficiency' is derived from the Latin word *efficientia*, the present participle of the verb *efficere*. *Efficere* means to bring about, accomplish, execute or produce (Barnhart, 1988; Klein, 2000; Morris and Morris, 1988; Shipley, 1984; Simpson and Weiner, 1989; Skeat, 1961). The infinitive is itself derived from a combination of *ex-* (after) with the Latin verb *facere*, to do or make (Barnhart, 1988; Klein, 2000).

The interpretation of efficiency has evolved in two directions. Efficiency was used in a philosophical and theological context to refer to the action of an 'operative agent' – God, as in, 'The manner of this devine efficiencie being farre above us' (Hooker, 1593, cited in Simpson and Weiner, 1989, p. 83). This use of the term is now generally obsolete.

The other direction of efficiency's evolution also derives from theology and is the basis for our contemporary use of the term. Efficiency came to be used to mean 'fitness or power to accomplish, or success in accomplishing, the purpose intended' (Simpson and Weiner, 1989, p. 84). The 'fitness or power to accomplish' interpretation of efficiency was taken from theological themes and, in the context of the rationalist spirit of the Enlightenment and the commercial activity of 18th-century Europe, applied more widely to the transient world. In doing so, the centre of gravity of efficiency interpretations shifted from a theological, spiritual basis to a Western-scientific, 'logical–positivist' realm. Evidence of this burgeoned in the literature of the 1800s.

Two threads are evident in this new approach to efficiency. First, the concept of efficiency is applied to the 'productive machine'. In 1827, Gilbert used the word efficiency in relation to physics: the work done by a force in operating a machine or engine (Simpson and Weiner, 1989). Similarly, 'efficiency' was used in relation to the 'organic machine' in biological literature as early as 1925 (Lotka, 1925). Borrowing from thermodynamics, Lotka defined efficiency as the fraction of energy (Q) converted to work (W).

A second thread in the contemporary use of the efficiency concept relates to the economics of resources and welfare. Efficiency began to enter the economic vocabulary in the 1800s (Simpson and Weiner, 1989). The most widely used interpretation of economic efficiency comes from the work of Vilfredo Pareto in the late 19th century. His work led to what is now referred to as allocative efficiency or simply Pareto efficiency.

Since the 1800s, and the wider application of the efficiency term, the number of efficiency concepts has burgeoned. As discussed below, efficiency concepts now include technical efficiency, production efficiency, profit efficiency, x-efficiency, allocative efficiency, scale efficiency, thermal and finite-time efficiency, managerial efficiency, dynamic efficiency, ecological efficiency, and many more.

In sum, the modern interpretation of efficiency can be traced to both its spiritual and scientific roots. It is a powerful concept that embodies the notion of fitness or power to accomplish, or success in accomplishing, the purpose intended.

A relatively new derivation of the 'efficiency' concept is the idea of 'eco-efficiency', which is the focus of this chapter. The 'eco-' prefix is commonly used in words borrowed from Greek such as *economy*, which originally referred to household management, and from 1651, the first recorded extension of the concept to the management of resources (Barnhart, 1988;

Skeat, 1961). Another example is *ecology*. This word, first coined by Haekel in 1866, represents an early example of the extension of the concept of 'house' to that of the 'environment-within-which-we-live' (Golley, 1993). In modern coinage the 'eco-' prefix has continued Haekel's tradition of broadening the meaning from the notion of 'house' to the 'environment and relation to it' (Barnhart, 1988, p. 313).

The 'eco-' prefix makes 'eco-'efficiency distinct from the other efficiency concepts. The 'eco-' prefix focuses efficiency on the 'environment and relation to it'. Specifically, the prefix adds a lens to the 'success in accomplishing' component of the efficiency concept. Through this lens, 'success' is seen to extend beyond simply whether the goal is achieved or not, to encompass a concern for the impact on the 'environment and relation to it' associated with the activity of achieving the goal. Often, in modern use of the term, this 'efficiency-success' is measured by using a ratio of useful outputs to inputs. The concern for environmental impact inherent in 'eco-'efficiency suggests a focus on those activities with environmental repercussions. Since economic activities impose significant pressures on the environment, it is reasonable to consider that economy–environment interactions form an important focus of the eco-efficiency concept.

Given the economy–environment interaction focus, the 'eco-' prefix also appears to align efficiency's 'purpose intended' towards sustainable development. This focus on sustainable development is implicit in many interpretations of eco-efficiency (such as the WBCSD interpretation). Following from these observations about the effect of the 'eco-' prefix on efficiency, a 'core meaning' (that is, a constancy of meaning that persists throughout different contexts) of the term eco-efficiency can be identified. Eco-efficiency could be generically described as 'a measure of the success (accounting for wider environmental impacts) of economic activities aimed at promoting sustainable development that is quantified as the ratio of useful outputs to ecological inputs'.

DISCIPLINARY PERSPECTIVES OF ECO-EFFICIENCY

The core definition of eco-efficiency mentioned above is interpreted through different disciplinary lenses. As with the proverbial parable of the blind men and the elephant, any single interpretation of efficiency is contextually bound to a particular set of disciplinary and epistemological assumptions. To shed light on the eco-efficiency concept and ratio, this section uses an epistemic encounter approach to illuminate the insights into eco-efficiency that emerge from several disciplines that have developed efficiency concepts as part of their core scientific enquiry: thermodynamics, economics and ecology.

Thermodynamic Approaches to Eco-efficiency

Efficiency has been a core focus of classical thermodynamics since the beginning of the science. This focus has developed primarily because of classical thermodynamics' conception during the Industrial Revolution and its preoccupation with increasing the efficiency of industrial-revolution machines (Khalil, 1990; Kondepudi and Prigogine, 1998; O'Connor, 1994). The concept of thermodynamic efficiency was first developed in connection with steam engines: an engine was more efficient if it could, for example, pump more water while using the same quantity of coal (Ayres and Nair, 1984).

The work of the early thermodynamicists led to an empirically precise definition of efficiency based on measures of physical, often observable, systems. Efficiency concepts within thermodynamics are all based on the same ratio:

$$Efficiency\ (\eta) = \frac{useful\ output}{input} \qquad (15.1)$$

Thermodynamic concepts of efficiency based on this ratio can be divided into thermal efficiency, efficiency based on ideal limits, finite-time efficiency, and energy-quality-adjusted efficiency measures. Insights from these concepts for eco-efficiency are summarized in Table 15.1.

As with any disciplinary perspective, care must be taken when using these concepts. Classical thermodynamic efficiency concepts are a product of the discipline's assumptions and the way it views reality. In particular, thermodynamic concepts could be criticized for being too preoccupied with machines of work (O'Connor, 1994), for assuming that systems deterministically tend toward equilibrium (Khalil, 1990), and for being based on the notion of an ideal 'reversible' system (Ruth, 1993).

These views have implications for the way classical thermodynamics would formulate the eco-efficiency concept. The preoccupation with controllable machines of work could imply that eco-efficiency is likewise controllable. In complex systems with non-linear feedback, this is unlikely to be the case. Also, in an 'equilibrial world', efficiency is assumed to converge on a unique final value through the relentless march towards equilibrium. Since non-equilibrium systems are ubiquitous in nature, a classical thermodynamic equilibrium-based approach to concepts such as eco-efficiency must be treated carefully.

*Table 15.1   Insights and lessons from classical thermodynamics,
              neoclassical economics and ecosystem ecology theories*

Efficiency concept	Insights and lessons for eco-efficiency
Classical thermodynamic theory	
Thermal efficiency	Provides a formulation for eco-efficiency concepts as the ratio of useful energy output to inputs
Efficiency measures based on ideal limits	Emphasizes that there are limits to eco-efficiency Is useful for identifying the theoretical savings that can be achieved in eco-efficiency Is useful for identifying the proximity to eco-efficiency limits
Finite-time efficiency	Emphasizes the trade-off between efficiency and speed of transformation
Efficiency measures adjusted for energy quality	Highlights the importance of energy quality Emphasizes that useful work should form the basis for an eco-efficiency that accounts for energy quality
Assumptions	Nature is controllable therefore eco-efficiency is controllable Eco-efficiency is focused on machines of work Equilibrium implies the level of eco-efficiency is computable and unique
Neoclassical economic theory	
Neoclassical economic production theory	
Technical efficiency	Focuses on the efficiency of the production process Focuses on those inputs and outputs that are commodified as part of the production function Focuses on direct inputs and outputs Emphasizes technology
Production efficiency	Emphasizes the need to consider prices when allocating resources Focuses on profit objective
x-efficiency	Helps to identify why the firm is not on the outermost production possibility frontier (perhaps because of unnecessary waste that has not been eliminated) Helps to identify waste reduction that can be achieved

Table 15.1 (continued)

Efficiency concept	Insights and lessons for eco-efficiency
Neoclassical welfare economics	
Allocative efficiency	Focuses eco-efficiency on arranging resources to maximize welfare
	Emphasizes the importance of internalising externalities
Intertemporal efficiency	Suggests rational consumers do consider time in their decisions to use natural resources, and these decisions are influenced by interest rates
Assumptions	Eco-efficiency achieved when the 'right context' is set
	Atomistic focus implies that neoclassical economic approach to eco-efficiency ignores wider system interdependencies
	Assumed reduced importance of the physical environment implies that eco-efficiency is less important than other efficiency concepts
Ecosystem ecology theory	
Ratios within and between trophic levels	Defines efficiency in terms of energy and matter flows
	Focuses on ecosystems service use by primary industry/biological sectors of the economy
Transformity	Emphasizes importance of accounting for energy quality in eco-efficiency
	Emphasizes importance of accounting for 'indirectness' in eco-efficiency
Maximum power principle	Raises the question of the role of evolution in influencing levels of efficiency
	Suggests systems are selected to operate at the eco-efficiency that generates maximum power
Assumptions	Eco-efficiency analyses require a judicious mix of holistic and reductionistic analyses
	Boundary definition is important
	The functionalist approach ignores some of the complex interactions in a system

Neoclassical Economic Approaches to Eco-efficiency

Since the current predominant theory in the economic discipline is neoclassical economics, the following will focus on a neoclassical interpretation of eco-efficiency. A focus on natural resource scarcity has been a major theme of economics since its inception (Randall, 1987). Such a concern naturally leads to a concern for the efficiency of resource use. As early as the Physiocrats (1750–80), notions of the environment and efficiency of resource use were alluded to. The classical school of economics (1775–1875) also pointed out that all resources (capital, labour, land) contribute to wealth. Another feature of early classical economists' thinking (Ricardo, Malthus), was their focus on natural resource constraints. However, following Adam Smith's treatise, outlining, among other things, a system for achieving an efficient allocation of resources, emphasis on the importance of natural resource constraints waned. Neoclassical economists have continued this trend, tending to focus efficiency concepts on the human welfare implications of resource allocations rather than on the imperative to avert resource extinction.

Efficiency remains a core concept of neoclassical economics (Leibenstein, 1966). In fact, 'many mainstream economists regard the domain of economics to be limited to matters of efficiency' (Woodward and Bishop, 1995, p. 104).

Efficiency in economics is not a single notion, but rather 'a multidimensional concept' (Helm, 1988, p. 13). These many efficiency concepts can be found in two main bodies of theory: production theory (such as technical efficiency, production efficiency) and welfare economics (such as allocative efficiency, intertemporal efficiency). Table 15.1 summarizes insights into eco-efficiency from neoclassical economic concepts.

A neoclassical economic approach to eco-efficiency is influenced by a particular world view about economic activity and the environment. In particular, neoclassical economics, and by implication its concept of eco-efficiency, has been criticized because of its mechanistic, deterministic and atomistic view of the economic system (Söllner, 1997).

The implication of this world view is that neoclassical economics assumes that, given the right conditions, the market machine will inevitably and instantly achieve equilibrium levels of eco-efficiency in its many guises. It is hard to find a justification for this view, since there is little empirical evidence that economic systems tend deterministically towards equilibrium. Instead, we see an economy characterized by 'non-equilibrium (and) self-reinforcing behaviour' (Christensen, 1991, p. 75).

Neoclassical economics also tends implicitly to view the economy as a closed system. As Sir John Hicks states, 'it is because the range of phenomena with which economists deal is so narrow that economists are so continually butting their head against its boundaries' (quoted in Norgaard, 1985, p. 388). The implications of this for eco-efficiency are twofold. First, a neoclassical approach to eco-efficiency tends to be restricted to the immediate, direct effects of an action within the closed system – wider flow-on effects are ignored. Second, closed-system assumptions lead to resource misallocation. The only way to avoid resource misallocation is to recognize that the economy is an open system from both economic and thermodynamic perspectives (Amir, 1994).

Ecosystem Ecology Approaches to Eco-efficiency

Ecology adds yet more efficiency concepts to what is already a crowded lexicon (see Table 15.1). As prominent ecologist Howard Odum (1971, p. 92) states, 'many names have been used to describe various kinds of efficiency, and definitions are not always clear'.

Concern for efficiency in ecosystem ecology theory has a shorter history than in thermodynamics or economics. According to Martinez-Alier (1987, p. 9), not until the mid-19th century did ecologists come to consider the efficiency and transformation of energy by plants and animals as a central question in their research. Lotka (1925) was among the first to apply the idea of efficiency directly to biological systems. By the 1940s, ecologists were calculating a variety of efficiency ratios.

Perhaps the most important contribution to the concept of ecological efficiency came from Raymond Lindeman (1941 and 1942). Lindeman was the 'first to implement Tansely's ecosystem concept in a quantitative effort to define the system and described and understand its dynamic behaviour' (Golley, 1993, p. 50). The contribution of Lindeman's coupling of thermodynamics and ecology was a watershed for ecosystem ecology's notion of efficiency. In particular, it enabled ecologists to quantify the energy and material flows through trophic levels and, therefore, to develop mathematical models.

By applying energy analysis, Lindeman defined ecological efficiency as:

$$Efficiency\ (\eta) = \frac{secondary\ consumers\ (or\ producers)}{primary\ consumers\ (or\ producers)} \quad (15.2)$$

Lindeman's work also led to a proliferation of research into the level of efficiency in ecosystems (see, for example, Chew and Chew, 1970; Golley, 1960, 1961, 1967, 1972; Kay and Schneider, 1992; Slobodkin, 1962; Wulff and Ulanowicz, 1989). The term ecological efficiency soon became popularized, and clearly became embedded in ecology as a result of Odum's book *Fundamentals of Ecology* (Eugene Odum, 1959).

Definitions of efficiency in ecology have received significant attention. Wiegert (1988, p. 34) defines efficiency in general terms as 'the ratio of some defined output or product to the input or cost'. Howard Odum (1971, p. 92) focuses on power flows for his definition. In his view, 'any ratio of power flows is an efficiency and there are many kinds of power ratios'. In a similar vein, Eugene Odum (1959, p. 53) defines ecological efficiency as 'ratios between energy flow at different points along the food chain. Such ratios, when expressed as percentages, are often called ecological efficiencies'. In ecological terms, then, ecological efficiency is defined uniquely as a ratio of energy and matter flows.

Discussion of efficiency concepts in ecological literature can be grouped into three areas: Eugene Odum's (Odum, 1959 and 1983) 'efficiency between and within trophic levels', Howard Odum's 'transformity' (Odum, 1971 and 1996), and the 'maximum power principle' (Odum and Pinkerton, 1955).

An ecosystem ecology perspective provides several insights into eco-efficiency. In particular, an ecological perspective:

- promotes a mix of holistic and reductionistic analyses of eco-efficiency (Koestler, 1978);
- emphasizes the importance of boundaries in an analysis of eco-efficiency (Golley, 1993; O'Neill et al., 1986; Odum, 1996);
- acknowledges complexity and questions an equilibrial view of systems (Golley, 1993; Hagen, 1992; Odum, 1983).

However, an ecological approach to eco-efficiency is firmly rooted in what Wiegert (1988) refers to as ecological energetics: a focus on energy flows through the ecosystem. This approach is limited in several ways. First, it ignores some complex interrelationships, such as interspecies relationships. Second, it emphasizes the quantitative rather than the qualitative and is therefore prone to the *pars pro toto* trap, taking the part for the whole. Finally, the putatively 'objective' view of eco-efficiency implied in energetics is misleading because the eco-efficiency concept is inherently subjective. The mere focus on efficiency in ecological research suggests a value judgement about the importance of efficiency.

Summary of Discussion on Disciplinary Eco-efficiency Interpretations

The preceding discussion has established that eco-efficiency has a core or 'timeless' meaning. This core meaning is overlaid by disciplinary accretions and must be uncovered through etymological and contextual analysis.

The three disciplinary perspectives just discussed provide a rich mix of potential approaches to eco-efficiency concepts. Table 15.1 is an attempt to draw together the many insights into eco-efficiency provided by selected efficiency concepts within each discipline. By presenting this range of different perspectives of eco-efficiency, I have tried to encourage a view that the perspectives of eco-efficiency are plural and intertwined. I have also presented these perspectives to promote tolerance and an acceptance that all perspectives can potentially provide important insights into eco-efficiency in appropriate contexts. In doing so, I hope to contribute to the policy-guiding potential of the eco-efficiency concept.

WHAT IS AN ECO-EFFICIENCY INDICATOR? A VIEW FROM SEMIOTICS

In addition to the lack of attention paid to the definition of eco-efficiency *per se*, the second issue I address in this chapter is the lack of a clear definition of just what is an eco-efficiency indicator. Without a clear understanding of what we mean by the term, we cannot hope to communicate fully the strengths, limitations and ken of what we are presenting to decision makers.

In order to define the term 'eco-efficiency indicator', we must first focus on the indicator concept in general. Current definitions of indicators and the terminology used in this area are particularly confusing. The indicators-related literature is full of sometimes contradicting and obtuse interpretations of what indicators are. A survey of environmental indicator literature shows significant confusion with terminology. An indicator has been defined as a parameter or a measure (Andreasen et al., 2001; Peng et al., 2002; Pykh, 2002), a model (Adriaanse, 1993), a metric (Bennett, 2002), and a value, a fraction, or a sign (Kurtz et al., 2001). Clearly, there is a need to develop a more rigorous definition of the concept of an indicator that is grounded in theory.

In order to define the term 'eco-efficiency indicator', we draw on semiotics – the general theory of signs. But, first, it is instructive to trace the etymological origins of the term 'indicator'. Etymologically, indicator traces back to the Latin verb *indicare*, meaning to disclose or point out, show, mention or make known or to act as a sign (Hammond et al., 1995; Simpson and Weiner, 1989). The use of the word 'indicator' has a long history in English, although its use in scientific endeavour is relatively recent. Simpson and Weiner (1989) present evidence of early use of the word in English dating back to 1666.

The use of the term 'indicator' in science was first recorded in 1842: 'The substance we use as an indicator . . .' (Grove, 1842 quoted in Simpson and Weiner, 1989, p. 861). In the area of environmental investigation, ecologists

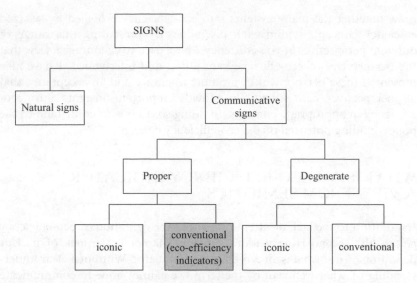

Source: Adapted from the classification by Clarke (1987).

Figure 15.1   Semiotics and signs

first used the term in the early 1900s to mean 'a group of plants or animals whose presence acts as a sign of particular environmental conditions' (Simpson and Weiner, 1989, p. 861). The term is now in common use in contemporary English language.

In its most general sense, an indicator can be thought of as a sign. In semiotics (the general theory of signs), a sign is defined as 'something which stands for something to somebody in some respect or capacity' (Gallopín, 1997, p. 14). An indicator is clearly something that stands for something to someone else. Therefore, an indicator can be considered as a particular form of sign.

Semiotics as defined by Pierce is a branch of logic and philosophy with the aim of 'singling out necessary, as opposed to contingent, features of signs interpreted by creatures capable of learning' (Clarke, 1987). The semiotics stemming from Pierce provides both a useful classification of signs and an insight into the core characteristics of those signs (and, therefore, eco-efficiency indicators as a particular form of sign). Clarke (1987) provides a three-tiered framework for classifying signs, as shown in Figure 15.1.

This framework is useful for defining eco-efficiency indicators, as they can be considered a particular form of sign that belongs to what can be termed 'conventional proper communicative signs' (shaded box in Figure 15.1).

Communicative signs are those that are produced 'with communicative intent and interpreted as such by their interpreters' (Clarke, 1987, p. 73). These can be compared with what Clarke refers to as 'natural signs' (those that are not produced with communicative intent). Several conditions are necessary for a sign to be a communicative sign. A sign 'X' is a communicative sign if and only if (Grice 1968):

1. X is produced by a communicator C with the intent of producing an effect E on some interpreter I; as
2. C intends that I recognize the intention of (1); and
3. I recognizes this intention, and if E were produced on I, then I's recognition of the intention of (2) would be the reason for E.

In other words, condition (1) requires that an effect on some interpreter be intended, and condition (2) adds that the communicator must intend for this effect to be recognized. Condition (3), in turn, requires that an interpreter perceives him or herself as the intended target of a display and that his or her response will not be a reflex response to a triggering stimulus (Clarke, 1987, p. 79).

Degenerate communicative signs satisfy conditions (1) and (2) only. Proper communicative signs, on the other hand, satisfy all three conditions. Eco-efficiency indicators can be regarded as proper communicative signs because, in a normative sense, they satisfy all three conditions – they are produced with communicative intent; this intent is aimed at informing decisions or changing behaviour; and they should be aimed at a clearly defined audience.

At the next level, iconic communicative signs are interpreted as representing objects by virtue of a similarity to those objects. For example, a person A may perform a jogging motion to indicate that she or he wants B to jog. In contrast, conventional communicative signs rely on some convention for their interpretation. The classical view of a convention is as a historical agreement reached by decree or stipulation. However, many conventions exist without such agreement. A broader definition of convention is 'an existing behavioural regularity based on the expectations and preferences of the members of a community' (Clarke, 1987, p. 85). The need to rely on some convention for interpretation is necessary because many communicative signs are essentially a model or abstraction of reality. Eco-efficiency indicators tend to adhere to both conceptual and scientific convention. Conceptually, eco-efficiency indicators are accepted as quantitative measures of some aspect of the environment. Scientifically, eco-efficiency indicators are quantified using conventional units such as joules for energy or kilograms for weight, and so on.

In summary, drawing on semiotics, eco-efficiency indicators can be defined in abstract as 'quantitative conventional proper communicative signs' of some aspect of the environment. This abstract definition can be used to build an operational definition of eco-efficiency indicators. At an operational level, eco-efficiency indicators require quantification. This is achieved by measuring variables.

In the mathematical sciences, the term 'variable' usually refers to some attribute of interest that takes on different values. More specifically, a variable is 'an operational representation of an attribute . . . of a system' (Gallopín, 1997, p. 14). Following from this and the core meaning of eco-efficiency mentioned above, the term 'eco-efficiency indicator' can be defined as:

> a measure of the success (accounting for wider environmental impacts) of economic activities aimed at promoting sustainable development that (1) is quantified as the ratio of useful outputs to ecological inputs; (2) uses clear scientific and theoretical conventions; and (3) is produced with communicative intent with the aim of informing the decisions of a clearly defined audience (Ibid).

CRITERIA FOR IDEAL ECO-EFFICIENCY INDICATORS

The third issue that requires attention in the eco-efficiency indicators literature is that of the criteria for selecting indicators. Defining the ideal characteristics of eco-efficiency indicators will help practitioners evaluate which indicators are best for their tasks. Contemporary indicators literature is replete with discussions on characteristics or criteria for ideal indicators (see, for example, Andreasen et al., 2001; Dale and Beyeler, 2001; Gallopín, 1997; Kurtz et al., 2001; Peng et al., 2002). A vast range of criteria has been proposed by many other authors, from the need for the indicator to be easily measurable and unambiguous (Dale and Beyeler, 2001), to the indicator's conceptual relevance and feasibility of implementation (Kurtz et al., 2001). However, little attempt has been made to integrate the many criteria proposed by these authors. We propose that the ideal characteristics of eco-efficiency indicators should usefully be grouped into theoretical and pragmatic considerations.

Theoretical Considerations

Theoretical basis
Eco-efficiency indicators must be grounded in theory – what Kurtz et al. (2001) refer to as 'conceptual relevance'. Grounding indicators in theory is

important because this helps the user map empirical measurements (or indicators) onto his or her model of reality (Hardi and DeSouza-Huletey, 2000). This grounding also helps to ensure eco-efficiency indicators measure the key aspects of the system in question. That is, indicators are more likely to be 'comprehensive' (Andreasen et al., 2001) and 'integrative' (Dale and Beyeler, 2001). Eco-efficiency indicators can draw on concepts from ecology, economics and thermodynamics. Ecological economics is another body of theory that offers a potential theoretical foundation for eco-efficiency indicators.

Philosophical bias
Ideal eco-efficiency indicators should be formulated in terms of broad philosophical or ethical frameworks. This need for a broad philosophical framework is particularly important for eco-efficiency indicators, as the target audiences may include decision makers having diverse political and ethical convictions. Ignoring this requirement can lead to inappropriate indicators. For example, specifying eco-efficiency indicators solely based on ecological theory is likely to disenfranchise those with socio-economic interests. As Wright (1991) argues, few indicators are without such bias. Because of the difficulty of removing bias, this criterion should be regarded as an ideal rather than an attainable goal.

Appropriate data transformations
Ideal eco-efficiency indicators are estimated using a sound methodology that employs appropriate data transformations (Ministry for the Environment, 1997). Raw data are rarely suitable for use as an indicator. That is, raw data nearly always need to be transformed into meaningful ratios, indices, or percentages. These data transformations must be scientifically credible, robust and standardized for the purpose intended.

Analytical validity
Analytical validity means the indicator should measure what it is designed to measure. This requires that the indicator responds to stress in a predictable manner and is sensitive to stress on the system (Dale and Beyeler, 2001). Communicating analytical validity is essential for the credibility of an indicator. This requires that the data transformations must be transparent and well documented (Gallopín, 1997; Ministry for the Environment, 1997). As well as providing users with the ability to determine how indicators have been estimated, transparency also allows others to reproduce the results.

Appropriate scale
Different indicators may be relevant at one scale but meaningless at other scales. According to Gallopín (1997), hierarchical systems theory shows

that 'different indicators of systems performance are usually required at different hierarchical levels of systems'. That is, eco-efficiency indicators selected to measure the performance of a single aspect of the environment in a single catchment could be different from indicators chosen to measure ecosystem performance at a biosphere level. An ideal eco-efficiency indicator will be one that is chosen at a scale relevant to the purpose of inquiry. According to Andreasen et al. (2001), 'the "best" scale depends on the scientific and management questions that are being asked'.

Efficient representation of a concept
Ideal eco-efficiency indicators should convey the maximum possible information about a theoretical concept (Gustavson et al., 1999). This involves the principle of parsimony – when many indicators are relevant to an aspect of interest, the simplest indicator is preferred over more complex indicators. Indeed, Peng et al. (2002) suggest that an important criterion for indicators is that they should be simple and easy to understand. Several techniques are available for identifying those indicators that convey the most information, including principal components analysis.

Pragmatic Considerations

In addition to theoretical considerations, there are a number of pragmatic considerations for choosing ideal eco-efficiency indicators. These are policy relevance, cost effectiveness, and clarity of message.

Policy relevance
The need for indicators (particularly national-level indicators) to be relevant to policy is a common theme throughout the indicators literature (Adriaanse, 1996; Mortensen, 1997; Peng et al., 2002; Walz et al., 1996). Gallopín (1997, p. 15) states, 'the most important feature of indicators compared to other forms of information is relevance to policy and decision-making'. An ideal eco-efficiency indicator can be used to evaluate government policy to assist decision makers to monitor progress towards policy objectives.

Data availability and cost effectiveness
The eco-efficiency indicator or set of indicators must be based on available information and be cost-effective (Alfsen and Saebo, 1993; Walz et al., 1996). In the words of Kurtz et al. (2001), these indicators must be 'feasible to implement'. The issue of cost-effectiveness is often overlooked (Gallopín, 1997). This issue also creates a tension with other ideal characteristics. For example, indicators that are theoretically sound may not

necessarily be cost-effective to monitor. From a pragmatic perspective, eco-efficiency indicators that are not cost-effective will not be implemented. Cost-effectiveness is a function of several aspects including data availability, data volume required, calculation complexity, and data processing required.

Clarity of message
Finally, drawing on semiotics, ideal eco-efficiency indicators must be able to communicate their message clearly to their audience (Alfsen and Saebo, 1993). Kurtz et al. (2001) suggest asking the question 'will the indicator convey information on [relevant] conditions that is meaningful to environmental decision-making?' Clarity of message also requires that the audience must be accurately defined and the best means of communicating with them considered (Ott, 1978). Hukkinen (2001, p. 313) suggests that the message of eco-efficiency indicators should be to ensure that 'individual actors perceive their everyday activities to be materially grounded in bundles of ecosystem services'. In general, eco-efficiency indicators should be easy to understand for the defined audience (Mortensen, 1997). The challenge of developing indicators that are easily understood should not be underestimated (Lindsey et al., 1997).

It is unlikely that any one eco-efficiency indicator will satisfy all these characteristics, so everyday use of indicators will inevitably involve trade-offs between these characteristics. For example, in pursuit of cost-effective indicators, it may be necessary to compromise on analytical validity or appropriate data transformations. In the final analysis, this list provides a benchmark for the development of high-quality eco-efficiency indicators rather than a list of characteristics that must be strictly adhered to.

A CRITIQUE OF ECO-EFFICIENCY INDICATORS

It is essential that those using eco-efficiency indicators appreciate the strengths and weaknesses of indicators. Unfortunately, there has been little debate about the relative strengths and weaknesses of eco-efficiency indicators in the literature. This lack of appreciation of such issues could hamper the ability of eco-efficiency indicators to guide policy making.

Limitations of Eco-efficiency Indicators

I will begin by laying bare some of the real and perceived limitations of eco-efficiency indicators. These indicators can be used to reinforce narrow perspectives of the environment or human–environment interface. By codifying the environment as indicators tied to a particular disciplinary perspective, there is a tendency to fall into a *pars pro toto* trap – where the part is considered as the whole. As Dale and Beyeler (2001, p. 5) suggest, when selecting 'only one or a few indicators, . . . the focus becomes narrow, and an oversimplified understanding . . . is promoted'. Such an approach can potentially lead down a treacherous path of incomplete information and ill-advised management practice. One way to reduce this problem is to remind the user constantly about the potential myopia inherent in using indicators.

The reliance on quantified indicators can lead to another problem – what Whitehead (1925) refers to as the 'fallacy of misplaced concreteness'. That is, by relying on quantified indicators, users are lulled into a (sometimes) false sense of security. Indicators printed in black and white are tangible, real, 'concrete' evidence. Often, however, indicators embody a number of assumptions and are always an estimate of the eco-efficiency phenomena of interest. An important role of an indicator practitioner is to provide clear information about the limits of the indicator presented.

Good eco-efficiency indicators (and indicators in general) will be based on a strong theoretical foundation. Unfortunately, a theoretical basis for indicators is often lacking, which has led to a situation where 'the use of environmental indicators continues to be *ad hoc* and sporadic' (Lindsey et al., 1997, p. 685). Without a strong theoretical context, indicators can miss key features or measure the wrong aspects of the system (Jorgensen, 2002).

The lack of a theoretical foundation also makes interpretation of indicators difficult, because theory is essential for mapping eco-efficiency indicators to their relevant contexts. As Waugh (1999, p. 200) points out, care is needed with numbers: 'A number on its own (take seven) has no meaning unless it is related to things outside of itself, i.e. seven dogs, seven cats, seven dots, or whatever'. Thus, all numbers, including eco-efficiency indicators, need to be based on a strong theoretical foundation that makes the indicators meaningful by tying them to a 'context'.

Another limitation is that eco-efficiency indicators are unavoidably biased. As Manoliadis (2002) states, 'indicator information implicitly reflects the values of those who develop and select them'. Most eco-efficiency indicators are constructed using information that is readily available, can be obtained at a reasonable cost, or conform to the convictions of the analyst. Therefore, it is important to be aware of this potential bias and to take care when interpreting eco-efficiency indicators.

Perhaps the most vigorous critique of indicators in general comes from Bradbury (1996), who argues that indicators *per se* are a legacy of an outmoded paradigm. In his opinion, indicators emerge 'effortlessly' from a simplistic, linear, equilibrial, reductionistic view of the world with its 'lust of lists – the desire to organise and codify' (Bradbury, 1996, p. 4). Scientists 'fall for their seductive charms, to create a sad Cartesian parody: *indico, ergo sum*' (Bradbury, 1996, p. 2). Bradbury (1996, p. 5) goes on to say:

> Indicators, despite their popularity, are the consequence of an approach to understanding the complexity of the world which is fundamentally and fatally flawed. . . . They are wrong, because they take reductionism, itself a suspect method . . . to a new pathological depth. They seek to reduce, to collapse, the dimensionality of some description of a complex system. . . . Like throwing shadows on a wall, they can never capture reality. They remain caricatures.

Bradbury (1996, p. 7) concludes by saying, 'it is time to learn to approach the complexity, the richness of the world with theory, data, models and tools which honour that richness instead of subverting it, which acknowledge that complexity instead of denying it'.

Dahl (2000, p. 41) echoes Bradbury's sentiment and suggests indicators are limited in their ability to assess 'the whole'. It is a characteristic of complex systems that they may show higher-order interactions that are not evident from a knowledge of the parts that are shown by indicators.

Strengths of Eco-efficiency Indicators

Despite their clear limitations, eco-efficiency indicators do have strengths, arising in part from the unique characteristics of the policy-making process itself. Bradbury's critique is itself limited in that context. His argument comes from the point of view of normative, objective, ideal science, but eco-efficiency indicators are primarily tools of policy analysis and management rather than objective science.

The real-world policy process does not follow the normative rational, scientific, comprehensive approach of Bradbury's model (Dye, 1981; Etzioni, 1967; Ham and Hill, 1984). Actual policy development is commonly disjointed and incremental; can involve mixed scanning (an approach that acknowledges that the important issues can proceed in a rational, linear way, while lower priority policies usually proceed in an incremental fashion) (Etzioni, 1967); and is more akin to 'muddling through' (Lindblom, 1959). In this context of imperfect information and limited resources, a reductionistic approach is often all that can be achieved. From a pragmatic perspective, indicators are a practical tool for informing 'messy' policy debates.

Furthermore, it is possible to reduce the 'indicators myopia' of the *pars pro toto* problem by acknowledging that indicators are not sufficient on their own for managing eco-efficiency. As Ott (1978, p. 3) states about environmental indicators in general, 'environmental indices, of course, are not the only source of information that is brought to bear on environmental decisions. Decision-making will be based on many other considerations besides indices and the monitoring data on which they are based'.

Eco-efficiency indicators have an important place in informing about the economy–environment context. Eco-efficiency indicators are one of a range of analytical tools useful for addressing ill-defined complex problems. In particular, eco-efficiency indicators are useful in this context for the following reasons:

- In the presence of such ill-defined problems it is often not possible to develop reliable, comprehensive models of the environment because of the lack of knowledge of many parts of the system. Instead, one must rely on more piecemeal information such as departure from benchmarks or time series of key variables over time (Cartwright, 1973). Indicators are particularly suited to these types of measurements.
- Indicators can accommodate an open system of information – that is, they are flexible and can accommodate new information as it becomes available.
- Indicators can accommodate the 'less-than-comprehensive analysis' aspects of some complex problems by tracking those aspects of the system amenable to measurement.
- Indicators can potentially provide information useful for understanding the complex interactions of a system.

CONCLUSIONS

In order to enhance the policy-guiding value of eco-efficiency indicators, several necessary theoretical issues need to be ironed out. First, it is important to clarify what is meant by eco-efficiency. Without a clear understanding of what this term means, there is a danger that eco-efficiency may be applied to situations where the concept is inappropriate. Second, we need to understand what the term eco-efficiency indicator means. Without a clear understanding of what an eco-efficiency indicator is, we cannot hope to communicate fully the strengths, limitations and ken of what we are presenting to decision makers. This chapter advocates using semiotics to define an eco-efficiency indicator as *a measure of some aspect of the environment that: (1) is quantified as a variable; (2) uses clear scientific and theoretical conventions; and (3) is produced with communicative intent to inform the decisions of a clearly defined audience.*

The third issue is how to select the most appropriate eco-efficiency indicators. There is a plethora of articles outlining criteria for ideal indicators in general. I have tried to relate these criteria to eco-efficiency and to add some order to the criteria by grouping them into theoretical and pragmatic considerations.

The fourth issue is the lack of debate about the relative strengths and weaknesses of eco-efficiency indicators in the literature. Although indicators can be criticized from several perspectives, they do have an important role to play in the context of ill-defined complex problems, such as occur in the realm of policy and management decisions.

This discussion of eco-efficiency indicators can conclude with the thoughts of the famous actor Maurice Chevalier. Upon being asked about the fate of being old, he replied it was so much better than the alternative (Doelman, 1976). This conclusion goes without saying. By addressing these four issues relating to eco-efficiency indicators, it is possible to improve their policy-guiding value and so improve the value of eco-efficiency indicators for policy.

REFERENCES

Adriaanse, A. (1993), *Environmental Policy Performance Indicators*, The Hague: Sdu Uitgeverij.

Adriaanse, A. (1996), 'Development of environmental policy performance indicators: designed for the Netherlands and extended with recent national and international experiences', proceedings of the Fenner Conference 'Tracking progress: linking environment and economy through indicators and accounting systems', Sydney: University of New South Wales, pp. 1–14.

Alfsen, K.H. and H.V. Saebo (1993), 'Environmental quality indicators: background, principles and examples from Norway', *Environmental and Resource Economics*, **3**, 415–35.

Amir, S. (1994), 'The role of thermodynamics in the study of economic and ecological systems', *Ecological Economics*, **10**, 125–42.

Andreasen, K., R. O'Neill, R. Noss and N. Slosser (2001), 'Considerations for the development of a terrestrial index of ecological integrity', *Ecological Indicators*, **1**, 21–35.

Ayres, R.U. and I. Nair (1984), 'Thermodynamics and economics', *Physics Today*, **37**, 62–71.

Barnhart, R.K. (1988), *Chambers Dictionary of Etymology*, New York: Chambers.

Bennett, J. (2002), 'Book review of Eological Indicators for the Nation', *Ecological Indicators*, **1**, 225–6.

Bradbury, R. (1996), 'Are indicators yesterday's news?', proceedings of the Fenner Conference 'Tracking progress: linking environment and economy through indicators and accounting systems', Sydney: University of New South Wales, pp. 1–8.

Business Council for Sustainable Development (1993), *Getting Eco-Efficient, Report of the Business Council for Sustainable Development, First Antwerp Eco-Efficiency Workshop*, Geneva: Business Council for Sustainable Development.

Cartwright, T. (1973), 'Problems, solutions and strategies: a contribution to the theory and practice of planning', *Journal of the American Institute of Planners*, **39**, 179–87.

Chatterjee, P. and M. Finger (1994), *The Earth Brokers: Power, Politics and World Development*, London: Routledge.

Chew, R.M. and A.E. Chew (1970), 'Energy relationships of the mammals of a desert shrub', *Ecological Monographs*, **40**, 1–21.

Christensen, P. (1991), 'Driving forces, increasing returns and ecological sustainability', in R. Costanza (ed.), *Ecological Economics: The Science and Management of Sustainability*, New York: Columbia University Press, pp. 75–87.

Clarke, D. (1987), *Principles of Semiotics*, London: Routledge and Kegan Paul.

Dahl, A. (2000), 'Using indicators to measure sustainability: recent methodological and conceptual developments', *Marine and Freshwater Research*, **51**, 427–33.

Dale, V. and S. Beyeler (2001), 'Challenges in the development and use of ecological indicators', *Ecological Indicators*, **1**, 3–10.

DeSimone, L.D., F. Popoff and World Business Council for Sustainable Development (2000), *Eco-efficiency: The Business Link to Sustainable Development*, MA: MIT Press.

Doelman, J.A. (1976), *Notes on the Art, Science and Relevance of CBA*, Newcastle: University of Newcastle.

Dye, T.R. (1981), *Understanding Policy*, New Jersey: Prentice Hall.

Energy Efficiency and Conservation Authority (2000), *The Dynamics of Energy Efficiency Trends in New Zealand: A Compendium of Energy End-Use Analysis and Statistics*, Wellington: Energy Efficiency and Conservation Authority.

Etzioni, A. (1967), 'Mixed-scanning: a "third" approach to decision making', *Public Administration Review*, **27**, 385–92.

Friend, G. (1998), 'EcoMetrics: integrating direct and indirect environmental costs and benefits into management information systems', *Environmental Quality Management*, **7**, 19–30.

Gallopín, G.C. (1997), 'Indicators and their use: information for decision-making', in B. Moldan and S. Billharz (eds), *Sustainability Indicators: Report of the Project on Indicators of Sustainable Development*, Chichester: John Wiley, pp. 13–27.

Glauser, M. and P. Muller (1997), 'Eco-effiency: a prerequisite for future success', *CHIMIA*, **51**, 201–6.

Golley, F.B. (1960), 'Energy dynamics of a food chain of an old-field community', *Ecological Monographs*, **30**, 187–206.

Golley, F.B. (1961), 'Energy values of ecological materials', *Ecology*, **42**, 581–4.

Golley, F.B. (1967), 'Methods of measuring secondary productivity in terrestrial vertebrate populations', in K. Petrusewicz (ed.), *Secondary Productivity of Terrestrial Ecosystems*, Warsaw: Institute of Ecology, pp. 99–124.

Golley, F.B. (1972), 'Energy flux in ecosystems', in J. Wiens (ed.), *Ecosystems Structure and Function*, Corvallis: Oregon State University Press, pp. 69–90.

Golley, F.B. (1993), *A History of the Ecosystem Concept in the Ecology – More Than the Sum of the Parts*, New Haven: Yale University Press.

Grice, H. (1968), 'Utterer's meaning, sentence-meaning, and word-meaning', *Foundations of Language*, **4**, 225–42.

Gustavson, K., S. Longeran and H.J. Ruitenbeek (1999), 'Selection and modelling of sustainable development indicators: a case study of the Fraser River Basin, British Columbia', *Ecological Economics*, **28**, 117–32.

Hagen, J.B. (1992), *An Entangled Banked: The Origins of Ecosystem Ecology*, New Brunswick: Rutgers University Press.

Ham, C. and M. Hill (1984), *The Policy Process in the Modern Capitalist State*, New York: Harvester Wheatsheaf.

Hammond, A., A. Adriaanse, E. Rodenburg, D. Bryant and R. Woodward (1995), *Environmental Indicators: A Systematic Approach to Measuring and Reporting on Environmental Policy Performance in the Context of Sustainable Development*, Washington: World Resources Institute.

Hardi, P. and J.A. DeSouza-Huletey (2000), 'Issues in analysing data and indicators for sustainable development', *Ecological Economics*, **130**, 59–65.

Helm, D. (1988), *Theoretical Concepts and Criteria of Appraisal: Consortia Paper One*, Wellington: Electricity Industry Task Force.

Hinterberger, F. and H. Stiller (1998), 'Energy and material flows', proceedings of the International Workshop: Energy Flows in Ecology and Economy – Advances in Energy Studies, Porto Venere, Italy, 27 May.

Hukkinen, J. (2001), 'Eco-efficiency as abandonment of nature', *Ecological Economics*, **38**, 311–5.

Jollands, N. (2003), *An Ecological Economics of Eco-Efficiency: Theory, Interpretations and Applications to New Zealand*, Massey University, PhD Thesis.

Jorgensen, E. (2002), 'Small mammals: consequenses of stochastic data variation for modelling indicators of habitat suitability for a well-studied resource', *Ecological Indicators*, **1**, 313–21.

Kay, J. and E.D. Schneider (1992), 'Thermodynamics and measures of ecological integrity', in D.E. McKenzie, D.E. Hyatt and V.J. McDonald (eds), *Ecological Indicators – Proceedings of the International Symposium on Ecological Indicators*, Fort Lauderdale: Elsevier, pp. 159–82.

Khalil, E.L. (1990), 'Entropy law and exhaustion of natural resources: is Nicholas Georgescu-Roegen's paradigm defensible?', *Ecological Economics*, **2**, 163–78.

Klein, E. (2000), *A Comprehensive Etymological Dictionary of the English Language*, Amsterdam: Elsevier.

Koestler, A. (1978), *Janus – A Summing Up*, London: Hutchinson.

Kondepudi, D. and I. Prigogine (1998), *Modern Thermodynamics: From Heat Engines to Dissipative Structures*, Chichester: John Wiley.

Kurtz, J., L. Jackson and W. Fisher (2001), 'Strategies for evaluating indicators based on guidelines from the Environmental Protection Agency's Office of Research and Development', *Ecological Indicators*, **1**, 49–60.

Lawn, P.A. (2003), 'A theoretical foundation to support the Index of Sustainable Economic Welfare (ISEW), Genuine Progress Indicator (GPI), and other related indexes', *Ecological Economics*, **44**, 105–18.

Leibenstein, H. (1966), 'Allocative efficiency vs X-efficiency', *American Economic Review*, **56**, 392–415.

Lindblom, C.E. (1959), 'The Science of "Muddling Through"', *Public Administration Review*, **19**, 79–88.

Lindeman, R.L. (1941), 'Seasonal food-cycle dynamics in a senescant lake', *American Midland Naturalist*, **2**, 636–73.

Lindeman, R.L. (1942), 'The trophic–dynamic aspect of ecology', *Ecology*, **23**, 399–418.

Lindsey, G., J. Wittman and M. Rummel (1997), 'Using indices in environmental planning: evaluating policies for wellfield protection', *Journal of Environmental Planning and Management*, **40**, 685–703.

Lotka, A.J. (1925), *Elements of Physical Biology*, New York: Dover Publications.

Manoliadis, O. (2002), 'Development of ecological indicators – a methodological framework using compromise programming', *Ecological Indicators*, **2**, 169–76.

Martinez-Alier, J. (1987), *Ecological Economics*, Oxford: Basil Blackwell.

Ministry for the Environment (1997), *Environmental Performance Indicators for Land, Air and Water*, Wellington: Ministry for the Environment.

Morris, W. and M. Morris (1988), *Morris Dictionary of Word and Phrase Origins*, New York: Harper and Row.

Mortensen, L.F. (1997), 'The driving force–state–response framework used by the CSD', in B. Moldan and S. Billharz (eds), *Sustainability Indicators: Report of the Project on Indicators of Sustainable Development*, Chichester: John Wiley, pp. 47–53.

Norgaard, R. (1985), 'Environmental economics: an evolutionary critique and a plea for pluralism', *Journal of Environmental Economics and Management*, **12**, 382–94.

O'Connor, J. (1994), 'Is sustainable capitalism possible?', in M. O'Connor (ed.), *Is Capitalism Sustainable? Political Economy and Politics of Ecology*, New York: Guilford Press, pp. 152–75.

Odum, E.P. (1959), *Fundamentals of Ecology*, Philadelphia: Saunders.

Odum, E.P. (1983), *Basic Ecology*, New York: Saunders College Publishing.

Odum, H.T. (1971), *Environment, Power, and Society*, New York: Wiley Interscience.

Odum, H.T. (1996), *Environmental Accounting – Emergy and Environmental Decision-making*, New York: John Wiley.

Odum, H.T. and R.C. Pinkerton (1955), 'Time's speed regulator: the optimum efficiency for maximum power output in physical and biological systems', *American Scientist*, **43**, 331–43.

O'Neill, R.V., D.L. DeAngelis, J.B. Waide and T.F.H. Allen (1986), *A Hierarchical Concept of Ecosystems*, Princeton, NJ: Princeton University Press.

Organisation for Economic Co-operation and Development (OECD) (1998), *Eco-efficiency*, Paris: OECD.

Ott, W.R. (1978), *Environmental Indices: Theory and Practice*, Ann Arbor: Ann Arbor Science.

Peng, C., J. Liu, Q. Dang, X. Szhou and M. Apps (2002), 'Developing carbon-based ecological indicators to monitor sustainability of Ontario's forests', *Ecological Indicators*, **1**, 235–46.

Pykh, Y. (2002), 'Lyapunov functions as a measure of biodiversity: theoretical background', *Ecological Indicators*, **2**, 123–33.

Randall, A. (1987), *Resource Economics – An Economic Approach to Natural Resource and Environmental Policy*, New York: John Wiley.

Randla, T., T. Kurissoo and V. Raivo (2002), 'On eco-efficiency and sustainable development in Estonia', *International Journal of Environment and Sustainable Development*, **1**, 32–41.

Ruth, M. (1993), *Integrating Economics, Ecology and Thermodynamics*, The Netherlands: Kluwer Academic Publishers.

Schaltegger, S. and R. Burritt (2000), *Contemporary Environmental Accounting: Issues, Concepts and Practice*, Sheffield: Greenleaf Publishing.

Schmidheiny, S. (1992), *Changing Course*, Cambridge, MA: MIT Press.

Shipley, J.T. (1984), *The Origins of English Words: A Discursive Dictionary of Indo-European Roots*, Baltimore, MD: John Hopkins Press.

Simpson, J. and E. Weiner (1989), *The Oxford English Dictionary*, Oxford: Clarendon Press.

Skeat, W. (1961), *An Etymological Dictionary of the English Language*, Oxford: Clarendon Press.

Slobodkin, L.B. (1962), 'Energy in animal ecology', in J.B. Cragg (ed.), *Advances in Ecological Research*, London: Academic Press, pp. 69–101.

Söllner, F. (1997), 'A reexamination of the role of thermodynamics for environmental economics', *Ecological Economics*, **22**, 175–201.

United Nations Conference on Environment and Development (1992), *Agenda 21*, New York: United Nations Conference on Environment and Development.

Walz, R., N. Block, W. Eichhammer, I. Hiessel, C. Nathani, V. Ostertag and M. Schon (1996), *Further Development of Indicator Systems for Environmental Reporting: Summary of Results*, Karlsruhe: Fraunhofer Institute for Systems and Innovation Research.

Waugh, A. (1999), *Time*, London: Headline Book Publishing.

Welford, R. (1997), *Hijacking Environmentalism: Corporate Responses to Sustainable Development*, London: Earthscan Publications.

Welford, R. (2003), 'Beyond systems: a vision for corporate environmental management for the future', *International Journal of Environment and Sustainable Development*, **2**, 162–73.

Whitehead, A.N. (1925), *Science and the Modern World*, New York: Macmillan.

Wiegert, R.G. (1988), 'The past, present and future of ecological energetics', in L.R. Pomeroy and J.J. Alberts (eds), *Concepts of Ecosystem Ecology: A Comparative View*, New York: Springer-Verlag, pp. 29–55.

Williams, J.M. (1999), 'Eco-efficiency for New Zealand', *New Zealand Engineering*, **54**, 37–8.

Woodward, R. and R. Bishop (1995), 'Efficiency, sustainability and global warming', *Ecological Economics*, **14**, 101–11.

World Business Council for Sustainable Development (1995), *Achieving Eco-efficiency and Business, Report of the World Business Council for Sustainable Development, Second Antwerp Eco-Efficiency Workshop*, Geneva: World Business Council for Sustainable Development.

World Business Council for Sustainable Development (2000), *Eco-Efficiency, Creating More Value with Less Impact*, Geneva: World Business Council for Sustainable Development.

Wright, J. (1991), *Indicators of Sustainable Energy Development: Information Paper No. 28*, Lincoln: Centre for Resource Management, Lincoln University.

Wulff, F. and R.E. Ulanowicz (1989), 'A comparative anatomy of the Baltic Sea and Chesapeake Bay ecosystems', in F. Wulff, J. Field and K. Mann (eds), *Network Analysis in Marine Ecosystems*, London: Springer-Verlag, pp. 232–58.

16. Eco-efficiency indicators applied to Australia and their policy relevance

Philip Lawn

INTRODUCTION

Broadly speaking, eco-efficiency is measure of the efficiency or effectiveness with which natural capital is transformed into human-made capital. Given the messages put across in the previous chapter and the conclusions drawn from the coevolutionary paradigm in Chapter 2, it is clear that eco-efficiency indicators must be developed on the basis of various understandings. While many such understandings exist, the number can be reduced to the following key short-list: (1) natural capital and human-made capital are complements, not substitutes; (2) humankind cannot overcome its dependence on the natural environment by 'dematerialising' economic activity; and (3) since humankind cannot control the evolutionary pathway of the global system, eco-efficiency solutions must be in keeping with a coevolutionary worldview. It will be argued in this chapter that the eco-efficiency ratios outlined in Chapter 2 are commensurate with these understandings. The eco-efficiency indicators are then calculated for Australia to reveal the extent to which Australia's use of its natural capital assets has progressed since the mid-1960s. By enabling one to identify where Australia has made particular gains and losses, it is shown that eco-efficiency indicators can provide valuable information for policy-makers.

ECO-EFFICIENCY, TECHNOLOGICAL PROGRESS, AND SUSTAINABLE ECONOMIC WELFARE

In Chapter 2, the two elemental categories of net psychic income and lost natural capital services were arranged to arrive at a measure of ecological economic efficiency (EEE). The EEE ratio was then decomposed to reveal the following four eco-efficiency ratios:

Ratio 1   Ratio 2   Ratio 3   Ratio 4

$$EEE = \frac{NPI}{LNCS} = \frac{NPI}{HMK} \times \frac{HMK}{RT} \times \frac{RT}{NK} \times \frac{NK}{LNCS} \qquad (16.1)$$

To recall, the order in which the four eco-efficiency ratios are presented is in keeping with the conclusions drawn from the linear throughput representation of the socio-economic process. As such, each eco-efficiency ratio represents a different form of efficiency pertaining to a particular sub-problem of the larger ecological economic problem of sustainable development. The four eco-efficiency ratios will now, along with their implications, be individually explained and discussed.

The Service Efficiency of Human-made Capital

Ratio 1 is a measure of the *service efficiency* of human-made capital. It increases whenever a given physical magnitude of human-made capital yields a higher level of net psychic income. An increase in Ratio 1 causes the uncancelled benefit (UB) curve in Figure 2.5 of Chapter 2 to shift upwards. This can be achieved by improving the technical design of newly produced goods and by advancing the means by which human beings organise themselves in the course of producing and maintaining the stock of human-made capital (thereby reducing such things as the disutility of labour and the cost of commuting and unemployment). A beneficial shift in the UB curve can also be achieved by redistributing income from the low marginal service or psychic income uses of the rich to the higher marginal service uses of the poor (Robinson, 1962). There is, however, a limit on the capacity for redistribution to increase Ratio 1 because an excessive approach to redistribution adversely dilutes the incentive structure built into a market-based system.

Figure 16.1 illustrates what happens to sustainable economic welfare when the UB curve shifts upwards. Because an increase in Ratio 1 augments the net psychic income yielded by a given amount of human-made capital, the UB curve shifts up to UB^1. The uncancelled cost (UC) curve does not move since the opportunity cost of creating and maintaining a given stock of human-made capital remains unchanged. Moreover, the maximum sustainable scale remains at S_S. However, sustainable economic welfare is no longer maximised at the prevailing macroeconomic scale of S_*. It is now desirable to expand the physical scale of the macroeconomy to the new optimal scale of S_*^1 where sustainable economic welfare now equals SEW_*^1.

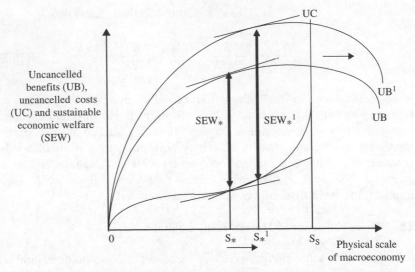

Figure 16.1   A change in sustainable economic welfare brought about by an increase in the service efficiency of human-made capital (Ratio 1)

Maintenance, Growth, and Exploitative Efficiencies

Changes in Ratios 2, 3 and 4 cause the UC curve to shift. Ratio 2 is a measure of the *maintenance efficiency* of human-made capital. It increases whenever a given physical magnitude of human-made capital can be maintained by a lessened rate of throughput. This can be achieved by developing new technologies that reduce the requirement for resource input either through: (1) the more efficient use of resources in production; (2) increased rates of product recycling; (3) greater product durability, or (4) improved operational efficiency. An increase in Ratio 2 causes the UC to shift downwards and to the right for the following reasons. First, it enables any given macroeconomic scale to be sustained by a reduced rate of resource throughput. Second, a lower rate of throughput means less natural capital requires exploitation that, in turn, means fewer lost natural capital services.

Ratio 3 is a measure of the *growth efficiency* or productivity of natural capital. This form of efficiency is increased whenever a given amount of natural capital is able to sustainably yield a greater quantity of low entropy resources and assimilate more of the high entropy waste generated by socioeconomic activity. Better management of natural resource systems and the preservation of critical ecosystems can lead to a more productive stock of

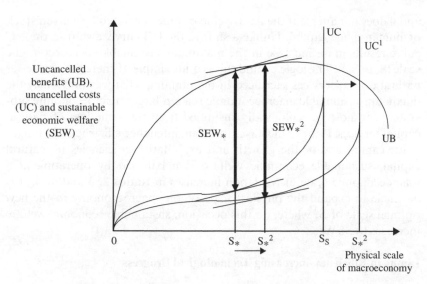

Figure 16.2   A change in sustainable economic welfare brought about by increases in the maintenance efficiency of human-made capital (Ratio 2), and the growth and exploitative efficiencies of natural capital (Ratios 3 and 4)

natural capital. How does an increase in Ratio 3 lead to a downward and rightward shift of the UC curve? An increase in the productivity of natural capital reduces the quantity of natural capital that must be exploited for the throughput of matter-energy needed to sustain the macroeconomy at a given physical scale. This allows a macroeconomy of a given physical scale to be sustained at the expense of fewer natural capital services.

Ratio 4 is a measure of the *exploitative efficiency* of natural capital. If Ratio 4 increases, fewer natural capital services are lost in exploiting a given quantity of natural capital. This, again, allows a macroeconomy of a given physical scale to be sustained at the expense of fewer natural capital services. In doing so, it leads to a downward and rightward shift of the UC curve. Increases in Ratio 4 can be obtained through the development and execution of more ecologically sensitive extractive techniques, such as the use of underground rather than open-cut or strip mining practices.

Figure 16.2 illustrates what happens to sustainable economic welfare when there is a beneficial shift of the UC curve. Because an increase in Ratios 2, 3 and 4 reduces the uncancelled cost of producing and maintaining a given macroeconomic scale, the UC curve shifts down and out to UC^1. However, the UB curve remains stationary since an increase in Ratios 2, 3 and 4 does not augment the net psychic income generated by a given stock of human-made capital. Unlike a shift in the UB curve, a shift in the UC curve results in an increase in the maximum sustainable macroeconomic scale (S_S to S_S^1). The logic behind this is quite simple. If there are now fewer natural capital services sacrificed in maintaining what was previously the maximum sustainable macroeconomic scale, a larger macroeconomic sub-system can now be ecologically sustained from the same loss of natural capital services. Prior to increases in the maintenance efficiency of human-made capital and/or the growth and exploitative efficiencies of natural capital, sustainable economic welfare is maximised by operating at a macroeconomic scale of S_*. Upon increases in Ratios 2, 3 and/or 4, it is desirable to expand the physical scale of the macroeconomy to the new optimal scale of S_*^2 where, on this occasion, sustainable economic welfare increases to SEW_*^2.

Limits to Efficiency-increasing Technological Progress

There is considerable debate surrounding how much and for how long human beings can rely on efficiency-increasing technological progress to reduce the uncancelled costs of the socio-economic process. Due to the bio-physical constraints outlined in Chapter 2, there are many people who believe the ability to increase Ratios 2, 3 and 4 is ultimately limited (Georgescu-Roegen, 1971; Pearce and Turner, 1990; Costanza et al., 1991; Folke et al., 1994; Daly, 1996; Lawn, 2000a). Ratio 2, for instance, is limited by the first and second laws of thermodynamics (nothing is eternally durable and 100 per cent recycling and production efficiency is impossible). Ratio 3 is limited by the inability to increase indefinitely the productivity of natural capital, while Ratio 4 is limited by the fact that at least some of the environment's instrumental functions are lost as a consequence of its exploitation (Perrings, 1986).

Conclusions regarding limits to increases in Ratio 1 are harder to draw because service, as a psychic rather than physical magnitude, is not subject to the same physical laws as the very goods that yield the service. Having said this, there is a probable limit on humankind's capacity to experience service (i.e. a point of satiation exists for everyone).[1] Thus, regardless of how well physical goods are designed, a given quantity of human-made capital is unlikely to yield ever-increasing levels of net psychic income.

THEORETICAL SUPPORT FOR THE ECO-EFFICIENCY INDICATORS

In this section, it is shown that the above eco-efficiency indicators are commensurate with the understandings outlined in the introduction of the chapter.

Eco-efficiency and the Complementary Relationship Between Natural and Human-made Capital

By keeping natural and human-made capital sharply distinct and having a separate magnitude for each, the eco-efficiency indicators recognise the unique nature of the two forms of capital. Moreover, natural and human-made capital are shown to be coupled in terms of the throughput of matter-energy that can only be provided by the natural capital stock. As such, the eco-efficiency indicators explicitly recognise the entropic connection between the two forms of capital. In doing so, they are clearly commensurate with the strong sustainability notion that natural and human-made capital are strictly complements, not substitutes.

To cast off any lingering doubts, consider the indicator effect of augmenting the stock of human-made capital at the expense of natural capital depletion. Because this course of action does not involve an increase in efficiency-increasing technological progress (since technological progress of this nature would allow human-made capital to be increased without having to liquidate natural capital), such an exercise ought not to be reflected by increases in either Ratios 2 or 3.[2] However, it would presumably lower Ratio 4 – a reflection of the increased opportunity cost of each additional disruption of natural capital. This would reduce the EEE ratio and, since it would undesirably shift the UC curve upwards, result in a decline in sustainable economic welfare. Many standard eco-efficiency exercises falsely reveal increases in the effectiveness of transformation in circumstances such as these.

Eco-efficiency and Humankind's Dependence on the Ecosphere

There is a growing view among many observers and some organisations that humankind can significantly overcome its dependence on the natural environment by dematerialising economic activity (Schmidheiny and Zoraquin, 1996; WCED, 1987; United Nations, 1999; WBCSD, 2000). In particular, it is believed that eco-efficiency gains can be made by shifting the emphasis of economic activity away from the production of goods (e.g. manufacturing industries) and towards the provision of services (e.g. the information technology and tourism industries). This is a fallacy (Lawn, 2001). As Figure 2.3 in Chapter 2 illustrated, goods (human-made capital) are the physical objects that yield the service (psychic income). Service is the welfare that flows from goods as they are either consumed (such as food and petrol) or worn out through use (such as clothes and consumer durables). As much as goods and services are distinct magnitudes, they are in no way independent magnitudes. While some economic activities are less resource intensive than others, thereby providing a higher level of service per unit of matter-energy expended, Costanza (1980) and Ayres and Ayres (1999) have shown there is very little difference in resource use intensity across industries. The disparity virtually disappears if one attributes to the so-called 'service industries' the resources required to produce the human-made capital necessary for such industries to function. Hence, there is no reason to believe that the resource intensity per unit of welfare can be reduced by shifting the emphasis of economic activity towards specific industries.

The eco-efficiency ratios outlined in equation (16.1) prevent the fallacious emergence of eco-efficiency improvements because, again, they keep natural and human-made capital separate and distinct. This ensures that the overall level of service or net psychic income can only rise if: (1) the quantity of human-made capital has increased, or (2) if there has been an increase in the service-yielding qualities of human-made capital. The former, however, does not constitute an eco-efficiency improvement. Critically, it does not lead to a rise in any of the four eco-efficiency ratios. Only (2) amounts to an eco-efficiency improvement which, importantly, is reflected by a rise in Ratio 1.

Of course, it is true that more service can be generated from a given resource flow if technological progress increases the rate of recycling and/or the degree of production efficiency. This is because a larger stock of human-made capital can be produced and maintained from a given rate of throughput which, *ceteris paribus*, leads to a higher overall level of service being generated. Importantly, it is correctly reflected by a rise in Ratio 2. However, Ratio 2 cannot rise without limit because, as previously explained, an increase in the maintenance efficiency of human-made capital is constrained by the first and second laws of thermodynamics. Given that increases in Ratios 3 and 4 are also biophysically constrained, the so-called dematerialisation of the socio-economic process, if actively pursued, will ultimately be revealed by the four eco-efficiency ratios as a Cornucopian pipedream. So, too, will the notion that humankind can overcome its dependence on the natural environment.

Eco-efficiency Solutions and the Coevolutionary Paradigm

The need for eco-efficiency indicators and solutions to be commensurate with the coevolutionary worldview is perhaps the greatest source of concern among their detractors. Critics of the eco-efficiency concept (such as Hukkinen, 2001) are consistent in their antagonism towards a theme underlying most eco-efficiency conceptions – i.e. that humankind can significantly augment the effectiveness with which it transforms natural into human-made capital by increasing its control over the global system. The notion of control of any sort is at odds with the coevolutionary worldview. Most eco-efficiency critics therefore argue that most of the claims made about potential eco-efficiency improvements are unrealistic. Furthermore, they believe such claims lead to the development of inappropriate, if not hazardous, policy prescriptions. To explain why, we need to examine an important implication of the coevolutionary worldview in greater depth.

A critical aspect of the coevolutionary paradigm that was not outlined in Chapter 2 is the concept of *surprise*. Surprising events occur because there is always a disparity between what humankind expects *ex ante* and what it experiences *ex post* – a consequence of the evolving relationships and feedback responses typically associated with two or more interdependent systems. The notion of surprise has been given implicit attention by economists ever since the ground-breaking work of Knight (1921). Unfortunately, the treatment of surprise has been confined to the distinction between *risk* and *uncertainty*. As Faber and Proops point out (1990), a coevolutionary paradigm requires a third category of surprise; namely, human *ignorance*.

Since the existence of surprising events restricts humankind's ability to predict future outcomes, then, for two good reasons, it is necessary to gain a better understanding of their source. To begin with, the precise nature and source of a surprising event determines the degree to which humankind can make valid predictions regarding future events. Secondly, without a comprehensive knowledge of the sources of surprise, humankind's ability to positively influence the evolutionary pathway of the global system is greatly reduced. To deal with surprise, Figure 16.3 serves as a diagrammatic representation of its various sources. Also included is a simple taxonomy of ignorance.

Risk and uncertainty
Figure 16.3 depicts two kinds of surprising events experienced by humankind. The first includes events where the range of all possible outcomes is *a priori* known. Humankind's understanding of the dynamic processes involved is sufficient to make useful, if not limited, predictions

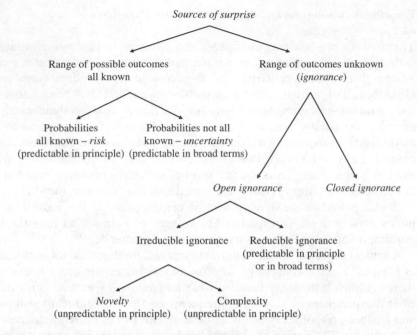

Source: Adapted from Faber, Manstetten and Proops, 1992, p. 84.

Figure 16.3   Sources of surprise and a taxonomy of ignorance

about the likely emergence of particular outcomes and events. Exactly how restricted humankind's predictive capacities are depends on its knowledge of the respective probabilities of each outcome emerging. Should all probabilities be known (e.g. it is known that there is a 60 per cent, 30 per cent and 10 per cent chance of X, Y and Z occurring), future outcomes are predictable 'in principle' (Faber et al., 1992). In these circumstances, one is dealing with *risk* since, if X is the desired outcome, there is a 40 per cent chance of it not occurring.

When the probabilities of a range of outcomes are not all known (it is known that X, Y and Z may occur, but the probability of each emerging is not), one is dealing with *uncertainty*. On this occasion, future outcomes are only predictable 'in broad terms' (Faber et al., 1992). Thus, humankind is restricted to saying little more than something about the probable future behaviour of a system and the range of future events and outcomes that might ensue (worst and best case scenarios). Clearly, when confronted with uncertainty, humankind's predictive powers are considerably weaker than in circumstances involving risk.

Closed and open ignorance

The second category of surprising events involves those where the range of all possible outcomes are not known. It is here where humankind suffers from *ignorance* (Faber et al., 1992). As the taxonomy of ignorance in the right-hand side of Figure 16.3 shows, ignorance comes in two forms – *closed* and *open* ignorance.

When a society deliberately overlooks its ignorance, that is, it chooses not to engage in further learning or research to determine if something is true, it is in a state of *closed ignorance*. Closed ignorance, particularly if it exists in the form of assumed omniscience (e.g. believing in the dematerial-isation of the socio-economic process), constitutes a significant barrier to humankind's capacity to positively influence the evolutionary pathway of the global system. In the event that a society is aware of its ignorance and, furthermore, chooses not to believe something until proven true, it is in a state of *open ignorance*. Only in a state of open ignorance is it possible for a society to fully experience novel and surprising events. Figure 16.3 indi-cates that open ignorance can be dichotomised into two forms – *reducible* and *irreducible* ignorance.

Reducible ignorance is ignorance that can be partially or fully overcome through learning and the application of the scientific method. Reducible ignorance exists because the stock of a society's knowledge is, at any moment in time, incapable of explaining and predicting the broadly explainable and predictable. Appropriate research eventually makes it pos-sible to explain an event that has already taken place and/or to predict a greater range of future events.

The second form of open ignorance – irreducible ignorance – is never amenable to scientific tools of learning and research. In this instance, out-comes have the potential to emerge that can never be *a priori* envisaged. As a consequence, irreducible ignorance involves a class of future events which are 'unpredictable in principle'. Humankind is unable to make even tenta-tive predictions about the likely range of all possible outcomes. Not sur-prisingly, irreducible ignorance severely restricts humankind's capacity to positively influence the evolutionary pathway of the global system.

Ignorance of the irreducible variety exists because of two ever-present factors. The first factor is *complexity* (Dyke, 1988). Here an outcome is unexpected because the complex nature of the processes underlying certain dynamic systems precludes the possibility of gaining a comprehensive understanding of them. In the second instance, irreducible ignorance stems from the emergence of *novelty*. Novelty arises because the parameters of dynamic systems are forever evolving. This leads to adaptive and somatic change in the short and medium terms, and genotypic change (bifurcation) in the long term (Capra, 1982). Novelty gives rise to irreducible ignorance because, in not knowing the initial boundary conditions governing the global system's evolutionary pathway, one cannot predict the future pathway of the global system either in principle or in broad terms.

The inevitability of surprise, in all its above described forms, obliges humankind to take note of the following. First, it cannot 'control' the evolutionary pathway of the global system. The increasing ability of humankind to manipulate the ecosphere does not translate to an equivalent increase in its ability to control the destiny of ecological and natural resource systems. Indeed, humankind can only hope to marginally increase its knowledge of the long-term impact that its own manipulative endeavours are having on the global system. For this reason, humankind is strictly confined to positively 'influencing' the pathway of the global system which, moreover, it can only do in circumstances where predictions can be made about the implications of its endeavours in principle and in broad terms.

Second, since the logos of the global system is characterised by uncontrollable coevolutionary processes decidedly more so than by human teleology, humankind must obey the logos of the global system. As Laszlo (1972, p. 75) puts it:

> There is freedom in choosing one's path of progress, yet this freedom is always bounded by the limits of compatibility with the dynamic structure of the whole (or global) system. (parentheses added)

It would appear, therefore, that only insofar as humankind learns to respect and obey the logos of the global system can it, in Boulding's words, 'move away from the slavery of evolution to the freedom of teleology' (Boulding, 1970, p. 18). Clearly, for humankind to maximise its limited capacity to positively influence the global system's pathway, it must recognise the circumstances under which it is a slave to the 'rules' governing coevolutionary processes (as opposed to being a slave to the process itself), and where its actions are most likely to bring to bear catastrophic future macrostates of the global system (i.e. where the impact of its own actions are unpredictable in principle).

Implications for the eco-efficiency ratios
Just how well do the four eco-efficiency ratios stack up against the coevolutionary worldview? Very well, it would seem. Because the eco-efficiency ratios emerge from the decomposition of the larger EEE ratio and reflect the conclusions drawn from the linear throughput model – itself a product of the coevolutionary paradigm – there is an implicit recognition that each sub-problem is an integral part of the larger ecological economic problem of sustainable development. That is, each eco-efficiency ratio takes account

of the possible impact that a particular activity can have on the global system. As such, there is a strong sense of interdependence between the four eco-efficiency ratios.

To demonstrate how, consider the following example. A new production technique enhances the strength of certain metals that, in turn, increases the durability of many newly produced goods. This augments the maintenance efficiency of human-made capital (increases Ratio 2). However, the production technique involves the use of a new chemical that, when released into the natural environment, impacts deleteriously on a range of ecosystems and the organisms contained within. This ultimately reduces the productivity of natural capital and leads to the degradation of certain natural resource assets. As a consequence, Ratios 3 and 4 decline – perhaps enough to cause the EEE ratio to fall.

Clearly, and unlike many eco-efficiency indicators developed in the past, genuine eco-efficiency improvements reflected by Ratios 1–4 will only be possible if the logos of nature is duly recognised. This, as we have seen, is a fundamental coevolutionary imperative that humankind must adhere to if it is to positively influence the coevolutionary pathway of the global system (i.e. increase the sustainable economic welfare generated by the socio-economic process). Indeed, failure to adhere to the logos of nature and other coevolutionary principles will more than likely be revealed in terms of a decline in the EEE ratio and its four component ratios.

CALCULATING THE ECO-EFFICIENCY INDICATORS FOR AUSTRALIA

Having provided theoretical support for the eco-efficiency indicators outlined in equation (16.1), they are now calculated for Australia. To do this, it is first necessary to obtain an index value for the five elemental categories of the linear throughput model. This can be achieved by compiling uncancelled benefit, uncancelled cost, human-made capital, natural capital, and throughput accounts. Four of these five accounts have been compiled for Australia for the period 1966–7 to 1994–5. Because the compilation of a throughput account was a profoundly difficult exercise, the annual consumption of energy was used as a proxy measure of resource throughput. Due to a lack of space in this volume and the extensive and unique nature of the study, a full explanation of the individual accounts, the items they comprise, data sources, and the methods of calculation can be found in Lawn (2000a). See the Appendix of this chapter for a very brief description of the individual accounts.

Australia's Ecological Economic Efficiency (EEE) Ratio

The EEE ratio is the ratio of uncancelled benefits (net psychic income) to uncancelled costs (lost natural capital services). It indicates, at the macro level, what advances a nation has made in terms of the efficiency with which it transforms natural capital and the low entropy resources it provides into service-yielding human-made capital. The EEE ratio for Australia over the period 1966/7 to 1994/5 is indicated by Table 16.1 and Figure 16.4. Both show that the EEE ratio increased from 2.41 in 1966/7 to a peak in 1973/4 of 2.85. The EEE ratio then declined to 1.86 in 1992/3 before rising slightly to 1.94 by 1994/5. By the end of the study period, the EEE ratio was much lower than its initial value (1.94 compared to 2.41).

Interestingly, the trend movement of the EEE ratio closely follows that of the Sustainable Net Benefit Index (SNBI) which was revealed in Chapter 2 (see Figure 2.6). This would indicate that the general decline in Australia's SNBI after 1973/4 was due as much to the inefficient allocation of resources as it was the depletion of its natural capital and the inequitable distribution of income. In what ways inefficiencies contributed to the decline in the SNBI is not altogether clear from the EEE ratio. This information is better revealed by the four eco-efficiency ratios that make up the larger ecological economic problem. It is towards these efficiency ratios that we now direct our attention.

Australia's Service Efficiency Ratio (Ratio 1)

A nation's service efficiency ratio is a measure of how well the total stock of human-made capital contributes to the net psychic income of its citizens (Ratio 1). Table 16.2 and Figure 16.5 reveal the service efficiency of Australia's human-made capital. Both show that Australia's service efficiency began at a value of 0.126 in 1966/7 (equivalent to an imputed service rate of 12.6 per cent). It then increased to a peak of 0.133 (13.3 per cent) by 1972/3. Apart from a small rise between 1979/80 and 1981/2, Australia's service efficiency ratio effectively declined thereafter. By the end of the study period (1994/5), the service efficiency ratio had fallen to 0.102 (10.2 per cent).

Given that technological progress has undoubtedly increased the ability of human-made capital to directly yield service (e.g. televisions now provide colour images, microwave ovens cook food in a fraction of the time of conventional ovens, and cars are less noisy and considerably more comfortable than those gone by), why would the service efficiency of human-made capital have declined over much of the study period? Although the uncancelled benefit account is not provided in this chapter (see Lawn,

Table 16.1   *Ecological economic efficiency (EEE) ratio for Australia, 1966/7 to 1994/5*

Year	Uncancelled benefits ($m at 1989–90 prices)	Uncancelled costs ($m at 1989–90 prices	Ecological economic efficiency (EEE) (a/b)
	a	b	c
1966–67	262 606	108 941	2.41
1967–68	282 956	112 830	2.51
1968–69	294 981	117 306	2.51
1969–70	306 639	122 265	2.51
1970–71	332 281	126 338	2.63
1971–72	347 843	130 902	2.66
1972–73	375 789	135 338	2.78
1973–74	401 192	140 820	2.85
1974–75	398 862	146 047	2.73
1975–76	405 100	150 430	2.69
1976–77	394 768	155 479	2.54
1977–78	391 465	159 814	2.45
1978–79	386 852	166 103	2.33
1979–80	367 096	171 962	2.13
1980–81	402 592	176 748	2.28
1981–82	412 625	182 239	2.26
1982–83	392 483	186 395	2.11
1983–84	406 404	190 907	2.13
1984–85	406 801	197 236	2.06
1985–86	415 492	202 215	2.05
1986–87	431 925	206 729	2.09
1987–88	457 233	211 570	2.16
1988–89	454 252	216 289	2.10
1989–90	447 247	224 187	1.99
1990–91	435 961	228 905	1.90
1991–92	448 485	233 111	1.92
1992–93	445 182	239 809	1.86
1993–94	455 611	243 097	1.87
1994–95	479 328	247 534	1.94

2000a, Table 14.1), it shows that Australia's psychic income increased at a much slower rate than its psychic outgo (e.g. the cost of such things as commuting, noise pollution, unemployment and so on). In other words, the stock of human-made capital was able to generate more psychic benefits but it came at the expense of considerably higher psychic disbenefits. Clearly, the incoming resource flow is being predominantly allocated to

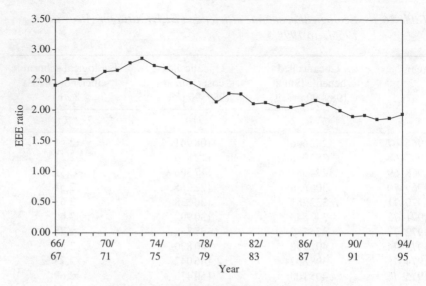

Figure 16.4   Ecological economic efficiency (EEE) ratio for Australia,
1966/7 to 1994/5

meet the already satisfied lower-order needs of most Australians. An insufficient proportion of the total resource flow is being allocated to satisfy emerging higher-order needs.

Australia's Maintenance Efficiency Ratio (Ratio 2)

As defined earlier in the chapter, the maintenance efficiency ratio is a measure of the throughput of matter-energy required to keep a given quantity of human-made capital intact (Ratio 2). For the purposes of this study, the maintenance efficiency ratio revealed in Table 16.3 and Figure 16.6 indicates the human-made capital maintained by Australia per petajoule of energy consumed. Table 16.3 and Figure 16.6 show that, in 1966/7, a petajoule of energy maintained $1154.2 million of human-made capital. This increased to a maximum of $1176.9 million by 1970/71 (when Ratio 2 was at its highest value). The quantity of human-made capital maintained per petajoule of energy consumed then declined very gradually to a low of $1070.8 million in 1989/90. By 1993/4, it had marginally recovered to $1098.0 million – still less than the initial 1966/7 figure. Ratio 2 was therefore lower in 1993/4 than in 1966/7.

The overall fall in Ratio 2 is particularly interesting because many studies on the energy efficiency of economic activity have indicated a steady

Table 16.2   Service efficiency ratio for Australia, 1966/7 to 1994/5

Year	Uncancelled benefits ($m at 1989–90 prices)	Human-made capital stock ($m at 1989–90 prices)	Service efficiency (Ratio 1) (a/b)
	a	b	c
1966–67	262 606	2 084 135	0.126
1967–68	282 956	2 225 354	0.127
1968–69	294 981	2 333 700	0.126
1969–70	306 639	2 434 665	0.126
1970–71	332 281	2 601 301	0.128
1971–72	347 843	2 707 916	0.128
1972–73	375 789	2 821 276	0.133
1973–74	401 192	2 995 896	0.134
1974–75	398 862	3 083 698	0.129
1975–76	405 100	3 153 572	0.128
1976–77	394 768	3 244 952	0.122
1977–78	391 465	3 319 701	0.118
1978–79	386 852	3 366 208	0.115
1979–80	367 096	3 416 009	0.107
1980–81	402 592	3 535 944	0.114
1981–82	412 625	3 532 734	0.117
1982–83	392 483	3 588 416	0.109
1983–84	406 404	3 682 232	0.110
1984–85	406 801	3 781 370	0.108
1985–86	415 492	3 825 766	0.109
1986–87	431 925	3 946 069	0.109
1987–88	457 233	4 071 717	0.112
1988–89	454 252	4 130 657	0.110
1989–90	447 247	4 224 225	0.106
1990–91	435 961	4 325 592	0.101
1991–92	448 485	4 384 474	0.102
1992–93	445 182	4 439 785	0.100
1993–94	455 611	4 585 704	0.099
1994–95	479 328	4 712 174	0.102

improvement (e.g. Reddy and Goldemberg, 1990; OECD, 1998; Weiszacker et al., 1998). The misleading nature of these studies arises because they are based on GDP/energy ratios instead of human-made capital/energy ratios, as has been calculated here. The problem with GDP/energy ratios is that a measure of GDP includes the cost of energy use. As such, energy appears in both the numerator and the denominator of the ratio. What's more, GDP

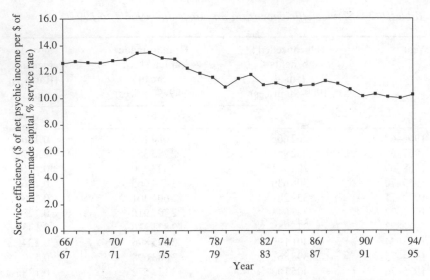

*Figure 16.5   Service efficiency ratio (Ratio 1) for Australia, 1966/7
          to 1994/5*

is often regarded as a useful if not imprecise indicator of the rate of a
nation's resource throughput (Daly, 1996). Consequently, a GDP/energy
ratio involves the division of two flows when an appropriate eco-efficiency
indicator demands the division between a stock magnitude (in this case
human-made capital) and a flow magnitude (energy consumption).

Australia's Growth Efficiency Ratio (Ratio 3)

The growth efficiency ratio is a measure of the productivity of natural
capital (Ratio 3). As presented in this study, Australia's growth efficiency
ratio represents the terajoules of energy entering the Australian macroeconomy relative to each unit of natural capital it has available for exploitation (Note: one petajoule equals 1000 terajoules). Australia's growth
efficiency ratio is revealed in Table 16.4 and Figure 16.7. The ratio increased
over the study period in all but the financial year of 1982/3. The ratio began
from a low of 2.31 in 1966/7 and increased to a high of 6.76 by 1993/4. The
increase in Ratio 3 over the study period suggests that Australia's natural
capital became progressively more productive (i.e. increasingly able to generate of flow of low entropy resources and assimilate high entropy waste).
This is misleading. Closer examination of Australia's natural capital
account and the sources of its energy consumption (see Lawn, 2000a,
Tables 14.5 and 14.6) reveal that the continued rise in Australia's energy

Table 16.3   Maintenance efficiency ratio for Australia, 1966/7 to 1994/5

Year	Human-made capital stock ($m at 1989–90 prices)	Total energy consumption (throughput) (petajoules)	Maintenance efficiency (Ratio 2) (a/b)
	a	b	c
1966–67	2 084 135	1805.8	1154.1
1967–68	2 225 354	1898.9	1171.9
1968–69	2 333 700	2025.9	1151.9
1969–70	2 434 665	2137.6	1139.0
1970–71	2 601 301	2210.3	1176.9
1971–72	2 707 916	2331.2	1161.6
1972–73	2 821 276	2447.8	1152.6
1973–74	2 995 896	2615.1	1145.6
1974–75	3 083 698	2694.5	1144.4
1975–76	3 153 572	2730.6	1154.9
1976–77	3 244 952	2905.6	1116.8
1977–78	3 319 701	2982.7	1113.0
1978–79	3 366 208	3050.9	1103.3
1979–80	3 416 009	3130.2	1091.3
1980 81	3 535 944	3146.1	1123.9
1981–82	3 532 734	3236.5	1091.5
1982–83	3 588 416	3122.9	1149.1
1983–84	3 682 232	3220.4	1143.4
1984–85	3 781 370	3369.6	1122.2
1985 86	3 825 766	3403.0	1124.2
1986–87	3 946 069	3514.8	1122.7
1987–88	4 071 717	3622.3	1124.1
1988–89	4 130 657	3832.1	1077.9
1989–90	4 224 225	3945.2	1070.7
1990–91	4 325 592	3946.6	1096.0
1991 92	4 384 474	4003.2	1095.2
1992–93	4 439 785	4079.2	1088.4
1993–94	4 585 704	4176.6	1098.0
1994–95	4 712 174	n.a.	n.a.

Note: n.a. denotes not available.

consumption was only made possible because Australia increased the depletion rate of its non-renewable energy stocks.

Given that a nation is ultimately dependent on renewable energy, a more cogent growth efficiency ratio is a *renewable* natural capital growth efficiency

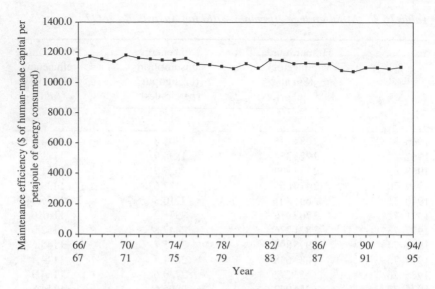

*Figure 16.6   Maintenance efficiency ratio (Ratio 2) for Australia, 1966/7
             to 1994/5*

ratio. This can be calculated by excluding the non-renewable resource
component of the natural capital stock and including only the consumption of renewable energy. Australia's renewable natural capital growth
efficiency ratio for the period 1966/7 to 1993/4 is revealed in Table 16.5 and
Figure 16.8. They both show that the renewable natural capital growth
efficiency ratio changed very little between the period 1966/7 and 1983/4
(1.24 in 1966/7 and 1.22 in 1983/4). However, by 1993/4, the ratio had
increased to a value of 1.52. This increase reflects the impact of stricter pollution standards. It is also a lagged response to the oil price shocks of 1973
and 1979. While this increase is an encouraging development, it must be seen
in the context of Australia's continuing reliance on non-renewable energy
sources. One would be hard-pressed to conclude that the capacity of
Australia's natural capital to provide a sustainable flow of energy has in any
way significantly increased.

Australia's Exploitative Efficiency Ratio (Ratio 4)

A nation's exploitative efficiency ratio is a measure of the opportunity cost
of natural capital services that a nation has foregone relative to the stock
of natural capital it has available for exploitation. The exploitative
efficiency ratio is calculated by dividing the estimated monetary value of

Table 16.4   *Natural capital growth efficiency ratio for Australia,*
1966/7 to 1994/5

Year	Total energy consumption (throughput) (Terajoules)	Natural capital stock ($m at 1989–90 prices)	Natural capital growth efficiency (Ratio 3) (a/b)
	a	b	c
1966–67	1 805 800	780 448	2.31
1967–68	1 898 900	777 952	2.44
1968–69	2 025 900	775 057	2.61
1969–70	2 137 600	772 290	2.77
1970–71	2 210 300	771 314	2.87
1971–72	2 331 200	769 665	3.03
1972–73	2 447 800	766 550	3.19
1973–74	2 615 100	762 221	3.43
1974–75	2 694 500	758 384	3.55
1975–76	2 730 600	754 000	3.62
1976–77	2 905 600	746 602	3.89
1977–78	2 982 700	739 869	4.03
1978–79	3 050 900	733 361	4.16
1979–80	3 130 200	727 961	4.30
1980–81	3 146 100	721 292	4.36
1981–82	3 236 500	714 341	4.53
1982–83	3 122 900	706 361	4.42
1983–84	3 220 400	700 039	4.60
1984–85	3 369 600	692 692	4.86
1985–86	3 403 000	681 766	4.99
1986–87	3 514 800	674 395	5.21
1987–88	3 622 300	666 835	5.43
1988–89	3 832 100	658 973	5.82
1989–90	3 945 200	651 192	6.06
1990–91	3 946 600	642 862	6.14
1991–92	4 003 200	634 924	6.31
1992–93	4 079 200	625 177	6.52
1993–94	4 176 600	618 259	6.76
1994–95	n.a.	608 912	n.a.

Note: n.a. denotes not available.

natural capital by the uncancelled cost of economic activity. The
larger/smaller is the ratio, the smaller/larger is the opportunity cost of
natural capital services sacrificed per dollar of available natural capital
(valued at 1989/90 prices). Australia's exploitative efficiency ratio is

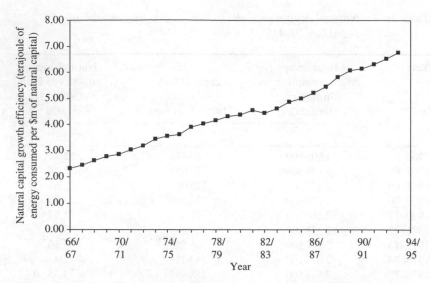

*Figure 16.7   Natural capital growth efficiency ratio (Ratio 3) for
              Australia, 1966/7 to 1994/5*

indicated in Table 16.6 and Figure 16.9. Both reveal that the exploitative
efficiency ratio declined in every year between 1966/7 and 1994/5. This
result suggests that the opportunity cost of exploiting natural capital for
the throughput of matter-energy increased continuously over the study
period. The decline in the exploitative efficiency ratio was considerable. The
ratio began at a value of 7.2 in 1966/7 and declined to a value of 2.4 by
1994/5. Whilst this result probably overstates the opportunity cost of
Australia's natural capital exploitation, it does reflect Australia's heavy
reliance on non-renewable resources, its lack of reinvestment into renewable resource substitutes, and its poor record of land management.

THE POLICY RELEVANCE OF ECO-EFFICIENCY INDICATORS

Much has already been said in earlier chapters about the accuracy of
various indicators and its implications for policy-making. Most of it can
also be directed at the eco-efficiency indicators calculated in this chapter.
For example, the calculation of certain items that make up the uncancelled
cost account involves assumptions and valuation methods heavily criticised
by Dietz and Neumayer (Chapter 9). In addition, the natural capital

Table 16.5   *Renewable natural capital growth efficiency ratio for Australia, 1966/7 to 1994/5*

Year	Total renewable energy consumption (throughput) (terajoules)	Renewable natural capital stock ($m at 1989–90 prices)	Renewable natural capital growth efficiency (a/b×1000)
	a	b	c
1966–67	192.0	154962	1.24
1967–68	187.7	155210	1.21
1968–69	189.8	155555	1.22
1969–70	180.9	156041	1.16
1970–71	191.4	158871	1.20
1971–72	194.2	161885	1.20
1972–73	190.7	164012	1.16
1973–74	197.2	165391	1.19
1974–75	203.9	167521	1.22
1975–76	206.2	169045	1.22
1976–77	199.5	169143	1.18
1977–78	199.4	169107	1.18
1978–79	198.5	168317	1.18
1979–80	193.5	168812	1.15
1980–81	207.2	168332	1.23
1981–82	211.3	168011	1.26
1982–83	204.4	167035	1.22
1983–84	203.5	166881	1.22
1984–85	217.0	167088	1.30
1985–86	215.1	167050	1.29
1986–87	217.7	167176	1.30
1987–88	220.8	167375	1.32
1988–89	231.6	167643	1.38
1989–90	233.9	168385	1.39
1990–91	239.4	168670	1.42
1991–92	225.2	168661	1.34
1992–93	246.7	167998	1.47
1993–94	254.2	167780	1.52
1994–95	n.a.	167537	n.a.

Note: n.a. denotes not available.

account is potentially beset with problems and weaknesses highlighted by England (Chapter 10). Moreover, the 'Cambridge controversy' raises serious issues regarding the compilation of a human-made capital account. Finally, one can also call into question the legitimacy of establishing a

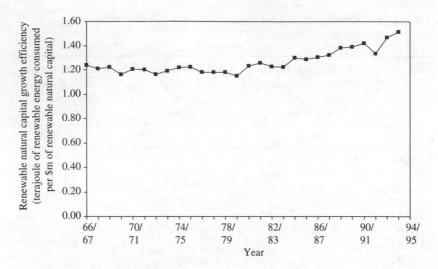

*Figure 16.8　Renewable natural capital growth efficiency ratio for
Australia, 1966/7 to 1994/5*

single index value for each of the elemental categories used to calculate the
eco-efficiency ratios.

Many of these issues and concerns were dealt with in Chapter 7,
although they were far from completely resolved. While these concerns
leave one decidedly more equivocal when drawing conclusions from the
eco-efficiency indicators presented in this chapter, they do not necessarily
extinguish their policy-guiding value. As Daly (1996, p. 115) reminds us,
the poorest approximation of a correct and highly desirable concept is
always better than an accurate approximation of an irrelevant or erroneous
concept. Given what has so far been said by the various contributors in
this book, it is clear that most mainstream performance indicators, while
often accurate approximations of various phenomena, constitute poor if
not entirely misleading indicators of a nation's sustainable development
performance. Conversely, the eco-efficiency indicators revealed in this
chapter provide a transparent overall picture of Australia's management
and use of its natural capital assets.

The question that needs to be answered is this: to what extent can the
general outlook of a nation's record of natural capital management be used
to inform its policy-makers? Perhaps it should first be stressed that it does
not enable policy-makers to make policy decisions regarding, for example,
the management of a specific river basin, a regional electricity market or a
particular city's transport network. What it does do, however, is enable

Table 16.6   Natural capital exploitative efficiency ratio for Australia, 1966/7 to 1994/5

Year	Natural capital stock ($m at 1989–90 prices)	Uncancelled costs ($m at 1989–90 prices)	Natural capital exploitative efficiency (Ratio 4) (a/b)
	a	b	c
1966–67	780448	108941	7.2
1967–68	777952	112830	6.9
1968–69	775057	117306	6.6
1969–70	772290	122265	6.3
1970–71	771314	126338	6.1
1971–72	769665	130902	5.9
1972–73	766550	135338	5.7
1973–74	762221	140820	5.4
1974–75	758384	146047	5.2
1975–76	754000	150430	5.0
1976–77	746602	155479	4.8
1977–78	739869	159814	4.6
1978–79	733361	166103	4.4
1979–80	727961	171962	4.2
1980–81	721292	176748	4.1
1981–82	714341	182239	3.9
1982–83	706361	186395	3.8
1983–84	700039	190907	3.7
1984–85	692692	197236	3.5
1985–86	681766	202215	3.4
1986–87	674395	206729	3.3
1987–88	666835	211570	3.2
1988–89	658973	216289	3.0
1989–90	651192	224187	2.9
1990–91	642862	228905	2.8
1991–92	634924	233111	2.7
1992–93	625177	239809	2.6
1993–94	618259	243097	2.5
1994–95	608912	247534	2.5

policy-makers to identify general policy shortcomings and establish appropriate policy goals. The latter can then be used to facilitate the emergence and subsequent implementation of more specific public policies.

For example, in Australia's case, the decline in the service efficiency ratio (Ratio 1) in most years since the early 1970s indicates that although the

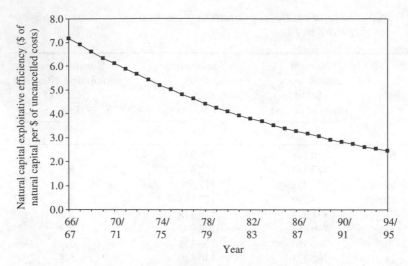

*Figure 16.9   Natural capital exploitative efficiency ratio (Ratio 4) for
          Australia, 1966/7 to 1994/5*

lower-order needs of most Australians are being adequately satisfied, the
continuing growth in the stock of human-made capital is coming at
the expense of higher-order need satisfaction. Rather than Australia's
uncancelled benefit (UB) curve shifting up as desired (see Figure 16.1), it
has probably been shifting down over the last 20 years, thereby contributing to the decline in Australia's sustainable economic welfare.

This evidence sends a signal to policy-makers that there is an urgent
need to focus on qualitative improvement, not quantitative growth.
Moreover, since the fall in Ratio 1 had much to do with the increased cost
of unemployment, commuting, noise pollution, crime, and a widening gap
between the rich and poor, Australian policy-makers need to concentrate
their policy attention on the social factors discussed in Chapter 2. Too
much of the incoming resource flow is being allocated to produce more
goods with little attention given to the indirect and mounting costs associated with Australia's persistent drive for growth. Clearly, current incentives
and disincentives – caused by such market distortions as the failure to publicly remunerate non-paid household work – are restricting the options
available to Australians and forcing them, on occasions, to make choices
that are not in their welfare interests. In addition, the Australian taxation
system is discouraging value-adding in production (qualitative improvement) by excessively taxing such 'goods' as income, wages and profit.

More also needs to be done by Australian policy-makers to reduce
unemployment. The continuing acceptance of high unemployment rates is

not only morally unjustified, it is unnecessary (Wray, 1998; Mitchell and Watts, 2002; and Tcherneva, 2003). Finally, Australian policy-makers need to overturn the growing imbalance between rich and poor. The public remuneration of non-paid work and a greater commitment to full employment would assist enormously in this regard.

As for the maintenance efficiency ratio (Ratio 2), which was lower at the end of the study period than the beginning, distorted incentives again appear to be the culprit. Coupled with a large increase in Australia's total energy consumption between 1966/7 and 1993/4, the fall in Ratio 2 indicates that most of Australia's recent technological innovation has been of the throughput-increasing variety. Throughput-increasing technological progress augments the resource flow passing through a nation's macro-economy. Examples include the development of a novel resource exploration method that leads to the discovery of a new oil deposit, a new resource extraction technique that allows a previously inaccessible mineral deposit to be exploited, and the development of a new use for a previously unwanted resource. Disconcertingly, little progress seems to have been made in terms of maintenance efficiency-increasing innovation. More therefore needs to be done by Australian policy-makers to encourage greater production efficiency, more durable goods, and higher rates of material recycling. Thus, at the very minimum, taxes should be imposed to discourage such 'bads' as resource depletion and pollution. If the imposition of these taxes were combined with a reduction in taxes on income, wages, and profit, Australian policy-makers would come closer to instituting what is now popularly termed ecological tax reform (Lawn, 2000b).

The policy-related message provided by Australia's growth efficiency ratio (Ratio 3) is somewhat less definitive because the rise in this ratio was the consequence of Australia's increasing rate of non-renewable resource depletion. In view of the decline in Australia's natural capital stock, it should be clear to policy-makers that Australia has failed to invest enough of the proceeds from its depletion of non-renewable resources into the cultivation of renewable resource substitutes. Without a policy overhaul in this area, it is unlikely that Australia could self-sustain its current rate of energy consumption into the future.

It was pointed out in Chapter 2 that a 'user cost' formula has been devised by El Serafy to calculate the portion of depletion profits that must be set aside to establish a replacement capital asset (El Serafy, 1989; Lawn, 1998). This so-called El Serafy Rule can be operationalised by compelling resource liquidators to establish a 'capital replacement' account in the same way it is necessary for most business managers to establish a superannuation fund for employees. This could be done through changes in accounting legislation.

On a positive note, the rise in Australia's renewable natural capital growth ratio since the early 1980s appears to have been induced, in part, by stringent pollution standards introduced at the national and state levels during the 1970s. However, since this rise can also be attributed to the oil price shocks of 1973 and 1979, a tax impost on depletion and pollution activities – by increasing the throughput cost of production – would boost the incentive of Australian producers to develop greener production techniques. This would bring about a much a larger rise in the renewable natural capital growth ratio than that experienced in the 1980s and 1990s. Furthermore, by asserting greater downward pressure on the uncancelled cost (UC) curve, such a policy would assist in increasing Australia's economic welfare.

Our attention finally turns to the evidential decline in Australia's exploitative efficiency ratio (Ratio 4). Again, the fall in Ratio 4 has much to do with Australia's reliance on non-renewable resources and its lack of suitable asset replacement. However, the largest contributing factor appears to be Australia's excessive rate of native vegetation clearance. While in some states of Australia vegetation clearance is strictly controlled, in other states (such as Queensland) it is not. A sensible policy response requires the establishment of co-ordinated clearance controls at the national level where, importantly, the federal government is better positioned to compensate affected land owners than state governments. Compensation is not only necessary for equity reasons, but to encourage land owners to conserve and manage protected vegetation.

CONCLUDING REMARKS

Contrary to some opinions, eco-efficiency indicators can be developed in a manner consistent with the coevolutionary paradigm and the conclusions drawn from the linear throughput representation of the socio-economic process. Despite some possible inaccuracies, appropriately developed eco-efficiency indicators can provide valuable information for policy-makers. The eco-efficiency exercise conducted on Australia demonstrates this point. What is more, the development and application of more robust valuation methods will only improve their policy-guiding value. Indeed, if just some of the policies suggested in this chapter were implemented by Australian policy-makers, much could be accomplished, I am sure, to overcome the welfare-declining impact of failing to embrace the notions of qualitative improvement, distributional equity, and natural capital maintenance.

APPENDIX

The individual items that make up the uncancelled benefit, uncancelled cost, human-made capital and natural capital accounts were all estimated in 1989/90 Australian dollar prices. The values of some items were drawn directly from Australia's national accounts (e.g. private consumption expenditure). However, the estimation of many items required the use of specific valuation techniques (e.g. the value of non-paid household work, the cost of noise pollution, and the cost of long-term environmental damage). The uncancelled benefit, uncancelled cost, human-made capital and natural capital accounts are briefly explained below. The valuation methods used to calculate each item that make up the individual accounts can be found in Lawn (2000a).

The Uncancelled Benefit (Net Psychic Income) Account

Since the reason for compiling an uncancelled benefit account is to ascertain the net psychic income enjoyed by Australian citizens, this account includes a number of psychic income and psychic outgo-related items. Once the values of these items are calculated, the sum of the latter is subtracted from the former to obtain a final measure of net psychic income. The psychic income-related items used to compile the uncancelled benefit account include:

- private consumption expenditure;
- an index of distributional inequality that is used to weight private consumption expenditure;
- services from consumer durables, public dwellings, and roads and highways';
- services from volunteer and non-paid household labour;
- public expenditure on health and education counted as consumption;
- an imputed value of leisure time;
- net producer goods growth;
- changes in the nation's net foreign assets/liabilities.

The psychic outgo-related items included in the uncancelled benefit account are:

- the cost of commuting, noise pollution, and private vehicle accidents;
- the direct disamenity cost of air pollution (assumed to be 40 per cent of the total cost of air pollution);
- the cost of unemployment and underemployment;

- the cost of crime and family breakdown;
- defensive private health and education expenditure;
- current expenditure on consumer durables.

The Uncancelled Cost (Lost Natural Capital Services) Account

The aim of the uncancelled cost account is to ascertain the natural capital services lost from the transformation of natural capital into service-yielding goods. The uncancelled cost account is divided into three categories to reflect the partial loss of the three instrumental functions of natural capital – namely, its source, sink and life-support functions. The lost source-related category includes the following items:

- the user cost of non-renewable resources (metallic minerals, non-metallic minerals, coal and gas);
- the cost of lost agricultural land;
- the user cost of timber and fishery resources;
- the cost of degraded wetlands.

Items included in the category related to lost sink-related functions of natural capital are:

- the cost of water, air, and solid waste pollution (the sink-related air pollution cost assumed to be 60 per cent of the total cost of air pollution); and
- the cost of ozone depletion.

Items included in the lost life-support services category are:

- the cost of long-term environmental damage; and
- an ecosystem health index. This index is used to weight the total of all uncancelled costs on the basis that many exploitative activities, such as mining, not only diminish the source and sink functions of natural capital, but also its life-support function.

The Human-made Capital Account

As explained in Chapter 2, ecological economists often refer to human-made capital in the Irving Fisher (1906) sense as all human-made objects subject to ownership that are capable of directly or indirectly satisfying human needs and wants. Included in the human-made capital account are:

- the public and private sector ownership of buildings and producer goods such as plant, machinery and equipment;
- business inventories;
- household dwellings;
- the stock of consumer durables (this includes durable household items and private motor vehicles);
- the stock of human labour (capitalised value).

The Natural Capital Account

The natural capital account is divided into renewable and non-renewable resources. Where possible, ecosystem services are incorporated into the value of some renewable resources (e.g. non-commercial native vegetation found in national parks and other conservation reserves). Wetlands and saltmarshes were also included in the renewable resource category. Items included in the non-renewable resource category are:

- sub-soil assets (metallic minerals, non-metallic minerals, coal, and gas);
- agricultural land.

Items included in the renewable resource category are:

- timber stocks;
- wetlands;
- saltmarshes;
- fishery stocks;
- livestock;
- water storage resources.

NOTES

1. Indeed, economists have a term for such a condition. It is referred to as a 'bliss point'.
2. In the case of renewable natural capital, it would involve the use of a resource flow in keeping with its regenerative capacities. In the case of non-renewable natural capital that does not regenerate, it would involve the cultivation of a renewable resource substitute to replace the declining non-renewable resource. This would keep the combined stock of natural capital intact.

REFERENCES

Ayres, R. and L. Ayres (1999), *Accounting for Resources*, Cheltenham, UK and Northampton MA, USA: Edward Elgar.
Boulding, K. (1970), *A Primer on Social Dynamics*, New York: Free Press.
Capra, F. (1982), *The Turning Point*, London: Fontana.
Costanza, R. (1980), 'Embodied energy and economic valuation', *Science*, **210**, 1219–24.
Costanza, R., H. Daly and J. Bartholomew (1991), 'Goals, agenda, and policy recommendations for ecological economics', in R. Costanza (ed.), *Ecological Economics: The Science and Management of Sustainability*, New York: Columbia University Press, pp. 1–20.
Daly, H. (1996), *Beyond Growth: The Economics of Sustainable Development*, Boston: Beacon Press.
Dyke, C. (1988), *The Evolutionary Dynamics of Complex Systems: A Study in Biosocial Complexity*, Oxford: Oxford University Press.
El Serafy, S. (1989), 'The proper calculation of income from depletable natural resources', in Y. Ahmad, S. El Serafy and E. Lutz (eds), *Environmental Accounting for Sustainable Development*, Washington DC: World Bank, pp. 10–18.
Faber, M., R. Manstetten and J. Proops (1992), 'Toward an open future: ignorance, novelty, and evolution', in R. Costanza, B. Norton and B. Haskell (eds), *Ecosystem Health: New Goals for Environmental Management*, Washington DC: Island Press, pp. 72–96.
Faber, M. and J. Proops (1990), *Evolution, Time, Production and the Environment*, Heidelberg: Springer.
Fisher, I. (1906), *Nature of Capital and Income*, New York: A.M. Kelly.
Folke, C., M. Hammer, R. Costanza and A. Jansson (1994), 'Investing in natural capital – why, what, and how', in A. Jansson, M. Hammer, C. Folke, and R. Costanza (eds), *Investing in Natural Capital*, Washington DC: Island Press, pp. 1–20.
Georgescu-Roegen, N. (1971), *The Entropy Law and the Economic Process*, Cambridge: Harvard University Press.
Hukkinen, J. (2001), 'Eco-efficiency as abandonment of nature', *Ecological Economics*, **38**, 311–16.
Knight, F. (1921), *Risk, Uncertainty, and Profit*, Boston: Houghton Mifflin.
Laszlo, E. (1972), *The Systems View of the World*, New York: G. Braziller.
Lawn, P. (1998), 'In defence of the strong sustainability approach to national income accounting', *Environmental Taxation and Accounting*, **3**, 29–47.
Lawn, P. (2000a), *Toward Sustainable Development: An Ecological Economics Approach*, Boca Raton: Lewis Publishers.
Lawn, P. (2000b), 'Ecological tax reform: many know why but few know how', *Environment, Development, and Sustainability*, **2**, 143–64.
Lawn, P. (2001), 'Goods and services and the dematerialisation fallacy: implications for sustainable development indicators and policy', *International Journal of Services, Technology, and Management*, **2**, 363–76.
Mitchell, W. and M. Watts (2002), 'Restoring full employment: the Job Guarantee', in E. Carlson and W. Mitchell (eds), *The Urgency of Full Employment*, Sydney: University of New South Wales Press, pp. 95–114.

OECD (1998), *Towards Sustainable Development: Environmental Indicators*, Paris: OECD.

Pearce, D. and R. Turner (1990), *Economics of Natural Resources and the Environment*, London: Harvester Wheatsheaf.

Perrings, C. (1986), 'Conservation of mass and instability in a dynamic economy-environment system', *Journal of Environmental Economics and Management*, **13**, 199–211.

Reddy, A. and J. Goldemberg (1990), 'Energy for the developing world', *Scientific American*, September, pp. 110–18.

Robinson, J. (1962), *Economic Philosophy*, London: C.A. Watts.

Schmidheiny, S. and F. Zorraquin (1996), *Financing Change: The Financial Community, Eco-Efficiency, and Sustainable Development*, Cambridge, MA: MIT Press.

Tcherneva, P. (2003), *Job or Income Guarantee?*, Centre for Full Employment and Price Stability, Working Paper No. 29, University of Missouri, Kansas City.

United Nations (1999), *The Global Compact and the Environment* (http://www.unglobalcompact.org/gc/unweb.nsf/content/enviroment.htm).

Weiszacker, E., A. Lovins and L. Lovins (1998), *Factor Four: Doubling Wealth – Halving Resource Use*, London: Earthscan.

World Business Council for Sustainable Development (WBCSD) (2000), *Eco-efficiency: Creating More Value With Less Impact* (www.wbcsd.org).

World Commission on Environment and Development (WCED) (1987), *Our Common Future*, Oxford: Oxford University Press.

Wray, R. (1998), *Understanding Modern Money: The Key to Full Employment and Price Stability*, Cheltenham, UK and Lyme, USA: Edward Elgar.

17. Material flow-based indicators for evaluation of eco-efficiency and dematerialisation policies

Stefan Giljum

POLICY BACKGROUND

Since the 1980s, a change in the complexity and scope of environmental problems in industrialised countries has been observed, away from local or regional environmental degradation through pollution towards more complex and global environmental issues associated with changes in production, trade, and consumption patterns (EEAC, 2003). Flows of energy and materials activated for socio-economic activities together with intensive use of land, represent the main anthropogenic pressures on ecosystems and entail most environmental problems currently on the European political agenda (EEA, 2003). In today's globalised economic system, industrialised economies are responsible for the major share of global environmental pressures, appropriating about 80 per cent of natural resources and producing 80 per cent of waste and emissions with only about 20 per cent of world population (von Weizsäcker et al., 1997).

This global responsibility is beginning to be addressed by environmental policy strategies in Europe and other OECD member countries. The European Commission (2001b) acknowledges that production and consumption activities within industrialised regions have environmental consequences in other world regions, in particular, developing countries. High levels of resource use are one major obstacle for the realisation of an environmentally sustainable development. The transformation towards a sustainable use of natural resources is therefore defined as one of four priority environmental policy areas in the European Union (EU) (European Commission, 2001a). Also, OECD environmental ministers have recently adopted a recommendation on material flows and resource productivity (OECD, 2004) that is aimed at better integrating resource flow-based indicators in environmental–economic decision making. De-coupling (or de-linking) economic growth from the use of natural resources and environmental degradation is regarded as the core strategy to achieve this transformation (OECD, 2002). Raising the eco-efficiency of production and consumption activities should allow the same or even more products to be produced while providing long-term quality service with significantly reduced inputs of materials, energy and land, and less pollution of the natural environment.

Traditional environmental policy in industrialised countries has focused on detoxification on the output side of the economy as well as the application of command-and-control mechanisms, such as critical load assessment and pollution abatement legislation. These regulation policies have been effective in decreasing local or regional environmental pressures and still play an important role in ameliorating environmental problems in circumstances where a reduction of specific substances with a high potential for negative environmental impacts, such as toxic substances is required. However, they are not suitable to tackle persistent environmental problems, such as high material and energy consumption. Nor do they initiate long-term dynamic solutions that would otherwise increase eco-efficiency across all economic activities – a consequence of the failure to set incentives to decrease environmental pressures beyond the agreed critical loads (Spangenberg and Verheyen, 1996). New approaches of environmental governance should take a systemic view of the economy–environment relationship, acknowledging that many current environmental problems are related to the overall scale of resource use rather than to toxicities of specific substances (Giljum et al., 2005). Thus, input-oriented policy strategies, such as the concept of dematerialisation (Hinterberger et al., 1997), are favoured as the means to tackling persistent environmental problems at their source, thereby reducing the potential of environmental harm in accordance with the precautionary principle, not simply by combating symptoms. Furthermore, input-oriented policies are often characterised by higher cost-effectiveness and allow targets to be achieved with less effort of control compared to output-focused strategies (Spangenberg et al., 1999).

The realisation of a dematerialisation policy requires the implementation of a balanced mix of policy instruments (Behrens, 2004). These instruments range from voluntary, de-centralised solutions to traditional regulations through nation-state institutions. A special focus should be put on market-based instruments since they allow decision-makers and economic actors to achieve environmental objectives in a cost-effective way. Compared to traditional regulation, market-based instruments are the drivers of technological innovation. For instance, a redesigned framework of taxes, subsidies, and certificates oriented towards a reduction of natural resource use can facilitate investment in higher eco-efficiency beyond fixed limits of, for example, emissions or waste generation. The increasing importance of market-based (and voluntary) instruments is also reflected in current trends in EU environmental policies (Jordan et al., 2003).

Monitoring success or failure of eco-efficiency and dematerialisation policies requires comprehensive and consistent information on the relations between socio-economic activities and resulting environmental consequences. Within ecological economics and industrial ecology, a number of approaches have been developed since the mid-1980s to provide relational information in biophysical terms (see, for example, Daniels and Moore, 2002 for an overview). Many ecological economists regard the use of physical units as a crucial requirement for sustainability-oriented analyses since pure monetary approaches possess a number of shortcomings, such as the insufficient reflection of physical scarcities, the systematic bias against the future due to discounting practices, or the assumption of complete substitutability between natural and man-made capital (e.g., Ekins, 2001; Rees and Wackernagel, 1999).

On the macro level, several approaches of physical accounting (for example, economy-wide material flow accounting and analysis (MFA), energy accounting and land use accounting) define system boundaries in accordance with the System of National Accounts (SNA). This structure allows direct integration of monetary and physical information within one accounting framework and thus enables the compilation of consistent data bases for policy-oriented analyses of economy–environment interactions. The usefulness of these integrated accounting schemes is also increasingly highlighted on the international level. A good example is the publishing of the United Nations' 'System for Integrated Environmental Economic Accounting (SEEA)' (for the latest version, see United Nations, 2003). With regard to assessing the material base and resource throughput of national economies, MFA has been established as a widely applied methodological approach and is recognised as a key tool for evaluating eco-efficiency policies (European Commission, 2003; OECD, 2004).

This chapter focuses on the policy relevance of the MFA approach and derived material flow indicators. The following section introduces the basic concept of economy-wide material flow analysis. Most important MFA-based indicators are presented in the third major section of this chapter. In the fourth major section, selected examples are given as to how these indicators are used for environmental and sustainability policy evaluations. The penultimate major section discusses the main shortcomings of the MFA approach and introduces possible extensions of the current

MFA framework. The main arguments are summarised in the final major section.

ECONOMY-WIDE MATERIAL FLOW ACCOUNTING

Material flow accounting and analysis builds on earlier concepts of material and energy balancing, as introduced, for example, by Ayres (1978).[1] Since the beginning of the 1990s, when first material flow accounts on the national level were presented (Environment Agency Japan, 1992), MFA has been a rapidly growing field of scientific interest and major efforts have been undertaken to harmonise methodological approaches developed by different research teams (Adriannse et al., 1997; Matthews et al., 2000). In an international working group on MFA, standardisation for economy-wide material flow accounting was for the first time achieved and published in a methodological guidebook by the Statistical Office of the EU (EUROSTAT, 2001).

Methodological Foundations

The principle concept underlying the economy-wide MFA approach is a simple model of the interrelation between the economy and the environment, in which the economy is an embedded subsystem of the environment and – similar to living beings – dependent on a constant throughput of materials and energy. Raw materials, water and air are extracted from the natural system as inputs, transformed into products, and finally re-transferred to the natural system as outputs (waste and emissions). To highlight the similarity to natural metabolic processes, the terms 'industrial metabolism' (Ayres, 1989) and 'societal metabolism' (Fischer-Kowalski, 1998a) were introduced as key interrelational terms.

According to the first law of thermodynamics (the law of the conservation of mass), total inputs must, by definition, equal total outputs plus net accumulation of materials in the system. This material balance principle holds true for the economy as a whole as well as for any subsystem (an economic sector, a company, a household). For a consistent compilation of an economy-wide material flow account, it is necessary to define exactly where the boundary between the economic and the environmental system is set, as only resources crossing this border are accounted. As described in the Integrated System of Environmental and Economic Accounts (SEEA) (United Nations, 2003), the economic sphere is defined in close relation to the flows covered by the conventional System of National Accounts (SNA). Thus, all flows related to the three types of economic activities included in the SNA (production, consumption and stock change) are referred to as part of the economic system. On the other hand, the environmental sphere comprises all resources other than products traded within the market system. Therefore, for MFA on the national level, two main boundaries for resource flows can be defined. The first is the boundary between the economy and the domestic natural environment from which resources (raw materials, water and air) are extracted. The second is the frontier to other economies with imports and exports as accounted flows.

Categories of Material Flows

Before outlining a comprehensive material balance scheme on the national level, the differences between the different types of material flows shall be explained. In its methodological guide, EUROSTAT (2001) distinguishes the various types of material flows according to the following scheme:[2]

- *Direct versus indirect*: Direct flows refer to the actual weight of the products and thus do not take into account the life-cycle dimension of production chains. Indirect flows, however, indicate all materials that have been required for manufacturing (i.e. up-stream resource requirements) and comprise both used and unused materials.
- *Used versus unused*: The category of used materials is defined as the amount of extracted resources which enters the economic system for further processing or direct consumption. All used materials are transformed within the economic system. Unused extraction refers to materials that never enter the economic system and thus can be described as physical market externalities (Hinterberger et al., 1999). This category comprises overburden and parting materials from mining, by-catch from fishing, wood and agricultural harvesting losses, as well as soil excavation and dredged materials from construction activities.
- *Domestic versus Rest of the World*: This category refers to the origin and/or destination of material flows.

In its methodological guide, EUROSTAT provides a standard classification of materials that should be applied in the compilation of material flow accounts at the national level. All physical material inputs of a socio-economic system can be attributed to three subgroups: solid materials, water and air. As water and air flows, in general, exceed all other material inputs by a factor of ten or more (especially if water cooling is also accounted for – see Stahmer et al., 1997) EUROSTAT recommends presenting water and air balances separately from solid materials. Thus, in the standard accounts, water should only be included when becoming part of a product. The group of solid materials is further classified into three main subgroups of material inputs:

- minerals (metal ores, industrial and construction minerals);
- fossil energy carriers (coal, oil, gas, peat); and
- biomass (from agriculture, forestry, fishery, and hunting).

A General Scheme for Economy-Wide MFA

A general material balancing scheme, including all relevant input and output flows, is presented in Figure 17.1. The material balance reveals the composition of the physical metabolism of an economy and depicts domestic material extraction, imports and exports in physical units, the physical growth of the economy's infrastructure, and the amount of materials released back to nature.

Material inputs to the economic system are either (1) accumulated within the socio-economic system (net addition to stock, such as infrastructure and durable consumer goods); (2) consumed domestically within the accounting period (in most cases one year) and thus cross the system boundary as waste and emissions back to nature; or (3) exported to other economies.

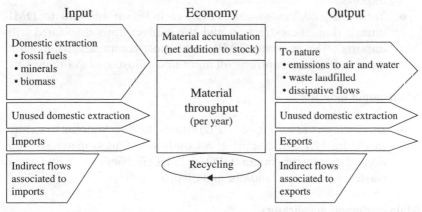

Source: adapted from EUROSTAT, 2001.

Figure 17.1 General scheme for economy-wide MFA, excluding flows of water and air

MATERIAL FLOW-BASED INDICATORS ON THE MACRO LEVEL

Within the internationally harmonised classification systems for environmental indicators, such as the pressure–state–response (PSR) framework of the OECD (1994) or the extended driving forces–pressures–state–impact–response (DPSIR) system used in the EU (EUROSTAT, 1999), material flow-based indicators are part of the pressure indicator group. These indicators identify and describe the socio-economic activities that exert pressures on the environment, such as agricultural or industrial production, transport and energy use.

Economy-Wide Material Flow-Based Indicators

A large number of resource-use indicators can be derived from economy-wide material flow accounts. These indicators can be grouped into (1) input, (2) output, (3) consumption and (4) trade indicators. The following selected indicators are most commonly used in MFA studies at the national level (EUROSTAT, 2001).

Main input indicators

- *Direct material input* (*DMI*) comprises all materials with economic value and which are directly used in production and consumption activities. DMI equals the sum of domestic extraction and imports.
- *Total material requirement* (*TMR*) includes, in addition to DMI, unused domestic extraction and the indirect flows associated with imports of an economy. TMR is the most comprehensive material input indicator, comprising all input flows illustrated in Figure 17.1.

Main output indicator

- *Domestic processed output* (*DPO*) equals the flow 'outputs to nature' in Figure 17.1 and comprises all outflows of used materials from domestic or foreign origin. DPO includes emissions to air and water, wastes deposited in landfills, and dissipative flows.

Main consumption indicators

- *Domestic material consumption* (*DMC*) measures the total quantity of materials used within an economic system, excluding indirect flows. Thus DMC is the closest equivalent to aggregate income in the conventional system of national accounts. DMC is calculated by subtracting exports from DMI.

- *Total material consumption (TMC)* includes, in addition to DMC, the indirect flows associated with imports and exports. TMC equals TMR minus exports and their indirect flows.

Main trade indicator

- *Physical trade balance (PTB)* expresses whether resource imports from abroad exceed resource exports of a country or world region and thus illustrates to what extent domestic material consumption is based on domestic resource extraction or on imports from abroad. A PTB can either be compiled for direct material flows (physical imports minus physical exports) or, additionally, by including indirect flows associated with imports and exports.

Eco-Efficiency Indicators

The compatibility of MFA with data from the System of National Accounts (SNA) enables direct relation of material flow indicators with indicators of economic performance, such as GDP. These interlinkage indicators quantify the eco-efficiency (or resource productivity) of an economic system by calculating economic output (measured in monetary units) generated per material input (in physical units), for example GDP/DMI.[3] Eco-efficiency indicators are thus suitable tools to monitor processes of de-linking or de-coupling of resource use from economic growth as the key strategy toward a more sustainable use of natural resources.

These economic–environmental indicators were applied to test the so-called Environmental Kutznets Curve (EKC) hypothesis[4] for material inputs (for example, Seppälä et al., 2001) and to define benchmarks for environmentally sustainable economic growth (Spangenberg et al., 2002).

From a sustainability point of view, it is crucial to distinguish between relative and absolute de-linking. In a situation involving relative increases in eco-efficiency, the amount of material inputs required to generate economic output diminishes in relative terms, while absolute levels of environmental pressures still increase. However, in order to be environmentally sustainable, levels of natural resource use must be dramatically decreased in absolute terms, particularly in industrialised countries – indeed, by a factor of up to ten (see Schmidt-Bleek, 1994). Strategies for raising eco-efficiency must therefore aim at absolute de-linking, a situation where environmental pressures decrease even in a growing economy. In order to achieve absolute de-coupling, increases in resource productivity must be higher than the rate of economic growth (Spangenberg et al., 2002).

Calculation Procedures for Material Flow Indicators

Indicators for direct material flows, such as DMI and DMC and their corresponding eco-efficiency indicators, can, to a large extent, be calculated using published national or international statistics. Concerning internationally available statistics, most common data sources are:

- data on extraction of fossil fuels published, for example, by the International Energy Agency (IEA) or the Industrial Commodity Statistics of the United Nations;
- data on extraction of metal ores and industrial and construction minerals published by reports from United States Geological Survey (USGS) or the Industrial Commodity Statistics of the United Nations;
- biomass extraction data published by the Food and Agricultural Organization of the United Nations (FAO), which provides an online database for agricultural, forestry and fishery production on the national level;
- international trade data in physical units published, for example, in the UN International Trade Statistics Yearbooks or in trade statistics by the European Statistical Office;
- GDP data sets published by the World Bank.

While data quality for biomass and fossil fuel extraction can be rated relatively high, statistics covering other material categories (in particular, construction minerals) are less comprehensive and less reliable. Here, in many cases, estimations of average per capita extraction numbers must be made and subsequently applied. Another problematic issue is the fact that international statistics normally report metal extraction in net weight, covering only the metal content of the primary extracted ore. In order to account for the total used in mining, one has to re-calculate crude ore extraction using information on average metal concentrations in specific countries as, for example, is provided by USGS country and commodity reports.

Data availability is in general lower with regard to unused domestic extraction (UDE) or indirect flows associated with traded products. Valuable information on UDE for abiotic minerals can be obtained from publications by the Wuppertal Institute for Climate, Environment and Energy in Germany (e.g. Bringezu and Schütz, 2001b). For UDE of biotic materials, specific literature (for example, reports from FAO fishery and forestry departments) has to be analysed since available information in existing MFA studies is very scarce.

Concerning indirect flows of traded products, two main calculation approaches can be distinguished. The first approach is based on a simplified life-cycle assessment (LCA) of products or product groups. 'Material intensity analysis (MAIA)' (Schmidt-Bleek et al., 1998) is an analytical tool to assess material inputs along the whole life cycle of a product. The Wuppertal Institute is one of the most important sources for data on indirect material flows (Bringezu and Schütz, 2001b; Schütz, 1999). This LCA-oriented approach is mainly suitable for the calculation of indirect flows associated with biotic and abiotic raw materials and products with a low level of processing. Applying this method to calculate indirect flows for semi-manufactured and finished products requires the compilation of an enormous amount of material input data at each stage of production. Therefore, indirect material flows have only been estimated for a very small number of finished products.

An alternative method for calculating indirect material flows on the macro level is to apply extended input–output (IO) analysis, which allows the comprehensive accounting of direct and indirect resource flows activated by final demand. The method used to link monetary input–output models with material flow accounts at the national level was developed by Femia, Hinterberger and Moll (Femia, 1996; Hinterberger et al., 1998). The major advantage of this approach compared to the LCA-based calculation is the fact that, for studies at the national level, only domestic material extraction and physical imports have to be known and linked to the monetary IO table in order to calculate direct and indirect material inputs and resource productivities of all sectors of the economic system. In the course of a research project funded by the European Union (Modelling opportunities and limits for restructuring Europe towards sustainability, MOSUS, see www.mosus. net), a global system of econometric input–output models is extended by world-wide material input data in physical units in order to evaluate different scenarios of European use of resources, including indirect effects induced by international trade flows in other regions of the world (Giljum et al., forthcoming).

Availability of Material Flow Indicators

The number of countries that have already compiled or currently are in the stage of compiling economy-wide material flow accounts according to the methodological guidelines presented above is rapidly increasing. So far, full MFAs have been presented for the USA, Japan, Austria, Germany and the Netherlands within the framework of two projects co-ordinated by the World Resources Institute (WRI) (Adriaanse et al., 1997; Matthews et al., 2000). In addition to a large number of studies presented by national statistical institutions in Europe, MFA input indicators for all former EU-15 countries were calculated in studies commissioned by the European Statistical Office (Bringezu and Schütz, 2001a; EUROSTAT, 2002). MFA studies exist for transition economies in Eastern Europe (Hammer and Hubacek, 2002; Moll et al., 2003; Mündl et al., 1999; Scasny et al., 2003) and for Australia (Poldy and Foran, 1999). Concerning countries in the global South (Africa, Asia excluding Japan and Latin America), economy-wide MFAs have been presented for Brazil and Venezuela (Amann et al., 2002), for Chile (Giljum, 2004), and for China (Chen and Qiao, 2001). As for the material basis of the global economy, a first estimation was presented by Schandl and Eisenmenger (2004). In the course of the above mentioned MOSUS project, the first time series of total material input for all countries of the world has been presented (Giljum et al., 2004).

POLICY-ORIENTED APPLICATIONS OF MATERIAL FLOW INDICATORS

The main purpose of economy-wide MFA is to provide aggregate background information on composition and changes of the physical structure of socio-economic systems. MFA represents a useful methodological framework for analysing economy–environment relationships and deriving aggregated environmental and integrated environmental–economic (eco-efficiency) indicators. These indicators provide policy-makers with information to help shift the policy focus from purely monetary analysis to integrating biophysical aspects (Kleijn, 2001). In this major section, examples shall be presented to demonstrate how material flow-based indicators are used for identification and evaluation of environmental and sustainability policy strategies.

Integrated Sustainability Modelling

Economic models can be extended by environmental data in physical units (such as material flows, energy consumption or land use) in order to consider environmental aspects in evaluation of (future) economic development strategies. The use of integrated environmental–economic models allows for quantification of the implications of economic growth, of structural changes, of technological changes in specific economic sectors and of changes in consumption behaviour (life-styles) in terms of the extraction of natural resources and the production of emissions and waste.

Analysis of material flows within a dynamic input–output type economic model was first performed in the project *Work and Ecology* that was carried out by three research institutions in Germany (Hans-Böckler-Stiftung, 2000). The integrated model was used to simulate and evaluate different sustainability scenarios and identify policy strategies to increase both eco-efficiency and employment in Germany (Hinterberger et al., 2002; Spangenberg et al., 2002). Another recent German modelling study (Fischer et al., 2004) illustrated the huge potential for economically profitable resource savings that still await exploitation. According to the results of this study, more than 170 billion euros could be saved in Germany on an annual basis through a 25 per cent dematerialisation of economic activities. The study also revealed that state revenue could increase by some 40 billion euros annually and, provided the resulting savings were not invested in wage increases, 700,000 new jobs could be created through dematerialisation efforts.

In the MOSUS project already mentioned above, a global system of econometric country models (Meyer et al., 2003) is extended by material input and land use data. This integrated economy–environmental model system is then used to simulate – in a truly global (multinational and multi-sectoral) view – different sustainability scenarios formulated for Europe's development until 2020. In particular, the model illustrates the consequences of implementing key environmental policy measures (such as eco-logical tax reform, a reform of the subsidy system or implementation of the Kyoto instruments) for economic growth, employment and aggregated environmental indicators such as material and energy use, both within Europe, and in other world regions.

Globalisation, Trade and Environmental Distribution

Material flow-based indicators are important tools to illustrate environmental consequences of economic specialisation in the division of labour between different world regions (Giljum and Eisenmenger, 2004). Since production and consumption activities in industrialised countries have environmental impacts far beyond their borders, links between international trade and the environment and problems related to emissions with global environmental implications (such as carbon dioxide) have to be taken into account in the evaluation of national sustainability strategies.

Recent studies on the physical trade relations between industrialised and developing regions reveal that industrialised regions are in general physical net importers of natural resources from other world regions. For some material categories of crucial importance for economic development (such as fossil fuels and basic metal products), a clear tendency towards an increasing physical trade surplus (imports higher than exports) can be observed (Muradian and Martinez-Alier, 2001). Although, in many indus-trialised countries, a process of relative dematerialisation is taking place (Adriaanse et al., 1997), South–North resource flows maintain or even increase their importance.

A recent material flow study analysing the external trade relations of the EU revealed that physical imports and associated indirect material flows are growing and increasingly substituting for domestic material extraction – in particular, with regard to fossil fuels and metal ores (Schütz et al., 2004). At the same time, countries in the global South, for example, in Latin America, show a significant increase in economic activities of primary sectors, such as metal and mineral extraction, agriculture, forestry and fisheries and related physical export flows (Fischer-Kowalski and Amann, 2001; Giljum, 2004). Through this global pattern of resource extraction and trade, environmental burden associated with extraction activities, such as high material, energy and land intensities, and the accumulation of haz-ardous wastes and/or emissions, is externalised to countries specialised, for example, in metal mining and processing. Policy strategies toward higher eco-efficiency therefore must be evaluated within a global perspective and take full account of the international interrelations associated with the increasing integration of world markets (Giljum et al., forthcoming).

Micro–Macro Links and Analyses of Rebound Effects

While this chapter focuses on eco-efficiency measures at the macro level, production and consumption patterns at the micro level determine the development of aggregated material flow-based indicators. Due to the consistent accounting framework, material flow-based indicators can be aggregated from the micro level via the sectoral level to the macro level and thus allow analysis of the macro effects of changes at the micro level.

Eco-intelligent products are a crucial step towards the realisation of environmentally sustainable development (Schmidt-Bleek, 1994). They can be defined as competitively priced services and products that yield maximum possible utility for the longest possible time, with a minimum of material, energy and land input, and minimum generation of waste and emissions. This means that, from a resource conserving point of view, designing eco-intelligent products, services and infrastructures requires from each investment in natural materials the extraction of the largest possible number of service units for the longest possible time span. The most common indicator used to measure eco-efficiency at the product level is *MIPS*, which stands for 'material input per service unit' (Ritthof et al., 2002). Several strategies can increase eco-efficiency (Hinterberger et al., 2004): (1) increasing resource efficiency at the process and production stage; (2) reducing material input by using alternative materials and by redesigning products; (3) resource optimisation at the utilisation stage; and (4) creating new eco-efficient services by longer and intensified usage of products.

Evaluation of macro effects of dematerialisation processes at the micro level are of crucial importance for the overall evaluation from the perspective of environmental sustainability. If higher material and energy efficiency results in lower production costs and real savings to customers, overall demand for these products is likely to increase – a phenomenon known as the 'rebound effect' (Binswanger, 2001). In the case of 'mature' products, which approach demand saturation, customers will spend savings on other goods and services, which may be more material-intensive. In the case of products with still expanding markets, the lower cost of purchasing the product will likely encourage consumers to buy more of them or replace them more often. Typical examples of this development are personal computers, digital assistants, and cellular phones (Ayres, 2000). Therefore, efficiency gains at the micro level can well go along with an increase in the overall material and energy consumption at the macro level. This highlights the need to implement policy instruments such as certificate trading systems or material input taxes which aim at limiting the absolute level of resource extraction and use (Hinterberger et al., 2004).

SHORTCOMINGS AND FURTHER METHODOLOGICAL DEVELOPMENTS OF MFA

Several important shortcomings and limits of the standard MFA method can be identified. The two main shortcomings are: (1) the aggregation of different qualities of material flows to derive aggregated indicators plus the weak links between MFA indicators and environmental impacts; and (2) the missing separation of the production (including inter-industry relationships) and the consumption sphere. This section presents possible approaches for extending the existing MFA framework to help overcoming these shortcomings.

(Dis)Aggregation and Valuation of Material Flows

One important methodological issue requiring consideration is the fact that big material flows in terms of weight (such as construction minerals or specific metal ores) dominate aggregated MFA indicators and can bias the interpretation of aggregated results. This is because detailed information on developments of other material groups or economic sectors is often diluted or obscured (Giljum, 2004). Collection and interpretation of MFA data should therefore always be carried out on a level that disaggregates material groups and, if possible, different economic sectors (see, also, the next minor section).

Another major point of critique is the fact that weight-based MFA indicators do not inform us of actual environmental impacts since qualitative characteristics of different material input or output flows cannot be adequately depicted by quantitative numbers. These different qualities are, however, an important factor in the evaluation of economic development from the perspective of environmental sustainability. The sole focus on the reduction of aggregated resource use is a necessary, but not sufficient, precondition for achieving environmental sustainability. Small material flows, which might be neglected in aggregated weight-based indicators, can have large environmental impacts. Therefore, the question arises as to which material use should be reduced to achieve a sustainable resource throughput regime (see Reijnders, 1998). Some authors (such as Brunner, 2002) state that MFAs are of no use if data presentation is not followed by a critical assessment of the meaning of the results in a policy context. Although problems related to weight-based aggregation are, in principle, recognised by the MFA community, and first evaluation procedures have been suggested (van der Voet et al., 2003), an internationally standardised procedure for considering qualitative differences in the quantitative concept of MFA is currently lacking.

In life cycle assessment (LCA), the development of a common framework for environmental impact assessment has been a major issue over the past ten years, however, there is general agreement on the most relevant impact categories and corresponding indicators (de Haes et al., 1999). Furthermore, a number of evaluation methods have been developed which allow one to aggregate different effects into an overall judgment of alternative options (see Notarnicola et al., 1998). Weighting approaches based on a distance-to-target determination represent one group of valuation methods and have been widely used within LCA (Seppälä and Hämäläinen, 2001). These valuation methods would be particularly appropriate when applied to MFA data, as valuation starts from physical flows and relates the critical load of a substance to the actual load of anthropogenic emissions of that substance (Goedkoop, 1995). At the macroeconomic level, a similar approach has been introduced under the term 'sustainability gap' (Ekins and Simon, 1999). The sustainability gap can be defined as the difference between the current level of environmental impact from a particular source and the sustainable level of impact according to sustainability targets derived from scientific considerations. However, sustainability gaps have so far only been estimated for air pollutants in the UK and Netherlands (Ekins and Simon, 2001) and have not been applied on a broader scale.

Physical Input–Output Tables (PIOTs)

The concept of economy-wide MFA regards a national economy as a black box and only distinguishes domestic resource extraction and physical imports on the input side and physical exports and aggregated waste and emissions on the output side, with changes in the physical stock balancing inputs and outputs. This means that MFA accounts do not provide information on developments at the level of economic sectors, in particular, on inter-industry relations, nor do they separate material inputs used for production processes from those directly delivered to final demand. Thus, MFA accounts and derived indicators do not, by themselves, allow one to analyse policy issues such as structural or technological change, or changes in consumption behaviour and life-styles and their respective implications for resource use.

From this perspective, physical input–output tables (PIOTs) can be regarded as a crucial further development of material flow accounts, erasing the deficiencies identified in relation to aggregated MFA accounts. Like economy-wide MFA, a PIOT lists the overall amount of materials flowing into and out of the socio-economic system. In addition, the sectoral disaggregation of data allows for analyses of resource intensities of the different branches and highlights the correlation of material inputs, produced goods and residuals in each sector. This subsequently provides information on the resource efficiency of production processes. As the symmetric physical input–output table is directly comparable to the MIOT, various possibilities for parallel studies of material and monetary flows arise. Residuals, such as air or water emissions, can thus be directly connected to the MIOT and scenarios on the impacts of specific policy strategies can be developed and analysed (Stahmer et al., 1997). Apart from accounting of direct material inputs of economic activities, the application of input–output analysis enables the calculation of indirect material flows activated in production chains. These indirect flows can then be attributed to categories of final demand (such as private consumption and exports) (Hubacek and Giljum, 2003).

However, since the compilation of a full set of PIOTs is a very work-and time-intensive task and requires the availability of highly disaggregated production and trade data as well as data on domestic material extractions and water use, only a few economy-wide PIOTs have been presented so far (see Statistisches Bundesamt, 2001 for Germany). It remains an open question whether the compilation of PIOTs will be integrated into standard environmental statistics in the future.

CONCLUSIONS

This chapter has attempted to illustrate the usefulness of material flow analysis and derived material flow-based indicators for evaluation of eco-efficiency and dematerialisation policies. It was argued that many persistent environmental problems, such as high material and energy consumption and related negative environmental consequences (such as climate change), are determined by the overall scale of industrial metabolism rather than toxicities of specific substances. The systemic approach for assessing economy–environment interrelations taken by the MFA concept is therefore important for the development of new strategies for environmental governance. Material flow-based indicators can be applied for a large number of policy issues related to the overall objective of de-coupling economic growth from natural resource use. These include links between the micro and the macro level (e.g. rebound effects), the consequences of globalisation and the increasing interrelations of markets at the world-wide level in terms of international environmental distribution, and scenario evaluation of policy strategies to reconcile different sustainability goals, such as continued economic growth and competitiveness, increased social cohesion through reduction of unemployment and income disparities, and the absolute reduction of environmental pressures.

NOTES

1. For a comprehensive review on the history of the development of MFA see Fischer-Kowalski (1998b) and Fischer-Kowalski and Hüttler (1999).
2. Note that for the categories of unused and indirect material flows, the terms 'ecological rucksacks' (Schmidt-Bleek, 1994) and 'hidden flows' (Adriaanse et al., 1997) are also used in the literature.
3. In the literature, also the reverse indicator, the material intensity of an economic system (for example DMI/GDP), is used.
4. The 'Environmental Kutznets curve' (EKC) hypothesis postulates a correlation in the shape of an inverted U relationship between economic affluence and negative environmental consequences, such as high material and energy use.

REFERENCES

Adriaanse, A., S. Bringezu, A. Hamond, Y. Moriguchi, E. Rodenburg, D. Rogich and H. Schütz (1997), *Resource Flows: The Material Base of Industrial Economies*, Washington DC: World Resource Institute.

Amann, C., W. Bruckner, M. Fischer-Kowalski and C. Grünbühel (2002), *Material Flow Accounting in Amazonia. A Tool for Sustainable Development*, Working Paper. No. 63, Vienna: IFF Social Ecology.

Ayres, R. (1978), *Resources, Environment and Economics*, New York: John Wiley.

Ayres, R. (1989), 'Industrial metabolism', in J. Ausubel (ed.), *Technology and Environment*, Washington DC: National Academy Press.

Ayres, R.U. (2000), *Resources, Scarcity, Growth and the Environment*, working paper No. 2000/31/EPS/CMER, Fontainebleau, France: INSEAD.

Behrens, A. (2004), *Environmental Policy Instruments for Dematerialisation of the European Union*, SERI background papers, No. 7, Vienna: Sustainable Europe Research Institute.

Binswanger, M. (2001), 'Technological progress and sustainable development: what about the rebound effect?', *Ecological Economics*, **36**, 119–32.

Bringezu, S. and H. Schütz (2001a), *Material Use Indicators for the European Union, 1980–1997: Economy-wide material flow accounts and balances and derived indicators of resource use*, EUROSTAT Working Paper. No. 2/2001/B/2. Wuppertal: Wuppertal Institute.

Bringezu, S. and H. Schütz (2001b), *Total Material Requirement of the European Union*, Technical Report 56, Copenhagen: European Environmental Agency.

Brunner, P. (2002), 'Beyond materials flow analysis', *Journal of Industrial Ecology*, **6** (1), 8–10.

Chen, X. and L. Qiao (2001), 'A preliminary material input analysis of China', *Population and Environment*, **23** (1), 117–26.

Daniels, P.L. and S. Moore (2002), 'Approaches for quantifying the metabolism of physical economies. Part I: Methodological overview', *Journal of Industrial Ecology*, **5** (4), 69–93.

de Haes, U., O. Jolliet, G. Finnveden, M. Hauschild, W. Krewitt and R. Müller-Wenk (1999), 'Best available practice regarding impact categories and category indicators in life cycle impact assessment', *International Journal of Life Cycle Assessment*, **4** (3), 167–74.

EEA (2003), *Europe's Environment: The Third Assessment*, Environmental Assessment Report. No. 10, Copenhagen: European Environment Agency.

EEAC (2003), *European Governance for the Environment*, European Environmental Advisory Councils, Working Group on Governance, The Hague.

Ekins, P. (2001), 'From Green GDP to the sustainability gap: recent developments in national environmental economic accounting', *Environmental Assessment Policy and Management*, **3** (1), 61–93.

Ekins, P. and S. Simon (1999), 'The sustainability gap: a practical indicator of sustainability in the framework of the national accounts', *International Journal for Sustainable Development*, **2** (1), 32–58.

Ekins, P. and S. Simon (2001), 'Estimating sustainability gaps: methods and preliminary applications for the UK and the Netherlands', *Ecological Economic*, **37**, 5–22.

Environment Agency Japan (1992), *Quality of the Environment in Japan 1992*, Tokyo.

European Commission (2001a), *On the Sixth Environmental Action Programme of the European Community – Environment 2010 – Our Future, Our Choice*, COM (2001) 31 final, Brussels: European Commission.

European Commission (2001b), *A Sustainable Europe for a Better World: A European Union Strategy for Sustainable Development*, The Commission's proposal to the Gothenburg European Council, Brussels: European Commission.

European Commission (2003), *Towards a Thematic Strategy for the Sustainable Use of Natural Resources*, COM(2003) 572 final, Brussels: DG Environment.

EUROSTAT (1999), *Toward Environmental Pressure Indicators for the EU*, Luxembourg: Statistical Office of the European Union.

EUROSTAT (2001), *Economy-Wide Material Flow Accounts and Derived Indicators. A Methodological Guide*, Luxembourg: Statistical Office of the European Union.

EUROSTAT (2002), *Material Use in the European Union 1980–2000: Indicators and Analysis*, Luxembourg: Statistical Office of the European Union.

Femia, A. (1996), *Input–Output Analysis of Material Flows: An Application to the German Economic System for the Year 1990*, Quaderni di recerca. No. 82. Ancona: University of Ancona.

Fischer, H., K. Lichtblau, B. Meyer and J. Scheelhaase (2004), 'Wachstums- und Beschäftigungsimpulse rentabler Materialeinsparungen [Growth and employment impulses of profitable material savings]', *Wirtschaftsdienst*, **84** (4), 247–54.

Fischer-Kowalski, M. (1998a), 'Society's metabolism', in G. Redclift and G. Woodgate (eds), *International Handbook of Environmental Sociology*, Cheltenham, UK and Lyme, USA: Edward Elgar.

Fischer-Kowalski, M. (1998b), 'Society's metabolism. The intellectual history of materials flow analysis: Part I, 1860–1970', *Industrial Ecology*, **2** (1), 61–78.

Fischer-Kowalski, M. and C. Amann (2001), 'Beyond IPAT and Kuznets curves: globalization as a vital factor in analysing the environmental impact of socio-economic metabolism, *Population and Environment*, **23** (1), 7–47.

Fischer-Kowalski, M. and W. Hüttler (1999), 'Society's metabolism. The intellectual history of materials flow analysis: Part II, 1970–1998', *Journal of Industrial Ecology*, **2** (4), 107–36.

Giljum, S. (2004), 'Trade, material flows and economic development in the South: the example of Chile', *Journal of Industrial Ecology*, **8** (1–2), 241–61.

Giljum, S., A. Behrens, M. Hammer, F. Hinterberger, J. Kovanda and S. Niza (2004), 'The material basis of the global economy', Presentation of data and implications for sustainable resource use policies in North and South. Presentation at the 2004 ConAccount Workshop, ETH Zurich.

Giljum, S. and N. Eisenmenger (2004), 'North–south trade and the distribution of environmental goods and burdens: a biophysical perspective', *Journal of Environment and Development*, **13** (1), 73–100.

Giljum, S., T. Hak, F. Hinterberger and J. Kovanda (2005), 'Environmental governance in the European Union: Strategies and instruments for absolute decoupling', *International Journal of Sustainable Development* **8** (1/2), 31–46.

Giljum, S., F. Hinterberger, C. Lutz and B. Meyer (forthcoming), 'Modelling global resource use: material flows, land use and input–output models', in S. Suh (ed.), *Handbook of Input–Output Economics in Industrial Ecology*, Dordrecht: Springer.

Goedkoop, M. (1995), *The Eco-Indicator 95: Final Report*, NOH Report. No. 9523, PRé consultants, Amersfoort, The Netherlands.

Hammer, M. and K. Hubacek (2002), *Material Flows and Economic Development. Material Flow Analysis of the Hungarian Economy*, Interim Report. No. 02–057, Laxenburg: International Institute for Applied Systems Analysis (IIASA).

Hans-Böckler-Stiftung (ed.) (2000), *Work and Ecology: Final Project Report*, Düsseldorf: Hans-Böckler-Stiftung.

Hinterberger, F., H. Hutterer and F. Schmidt-Bleek (2004), *Eco-Efficient Innovation. State of the Art and Policy Recommendations*, EU Regional Stakeholder Workshop on eco-efficiency, Paris.

Hinterberger, F., F. Luks and F. Schmidt-Bleek (1997), 'Material flows vs. "natural capital": what makes an economy sustainable?', *Ecological Economics*, **23** (1), 1–14.
Hinterberger, F., S. Moll and A. Femia (1998), *Arbeitsproduktivität, Ressourcenproduktivität und Ressourcenintensität der Arbeit. Graue Reihe des Instituts für Arbeit und Technik*, No. 1998–02, Wuppertal: Wuppertal Institute.
Hinterberger, F., I. Omann and A. Stocker (2002), 'Employment and environment in a sustainable Europe', *Empirica*, **29**, 113–30.
Hinterberger, F., S. Renn and H. Schütz (1999), *Arbeit – Wirtschaft – Umwelt. Einige Indikatoren sozialer, wirtschaftlicher und ökologischer Entwicklung im Zeitablauf*, Wuppertal: Wuppertal paper no. 89. Jänner.
Hubacek, K. and S. Giljum (2003), 'Applying physical input–output analysis to estimate land appropriation (ecological footprints) of international trade activities', *Ecological Economics*, **44** (1), 137–51.
Jordan, A., W. Rüdiger and A. Zito (2003), *Has Governance Eclipsed Government? Patterns of Environmental Instrument Selection and Use in Eight States and the EU*, CSERGE Working Paper No. EDM 03–15, Norwich: University of East Anglia.
Kleijn, R. (2001), 'Adding it all up. The sense and non-sense of Bulk-MFA', *Journal of Industrial Ecology*, **4** (2), 7–8.
Matthews, E., S. Bringezu, M. Fischer-Kowalski, W. Huetller, R. Kleijn, Y. Moriguchi, C. Ottke, E. Rodenburg, D. Rogich, H. Schandl, H. Schuetz, E. van der Voet and H. Weisz (2000), *The Weight of Nations: Material Outflows from Industrial Economies*, Washington DC: World Resources Institute.
Meyer, B., C. Lutz and I. Wolter (2003), *Global Multisector/Mulitcountry 3: E Modelling From COMPASS to GINFORS*, Osnabrück: Institute for Economic Structures Research.
Moll, S., S. Bringezu and H. Schütz (2003), *Resource Use in European Countries. An Estimate of Materials and Waste Streams in the Community, Including Imports and Exports Using the Instrument of Material Flow Analysis*, Copenhagen: European Environment Agency.
Mündl, A., H. Schütz, W. Stodulski, J. Sleszynski and M. Welfens (1999), *Sustainable Development by Dematerialization in Production and Consumption: Strategy for the New Environmental Policy in Poland – Report 3*, Warsaw: Institute for Sustainable Development.
Muradian, R. and J. Martinez-Alier (2001), 'South North materials flow: history and environmental repercussions', *Innovation*, **14** (2), 171–88.
Notarnicola, B., G. Huppes and N.W. van den Berg (1998), 'Evaluating options in LCA: the emergence of conflicting paradigms for impact assessment and evaluation', *International Journal of Life Cycle Assessment*, **3** (5), 289–300.
OECD (1994), *Environmental Indicators: Core Set*, Paris: OECD.
OECD (2002), *Indicators to Measure Decoupling of Environmental Pressure From Economic Growth*, SG/SD(2002)1, Paris: OECD.
OECD (2004), 'Recommendation on material flows and resource productivity', Adopted by the OECD Council on 21 April 2004. Paris: OECD.
Poldy, F. and B. Foran (1999), *Resource Flows: The Material Basis of the Australian Economy*, Working Document. No. 99/16. Canberra: CSIRO.
Rees, W. E. and M. Wackernagel (1999), 'Monetary analysis: turning a blind eye on sustainability', *Ecological Economics*, **29**, 47–52.

Reijnders, L. (1998), 'The Factor X debate: Setting targets for eco-efficiency', *Journal of Industrial Ecology*, **2** (1), 13–22.

Ritthof, M., H. Rohn and C. Liedtke (2002), *MIPS berechnen. Ressourcenproduktivität von Produkten und Dienstleistungen*, Wuppertal Spezial No. 27, Wuppertal: Wuppertal Institute.

Scasny, M., J. Kovanda and T. Hak (2003), 'Material flow accounts, balances and derived indicators the Czech Republic during the 1990s: results and recommendations for methodological improvements', *Ecological Economics*, **45** (1), 41–57.

Schandl, H. and N. Eisenmenger (2004), *Global Resource Extraction*, Poster presented at the 8th International Conference of the International Society for Ecological Economics (ISEE), Montreal.

Schmidt-Bleek, F. (1994), *Wie viel Umwelt braucht der Mensch? MIPS – das Maß für ökologisches Wirtschaften*, Birkhauser, Berlin, Basel.

Schmidt-Bleek, F., S. Bringezu, F. Hinterberger, C. Liedtke, J. Spangenberg, H. Stiller and M. Welfens (1998), *MAIA. Einführung in die Materialintensitätsanalyse nach dem MIPS-Konzept*, Birkhauser, Berlin, Basel.

Schütz, H. (1999), *Technical Details of National Material Flow Accounting (Inputside) for Germany*, Wuppertal: Wuppertal Institute.

Schütz, H., S. Bringezu and S. Moll (2004), *Globalisation and the shifting environmental burden. Material trade flows of the European Union*, Wuppertal: Wuppertal Institute.

Seppälä, J. and R. Hämäläinen (2001), 'On the meaning of the distance-to-target weighting method and normalisation in life cycle impact assessment', *International Journal of Life Cycle Assessment*, **6** (4), 211–18.

Seppälä, T., T. Haukioja and J. Kaivo-oja (2001), 'The EKC Hypothesis does not hold for direct material flows: environmental Kuznets curve hypothesis tests for direct material flows in five industrial countries', *Population and Environment*, **23** (2), 217–38.

Spangenberg, J., F. Hinterberger, S. Moll and H. Schütz (1999), 'Material Flow Analysis, TMR and the MIPS-concept: a contribution to the development of indicators for measuring changes in consumption and production patterns', *International Journal for Sustainable Development*, **2** (4), 491–505.

Spangenberg, J., I. Omann and F. Hinterberger (2002), 'Sustainable growth criteria. Minimum benchmarks and scenarios for employment and the environment', *Ecological Economics*, **42**, 429–43.

Spangenberg, J. and R. Verheyen (1996), *Von der Abfallwirtschaft zum Stoffstrom-Management*, Bonn: Friedrich-Ebert-Stiftung.

Stahmer, C., M. Kuhn and N. Braun (1997), *Physische Input-Output-Tabellen 1990*, Wiesbaden: Statistisches Bundesamt.

Statistisches Bundesamt (2001), *A Physical Input–Output Table for Germany 1995*, Wiesbaden: Statistisches Bundesamt Deutschland.

United Nations (2003), *Integrated Environmental and Economic Accounting 2003*, New York: United Nations.

van der Voet, E., L. van Oers and I. Nikolic (2003), *Dematerialisation: Not Just a Matter of Weight*, CML Report. No. 160, Centre of Environmental Science (CML), Leiden: Leiden University.

von Weizsäcker, E.U., A. Lovins and H. Lovins (1997), *The Factor Four*, London: Earthscan.

PART VI

Concluding assessments of sustainable
development indicators

18. Sustainable development indicators and human needs

John Peet

INTRODUCTION

A former Director-General of UNESCO (Mayor, 1977) suggested a few years ago that:

> All over the world, the citizens of today are appropriating the rights of the citizens of tomorrow, threatening their well-being and at times their lives. . . . Caught in the vortex of the immediate, oppressed by urgency, we do not have time to shape our actions or think about their consequences. We are hurtling into the future, without any brakes and in conditions of zero visibility.

I believe these views need to be taken very seriously. 'Hurtling into the future, without any brakes and in conditions of zero visibility' accurately describes my concerns and those of many people I know. Yet present-day leaders of government and commerce in most countries persist in addressing problems by promoting simplistic responses, mostly directed at generating more economic growth as the means to create a marvellous future.

I do not think these ideas hang together economically, let alone socially or environmentally. That is why I want to develop some thoughts about the notion of complexity, in order to encourage an understanding that reality is not too complex to do something about it. Like economics, complexity is actually part of everyone's everyday experience, and does not need to be 'left to the experts'.

But first, I sound a note of warning about dealing with complexity. A humorist put it succinctly many years ago, when he wrote that: 'For every human problem, there is a neat, simple solution; and it is always wrong'.

I believe it is the desire of all people that the personal, social, economic and environmental systems upon which they depend jointly remain healthy and viable into the long-term future. According to Steve Hatfield Dodds (1999), the needs of humans cannot be separated from those of the total system of life on Earth:

The truly good society is one which combines justice and the highest human freedoms to promote the well-being of all of its members, both present and future, while protecting the integrity and beauty of the Earth and all its life. This implies that 'the good society' and 'sustainable development' are effectively interchangeable terms, but raises other questions about the nature and inter-pretation of freedom and justice.

The suggestion that there may be consensus about the links between the good society and sustainable development raises issues of how we tell whether our decisions are leading us in a positive or a negative direction. That, to me, is the key question facing us. Without a clear understanding of its nature and meaning we will never know how to begin to construct an answer. Clearly, issues of value and meaning are central to discussions in this area, and need to be clarified as essential prerequisites to identification and understanding of the question. That, however, has not stopped a gen-eration of policy advisors from putting forward enough indicators of what-ever it is that they are concerned about to flood our bookshelves. Most of them fail to address Mencken's concern. We need better tools.

THE ISSUE OF NEED

In this context, Salah El Serafy (1997, pp. 4–5) asked the following: 'Are humans appropriating too much of the natural wealth at the expense of other species? And are the rich taking more than their fair share away from the needy?'

I and many others would have to answer 'yes' to both questions. From my viewpoint, the needs I see around me are often not being met. 'The market' is seen by those in positions of political or economic power to be the way to respond to need nowadays, but it is not working for many people. Nor, in my opinion, can it be expected to. Again, I assert that we need better tools.

While an ethically-based socio-economic response to the needs of people is urgently needed, at the same time, we should also acknowledge the equally important, but often less obvious, needs of the 'natural wealth' – the ecosystems of our countries and of the Earth as a whole. The policy imperative of 'strong' sustainability requires that society is seen as inextric-ably connected to the environment within which it exists.

Sustainable living, often referred to as sustainable development, implies an agenda for change, since few of its attributes are obviously satisfied today, in most societies. In order for it to happen, people and communities first need to know where they are in order to be able to determine whether or not they are making progress towards where they want to go.

The criteria they use must be selected in accordance with the goal, and also be consistent with a community-based ethic of how best to move towards it.

Human Needs

As a start towards addressing this issue, I assert that an understanding of the needs of people must come through processes rooted in the third (voluntary) sector, which has existed for tens of thousands of years but is usually less well represented in policy groups and processes than the two dominant sectors, government and commerce. In my opinion, it is crucial that the third sector be directly involved under its own terms. It should not be treated as invisible, required to follow the rules of the market, or be limited to statutory requirements.

In recent years, development workers in Central and South American countries have produced some important related ideas, directly relevant to the issues we are addressing. For example, Manfred A. Max-Neef (1991) has asserted that 'Development is about. . . . allowing people the greatest improvement in . . . Quality of Life' [which in turn] 'depends on the possibilities people have to adequately satisfy their fundamental human needs'. Further to this:

- Fundamental human needs are finite, few and classifiable.
- Fundamental human needs are the same in all cultures and in all historical periods. What changes, both over time and through cultures, is the way or the means by which the needs are satisfied.

Max-Neef has classified human needs into nine fundamental categories: subsistence, protection, affection, understanding, participation, idleness, creation, identity and freedom.[1]

- The needs are all necessary, all equal.
- Any human need that is not adequately satisfied reveals a human poverty.
- There are multiple poverties, not just one kind of poverty. . . . every poverty, if extended beyond a threshold, leads to a pathology, a sickness.

Examples of poverties include:

- the poverty of subsistence (due to insufficient income, food, shelter, etc);

- the poverty of protection (due to inadequate health systems, violence, the arms race, etc);
- the poverty of affection (due to authoritarian government, oppression, exploitative relationships, etc);
- the poverty of understanding (due to poor quality of education, etc);
- the poverty of participation (due to marginalisation and discrimination against women, children and minorities, etc);
- the poverty of identity (due to imposition of alien values on local/regional cultures, etc).

Every poverty, if extended beyond a threshold, leads to a pathology, a sickness. This analysis leads to a classification of different kinds of satisfiers of fundamental needs. For example:

- Destroyers are satisfiers that address one need but end up destroying that need and others as well. As examples, the arms race, bureaucracy and authoritarianism promise protection, but also stifle subsistence, affection, participation and freedom, while they increase insecurity.
- Pseudo-satisfiers are appealing, but they only promise to fill needs; they don't actually do so. Examples include advertising, chauvinistic nationalism, prostitution, charity and aggregate economic indicators, such as gross domestic product (GDP).
- Inhibitors satisfy one need but inhibit another. For example, an over-protective family provides protection but inhibits affection, understanding, participation, identity and freedom. Obsessive economic competitiveness provides a form of freedom, but stifles subsistence, protection, affection, participation and identity.
- Singular satisfiers satisfy one need while steadfastly ignoring others. Insurance, guided tours, professional armies and curative medicine are examples.
- Synergic satisfiers meet several different needs at once. Breast-feeding, popular education, barefoot doctors, democratic trade unions, educational games, preventive medicine, music, art, cooking and ornamentation are examples.

The aim in applying this understanding of human needs is to move from the negatives – the destroyers, pseudo-satisfiers and inhibitors – to the positives, especially the synergic, satisfiers. By this process, a structured understanding of the underlying fundamental needs and satisfiers, relevant to each society, is developed. Ideally, that result would feed through into that government's economic and social policy development processes but, as yet, there is little evidence of this superseding the more traditional economic understanding of human need as reflected in individual, preference-driven 'demand' in the marketplace.

Max-Neef's approach has the great strength of linking the most basic of human needs – most easily understood at the individual level – with the needs of the social system within which the individual lives and interacts with others.

The Ethical Basis of an Approach to Human Needs

The key element in finding out if people's needs are being satisfied is prior determination of an ethical principle against which the nature and extent of satisfaction of fundamental or basic needs can be evaluated. That evaluation can then be done by identifying indicators which must measure not only quantity of possessions or of income, but complex aspects of the quality of life.

Indicators, then, must reflect the state of satisfaction of each basic need, according to the requirements of an ethical principle. As a working base, I put forward an ethical principle which has been found to be acceptable to several community groups with which we are involved. It has been developed out of extended discussions and summarises the consensus reached. The ethic reads (Peet and Peet, 1998):

> All people have their basic needs satisfied, so they can live in dignity, in healthy communities, while ensuring the minimum adverse impact on natural systems, now and in the future.

If we are to change the direction of society towards sustainable living, we must first identify and understand both the overall direction that the system is currently following, and that which we wish it to follow. The goal will be an expression of overarching values which we, as a society, choose to guide us as we journey into the future. Whether the values which guide us are democratically chosen or imposed by a powerful elite will drastically affect both the ends and the means – the goal destination and the journey.

Once we know in what direction we are going, we will want to be sure that we travel well and reach our goal. This means, if we are serious about the goal of sustainable living, that we have to ensure that the system as a whole – society in its natural environment – is healthy and viable for the long term. We must also make sure that all of the parts – the subsystems such as people, families and communities, economy and so on – are in themselves healthy and viable for the long term, and are all contributing to the health and viability of the whole. The criteria that we use to tell us whether we are making progress towards our goal are the indicators.

How we select those indicators will govern the ways in which we make our journey towards our goal. Selecting indicators in order to concentrate on the most pressing needs becomes a touchstone for dealing with the apparent complexity that emerges.

Critical Needs of a System

To illustrate what it means to concentrate on the most pressing needs, let me give an everyday example learned in first aid classes. In the event of discovering someone injured as the result of an accident, the first priority is to determine whether their life is in danger, and if so, take immediate action to preserve it. The three primary items on the first-aider's checklist are, in order, something like: stop the bleeding; start the breathing; and treat for shock.[2]

Our first concern is with those parts where a person's (i.e. the system's) viability is under the most severe threat. By fixing up those things that are in deficit first, one ensures that the rest of the system will be better able to recover and improve its health and viability. As a simple example, a single, small loose screw on a bike may render the whole machine very dangerous (unviable) for the user, and is therefore a high priority for attention.

INDICATORS

All of us use indicators, of one form or another, to help us understand the world around us and control our responses to it, and this is necessary for everyday life. Familiar examples are the temperature of one's skin, the level of one's bank balance and the facial expressions of people one meets. The more complex the system in which we live, and within which we need to control even simple decisions (choice of clothing to wear, weekly expenditure, attitude towards others), the more we rely on indicators. But to avoid information overload, we must also avoid watching more indicators than are strictly necessary. In practice, the ones to which we pay most attention are the 'red light' indicators that indicate the need for urgent action. These include the car horn when one steps into the road without looking, the 'OD' that indicates overdraft in the bank balance and the hungry baby's cry. In this chapter, I describe a framework that can assist in identifying those 'red light' indicators in any complex system, since they are the ones which need the most urgent attention in order to ensure sustainability.

There is a voluminous literature on indicators of sustainable development, but in my opinion, it is generally fragmented, often parochial, missing vital information, and in particular, it lacks an overall organising framework. In this context I am reminded of Lord Rutherford's famous dictum: 'All science is either physics or stamp collecting' (Birks, 1962). In my opinion, indicators come out of contexts that represent either physics or stamp collecting. We are faced, daily through the media, with a plethora of indicators, usually representing some 'favourite' criteria, with little or no coherent, whole-system place or relevance to our complex system. The common pressure–state–response (PSR) system, for example, is widely used, but is out of date and known to suffer from an inability to account for system relationships and dynamics.

In this context, it is useful to be reminded of Ashby's Law of Requisite Variety, coming from general systems theory: 'Only variety can cope with variety'. Put another way, if we want to control a complex system (such as a society), design and operation of the controls must fully reflect the system's complexity. It cannot be expected that questions such as those involved in the development of policy for sustainable development can be answered simplistically, no matter how strong the pressures (often political or time-related) to do so may be. They will inevitably, as Mencken's home-spun advice confirms, be wrong.

As a response to this problem, I develop some ideas about complexity, and describe a framework which can help us identify key determinants of the health and viability of *any* system. I do this in order to encourage the idea that reality is not too difficult for people to do something about it. Complexity is part of everyday experience, and does not need to be 'left to the experts'. How we respond to a complex systems understanding of reality is a separate issue from developing that understanding in the first place.

CONTROL OF SYSTEMS

How does one ensure that identification of a community need is linked with the means for its satisfaction? Simply identifying an indicator is obviously not enough to ensure that the need is satisfied. A control system is required.

Figure 18.1 illustrates a simple, self-controlling system: a household water tank. The ballcock and float mechanism ensure that the water in the tank is automatically refilled after being drained, so it always returns to the 'correct' level.

A more generic representation of this system is given in Figure 18.2, which shows that the process is dependent upon a 'goal' being set – namely the 'correct' water level. In practice, the goal is achieved by design of the mechanism whereby the ballcock moves in order to open or close the inflow valve. Measurement alone is not enough, nor is action alone; both are needed, simultaneously, for the system to function properly.

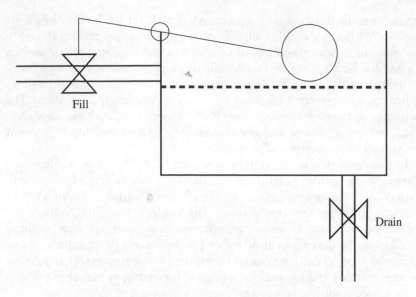

Figure 18.1   Household water tank – a simple, self-regulating system

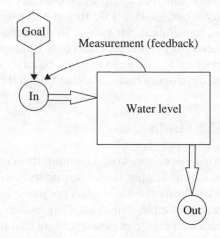

Figure 18.2   Generic household water tank system

In this context, selection of an appropriate measurement is only the first step towards an indicator. Unless the measurement is able to be compared with a realistic and achievable goal, and the result communicated to a control mechanism, it cannot be used to enable corrective action to be taken to refill the tank.

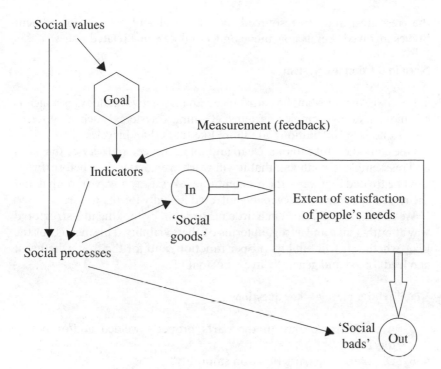

Figure 18.3   Satisfying people's needs as a social control system process

If we use this insight to address the questions implicit in our aim to determine how to satisfy people's needs, we find a situation of the type sketched in Figure 18.3.

Measurement of the extent to which needs are satisfied provides, via selected indicator(s), the feedback which, linked with a *goal* determined using *social values*, enables *social processes* to be 'informed' of the need or otherwise to carry out corrective action.

Social processes – which will obviously include policy at local or central government level – may then be invoked to achieve outcomes which 'close the loop', satisfy the needs, and hence improve community well-being. The outcomes may be achieved by either or both inflow of social goods and outflow of social bads.

The whole process is 'driven' by the social values which determine the nature of the goal and the selection of indicators. These values are essentially moral. How they are determined is, of course, a key question in the overall process, because it is those values that determine which social criteria (indicators) are chosen to represent the state of satisfaction of people's needs. In my opinion, they must come out of community processes that resource, and are resourced by, the local and central government bodies involved. Let us now move on to look at some related issues.

Need in a Complex System

The writer Alistair Mant has introduced an instructive analogy, as a means of understanding complex systems: 'Complex systems, such as governments and large institutions, are more like frogs than bicycles'.

One can take a bike to bits, clean and oil it, inspect and service the parts and reassemble it, confident that it will work even better than before. Frogs can't be treated that way – the moment one takes away any part, both it and the rest of the frog are irreversibly affected, usually for the worse.

We can develop this idea in a little more detail by looking in a structured way at both a bike and a frog, in terms of their viability. This means, for the bike, whether it will fulfil its proper function, and for the frog, whether it can feed, breed and generally live a normal life.

Viability of a bicycle – key questions

- Are the frame and all the parts properly welded and/or bolted together?
- Do all moving parts function smoothly?
- Can the rider go where he/she wants to go, starting and stopping when needed?
- Will it work well in all weathers?
- Can it be used by other people, on and off the road?
- Can it be seen and avoided by other road users?

The basic requirements for viability of a bike are all mechanical, and all are easily achieved by use of an oilcan, spanner, screwdriver or spare parts.

A bike is a 'stand-alone' system, which can exist without any connection to its surroundings. All the parts of a bike are interrelated, and all are simultaneously necessary for a reliable machine that is safe and fun to ride. In some respects, an even better example than a bicycle would be a boat. If one takes away any important part of a boat, it may sink!

Viability of a frog – key questions

- Can it survive and breed in its normal environment?
- Has it the ability to see, eat food, mate, identify danger?
- Can it physically move around, to find food, a mate or evade predators?

- Does it have the ability to survive cold, heat, drought or flood?
- If its surrounding environment changes, can it modify its behaviour in order to survive?
- Does it live in a stable relationship with other living things in its natural environment?

The basic requirements for viability – or sustainability – of a frog are quite complex, much more so than for the bike. They are hard to evaluate, mainly because we do not know enough about these requirements. None can be fixed up with a tool such as a spanner or screwdriver. Just as importantly, the requirements for a frog's viability are intimately bound up with, and connected in many complex ways to the viability of its surrounding ecosystem – soil, water, other living things, chemicals, climate and so on – in ways that we are still trying to understand.

A frog can never 'stand alone', either. It is at all times intimately connected to, and totally dependent on, the environment which gives it life. These are interrelated, and all are simultaneously necessary for the frog to survive and breed.

In this analogy, nature and society – and the economy – are frogs, not bicycles. They are very complex wholes, with interconnected parts and relations between them that even now, with centuries of scientific understanding behind us, we still barely understand. It is of central importance in this discussion that, in a complex system, a part can only be understood in the context of the whole; it has no independent existence (Capra, 1996).

According to Hinterberger et al. (2000, p. 277), even if some well-known basic principles of sustainability are accepted, complexity also gives rise to two problems that are often overlooked:

> From the viewpoint of natural sciences, it is impossible to measure if, or to what extent, the principles are observed. (This is due to the complexity of nature.)
> From the viewpoint of social sciences, it is impossible to implement, accomplish and control the observance of those principles. (This is due to the complexity of societies.)

Potentially, the most useful response to these problems comes from the coevolutionary approach of Norgaard (1994). On the one hand, he describes the conventional, 'linear' view of knowledge giving rise to new techniques and new forms of social organisation which, by the use of natural resources, are assumed to lead to an economic output. A coevolutionary perspective, on the other hand, stresses the interdependence of variables in the societal process of development (Hinterberger et al., 2000, p. 286).

From the mainstream linear viewpoint, norms and the environment are exogenous, or independent of economic development. From the coevolutionary viewpoint, values, knowledge, social organization, technologies and the natural environment influence each other in such a way that development is the coevolution of the total system. From the latter perspective, 'everything is symmetrically related to everything else. Nothing is exogenous' (Norgaard, 1994, p. 35). In such a situation, sustainable development is no longer a simple concept and cannot be mechanistically operationalised.

The policies and understandings of our decision-makers, however, especially politicians and the economists who advise them, are still based predominantly on the bike principle. They divide up society into neat parts and assign them to policy boxes, to be dealt with by some or other government department or ministry.[3] Each is set up as if it exists separately, albeit connected to other parts (as with a bike) rather than being seen as organic parts of a living entity (society as a whole existing and evolving within its environment – as with a frog) in which everything is connected to, and is dependent on, everything else.

If things in our society are judged not to be functioning well, the usual response of government is to pull the institutions and structures apart and put them back together again – sometimes in different ways – as if they were bikes. Examples that spring readily to mind in countries such as my own (New Zealand) are state-run hospitals, schools, and the electricity system. Although there has been more than a decade of such 'reforms', there is still no clear evidence that they have actually been of any real economic or social benefit to the total system of people, families, society and environment.

THE GENERIC NEEDS OF COMPLEX SYSTEMS

I now move on from human needs, to address the needs of complex systems in general. This uses a technique developed by Hartmut Bossel (1998 and 1999), independently of, but with remarkable generic similarities to, that of Max-Neef. It involves an analytical framework that does two main things (Peet and Bossel, 2000):

- relates the use or abuse of natural resources to ultimate human well-being through technology, economy, politics, and ethics; and
- allows people to order and see the relationships between the structures that can be identified in the natural, economic, human, and social systems.

Every system has a number of fundamental properties which are a direct reflection of the properties of the environment – the context – within which it exists. As Max-Neef showed, there are fundamental human needs which are the same everywhere. The same thing applies to systems in general. If one generalises this idea, as Bossel has done, one can show that every system – whether living or manufactured – has entirely general properties that Bossel calls *orientors*. These properties influence not just the structure and function of the system itself, but also influence (orient) that system's behaviour towards its surrounding environment. A *basic orientor* is more fundamental, and relates to the system's overriding goal or driver – in this chapter, the goal of sustainability.

Figure 18.4 shows a generalised *system* within its *environment or context*, incorporating Bossel's list of fundamental properties of system environments. The basic orientors ('inside' the system) that relate to the *fundamental properties* of the system's *environment* ('outside' the system), are described in Table 18.1. Each of them has a direct relationship to the corresponding fundamental properties of the system environment. Each basic orientor reflects a fundamental need of the system, in that a lack of satisfaction of any of them may render the entire system unviable (unsustainable).

To ensure viability and sustainability of the system, a sufficiency of each basic orientor must be ensured. This point is virtually identical to that of Max-Neef, where there are multiple needs, each one of which must be

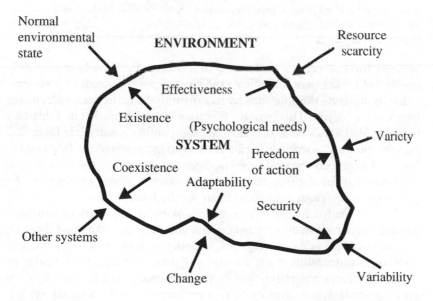

Figure 18.4   Generalised system within its context or environment

*Table 18.1   Bossel's basic system orientors and fundamental properties of
the system's environment*

Existence: Ensure the immediate survival and subsistence of the system in the normal environmental state.

Effectiveness: Over the long term be effective (not necessarily efficient) in securing from, and exerting influence on, its environment.

Freedom of action: Have the ability to cope in different ways with the challenges posed by environmental variety.

Security: Be able to protect against the detrimental effects of environmental *variability*, such as fluctuating and unpredictable conditions outside the normal environmental state.

Adaptability: Be able to change parameters and/or structure in order to generate more appropriate responses to challenges posed by change.

Coexistence: Be able to modify behaviour to account for behaviour and orientors of other systems (i.e. actor systems) in the environment.

Three additional basic orientors may be needed in some situations involving living creatures:

Reproduction: Self-replicating systems must have the opportunity to reproduce.

Psychological needs: Sentient beings (which can feel pain) have psychological needs.

Responsibility: Conscious actors – humans – are responsible for their actions and must comply with an ethical reference.

---

satisfied for the person to be free of poverty. In Bossel's framework, unsatisfied basic orientors indicate the most important needs of a system.

Let us illustrate the approach by relating it to the earlier examples of the frog and the bicycle. This requires that we go through the list in Table 18.1 to ensure that all six basic orientors are independently satisfied. Table 18.2 puts the questions identified earlier relating to the needs of the frog and the bike against the corresponding basic orientors. Note that the *reproduction* basic orientor for the frog has not been included, since (for comparative purposes), no obvious equivalent exists for the bike.

This table helps us appreciate that, looking at any part in isolation, whether it is of a bicycle or a frog, is not good enough. We must focus on the whole system in its entirety. But, in doing so, if we want to ensure viability or sustainability, we must also prioritize our actions. Clearly, we should concentrate our attention on those orientors which show the most pressing needs. Let us now move to a significantly more complex system: a family.

Table 18.2   Basic orientors for a bicycle and a frog

Basic orientor	Bicycle	Frog
Existence	Are the frame and all the parts properly welded and/or bolted together?	Can it survive and breed in its normal environment?
Effectiveness	Do all moving parts work smoothly?	Can it see, eat food, mate, identify danger?
Freedom of action	Can the rider go where he/she wants to go, starting and stopping when needed?	Can it physically move around to find food, a mate or evade predators?
Security	Will it work well in all weathers?	Does it have the ability to survive cold, heat, drought or flood?
Adaptability	Can it be used by other people, in different places?	If its surrounding environment changes, can it modify its behaviour in order to survive?
Coexistence	Can it be seen and avoided by other road users?	Does it live in a stable relationship with other living things in its natural environment?

Since we are dealing with sentient beings, we add the *additional orientor of psychological needs*. We could also include that of reproduction but, in practice, this is seldom the reason for any lack of viability of a family unit.[4]

Note that the *ethical reference* basic orientor is normally incorporated into the process of choosing the other basic orientors. In other words, indicators which satisfy the ethical reference (which refers to the overall viability of the family) are preferentially selected over indicators that do not.

The overall (Bossel) approach described here appears to be valid much more widely, and has been applied in practice in a number of different situations, including the viability of a critically-endangered NZ bird species, the roadworthiness of a motor vehicle, and a nation (NZ) (Peet and Bossel, 2000). Current work involves its application to a major NZ city in its surrounding regional (watershed) system).

More Complex Systems

The requirements for viability of a family are understandably more complex than those for a frog, let alone a bicycle. When we turn our attention to even

Table 18.3   Indicators of viability of a family

Basic orientor	Possible indicators of viability
Existence	Availability of shelter, food, clothing, water, sanitation, life expectancy
Effectiveness	Work hours necessary for life support
Freedom of action	Family income, job opportunities, health, mobility
Security	Safety of neighbourhood, social security, family savings
Adaptability	Participation in education and training, flexibility, cultural norms
Coexistence	Possession of social skills, language and culture compatibility
Psychological needs	Levels of emotional stress, anxiety, dissatisfaction, family quarrels

more complex systems, the number of factors to be taken into account increases substantially. This is because such systems often have a considerable direct effect on their environment. For example, a frog or two – or even a pond-full of frogs – will seldom have a major effect on the wetland within which they exist, but human settlements have effects on their environments that are often large and frequently damaging. If a system can only survive in the short term by severely depleting the resources of its surrounding environment, then the long-term sustainability of both is likely to be questionable.

In situations such as these – common when we address issues of sustainability of societies – we need two sets of indicators, one for the system itself and another for its influence on the surrounding environment. It is not good enough to consider only the human system. Since any future of humanity is inextricably bound up with the viability of the environment within which people exist, they must be considered together.

This immediately brings us back to the question of the ethical understandings and values we apply in pursuit of our relationship with the environment to ensure the system in which we live (including other people) is as sustainable as our own parts in it. Long-term factors and preservation of options for future generations are essential parts of our ethical position. Given our lack of deep scientific understanding of the ecosystems, societies, and economies which sustain us, I suggest we should adopt a precautionary principle when developing policies likely to have significant environmental or social consequences.

Table 18.4   System orientors and human needs

Bossel's basic system orientors	Max-Neef's human needs
Existence	Subsistence
Effectiveness	Understanding, idleness
Freedom of action	Freedom
Security	Protection
Adaptability	Creation
Coexistence	Participation
Psychological needs	Affection, identity

A Generic Approach to Needs

From the description of approaches used by Max-Neef and Bossel, it will be apparent that there is a remarkable similarity between Bossel's basic system orientors and Max-Neef's human needs, which is perhaps not accidental given the generality of the approaches used by them. Bossel has mapped Max-Neef's nine human needs onto his seven basic orientors (Table 18.4). In doing so, he has combined two pairs of Max-Neef's needs (also see Chittenden, 2000).

When is a Need 'Satisfied'?

Yet another question is: what does it take to satisfy a deficit in a basic need or orientor? Probably the best answer is to use the analogy that, if one is starving, one does not need or want a gourmet meal. A simple dish of nutritious staple foods is entirely appropriate. In other words, *sufficiency* is the appropriate response to *deficiency*. To achieve one's full humanity, a sufficiency of everything important is necessary; a surfeit of any one thing is no substitute for a basic deficit of another. The same applies to deficits affecting the viability of any system, from a family, to a community, to a society, and up to and including the whole Earth system.

But how does one evaluate 'sufficiency' to the satisfaction of those involved? This involves a number of tricky questions, but I believe a participatory process is the foundation of any such outcome.

Stakeholder Involvement

How can, for example, local knowledge and accumulated wisdom of settler and indigenous peoples alike be incorporated into the process of determining whether a system is viable, and whether it is making progress towards its goal? Expert scientific knowledge will influence the process of search and selection of indicators that can appropriately reflect basic need satisfaction. The process should, however, actually be shaped by the values of a much wider community than that of experts. In the context of the proposed approach, their values would, I feel, be most appropriately summarised through the ethics of the process used to select indicators.

A process such as this would benefit markedly from, for example, Funtowicz and Ravetz's (1991) suggestions of 'extended peer reviews within post-normal science' (also see Hayward, 1997).

PUTTING THESE IDEAS INTO PRACTICE

The process of constructing a system of indicators for assessing the viability of systems and, in particular, progress towards sustainable development, can be broken down into five main tasks:

1. Identify the overarching goal. In my view, 'sustainable living' is appropriate.
2. Adopt an ethical framework that provides an inclusive approach to guide our relationship with other, living and nonliving, human and non-human systems on which we depend or whose fate we influence in one way or another, now and in the future. In my opinion, the statement given above ('All people have their basic needs satisfied, so they can live in dignity, in healthy communities, while ensuring the minimum adverse impact on natural systems, now and in the future.') is appropriate.
3. Identify and develop sufficient knowledge about the participating sector subsystems we have to include within the 'total system' boundary, and their role and function in the sustainability of the total system.
4. For each participating sector subsystem, find indicators to answer the questions:
   - what is the viability (i.e. level of satisfaction of each basic need or orientor) of the sector subsystem itself) ?; and
   - how does each sector subsystem contribute to the viability of the total system within which that subsystem exists?
5. Define the indicators clearly and unambiguously, quantitatively or qualitatively as appropriate.

I remind the reader at this point, that the task is to define indicators that are representative of the *weakest* features of the system, with respect to the particular need or orientor question being addressed. To use a well-known analogy, a chain is only as strong as its weakest link; there is no point in strengthening links that are already strong enough, when one or more of the other links is obviously in a weak state.

Being Fully Human

Putting this framework together reiterates the importance of addressing the key question, which is likely to be something like: What is our real goal? When we have answered that question (through identifying our moral position and creating an ethical statement that reflects it), our measures of physical and other resource flows, for example, will help tell us what it 'costs' nature for us to maintain economic activity, and the extent to which our structures are viable and sustainable.

Once this has been done, we will be able to answer the important question of sustainable development, namely 'whether all people have their basic needs satisfied so they can live in dignity, while ensuring the minimum adverse impact on the natural world, now and in the future'.

So how does one start to reduce poverty and inequity, while at the same time keeping as much as possible of the infrastructure and economy of the nation under some degree of social control, as well as reducing fossil fuel use by converting to renewable energy sources?

Clearly, this is a tall order! However, without it, I believe society will remain hooked into perpetually searching for the political–economic 'magic bullet' that will ensure poverty alleviation, not realising that the key to poverty alleviation requires attention to the system in its entirety.

To solve the problems of the whole system requires very careful design and testing of the means of satisfying basic orientor deficiencies without causing deterioration in others. With so many interconnections, an action in one part of the system may have ramifications that go far beyond its immediate subsector boundaries. Clearly, Max-Neef's 'synergic satisfiers', which meet several different needs at once, are ideal in this situation. However, with the help of Bossel's framework described here, we can identify the areas where there is evidence of 'bleeding', and concentrate attention on them as a matter of priority.

Policy development in these areas will require the best of transdisciplinary cooperation between specialists, carefully guided by, and accountable to, the general public. It is not enough to use only one approach, such as the currently-fashionable mainstream (neoclassical) economic theory and its derivatives. A multiplicity of perspectives is required to ensure that as much of the full complexity of the whole system of which we are part is taken into account in our policymaking. In this context, Norgaard's coevolutionary approach, described above, has a lot to offer.

CONCLUSIONS

What I am suggesting is closely related to calls that have been made over recent years, in many countries, to change the ways in which society organises its priorities. To many, including myself (Peet, 1992; Peet and Peet, 2002), it means using the values determined through community-based processes to design a new economics – an ecological economics of sustainability (see, for example, Costanza et al., 1997; Robertson, 1997; Diesendorf and Hamilton, 1997; AtKisson, 1999; Edwards-Jones et al., 2000; Daly and Farley, 2004).

In my opinion, it is only when the political economy is guided by a clear goal and firm ethical principles that it can go beyond narrow economic theory and simple technical expediency. Only when it is guided by an understanding of the interdependence of all parts of the total system of people, society, economy, and environment will sustainable outcomes be achievable. I believe this requires a move to a new democracy – from the politics of self-interest to the politics of generosity – where there is understanding of 'enough' and commitment to satisfaction of the *needs* of all (human and non-human) before satisfying the *greeds* of a few.

ACKNOWLEDGEMENT

I warmly record debts of gratitude to my friend and colleague Hartmut Bossel, the source of much of the theoretical material presented here, and to my wife and helpmeet, Katherine Peet, for continually helping me towards better understanding the 'big picture'.

NOTES

1. Each need occurs at four different levels of activity: being, having, doing and interacting.
2. Note that these refer, respectively, to the *existence*, *effectiveness* and *security* basic orientors. If life itself is severely at risk, even the fundamental basic orientors have a priority ranking, in order to preserve the system. Normally when dealing with complex systems, things are not quite so critical, and the requirement is to satisfy all basic orientors simultaneously, with priority given to those that are in deficit.
3. It is worth noting that, at the same time as many state enterprises are being cut down, big businesses are getting even bigger, through takeovers and amalgamations. The extent of real competition in the marketplace is in many sectors somewhat questionable after such amalgamations.
4. Arguably, the converse is also true.

REFERENCES

AtKisson, A. (1999), *Believing Cassandra: An Optimist Looks at a Pessimist's World*, White River Junction, VT: Chelsea Green Publishing.

Birks, J.B. (1962), *Rutherford at Manchester*, London: Heywood & Co.

Bossel, H. (1998), *Earth at a Crossroads: Paths to a Sustainable Future*, Cambridge, UK: Cambridge University Press.

Bossel, H. (1999), *Indicators for Sustainable Development: Theory, Method, Applications. A report to the Balaton Group*, 161 Portage Avenue East, 6th floor, Winnipeg, Manitoba, Canada R3B 0Y4. (ISBN 1-895536-13-8), 'International Institute for Sustainable Development (IISD)'.

Capra, F. (1996), *The Web of Life: A New Synthesis of Mind and Matter*, London, UK: Flamingo/HarperCollins.

Chittenden, D. (2000), 'System and human needs', ME thesis, University of Canterbury, Christchurch, New Zealand, November.

Costanza, R., J. Cumberland, H. Daly, R. Goodland and R. Norgaard (1997), *An Introduction to Ecological Economics*, Boca Raton, FL: CRC Press/St Lucie Press.

Daly, H. and J. Farley (2004), *Ecological Economics: Principles and Applications*, Washington, DC: Island Press.

Diesendorf, M. and C. Hamilton (eds) (1997), *Human Ecology, Human Economy: Ideas for an Ecologically Sustainable Future*, St Leonards, NSW: Allen and Unwin.

Dodds, S. Hatfield (1999), 'Paradigms for sustainability: consumerism, well-being, and the social space', in *Grounding the Paradigm*, ANZSEE National Conference, Griffith University, Brisbane, 5–7 July 1999.

Edwards-Jones, G., B. Davies and S. Hussain (2000), *Ecological Economics: An Introduction*, Oxford, UK: Blackwell Science.

El Serafy, S. (1997), 'Distribution as an ethical link between economics and ecology', *Ecological Economics Bulletin, International Society for Ecological Economics*, **2** (4), 4–5.

Funtowicz, S. and J. Ravetz (1991), 'A new scientific methodology for global environmental issues', in R. Costanza (ed.), *Ecological Economics: The Science and Management of Sustainability*, New York: Columbia University Press.

Hayward, B. (1997), 'Talking ourselves green? a "deliberative" approach to sustainability', paper delivered as part of the 'Symbols of Sustainability' lecture series, Lincoln University, Canterbury, New Zealand, 5 March–11 June.

Hinterberger, F., F. Luks, M. Stewen and J. van der Straaten (2000), 'Environmental policy in a complex world', *International Journal of Sustainable Development*, **3** (3), 276–96.

Max-Neef, M. (1991), *Human Scale Development: Conception, Application and Further Reflections*, New York and London: Apex Press.

Mayor, F. (1997), From an address at the opening of the third meeting of Agenda for the Millennium: Ethics of the Future, Rio de Janeiro, 2–5 July.

Norgaard, R. (1994), *Development Betrayed: The End of Progress and a Coevolutionary Revisioning of the Future*, London: Routledge.

Peet, J. (1992), *Energy and the Ecological Economics of Sustainability*, Washington, DC: Island Press.

Peet, J. and H. Bossel (2000), 'An ethics-based system approach to indicators of sustainable development', *International Journal of Sustainable Development*, **3** (3), 221–38.

Peet, J. and K. Peet (1998), 87 Soleares Avenue, Christchurch 8008, New Zealand.

Peet, K. and J. Peet (2002), 'Stolen from future generations? The need to move to a political economy of generosity', ANZTSR (Australia and New Zealand Third Sector Research) Conference, Unitec, Auckland, 27–9 November.

Robertson, J. (1997), *The New Economics of Sustainable Development: A Briefing for Policy Makers*, a report for the European Commission, May 1997 (downloadable from the Turning Point 2000 web site www.the-commons.org/tp 2000).

19. Selecting headline indicators for tracking progress to sustainability in a nation state

Murray Patterson

INTRODUCTION AND CONTEXT

The purpose of this chapter is to provide guidance to readers on how to best select a national level headline indicator of sustainability, by reflecting on the experience of New Zealand. A fuller and more substantive account of the New Zealand sustainability indicators project can be obtained by referring to the publication *Headline Indicators for Tracking Progress to Sustainability in New Zealand* commissioned by the New Zealand Ministry for the Environment (Patterson, 2002).

History and Rationale for Sustainability Indicators

Indicators of all aspects of society are becoming increasingly important and evident in our everyday life. There is a daily barrage of indicators and indexes that are reported in our newspapers and appear on our television screens. Economic indicators, particularly gross domestic product (GDP), have also assumed a very important place in public policy debates and analysis. For all this, indicators are a relatively recent phenomenon, with even the GDP only really being used since the post-Second World War period.

There is an overwhelming bias towards economic indicators in public policy. In response to this, in the 1960s and 1970s, as social issues assumed more importance, the *social indicators movement* attempted to establish social measures of progress (Fox, 1985). There were, however, few 'success stories' of social indicators and indexes of progress in terms of getting the political acceptance for them that many had hoped for. Perhaps the Human Development Index indicator developed by the United Nations (1990) is one of the few social indicators that did emerge with some credibility and acceptance. In the 1980s and 1990s, as the environmental movement became increasingly dissatisfied with conventional

economic measures of progress, there was a concerted effort by governments, NGOs and academic researchers to establish environmental sustainability indicators.

The 1990s was a remarkable decade for the development of sustainability indicators theory and practice. The field grew extremely rapidly and
diversified into a wide variety of approaches. Much of the development was
driven through international agencies like the United Nations, the OECD,
the World Bank and the European Union. One major line of development
was the attempt to adjust and modify the System of National Accounts
(SNAs) to cover environmental factors. Accordingly, the System of
Integrated Economic and Environmental Accounts (SEEA), which was
released by the United Nations (1993), provided an official basis for integrating economic and environmental statistics within the SNA framework.
The SEEA represented the first major change in the SNA since its inception in 1953. This environmental accounting initiative has already had a
major impact on how many countries compile and report their economic
accounts. The top level indicator used in environmental accounting is the
'green GDP', which attempts to simultaneously measure economic and
environmental progress. This indicator has been developed for very many
countries including the United States, the United Kingdom and Australia.

The second main trend in the development of sustainability indicators is
represented by the initiatives of the United Nations and the OECD to standardise the collection of environmental indicators across nations to allow
the environmental performance of nations to be tracked and monitored
against each other. The OECD has developed, within its pressure–state–
response framework, a core set of environmental indicators. The United
Nations, through their Commission on Sustainable Development, have in
recent years focused on the integration of environmental statistics with economic and social measures of progress.

The emergence of the call for greater government accountability and
policy performance evaluation has also had a significant impact on the
development of sustainability indicators. The 'measure to manage' philosophy is a prevalent feature and a driving force behind many of the indicator systems that are being developed – e.g. the Dutch Policy Performance
Indicators. There is an increasing emphasis on monitoring and analysing
the effectiveness of environmental policies by using indicator systems.
Public awareness and the public's 'right to know' about trends in the environment is another strong rationale driving the rapid development of sustainability indicators. Many of these indicator initiatives exist at the local
or regional level (e.g. Sustainable Seattle) and are driven by community
involvement. There are now some very good examples of regional level
sustainability reporting projects (particularly in Canada). Business level

environmental reporting and indicators are also starting to emerge – e.g. the Trucost Indicator in New Zealand.

The rationale behind all of these sustainability indicator initiatives is based on the premise that, as a community (or nation), we need to know how we are performing economically, socially and environmentally. Without this information, we cannot rationally plan for the future and monitor progress towards any goals we may set. This applies to all levels and dimensions of decision-making in the regional community and ranges across the public and private sectors.

The need to move beyond treating 'economic', 'social' and 'environmental' indicators separately, is another clear trend emerging in the international indicators scene. Even the most conservative agencies, such as the World Bank, are moving in this direction with its Total Wealth Indicator – an attempt at integrating all of these dimensions of progress. Accordingly, the current study of the feasibility of sustainable development indicators in New Zealand is also focusing on simultaneously measuring economic, social and environmental progress in a composite index.

What is a Headline Indicator of Sustainability?

Many indicators measure different aspects of sustainability performance, often at a localised level. Although these indicators are useful in the management of specific resources and ecosystems, they give no information about the overall performance of the system. In fact, decision-makers are often overwhelmed by the sheer quantity and complexity of indicators to the extent that indicators become counterproductive.

Headline indicators are about trying to *reduce the complexity to a manageable and understandable level* and to capture the communication power of a single number. They measure the overall performance of the system in terms of broad economic, social and environmental goals. The main audience of headline indicators should ideally be the general public. In the economic area, well-known headline indicators that measure economic performance are the GDP and the inflation rate index. The meaning of these economic indicators is instantly apparent to the public and politicians and is therefore often reported without any explanation in the media.

There is very good evidence that accurate, accessible, headline information does influence decision-making. A case in point is the use of the high-level economic and financial indicators (such as GDP or inflation index) and their highly influential impact on decision-making and public policy. For example, Anielski et al. (2001) argue that the United States had no labour market policy until the unemployment rate was codified into the USA Statistical Framework in the 1940s and 1950s.

When it comes to sustainable development, a headline indicator has to encapsulate the essential characteristics of social, economic and environmental progress. This often, but not necessarily, requires the headline indicator to be a composite index – that is, an index made up of a hierarchical structure of sub-indexes and variables. This is because one single variable is unlikely to be capable of capturing all the behaviour one wishes to measure, whether it be economic, social, or environmental behaviour.

The literature contains a wide range of potential headline sustainability indicators. These include: the ecological footprint, genuine savings, the genuine progress indicator/index of sustainable economic welfare, material flow indicators, environmental sustainability index, consumption pressure index, and living planet index, among others. Several of these indicators are evaluated below.

New Zealand Initiatives in Sustainability Indicators

New Zealand has been relatively slow in developing sustainability indicator systems and environmental accounts. In the early 1990s, there were a number of joint efforts by the Ministry for the Environment and the Department of Statistics (1990 and 1991) to promote state-of-the-environment reporting in New Zealand. These reports were very wide-ranging and contained recommendations to explore integrative economic–environmental accounting and environmental indicator systems. Progress was slow and piecemeal, with an abortive attempt to initiate environmental accounting that was accompanied by a loss of impetus in environmental indicators development that endured well into the mid-1990s. The Department of Statistics did, however, publish compendiums on environmental statistics such as *Measuring Up* while the Ministry for the Environment released a national State of Environment Report. Nonetheless, there was no attempt to establish environmental indicators.

Eventually, in 1996, the Ministry for the Environment's Environmental Performance Indicators (EPI) programme was established with significant funding (approximately NZ$3 million per year) being devoted to setting up a national system of environmental indicators. A number of areas were selected for indicator development including: land, air, fresh water, climate change, ozone, marine environment, terrestrial and freshwater biodiversity, waste, transport, energy, pests, weeds and disease, urban amenity and landscape values and toxic contaminants. A great deal of effort was put into securing the support of regional councils and science providers, as well as identifying indicator variables through a consultative process. As yet, however, no indicator data series have been directly produced by the EPI programme. Only ecological footprint indicators for New Zealand and its regions have been produced (as well as a related calculator), but this initiative has resulted from *Recommendation 1* of Patterson's (2002) report rather than directly from the EPI programme.

Progress in the area of environmental accounting (integrating economic and environmental data and indicators) has been slower still. In the late 1980s, Wright (1989) called for the establishment of environmental accounts in New Zealand, but Statistics New Zealand concluded, in the early 1990s, that setting up environmental accounts in New Zealand 'was not feasible'. Regional level environmental accounts have, nonetheless, been set up for the Northland, Auckland and Waikato regions and are available on an interactive database called *Eco*Link (McDonald and Patterson, 1999). This work was sponsored by ten collaborating councils and the Ministry for the Environment. The decision to produce national environmental accounts was announced in the 2000 New Zealand government budget but progress has been slow and the funding inadequate.

Goldberg (1999) provided a review of *Indicators of Sustainable Consumption* for Statistics New Zealand. It examined the applicability of 28 sustainable consumption indicators for New Zealand. The review concluded that such indicators were relevant to New Zealand, but although the required social and economic data were available, the paucity of environmental pressures data was problematic in terms of implementing such a framework in New Zealand.

The measurement of social progress is an allied field that needs to be briefly mentioned here, particularly if New Zealand is to establish a composite index of 'social', 'economic' and 'environmental' performance. The most comprehensive measure of social progress (or lack of it) is the construction of the New Zealand Deprivation Index using data from the 1991 and 1996 census. This index measures social deprivation at the mesh block level using a composite index of nine variables (Crampton et al., 2000). There have also been other attempts at measuring social progress, poverty, income inequality, and related measures – for example, Easton (1995a and 1995b); Stephens et al. (1995); and Davis et al. (1996).

THEORETICAL BASES TO SUSTAINABILITY INDICATORS

Before we proceed with an evaluation of sustainability indicators, we must first establish the theoretical bases for the underlying concept of 'sustainability'. Unfortunately, little of the 'sustainability indicators' literature addresses this critical issue. Instead, the approach tends to be to select indicators that have an intuitive and pragmatic appeal, without fully defining the concept of 'sustainability' itself. In places, the literature comes seriously close to measurement without theory. Indeed, there is often an 'absent referent', where what is being measured has no transparent or explicit theoretical basis.

It is clear from the burgeoning literature on sustainability that there is no one definition of sustainability and different disciplines interpret the concept in fundamentally different ways. A comprehensive review of the Sustainable Development literature by Pezzoli (1997a and 1997b) categorises these interpretations across 11 fields: policy and planning; social conditions; environmental law; environmental sciences; eco-design and the environment; ecological economics; eco-philosophy; environmental values and ethics; environmental history and geography; utopianism, anarchism and bioregionalism; and political ecology.[1]

Ecological Interpretations

Ecologists since the early 1970s have started to apply ecological principles to the analysis of human sustainability issues. Ehrlich et al. (1973), Watt (1973), Odum (1971) and Dasmann (1972) encapsulated and formalized much of the early ecological sustainability theory. Watt (1973), for example, established 14 'core principles' of environmental science based on the 'fundamental variables' of matter, energy, space, time and diversity. Similar principles are outlined by Miller (1993) and Cronin's (1988) *Ecological Principles of Resource Management* that was published by the New Zealand Ministry for the Environment.

From this literature emerged a number of theoretical bases for defining sustainability ranging across various scales/levels of ecological organisation (biosphere, ecosystem and community levels) and paradigms within the discipline of ecology (equilibrium and non-equilibrium paradigms).

Equilibrium ecology

At the ecosystem level of organisation, the central idea is that of succession. Ecological succession is the progressive development of a community of animals, plants and microorganisms from an 'immature' state to a 'climax'. The climax community is relatively stable, diverse and energetically efficient. It essentially exists at a steady or dynamic equilibrium state. For example, after some catastrophic event, the vegetative cover in any locality will inexorably move to a dynamic equilibrium point such that a fire clearing of a forest may bring about a successional sequence that starts with bare ground and ends with a mature forest.

The concept of ecological succession can be traced back to the work of Clements (1916). According to Clements's theory of ecological succession, an ecological community advanced from its embryonic stage of development – i.e. gradually progressed through a series of stages to reach maturity – such that the 'climax' state was the most stable and supported the greatest diversity of species. In the absence of external changes, the theory held that the climax state would persist, seemingly indefinitely, with very little structural change. Thus, as the community matured, it progressively established its environment. According to Clements, however, the developing equilibrium between the plant community and its physical environment was not necessarily static. Clements preferred to characterise the climax state as a 'dynamic equilibrium' to account for the constant adjustments the community made in response to environmental fluctuations. This line of thinking culminated in Odum's (1969) landmark article that both explained the ecological succession process in terms of 24 ecosystem attributes and visualised ecosystem development in terms of smooth, predictable changes from the 'developmental stage' to the 'mature stage' at climax.

Essentially an *equilibrium paradigm of ecology* developed, with ecosystems being maintained in a 'state of balance' through the mechanism of homeostasis. Feedback mechanisms ensured that if the ecosystem was disrupted by a 'perturbation', such as a fire or flood, it was returned to its original state through a self-correcting feedback mechanism. This equilibrium idea of ecology dominated the discipline until quite recently. However, the central tenet of this view of ecosystems was that mature and species-diverse ecosystems are more stable (sustainable) and therefore more desirable than less diverse ecosystems.

Under the equilibrium paradigm of ecology, the definition of ecological sustainability is straightforward – that is, it occurs when an ecological system has reached it climax stage. At this climax state, the system is energetically efficient with energy inputs required only for maintenance and not growth; it is diverse in terms of spatial and species heterogeneity; it is complex in terms of niche specialisation and lifecycle roles of species; it is a closed system with respect to many nutrient cycles; it has highly developed feedback control (k selection); it is resistant to external perturbations; and it has low entropy and high information. All of these characteristics ensure that the ecosystem can be sustained indefinitely at this steady-state position. Under this equilibrium paradigm, the definition of ecological sustainability is not only straightforward, but so are the resource management principles under this paradigm – viz, the ability to *plan rationally* for environmental *goals* is relatively simple in a system where the successional pathway is *predictable* and its *endpoint* (*climax community*) is *known* and *desirable*. Much of the traditional resource management literature (e.g. Burton and Kates, 1965) and arguably the New

Zealand Resource Management Act 1991 is predicated on this equilibrium paradigm.

Non-equilibrium ecology
The equilibrium paradigm of ecology was challenged for the first time in the early 1970s. Having said this, it took the best part of a couple of decades for a non-equilibrium view of ecosystems to be accepted by the majority of ecologists.

Although the stability–diversity controversy has a long history in ecology, the watershed paper on this topic was published by May in 1972. May's (1972) mathematical paper clearly demonstrated that diverse communities are not necessarily stable, as assumed in the equilibrium paradigm. May showed that 'a too rich a food web connectance, or a too large an average interaction strength, . . . leads to instability . . . The larger the number of species, the more pronounced the effect.' May (1974) drew the attention of ecologists to another sobering fact – because the simplest of non-linear equations were capable of giving rise to chaotic and therefore intrinsically unpredictable behaviour, the hope of 'deriving simple laws for (ecological) systems in which non-linearity is the norm, is illusory'. From this point onwards, a great deal of empirical evidence pushed theoretical ecologists toward a non-equilibrium view of the world. The equilibrium paradigm was thus overturned.

Perhaps the best summary of the non-equilibrium paradigm is that of De Angelis and Waterhouse (1987). Under this alternative paradigm, it is not assumed that equilibrium points do not exist. Rather, De Angelis and Waterhouse, in endorsing Wiens (1984), depicted ecological communities as existing in a spectrum that ranged from stable equilibrium points (biotically interactive, few stochastic effects) to non-equilibrium systems (weakly interactive, large stochastic effects). It is important to note that, for a given community/ecosystem, there is no one given equilibrium point where the system will tend to stay the same forever.

Kay and Schneider's (1994) thermodynamic analysis of ecosystem behaviour essentially came to the same conclusion as May (1972 and 1974). Kay and Schneider's analysis was based on population modelling that revealed a lack of any single optimum or homeostatic ecological state, as assumed in the succession (equilibrium) model.

Under the new, 'non-equilibrium' paradigm, the interpretation of the ecological sustainability concept becomes more difficult and problematical, since there is, contrary to the equilibrium position, no steady-state or climax end-point. From a sustainability perspective, the best one can hope for is that the ecosystem *persists* over time, by maintaining itself within upper and lower biophysical limits represented by 'floors' and 'ceilings'.

Under this *persistence* model, decline in species numbers and ecosystem functions is permissible as long as the system persists. Unfortunately, for many, this ecological reality is unsatisfactory, particularly for those approaching the definition of ecological sustainability from a normative perspective that presumes the existence of a 'balance of nature'.

Holling's 'resilience'
Holling (1973) defined the concept of ecological resilience, which is widely used as a definitional basis for ecological sustainability. Holling's resilience concept can be considered a compromise between equilibrium and non-equilibrium ecology. Holling (1973) believes there are four phases that describe the dynamics of the ecosystem in terms of his well-known 'Figure 8' diagram. They include the following:

1. *Exploitation*: This is the early phase of ecosystem development where it is dominated by opportunistic pioneer species.
2. *Conservation*: This is equivalent to the climax stage where the ecosystem 'consolidates' and is relatively stable.
3. *Release*: The ecosystem structure begins to break down due to some external perturbation – e.g. pest outbreak, fire, storm.
4. *Reorganisation*: At this stage, it is possible for the ecosystem to return to the same 'equilibrium point' or flip to another 'equilibrium point'.

According to this resilience concept, the ecosystem has the ability to absorb change and ideally benefit from it. But, since systemic change can be expected, an ideal steady-state end-point cannot be assumed to exist. Odum (1996) has described a similar picture of ecosystem dynamics using his energy flow nomenclature – what he has termed as the *pulsing paradigm*.

Economic Interpretations

Economists, particularly in the 1980s and 1990s, have developed a number of interpretations of sustainability which now form the basis of several important headline indicators of sustainability.

Capital theory: intergenerational equity
Economic interpretations of sustainability often draw on capital theory which was first developed and applied to manufactured capital but now includes natural capital (natural resources). Under this theoretical framework, it is asserted that a necessary and sufficient condition to achieve sustainability is that the total amount of capital (natural, manufactured,

human, social) must be at least maintained from generation to generation. This draws very much on Hicks's (1946) idea of sustainable income:

> . . . it would seem that we ought to define a man's [sic] income as the maximum value, he can consume during a week, and still expect to be as well off at the end of the week as he was at the beginning.

The weak sustainability definition applies the idea of Hicksian (sustainable) income to the sum total of manufactured and natural capital (Faucheux et al., 1997). That is, as long as the sum of manufactured capital and natural capital is maintained from generation to generation, the economy/society is considered to be 'sustainable' (Solow, 1986; Hartwick, 1978). Under this condition, the flow of goods and services (derived from the capital stock) can at least be maintained, thereby meaning the level of human welfare is also continuously maintained.

It is assumed under the weak sustainability interpretation of sustainability that manufactured capital can substitute for losses in natural capital. The fact that natural capital (natural resources) is being depleted or degraded is of no consequence under this model so long as the formation of manufactured capital makes up for losses in natural capital. Whether manufactured natural capital is a true substitute for natural capital becomes a critical and a fundamental issue. If, for example, a wetland (natural capital) is lost, it is assumed under the weak sustainability argument that substitutes for the lost ecosystem services provided by a wetland can readily be found. In the case of a wetland, the relevant ecosystem services include flood control, disturbance buffering, habitat, nutrient cycling and water regulation. In some cases, manufactured substitutes, such as a dam, can provide flood control services, but in other cases it is difficult to envisage how a manufactured form of capital can substitute for the loss of unique habitat/refugia. The weak sustainability perspective therefore provides an optimistic view of the role of technology and innovation in overcoming resource scarcity and environmental problems. It is assumed that, through market forces, the loss of ecosystem functions and services can be overcome by providing the appropriate incentives for technological innovation.

Pearce and Atkinson (1993) present the formalism for the weak sustainability indicator. They formulate the following simple savings rule to gauge the sustainability rating of a nation's economy at a given point in time.

$$Z > 0 \quad \text{if } (S/Y) > [(D_M/Y) > (D_N/Y)] \tag{19.1}$$

where Z = the sustainability index for a nation; S = savings, or the accumulation of capital; D_M = the value of depreciation on manufactured capital; D_N = the value of depreciation on natural capital; and Y = national income.

The genuine savings index (which is evaluated in a later section) represents an attempt to operationalise an indicator based on this formula. Pearce and Turner (1990) argue the importance of maintaining constant natural capital stock (i.e. strong sustainability) as a condition for achieving sustainable economic development. They challenge the weak sustainability argument that manufactured capital can always substitute for natural capital within production processes by identifying five reasons why such substitution is often impossible and why sustained economic development requires the maintenance of a constant stock of natural capital.

Welfare theory: internalising externalities

Both the weak and strong sustainability indicators involve the measurement of the capital stock. Unfortunately, however, the theoretically valid operational measurement of capital stock has been a long recognised area of difficulty in economic theory (Blaug, 1974). For this reason alone, some economists prefer to measure *flows* of goods and services rather than *stock* levels. Flow measurements, such as the GDP, or an adjusted green GDP, are much easier to operationalise. Such measurements, of course, tell us nothing about the wealth transfer between generations and are therefore avoided by some economic theorists.

From a welfare perspective, the GDP has been widely criticised as an indicator of human welfare, primarily because it adds up 'goods' and 'bads'. If, for example, there are more car accidents per year, the GDP will increase due to hospital and medical expenses but, quite clearly, in this case, human welfare will have decreased. The same logic applies to the cost of pollution as reflected in health costs, abatement costs, regulatory costs and so forth. Second, the GDP only values goods and services that have a market value. Many ecological goods (air, water, biodiversity) have no market value and therefore do not enter into GDP calculations. Unpaid household work also has no market value and therefore is also ignored by the GDP. Third, distributional effects are also not factored into GDP calculations. The last marginal unit of income for a poor person is more valuable than the last marginal unit of income for a rich person, although the GDP incorrectly assumes this not to be the case.

Economic theorists have long recognised the shortcomings of the GDP indicator (e.g. Mishan, 1967). However, it has only been in relatively recent times that economists, such as Daly (1994), have set the theoretical foundations for adjusting the conventional GDP to take account of social and environmental factors. Specifically, this has led to the Index of Sustainable Welfare (ISEW) and the Genuine Progress Indicator (GPI) as alternative measures of welfare/progress (see Chapters 2 and 7–9). These indicators are further discussed in a later section of this chapter.

Thermodynamics and Ecological Economics Interpretations

Ecological economists, such as Daly (1973), Costanza (1991) and Georgescu-Roegen (1971), present a biophysical view of the economy that is in stark contrast to the models presented in the previous major section, all of which involved monetisation of capital stocks and flows.

In ecological economics, the economic system is considered to be a 'sub-system' of the biophysical system. The economic system uses low entropy energy inputs (fossil fuel, nuclear energy) and low entropy matter resources (minerals, biomass, water). These inputs are transformed, sometimes stored, but ultimately degraded into high entropy emissions that flow back into the biophysical environment. Fundamentally, there are a number of sustainability issues that arise from this model:

1.   To what extent does the economy occupy the space of the biosphere? Estimates by Vitousek et al. (1986) indicate that the economy has appropriated 40 per cent of the net primary productivity of the terrestrial biosphere. The ultimate physical limit cannot exceed 100 per cent and, certainly to have a safety margin, it has been argued that realistically this limit could be more like 80 per cent.
2.   To what extent does the economy's sustainability depend on the biosphere as a *source* of resources? Many resources are clearly finite and depletable – e.g. fossil fuels, minerals, land, and so forth. Economic growth cannot be sustained indefinitely if these resources are depleted or degraded.
3.   To what extent does the economy's sustainability depend on the *sink* functions of the biophysical environment? For many industrial wastes and emissions, the biophysical environment can efficiently purify and absorb such pollutants. However, there are critical thresholds beyond which the environment cannot cope with ever-increasing levels of pollutants. For instance, at a local level, a lake might become eutrophied, or on a global scale, the biophysical environment only has a certain capacity to absorb greenhouse gas emissions.
4.   To what extent are there critical limits to the ability to recycle material wastes? Despite the rhetoric of zero waste campaigns, this is a physical impossibility. The Second Law of Thermodynamics – the Entropy Law – tells us that degraded energy outputs can never be recycled and there are severe limits on the degree of recycling of materials (mass).

From a biophysical perspective, ecological economists, such as Goodland and Daly (1993), believe sustainability requires the minimisation of energy and material 'throughput' (see also Chapter 2). It is in this tradition that aggregative-level material flow indictors have been developed to track sustainability progress in terms of measuring the reduction of the material throughput/intensities of nations (Adriaanse et al., 1997; also see Chapters 16 and 17).

Public Policy and Planning Theory

Policy agencies, in particular, have promoted perspectives on sustainability that attempt to 'integrate' the social, economic and environmental dimensions of sustainability. This is seen as a 'more balanced' approach, whereby decision-makers can put social and economic policy objectives alongside environmental objectives. This integrative perspective on sustainability is advocated by planning and policy theorists (e.g. Cairns and Crawford, 1991; Mitchell, 1997). Such theoretical approaches lead naturally to *composite indicators* that simultaneously measure social, economic and environmental performance.

A good example of this approach is the New Zealand Government's *Environment 2010 Strategy* published by the Ministry for the Environment (1994). It defines sustainable development as having three *equal* components – economic, environmental and social. The economic dimension concerns the policy goal of maximising economic efficiency and improving economic competitiveness. The social dimension is concerned with issues of social equity, income distribution, social cohesion and justice. Finally, the environmental dimension is concerned with sustainable management of the biophysical environment which, in the New Zealand case, implies environmental management in accordance with the principles and purposes of the Resource Management Act of 1991. While this concept of sustainable development indicates that all of three dimensions are intricately interlinked and interdependent, it unfortunately gives few clues about how sustainable development can be precisely defined beyond the sum total of its component parts. However, implicit in this meaning of the sustainable development is the idea of 'trade-off' or 'balance' – something which is inconsistent with the Ministry for the Environment's advocacy for 'environmental bottom-lines' that, realistically, does not permit trade-offs.

The so-called 'ecosystem approach' (sic) to sustainable development advocated by the Canadian Government also promotes the idea of a balance or integration between environment, economy and community (Canadian Council of Ministers of the Environment, 1996). The Ontario Ministry of the Environment (1992) makes their intent quite clear by stipulating that 'ecological goals should be treated equally, and considered at the same time, as economic and social goals'.

The Wuppertal Institute in Germany also advocates a composite inter-pretation of sustainable development as reflected in a publication by Spangerberg and Bonniot (1998). To quote directly from this publication:

> Sustainability definition is a composite and an ambiguous policy target. It com-prises environmental, economic and social criteria with equal importance – neither environment deregulation or violating human dignity by poverty or other threats, nor public and private bankruptcy can be acceptable elements of a sustainable society.

CRITERIA FOR EVALUATING HEADLINE SUSTAINABILITY INDICATORS

General Criteria for Indicator Selection

A number of previous studies (e.g. Opschoor and Reijnders, 1991; Ministry for the Environment, 1996; and Gallopín, 1997) have identified the desir-able characteristics of 'good' public policy indicators. They include the following:

1. *Clarity of the message.* An important criterion is that the potential audience should understand what the indicator is attempting to convey. Most members of the public instantaneously understand the implica-tions of a drop in the unemployment rate, or a drop in the inflation index. A drop in the inflation index is seen as being 'good', and a rise in the inflation index is seen as being 'bad'. A government needs, for example, to reassure itself that the public would instantaneously understand what a drop in the sustainability index means, if it was to be used as a public indicator.

2. *Scientific and theoretical basis.* The theoretical basis of the indicator must be made explicit, and possible theoretical short-comings must be minimised. The standard criteria of scientific measurement should be met in applying the indicator (see Ziman, 1984). The credibility of a nation's proposed sustainability indicators will inevitably be under-mined if these standards of scientific practice are not adhered to. In this particular case, any headline indicator should be based on sound theory. In this way, the ecological principles discussed earlier in this chapter should inform the construction of the 'environmental' sub-index of any headline indicator of sustainable development.

3. *Philosophical bias.* Indicators should not be formulated in terms of narrow ethical, theoretical, or philosophical frameworks. Since the target group may include decision-makers from various political and ethical convictions, non-compliance with this requirement renders an indicator immediately inappropriate. Having said this, few indicators are without such biases (Wright, 1991), and therefore this criterion should be seen as an ideal rather than an attainable goal.

4. *Appropriate data transformation.* Raw statistical data rarely make good indicators. Indicators nearly always need to be expressed as ratios, indices, percentages, or in terms of some sort of arithmetical transformation. These data transformations should incorporate relevant reference points in order to facilitate the comparison of changes to the indicators through time.

5. *Timeliness.* Indicators must be made available to the potential target group as soon as possible after the date which they are referring to. Quarterly indicators should be made available within a few weeks, whereas longer delays are permissible for annual indicators. Inordinate time delays can diminish the value of the indicators to decision-makers and target groups.

6. *Data cost and availability.* The data must be readily available and at a reasonable cost. Preferably, the time-series data which the indicator is based on should span several decades with a high probability of future availability.

7. *Efficient representation of a concept.* The indicator should, as much as possible, convey the maximum information about a particular theoretical concept. As Vos et al. (1985) put it, indicators 'are thriftily selected data assumed to have a causal relationship with a theoretical concept'.

8. *Designed for the appropriate audience.* Indicators, whether they are social, environmental, or economic, should be designed to suit different target groups. It is often falsely assumed that a multi-purpose indicator can be developed to suit all audiences. A useful distinction concerning the design of indicators to suit the appropriate audience is provided by Braat (1991):

    (a) *Professional analysts and scientists.* This group is most interested in raw data which can be analysed statistically. They generally prefer many information bits per message conveyed.

    (b) *Policy-makers.* Policy-makers prefer data which are related to policy objectives, evaluation criteria, target, and threshold values. The information should be condensed to a few bits per message.

    (c) *The public.* The public is assumed to prefer unambiguous messages, free of redundancy, in a single bit of information.

Specific Criteria Relevant to the New Zealand Project

The project brief with the New Zealand Ministry for the Environment outlined the more specific requirements concerning the type of indicators
required for the New Zealand sustainability indicators project:

1. *Performance indicators.* It is intended that the headline sustainability
    indicators will serve as performance indicators in the sense of inform-
    ing us if 'things are getting better' or 'things are getting worse'. This
    necessarily implies some reference point or benchmarking system.
    Such reference points or benchmarks could include policy targets,
    comparisons with other countries, environmental standards, and
    departures from a base year.
2. *Inclusion of all dimensions of sustainable development.* The New
    Zealand government sought an overall indicator of sustainable devel-
    opment to encapsulate the 'economic', 'social' and 'environmental'
    dimensions of the sustainable development concept. The economic
    dimension would measure attributes such as economic growth, eco-
    nomic efficiency, and wealth creation; the social dimension, issues
    such as equity, justice and availability of social services; and the
    environmental dimension would measure attributes such as envi-
    ronmental quality, sustainable resource use and maintenance of
    biodiversity.
3. *Long-term availability of data.* The New Zealand government indi-
    cated the importance of being able to backdate selected indicators
    several years in order to establish trends. The selected indicators should
    also be suitable for long-term repeated measurements. Care is therefore
    needed to ensure that whatever variables are selected, there is a consis-
    tent historical time series and a good prospect that these time series will
    be maintained into the future. This requires liaison with statistical
    agencies, science providers, and the Ministry for the Environment's EPI
    programme.

EVALUATION OF POSSIBLE HEADLINE SUSTAINABILITY INDICATORS FOR NEW ZEALAND

We now evaluate a number of headline indicators of sustainability against
the criteria outlined in the previous section. The results of this evaluation
are summarised by Table 19.1.[2]

Table 19.1 Evaluation of headline sustainability indicators against each selection criterion

	Clarity of message and public acceptance	Scientific and theoretical basis	Timeliness	All dimensions of sustainable development	Explicit performance criteria	Data availability	Cost	Availability of long-term data series
Ecological Footprint	XXXX	XX	XXX	X	XXX	XXXX	XXXX	XXXX
Environmental Sustainability Index	XXX	XX	XXXX	X	XX	XX	XXXX	XXX
Green GDP	XXXX	XXX	XXX	XXXX	XXX	XX	XXX	XX
Genuine Savings Index	X	XXX	XXX	XX	XXX	XX	X	XX
Material Flows Indicator	X	XX	XX	X		X	X	X
Consumption Pressure Index	XXX	X	XXXX	X		XX	XXX	X
Living Planet Index	XXX	XXX	XX	XX	XX	XX	XXXX	X
Composite Environmental Performance Index	XX	XXX	XXXX	XX	XX	X	X	XX
NZ Composite Sustainable Development Index	XXX	XXXX	XX	XXXX	XXX	XXXX	XXX	XXX

Notes:
XXXX = Excellent
XXX = Good
XX = Fair
X = Poor

Ecological Footprint

The ecological footprint is a headline sustainability indicator in two senses. First, it measures the *total ecological cost* (in land area) of supplying all the goods and services to a particular human population (see also Chapter 12). The ecological footprint recognises that people not only *directly* require land for agricultural production, roads, buildings and so forth, but land is *indirectly* embodied in goods and services. In this sense, the ecological footprint makes visible the 'hidden' ecological cost of an activity or population.

A second and more controversial interpretation of the ecological footprint as a sustainability indicator invokes the idea of 'carrying capacity'. Carrying capacity in ecology is the maximum population a given land area can support indefinitely. This idea is relatively straightforward when applied to well-defined biological populations. The idea, however, becomes much more controversial when applied to human populations. A good example of this controversy is the *Limits to Growth* study, which predicted a decline in global human population as it overshot its carrying capacity (Meadows et al., 1972). Some proponents of the ecological footprint argue that the total embodied land area required by a population should not overshoot its actual productive land area.

Other theoretical and methodological problems associated with the ecological footprint include the following:[3]

1. Why is embodied land used as the only numeraire of sustainability? Land is not the only scarce natural resource, so why should it be the only resource entered into the calculations? Arguments alluding to the non-sustainability of land are not compelling, as it could be argued that other natural resources also do not have substitutes (e.g. solar energy).
2. Not all land is the same in terms of its productive quality and other attributes. Wackernagel and Rees (1996) attempt to overcome this criticism by using yield factors and other equivalence factors, but this approach is viewed by many as far from satisfactory.
3. The spatial boundaries used in the analysis have a critical impact on the calculations, but these are hard to select in a non-arbitrary way.

Notwithstanding these theoretical problems, the ecological footprint scores well against most of the evaluation criteria in Table 19.1:

- clarity of message and public acceptance (excellent);
- timeliness (good);

- explicit performance criteria (good);
- data availability (excellent);
- cost (excellent);
- availability of long-term data (excellent).

One particular weakness of the ecological footprint in terms of New Zealand requirements is that it only attempts to cover the 'environmental dimension' of sustainable development and in doing so only covers one resource input (land) and one pollutant (carbon dioxide). This is clearly an inadequate coverage of resources and pollutants, as well as their impact, even though land is an all-pervasive resource and carbon dioxide is critical in terms of climate change.

The particular strength of the ecological footprint is that it provides a vivid indicator of ecological appropriation which is easily understood. This has led to the ecological footprint being one of the most successful indicators of sustainability, judged by its widespread use and application (Costanza, 2000). Because of its attractiveness as a public indicator, as well as its relatively low cost and ease of implementation, the New Zealand government, on the recommendation of Patterson (2002), has adopted the ecological footprint indicator (refer to www.mfe.govt.nz).

Environmental Sustainability Index

The Environmental Sustainability Index (ESI) is a composite measure of overall progress towards environmental sustainability of 122 countries, which was developed by the World Economic Forum (2001). It is based on 67 underlying variables, measuring five components of environmental sustainability – the state of environmental systems; stresses on environmental systems; human vulnerability to environmental change; social and institutional capacity to cope with environmental change; and global stewardship.

The World Economic Forum (2001) took some care to construct the ESI in terms of statistical procedures. Certainly, issues such as the normalisation of data and weighting systems have been well addressed. In spite of this, the ESI has received a number of negative reviews (e.g. Jesinghaus, 2001). The inclusions of the parameters 'global stewardship', 'social and institutional capacity' and 'reducing vulnerability' (worth 60 per cent of the index) appeared to bias the ESI in favour of developed countries. Arguably, these factors have little or nothing to do with achieving environmental outcomes and therefore should not be incorporated into the index. Their inclusion clearly brings the theoretical basis of the index into question and, indeed, prompted the suggestion that the ESI has an ideological bias towards rich countries.

Overall, the ESI gains a similar assessment to the ecological footprint in that it scores well in terms of clarity of message and public acceptance (good); timeliness (excellent); explicit performance criteria (fair); data availability (good); cost (excellent); and availability of long-term data series (good). However, like the ecological footprint, it also scores poorly in terms of covering all dimensions of sustainable development (poor) and scientific and theoretical basis (fair).

There are also real concerns about how well adapted the ESI is to the New Zealand context and concerns. For example, soil erosion, arguably one of New Zealand's most significant environmental problems, is not captured by the ESI. Other factors included in the ESI, such as 'acidification exceedence' are not important in New Zealand. If the New Zealand government is committed to constructing a composite indicator of sustainability for New Zealand, an index tailor-made to suit New Zealand circumstances is likely to be more appropriate (refer to Patterson (2002) for such guidelines). Thus, in the New Zealand context, the ESI's role should be confined to that of a general indicator for broadly comparing New Zealand's performance with other countries.

Green GDP (including the ISEW and GPI)

Patterson (2002) concluded that the 'green' GDP has a stronger theoretical basis than the ecological footprint and the ESI. The foundations of green GDP are firmly grounded in welfare theory. It therefore provides a theoretically justifiable way of overcoming some of the well-known weaknesses in the conventional GDP. The operationalisation of this indicator does, however, critically depend on our ability to monetise the externalities *validly and reliably*. This is a controversial area in welfare economics (see Blamey and Common, 1994). The estimation of green GDP also depends on being able to correctly and comprehensively identify all of the externalities. However, a 'recipe book' approach, which is often followed in measuring green GDP, may not identify all the externalities relevant to New Zealand. Clearly, care needs to be taken in this regard.

A further advantage of green GDP is that it scores highly according to the 'clarity of message and public acceptance' criteria (excellent). The public, politicians and decision-makers, seem readily to recognise how the GDP measurement has been adjusted for environmental and social factors. The use of amoeba or spider diagrams also enables detailed data and trends in green GDP to be made apparent. The presentation of the component trends in the GPI for the Canadian province of Alberta is a good example of this (Anielski et al., 2001).

In sum, green GDP scores well for most of the criteria, including: clarity of message and public acceptance (excellent); timeliness (good); all dimensions of sustainable development (excellent); explicit performance criteria (good); and cost (good). There are, however, limitations in respect to the data availability (fair) and availability of long-term data series (fair).

The Australian GPI, which goes beyond green GDP to establish a measure of sustainable economic welfare (see Chapters 2 and 7), provides a good template for data requirements for a New Zealand indicator (refer, also, to Hamilton and Saddler, 1997). There are 22 items in the Australian GPI of which six are readily available in New Zealand in monetised terms. Essentially, to calculate the other 16 items, two sets of data are required: (1) physical/non-monetary quantification of the variable (e.g. hectares of land degraded, number of unemployed people and so on); and (2) pricing data for each of the physical/non-monetary variables (e.g. $/hectare for land degradation or $/person for the cost of unemployment). In most cases, in New Zealand, the physical/non-monetary data do not readily exist and will need to be either estimated or collected. This will require a considerable effort. The price data are even scarcer given the lack of non-market valuation studies in New Zealand. In most cases, standard values would need to be sourced from international literature and data bases. While such information would be reasonably reliable, it might not accurately reflect New Zealand conditions.

Despite these data problems, Patterson (2002) recommended to the New Zealand government that it construct a green GDP fashioned on the Australian GPI. Patterson concluded that the GPI 'covered all dimensions of sustainable development, is easy to understand, is theoretically sound and it is practically achievable within a reasonable budget'.

Genuine Savings Index

The genuine savings index draws on capital theory which has a rich, yet controversial, history in economics (see Chapter 6). In particular, the idea of Hicksian income, which is the concept upon which the index is based, is well supported on theoretical grounds. In spite of this, some theorists (e.g. Faucheux et al., 1997) have questioned the idea of applying the concept of capital to natural resources. Certainly, there are well-known methodological problems concerning the measurement of capital which have been highlighted in the so-called 'Cambridge controversy' of the 1960s (Blaug, 1974), and these problems become even more acute when applied to the measurement of natural capital.

A further weakness of this indicator is that it depends on understanding the concept of 'capital', which is an economic concept not familiar to most.

In fact, in popular parlance, 'capital' has a variety of meanings not all of which correspond to how it is used in the context of the genuine savings index. This all leads to the genuine savings index being a poor indicator for public use.

Hamilton (2001) has calculated the genuine savings index for 35 countries, based on four categories of natural capital (energy, minerals, forests and damage caused by carbon dioxide). Of the 35 countries measured in 1997, New Zealand ranks 15th, with a positive genuine savings of US$ 1460 per capita. As discussed in Patterson (2002), there are serious problems with the reliability and validity of the calculation of Hamilton's (2001) indicator. First, it is questionable how accurate the depreciation data are for energy, minerals, forests and carbon dioxide damage. Second, these four variables form an inadequate basis for measuring natural capital since they omit many important natural resources (e.g. water, land, soils, biodiversity and the atmosphere). There is also a bias towards energy use and carbon cycling. If, however, the New Zealand government is willing to live with these measurement limitations, the operationalisation of a genuine savings index for New Zealand is a practical proposition in terms of cost and data considerations.

On the other hand, if the New Zealand government wants a more theoretically defensible and comprehensive index, then there are significant data issues to be resolved. A time series of manufactured capital accounts certainly exist in New Zealand. However, no comprehensive natural capital accounts exist, and it would be an extremely difficult and costly task to construct them from both a practical and methodological point of view. Even with Statistics New Zealand planning to establish natural resource accounts for New Zealand, the prospect of full natural capital accounts is a very long-term prospect.

As a consequence of these considerations, the genuine savings index scored relatively poorly in comparison with the other headline indicators considered:

- clarity of message and public acceptance (poor);
- scientific and theoretical basis (good);
- timeliness (poor);
- all dimensions of sustainable development (fair);
- explicit performance criteria (good);
- data availability (fair);
- cost (poor);
- availability of long-term data series (fair).

Other Headline Indicators

The report *Headline Indicators for Tracking Progress to Sustainability in New Zealand* by Patterson (2002) also systematically covered a number of other possible headline sustainability indicators for New Zealand. Specifically these indicators included:

- material flows indicators;
- consumption pressure index;
- living planet index;
- composite environmental performance index, based on aggregating the environmental themes of climate change, ozone depletion, acidification, eutrophification, toxic substances, solid wastes and disturbance (noise) (refer to Hope and Parker, 1995);
- composite sustainable development index, covering economic, environmental and social performance components as proposed and outlined by Patterson (2002).

Recommendations and Outcomes of the Evaluation Process

Table 19.1 summarises the evaluation of nine headline indicators of sustainability across the eight evaluation criteria. The ecological footprint and green GDP are ranked the highest in terms of their clarity of message and public acceptance. This is consistent with the fact that these two headline indicators are the most widely used. Most of the headline indicators only focussed on ecological sustainability – often in a restricted way – which leads to relatively low scores for reflecting all the dimensions of sustainable development. Conversely, green GDP and the proposed Composite Index of Sustainable Development most adequately reflected all aspects of the sustainable development concept. A significant weakness in all of the headline indicators was the lack of explicit performance criteria, with the ecological footprint (carrying capacity), genuine savings index (intergenerational equity), and green GDP (maximisation of welfare) standing out as having explicit performance criteria, albeit controversial ones. In terms of practicalities (data availability, cost, long-term data availability), the ecological footprint rated the highest.

Based on an evaluation identical to that spelt out in this chapter, four specific recommendations were made to the New Zealand government:

- *Recommendation 1*: The ecological footprint should be implemented as a stand-alone headline indicator of *ecological sustainability*. It is easily implemented, at low cost, and would be readily understood by the general public.

- *Recommendation 2*: A more comprehensive indicator of ecological sustainability should be developed. This would be a *composite index* that systematically covers source and sink functions of the biophysical environment, pressure and state indicators and representatively encapsulates all aspects of the biophysical environment and ecological functioning. This could be completed at a moderate cost.
- *Recommendation 3*: The genuine progress indicator (GPI) should be constructed for New Zealand to enable the economic, social, and environmental dimensions of sustainable development to be encapsulated in one index. It would be sensible to use the Australian GPI methodology (Hamilton and Saddler, 1997) as an initial template and draw on Australian expertise gained in its construction.
- *Recommendation 4*: Investigations should be undertaken to construct a composite index of sustainable development for New Zealand, which explicitly measures the economic, social and environmental aspects of progress. A proposal for describing how this could be done is outlined by Patterson (2002). This proposal argues that the economic dimension be measured by GDP, the social dimension by the New Zealand Deprivation Index, and the environmental dimension by the index referred to in *Recommendation 2*.

CONCLUSIONS

The New Zealand government is devoting increasing attention to sustainable development. In August 2002, it released *The Government's Approach to Sustainable Development*, outlining the actions New Zealand had taken to improve its environmental, economic, and social sustainability. At the same time, Statistics New Zealand (2002) released its work on sustainable development indicators. More recently, the New Zealand government has continued its interest in sustainable development by setting out its *Programme of Action for Sustainable Development* (Department of Prime Minister and Cabinet, 2003). Sustainable development is clearly on New Zealand's policy agenda.

Many challenges have emerged as a result of the policy attention given to sustainable development. One significant challenge is how to communicate to decision-makers and the public the progress made towards sustainable development in terms of a headline indicator of sustainability. This chapter has demonstrated that there are a number of realistic choices for selecting such an indicator. Since each indicator has its own unique set of advantages and disadvantages, careful consideration must be taken before final selections are made. It is hoped that the evaluation presented in this chapter will not only prove helpful to the New Zealand government, but lessons can be drawn from it that will be both invaluable and applicable to other nation states.

NOTES

1. We restrict our discussion of sustainability concepts to those: (1) that are amenable to operational measurement (2) that emerged in the modern era. It is of course wrong to suggest that the 'sustainability' concept is a modern concept perhaps attributable to the first wave of environmental literature in the 1970s, such as the 'Limits to Growth' study. The idea is much older than that. Most modern interpretations of the sustainability concept can be traced back to the writings of the Classical Economists from the late 1700s to the late 1800s: Malthus, Ricardo, Marx, Mill and Jevons. For a full account of classical interpretations of sustainability refer to Patterson (2002).
2. Please note that although this evaluation is carried out in the New Zealand context, many of the conclusions are relevant to any nation seeking to establish a headline indicator of sustainability. In addition, Patterson (2002) involved the evaluation of twelve sustainability indicators. Due to space limitations, the coverage in this chapter is restricted to four key indicators.
3. See Chapter 11 where Wackernagel et al. have replied to some of these criticisms.

REFERENCES

Adriaanse, A., S. Bringezu, S. Hammond, Y. Moriguchi, E. Rodenburg, D. Rogich and H. Schutz (1997), *Resource Flows: The Material Basis of Industrial Economics*, Washington DC: World Resources Institute.

Anielski, M., M. Griffiths, D. Pollock, A. Taylor, J. Wilson and S. Wilson (2001), *Alberta Sustainability Trends 2000: The Genuine Progress Indicators Report 1961 to 1999*, Alberta: Pembina Institute for Appropriate Development.

Blamey, E. and M. Common (1994), 'Sustainability and the limits of pseudo market valuation', in J.C.J.M. van den Bergh and J. van der Straaten (eds), *Towards Sustainable Development: Concepts, Methods and Policy*, Washington DC: Island Press, pp. 165–205.

Blaug, M. (1974), *The Cambridge Revolution: Success or Failure?*, London: Institute of Economic Affairs.

Braat, L. (1991), 'The predictive nature of sustainability indicators', in O. Kuik and H. Verbruggen (eds), *In Search of Indicators of Sustainable Development*, Dordrecht: Klumer Academic Publishers, pp. 57–70.

Burton, I. and R. Kates (1965), *Readings in Resource Management and Conservation*, Chicago: University of Chicago Press.

Cairns, J. and T. Crawford (1991), *Integrated Environmental Management*, Chelsea: Lewis Publishers.

Canadian Council of Ministers of the Environment (1996), *A Framework for Developing Ecosystem Health Goals, Objective and Indicators: Tools for Ecosystem-Based Management*, Manitoba: Canadian Council of Ministers of the Environment.

Clements, F. (1916), *Plant Succession: An Analysis of the Development of Vegetation*, Washington DC: Carnegie Institution of Washington.

Costanza, R. (ed.) (1991), *Ecological Economics: The Science and Management of Sustainability*, New York: Columbia University Press.

Costanza, R. (2000), 'The dynamics of the ecological footprint concept', *Ecological Economics*, **32**, 341–5.

Crampton, P., C. Salmond, R. Kirkpatrick, R. Scarborough and C. Skelly (2000), *Degrees of Deprivation in New Zealand: An Atlas of Socio-Economic Difference*, Auckland: David Bateman.

Cronin, K. (1988), *Ecological Principles for Resource Management*, Wellington: Ministry for the Environment.

Daly, H. (ed.) (1973), *Toward a Steady State Economy*, San Francisco: W.H. Freeman.

Dasmann, R. (1972), *Environmental Conservation*, New York: Wiley.

Davis, P., P. Howden-Chapman and K. McLeod (1996), 'The New Zealand socio-economic index: a census-based occupational scale of socio-economic status', in *Socio-Economic Inequalities and Health*, Wellington: Institute of Policy Status, Victoria University of Wellington.

De Angelis, D. and J. Waterhouse (1987), 'Equilibrium and non equilibrium concepts in ecological models', *Ecological Monographs*, **57**, 1–21.

Department of Prime Minister and Cabinet (2003), *Sustainable Development for New Zealand – Programme of Action*, Wellington: Department of Prime Minister and Cabinet.

Easton, B. (1995a), 'Poverty in New Zealand: 1981–1993', *New Zealand Sociology*, **10** (2), 182–213.

Easton, B. (1995b), *Lower Incomes in Wellington City*, Wellington: Wellington City Council.

Ehrlich, P., A. Ehrlich and J. Holden (1973), *Human Ecology: Problems and Solutions*, San Francisco: W.H. Freeman.

Faucheux, S., E. Muir and M. O'Connor (1997), 'Neo-classical natural capital theory and "weak" indicators of sustainability', *Land Economics*, **73** (4), 523–8.

Fox, K. (1985), *Social System Accounts: Linking Social and Economic Indicators Through Tangible Behavior Settings*, Dordrecht: D. Riedd.

Gallopín, G. (1997), 'Indicators and their use: information for decision-making', in B. Moldan and S. Billharz (eds), *Sustainability Indicators: Report on the Project on Indicators of Sustainable Development*, Chichester: Wiley, pp. 11–27.

Georgescu-Roegen, N. (1971), *The Entropy Law and the Economic Process*, Massachusetts: Harvard University Press.

Goldberg, E. (1999), *Indicators of Sustainable Consumption: Messages for Policy Makers*, Wellington: Statistics New Zealand.

Goodland, R. and H. Daly (1993), 'Why Northern income growth is not the solution to Southern poverty', *Ecological Economics*, **8**, 85–101.

Hamilton, C. and H. Saddler (1997), *The Genuine Progress Indicator: A New Index of Changes in Well-Being in Australia*, Discussion Paper N. 14, Canberra: Australia Institute.

Hamilton, K. (2001), *Indicators of Sustainable Development: Genuine Savings*, Washington DC: World Bank.

Hartwick, J. (1978), 'Investing returns from depleting renewable resource stocks and intergenerational equity', *Economic Letters*, **1**, 85–8.

Hicks, J. (1946), *Value and Capital*, Oxford: Oxford University Press.

Holling, C.S. (1973), 'Resilience and stability of ecological systems', *Annual Review of Ecological Systems*, **4**, 1–23.

Hope, C. and J. Parker (1995), 'Environmental indices for France, Italy and the United Kingdom', *European Environment*, **5**, 13–19.

Jesinghaus, J. (2001), *The World Economic Forum's Environmental Sustainability Index: Strong and Weak Points*, European Commission.

Kay, J. and E. Schneider (1994), 'Embracing complexity: the challenge of the ecosystem approach', *Alternative*, **20** (3), 32–8.

May, R. (1972), 'Will a large complex system be stable?', *Nature*, **238**, 413–14.

May, R. (1974), 'Biological populations with non-overlapping generations: stable points, stable cycles and chaos', *Science*, 645–7.

McDonald, G. and M.G. Patterson (1999), *EcoLink Overview Report*, Palmerston North, New Zealand: Massey University.

Meadows, D.H., J. Meadows, J. Randers and W. Brehens (1972), *The Limits to Growth*, Washington: Earth Island.

Miller, T. (1993), *Environmental Science: Sustaining the Earth*, Belmont: Wadsworth.

Ministry for the Environment and Department of Statistics (1990), *State of the Environment Reporting in New Zealand*, Wellington: Ministry for the Environment and Department of Statistics.

Ministry for the Environment and Department of Statistics (1991), *Reporting on State of the Environment Information*, Wellington: Ministry for the Environment and Department of Statistics.

Ministry for the Environment (1994), *Environment 2010 Strategy: A Statement of the Government's Strategy on the Environment*, Wellington: Ministry for the Environment.

Ministry for the Environment (1996), *National Environmental Indicators: Building a Framework for a Core Set*, Wellington: Ministry for the Environment.

Mishan, E. (1967), *The Costs of Economic Growth*, London: Staples.

Mitchell, B. (1997), *Resource and Environmental Management*, Essex: Longman.

Odum, E. (1969), 'The strategy of ecosystem development', *Science*, **164**, 262–70.

Odum, H. (1971), *Environment, Power and Society*, New York: Wiley.

Odum, H. (1996), *Environmental Accounting: Emergy and Environmental Decision Making*, New York: Wiley.

Ontario Ministry for the Environment (1992), *Toward an Ecosystem Approach to Land Use Planning: Discussion Paper*, Ottawa: Ministry for the Environment.

Opschoor, H. and L. Reijnders (1991), 'Towards sustainable development indicators', in O. Kuik and H. Verbruggen (eds), *In Search of Indicators of Sustainable Development*, Dordrecht: Klumer Academic Publishers, pp. 7–28.

Patterson, M.G. (2002), *Headline Indicators for Tracking Progress to Sustainability in New Zealand*, Wellington: Ministry for the Environment.

Pearce, D. and G. Atkinson (1993), 'Capital theory and the measurement of weak sustainability', *Ecological Economics*, **8**, 103–8.

Pearce, D. and K. Turner (1990), *Economics of Natural Resources and the Environment*, London: Harvester Wheatshelf.

Pezzoli, K. (1997a), 'Sustainable development: a transdisciplinary overview of the literature', *Journal of Environment Planning and Management*, **40** (5), 549–74.

Pezzoli, K. (1997b), 'Sustainable development literature: a transdisciplinary bibliography', *Journal of Environment Planning and Management*, **40** (5), 575–601.

Solow, R. (1986), 'On intergenerational allocation of natural resources', *Scandinavian Journal of Economics*, **88** (1), 141–9.

Spangerberg, J. and O. Bonniot (1998), *Sustainability Indicators – A Compass on the Road Toward Sustainability*, Wuppertal, Germany: Wuppertal Institute.

Statistics New Zealand (2002), *Monitoring Progress Towards a Sustainable New Zealand*, Wellington: Statistics New Zealand.

Stephens, R., C. Waldegrave and P. Frater (1995), 'Measuring poverty in New Zealand', *Social Policy Journal of New Zealand*, **5**, 88–112.

United Nations (1990), *Human Development Report*, New York: Oxford University Press.

United Nations (1993), 'Integrated environmental and economic accounting', *Handbook of National Accounting*, Series F No. 61, New York: United Nations.

Vitousek, P. (1986), 'Human appropriation of the products of photosynthesis', *Bioscience*, **34** (6), 368–73.

Vos, J., J. Feenstra, I. de Boer, Z. Braat and J. van Baalen (1985), *Indicators of the State of the Environment*, Amsterdam: Institute for Environmental Studies, Kee University.

Wacknernagel, M. and W. Rees (1996), *Our Ecological Footprint: Reducing Human Impact on the Earth*, Philadelphia: New Society Publishers.

Watt, K. (1973), *Principles of Environmental Science*, New York: McGraw Hill.

Wiens, J. (1984), 'On understanding a non-equilibrium world: myth and reality in community patterns and processes', in D.R. Strong, A.B. Thistle and D. Simberloff (eds), *Ecological Communities: Conceptual Issues and Evidence*, Princeton, New Jersey: Princeton University Press, pp. 439–57.

World Economic Forum (2001), *2001 Environmental Sustainability Index*, Yale Centre for Environmental Law and Policy.

Wright, J. (1989), *Natural Resource Accounting: A Technique for Improving Planning in New Zealand*, Information Paper No.12, Lincoln College: Centre for Resource Management.

Wright, J. (1991), *Indicators of Sustainable Energy Development*, Information Paper No. 28, Lincoln College: Centre for Resource Management.

Ziman, J. (1984), *An Introduction to Science Studies: The Philosophical and Social Aspects of Science and Technology*, Cambridge: Cambridge University Press.

Index